States of Disconnect

STATES OF DISCONNECT

The China-India Literary Relation
in the Twentieth Century

ADHIRA MANGALAGIRI

COLUMBIA UNIVERSITY PRESS *NEW YORK*

Columbia University Press
Publishers Since 1893
New York   Chichester, West Sussex
cup.columbia.edu
Columbia University Press wishes to express its appreciation for assistance given
by the Wm. Theodore de Bary Fund in the publication of this book.
Copyright © 2023 Columbia University Press
All rights reserved

Library of Congress Cataloging-in-Publication Data
Names: Mangalagiri, Adhira, author.
Title: States of disconnect : the China-India literary relation in the twentieth century /
Adhira Mangalagiri.
Description: New York : Columbia University Press, [2023] |
Includes bibliographical references and index.
Identifiers: LCCN 2022014164 (print) | LCCN 2022014165 (ebook) | ISBN 9780231205689 (hardback ;
acid-free paper) | ISBN 9780231205696 (trade paperback) | ISBN 9780231556118 (ebook)
Subjects: LCSH: Chinese literature—20th century—History and criticism. |
Indic literature—20th century—History and criticism. | Transnationalism
in literature. | Comparative literature—Chinese and Indic. | Comparative literature—
Indic and Chinese. | LCGFT: Literary criticism.
Classification: LCC PL2274.2.I5 M36 2023 (print) | LCC PL2274.2.I5 (ebook) |
DDC 895.109/005—dc23/eng/20220810
LC record available at https://lccn.loc.gov/2022014164
LC ebook record available at https://lccn.loc.gov/2022014165

Columbia University Press books are printed on permanent and durable acid-free paper.
Printed in the United States of America
Cover design: Milenda Nan Ok Lee
Cover image: Shamsher Bahadur Singh, *Kuch Kavitāeṁ va Kuch aur Kavitāeṁ*
[Some poems and some more poems] (New Delhi: Radhakrishna Prakashan, 1984),
70–71. Courtesy of Rajkamal Prakashan.

Contents

Note on Transliteration and Translation

I USE THE pinyin system of transliteration for all Chinese words and titles, and, for the sake of consistency, I provide traditional Chinese characters throughout. I transliterate and provide diacritical marks for all Hindi and Urdu words and titles as given in the *Oxford Hindi-English Dictionary*, edited by R. S. McGregor (1993). For proper nouns, I have retained the customary transliterations and omitted diacritical marks—for instance, Agyeya instead of Ajñey. I render all quotations in English translation, and, unless indicated otherwise, all translations are mine.

States of Disconnect

Introduction

States of Disconnect

ENVISION A WORLD in which the act of traversing national borders, literally and literarily, cannot be taken for granted. Nation-states assert increasing degrees of geopolitical and epistemological primacy. Transnational exchange wanes, cross-border communication fails, hostility toward national others rises, the state overdetermines being. The world no longer comes into view as an interconnected totality; that imagination fragments into a reification of national categories and an advance of reactionary nationalisms. How can we think the transnational in such a world? We may reach for metaphors of mobility—networks, flows, circuits—in an effort to discursively transcend the national. But these patterns of thought only remind us of our deep conceptual imbrication in paradigms of globalization, which render national borders porous and set things in circulation but do so while integrating difference into a homogenizing, exploitative system. A globalized consciousness no longer offers an emancipatory antidote to the parochial. As the national and the global, mirrored horizons of hegemony, close in, relation across the nation's borders and beyond its thought-formations becomes severed, interrupted, or rendered absent. Our ability to apprehend the transnational thus wears away. I name this crisis of transnationalism disconnect.

This book dwells in disconnect. It studies moments of transnationalism in crisis, as indexed in texts that register the impossibility or undesirability of relating with national others and grapple with the fate of transnationalism in the face of a nationalism that turns its gaze ever inward.

Rather than bracketing away such uncomfortable expression by furnishing narratives of textual circulation, contact, and connectivity as possible correctives—a gesture that betrays a reliance upon the logics of globalization—I seek instead to confront head-on the breakdown and failures of transnational relation, and to do so while articulating a critical stance against the exclusionary rhetoric of the nation-state. The literary texts studied here alert us to the fact that a crisis of transnational relation is as much a crisis of aesthetics and hermeneutics as it is one of collective political life. A central claim of this book is that attending to the affordances of literature, the intricacies of imagination and interpretation, makes possible an ethics of transnational relation when none seems at hand, when expressions of hostility and fraught silences seem to drown out calls for solidarity and partnership.

At stake is comparison. The task of literary comparison, as practiced under the label of what has been termed "new world literature," has tended recently to model itself methodologically on processes of globalization.[1] The literary work of tracking the transmission of texts across national borders, the transfer of meaning across languages, and the traffic of ideas along routes of circulation, can correspond, in the final analysis, with the master narrative of the movements of global capital. And, further, if models of mobility conventionally comprise one side of comparison, an affective alignment with affinity could be said to characterize the other. Comparison is often regarded as bearing stories of literary kinship or as uncovering unexpected aesthetic alliances. How can we harness comparison to reckon instead with the uncomfortable rhetoric of insularity? And how can we do so while contending with a waning of globalized connectivity and the attendant erosion of those forms of transnational thought once easily at hand?

States of Disconnect casts these questions through the case of a single comparison, one that has been posed for so long and so vigorously—by thinkers as illustrious as Hegel and Marx and their many generations of interlocuters—that the pairing now seems a foregone conclusion: that of China and India. As constituents of a single comparative unit, China and India have long occupied a central position in both the history of modern intellectual thought and in the discourses of our current everyday.[2] In its contemporary manifestations, the China-India comparison, many argue, holds stakes so high as to "shape the global future."[3] A quintessential instantiation of comparison at work, the China-India pairing serves as a fitting case through which to rethink the task of comparing across national borders. This book begins from the ends of this already established and frequently evoked comparative unit in order to examine the techniques of comparison that have comprised, and continue to inform, its intellectual lineage. While much of this lineage has involved exercises of China-India thought in pursuit of some greater unity or oneness, I am interested in texts that engage in thinking China and India together but that do so while expressing an aversion or resistance to the pairing. These are texts of disconnect: they capture a moment of transnationalism in crisis.

The Chinese and Hindi texts of disconnect studied here range from the early years of the twentieth century to the 1960s. Twentieth-century writings that think China and India together in gestures of collaboration, emulation, admiration are better known and more readily studied, but this period also bore texts that register the discomforting rhetoric of China-India fracture and distance, expression that is reticent at best and exclusionary at worst. This second category remains unstudied in large part because such texts run counter to the fundamentally humanist ethos of literary comparison. But, as nation-states become increasingly bounded, it has become all the more urgent to train the critical eye upon precisely that which comparison has tended to look away from, to find ways of comparing capable of apprehending disconnect. Reading texts of disconnect from the past could help cultivate a literary sensibility for making sense of a world rife with division, and could articulate the indispensability of the literary—and, more broadly, the humanistic—to such a world. These hopes sustain the book.

In what follows here, I consider each of the terms that comprises this book's title. The first part maps the disciplinary home of the book by making a case for comparative literature—given its history and unique critical perspective—as particularly well suited to reading disconnect. The second charts a history of the China-India comparative unit, an intellectual complex that resides at the heart of how we conceptualize the modern nation-state, and considers the language politics of reading this comparison as inscribed in Chinese and Hindi. The third discusses "literary relation" as offering possibilities for transnational thought against the more familiar terminology of "political relations." The fourth introduces three "states" of disconnect—friction, ellipsis, and contingency—as the conditions of possibility that give rise to the texts studied in this book. Each state designates a particular crisis of transnationalism as registered in literary form, and together the three comprise a critical vocabulary of disconnect. The final section traces the trajectory of the book's chapters, which tell a story of China-India literary relation through the twentieth century that contends with the capacious yet tenuous binds of disconnect.

Comparison and Disconnect

How can we apprehend disconnect through comparison? At first glance, disconnect and comparison may seem antithetical, the latter locked in a drive to sublimate the former. This was arguably the case when comparison began to take shape as a formal mode of analysis. Comparison stems in one direction from the development of scientific knowledge in the Enlightenment period, when "comparative analysis" entailed a method for discerning from seemingly distant objects universal laws by which to understand all natural and human phenomena.[4] Conducting comparison involved positioning objects of study in contiguity—collapsing distance and difference—in order to discern patterns and taxonomies, to study one according to the rules of another, or to amass a varied sample against which to test general principles. The comparative analysis of literature furthered this scientific tradition by concerning itself with drawing together disparate literary works (across time, languages, cultures) in the hopes that doing so may yield principles of human genius.[5] Following this tradition of positioning comparative literature on the "border-lands of Science and Literature" as Hutcheson M. Posnett put it in 1886, comparison seems to offer a blueprint for overcoming disconnect, not for dwelling within it, as this book proposes.[6]

Yet comparative literature exceeds its positivistic impulses in its longstanding commitment to a deeply political agenda. The discipline emerged, in René Wellek's words, "as a reaction against the narrow nationalism of much nineteenth-century scholarship."[7] Indeed, early articulations of comparative literature evince a palpable desire to oppose through the study of literature what Hugo Meltzl referred to in 1877 as an "unhealthy 'national principle'": a prevailing sense that "every nation considers itself . . . superior to all other nations."[8] Since these words appeared in the early issues of comparative literature's first journal, founded under Meltzl's editorship, the discipline has survived despite its lack of consensus over what constitutes its materials or methods (in fact, enduring disagreements over these thorny questions have served variously to enliven comparative literature and declare it dead). What has held the discipline in shape, through the twentieth century and into the twenty-first, is its constant attunement to the power-inflected fragmentation, boundedness, and containment national borders wreak, and a shared belief among its practitioners that the study of literature can meaningfully confront and counter such violence. It is no coincidence, then, that so many of comparative literature's founders "stood themselves at the crossroads of nations or, at least, on the borders of one nation," a perspectival position that brings into sharp focus the divisiveness of national borders, the violence of exclusionary nationalisms, and the vast peripheries beyond centers of national power.[9] The discipline thrived in the writings of exiles, émigrés, and outcasts, particularly in the 1930s and 1940s, when comparative literature took root in America under the shadow of fascism and persecution, registered in the writings of expatriate European philologists, Wellek among them, alongside Leo Spitzer, Erich Auerbach, and others. Comparative literature has since inhered, more so than any other discipline, in a critical ethos marked by displacement, estrangement, disinheritance, unhomeliness.

Such a discursive orientation aligned comparative literature with the concerns of postcolonial theory in the 1980s and 1990s. While the postcolonial critique initially chafed against comparative literature's Eurocentric origins and, in turn, was met with some resistance, scholars at the time convincingly argued that postcolonialism in fact proved "truer to the foundational disposition of comparative literature" given that both emerged from "melancholia, *Heimlosigkeit* [homelessness], cultural ambivalence, consciousness of linguistic loss, confusion induced by 'worlding' or global transference, amnesia of origins, fractured subjectivity, [and] border trauma."[10] As comparative literature passed from an "age of multiculturalism" into an "age of globalization" in the new millennium, its European canons and methods underwent radical deconstruction, but its keen attunement to the limits of national categories and nation-based epistemologies formed a thread of continuity during that time of transition.[11]

States of Disconnect inherits this strand of comparative literature's historical legacy. Disconnect, as I conceive of it, aligns less with the scientific notion of distance between disparate texts, a lack of historical or aesthetic link that must be furnished in service of mastery over the fruits of human creativity or of a unified humanity. To be clear, this book is not concerned with forging links between texts hitherto deemed distant or with building interpretive bridges between nationally differentiated texts yet to be read together. Rather, extending what I see as comparative literature's core preoccupation, disconnect signals moments when the ascending primacy of the nation as a conceptual unit—and the machinations of the nation-state in enforcing that primacy—engender a crisis of transnational relation. Throughout this book, I use the term "disconnect" to mark this crisis through its inscription in Chinese and Hindi literary texts written during key junctures of the twentieth century, when the impossibility or undesirability of thinking China and India together becomes heightened. The task at hand is to find in literary practice possibilities for apprehending the breakdown of transnational relation ethically.

In recent decades, comparative literature's pursuit of exceeding and exploding the nation-state's hold over literature seems to have reached its apogee in world literature's revival. The resurgence of world literature at the turn of the twenty-first century indicates, in large part, the deep impact of the postcolonial intervention. The rapid expansion of comparative literature's purview beyond Europe and into the textual archives of the world bespeaks a desire to provincialize Eurocentric grounds of comparison. At the same time, however, world literature has struggled to reconcile its markedly humanist ethos with its own rootedness in capitalist exploitation. In an early articulation of the concept of world literature, Marx and Engels famously forewarned of comparison's complicity with a global capitalist system and its inherent inequities: "From numerous national and local literatures, there arises a world literature"; bourgeois greed expands outward ever, in search for new, untapped resources to exploit in the quest to create "a world after its own image."[12] From its Goethean conception to its twenty-first-century iteration, world literature has engendered an eagerness to read the world itself as text— as the "thing woven" in the etymological sense of the word— yielding a view of the world as an inextricably interconnected fabric. The admirable ambition of such a worldview, however, obscures its epistemological reproduction of the patterns and movements of capital, which similarly assume a certain porousness of national borders and maintain a certain faith in mobility and circulation. These foundational beliefs reveal world literature's deep dependency on paradigms of globalization and its attendant systems of hyperconnectivity borne of texts, ideas, peoples, commodities in constant motion. Uncovering a repeated conflation between recent conceptions of world literature and capitalist globalization, Pheng Cheah describes the "allure of the market metaphor for understanding literature's worldliness" as a promised "liberation from a national framework's stifling strictures" on literary practice and criticism.[13] "Just as contemporary global markets and the liberalization of trade and financial flows have brought about the erosion of national-state regulated economies," Cheah writes, "so too the globalization of literary exchange and production is said to lead to the emergence of world literature, a form of literature that has rendered merely national literature obsolete and illusory."[14] Buoyed by visions of total connectedness and boundless mobility, visions conjured by the forces of the global market, recent theories of world literature have undeniably succeeded in exceeding national limits, but have done so through an often unacknowledged reliance on the logics of globalization. Such a reliance not only diminishes literature's "worldly force" by placing literature in a derivative and reactive position to capital, but, further, a critical dependence on models of hyperconnectivity in the study of literature risks methodologically perpetuating the exploitative and uneven workings of globalization even when intended as critique.[15]

An approach to transnational comparison founded upon the premise of global connectedness may have lived more comfortably in a world steeped in the cross-border affordances of globalization. Now, stepping into the twenty-first century's third decade, the stakes of transnational comparison seem to have shifted. What can such comparison offer a world caught in the resurgence of authoritarian politics, the failures of democracy, crises of migration, rampant ethnoreligious violence, a globe in lockdown, and a planet in decline? These realities may not all be singular to our particular moment, and yet, for a generation of comparatists confronting the disintegration of the only norm they have borne witness to—the profits of neoliberal globalization and its chimeral horizons of unbounded openness—the disciplinary tenor and tools of the past no longer seem adequate.

A critical attunement to disconnect allows comparison to exceed its reliance on the models and methods of globalization, that paradigm of transnationalism that has reigned dominant for the last two centuries. *States of Disconnect* approaches the study of transnational relation from the perspective of those ruptures that upend visions of the world as endlessly interconnected. I harness a comparatist lens to look not only across or through but also *at* national borders, and to study these not only as permeable constructs but also as barriers, both real and imagined, erected and enforced to impede transnational exchange and erode transnational sentiment. Disconnect thus takes shape against, on one hand, the impulse toward hyperconnectivity in the study of transnationalism, wherein national borders easily dissolve to yield globalized circulation and connection, and on the other, the kind of national overdetermination of literary work that once fueled comparative literature's inception and now looms again. I read texts that imaginatively bring China and India together, but that do not (or, in many cases, cannot) traverse the national borders of China and India and that champion insularity at the cost of China-India alliance. Much of this literary expression evokes a certain discomfort, but this is precisely the challenge this book takes up: How can we read uncomfortable expressions of hostility, antagonism, or misunderstanding ethically, in texts that refuse to sate our critical appetite for transnational connection and affinity?

This book, therefore, shares with comparative literature's founding figures a core concern with finding in literary practice—writing, reading, translation—possibilities for ethical ways to relate with national others in a hostile world. I extend this disciplinary impulse to current debates in world literature by seeking an approach to comparison that strives to make sense of a world in which global connectedness is no longer self-evident. Each of the texts that comprise this book's archive engages in the practice of thinking China and India together—and, thus, in discourses of comparison—but does so while calling into question, instead of unequivocally celebrating, the basis and value of that pairing. Approaching comparison from the perspective of its discontents, I explore the ability of comparison to offer tools for apprehending disconnect on its own terms and to engender reading practices that unexpectedly draw from lapses in connection an ethics of transnational relation.

The China-India Comparative Unit

The practice of thinking China and India together, as a coherent pairing, has occupied a position of much centrality and notoriety in the history of comparative thought. Hegel was certainly not the first to think China and India together, and yet he figures as somewhat of a progenitor in that so much of China-India comparative thought remains indebted to and rebels against his writing. In an infamous statement that has since acquired a citational life of its own, Hegel declared, "China and India lie, as it were, still outside the World's History, as the mere presupposition of elements whose combination must be waited for to constitute their vital progress."[16] Hegel draws China and India together in a relation of similarity, both positioned on the path toward freedom at once at the beginning, in the "childhood" of history, and wholly outside it in their perpetual "fixedness," their inability to advance beyond infancy.[17] The equivalence Hegel constructs between China and India then gives way to a series of contrasts: China stands for unity, India for diversity; China is nothing but the state (the emperor), India "presents us with a people, but no State"; in China, we find a "moral despotism," in India there is no morality, only chaos and "confused dreams."[18]

Rectifying Hegel's misconceptions interests me less than the specific technique of comparison at work here.[19] In Hegel's thought, China and India come together under the critic's hand even as Hegel presents the pairing as natural. Hegel justifies yoking China and India together through various historical determinisms in an effort to convince his reader of the inherent comparability of the two. The critic's role as the architect of the pairing consequently imposes upon the entities compared a normative standard or grounds for comparison. The fruits of the pairing—the series of contrasts between China and India—emerge through the exercise of measuring each in relation to this externally imposed norm, here the Hegelian notion of freedom. In its most violent iteration, this practice of comparison bears striking affinity with much of the discourses of the civilizing mission: in the hands of the colonizer, comparison as "similarities and differences" (read: proximity to and deviation from the norm) provided an easy logic by which to justify imperial expansion, material exploitation, and epistemic subjugation.

Hegel's treatment of China and India in *The Philosophy of History* may offer more of a cautionary tale of comparison than a model for emulation, but his lectures lay bare how crucial a position the China-India comparative unit occupies in conceptualizations of the modern state. For Hegel, history is the development of spirit, or the process through which the world attains its consciousness of freedom. And it is the structure of the modern state that affords this consciousness of freedom, wherein "the private interest of its citizens is one with the common interest of the State; when the one finds its gratification and realization in the other."[20] The whole process of history moves toward the establishment of this modern state—an ideal system of governance under which the interests of the state and those of the individual align in perfect synthesis—and, consequently, toward the development of spirit. If China and India "lie outside the World's History," incapable of attaining the rational heights of the modern state, China and India (along with Persia, which together constitute the "Oriental World") mark the presence of the modern state in the negative. The Orient presents the comparison against which the modern state takes shape, the limit against which the realization of spirit becomes possible. From the shadowy peripheries of history to which Hegel relegated the Orient, China and India emerge to enact a constitutive role in bringing the modern state into view.

The China-India comparative unit similarly figured in conceptions of the modern nation state envisaged in China and India in the late nineteenth and early twentieth centuries. As Chinese intellectuals and statesmen sought a postdynastic state structure, many looked to the West as a model of modernity at the same time as they condemned the West's colonial ambitions. While the Western modern state—of the kind Hegel wrote of—figured as an ideal, Chinese intellectuals also recognized that the national strength and autonomy they sought found resonance in the many nationalist struggles ongoing across the colonized world.[21] India proved of particular interest to those seeking alternatives to the Western pathway into modern statehood. In contrast to the kind of decontextualized and dehistoricized China-India comparison Hegel had epitomized, a new idiom of China-India comparison emerged from the writings of intellectuals such as Qing reformer Kang Youwei 康有為, his student Liang Qichao 梁啓超, and the revolutionary scholar Zhang Taiyan 章太炎. In an anticolonial effort to wrest the act of thinking China and India together away from the legacies of European hegemony, these intellectuals recovered what they framed as a millennia-long history of China-India connection, unmediated by the West. The idea of "two thousand years" of China-India intercourse, famously outlined by Liang Qichao in his 1924 speech welcoming the Nobel laureate Rabindranath Tagore to China, came to serve as an anticolonial rejoinder in pan-Asian thought of the time.[22] China and India enjoyed thousands of years of uninterrupted intercourse and exchange, the narrative ran, until Western encroachment ("the White Disaster," as Okakura Kakuzō termed it) fragmented Asia asunder.[23] For pan-Asians like Zhang Taiyan, only a reunion between China and

India could "form a protective shield over Asia," defending against Western and Japanese imperialism alike.[24]

Mirroring Chinese intellectuals' interest in India, Indian intellectuals and radicals, many holding vastly divergent views of how best to achieve decolonization, looked to China as they furthered their political visions. Tagore, now a seminal figure in China-India thought of the early twentieth century, famously called for an antinationalist and antimaterialist pan-Asianism, "an alternative cosmopolitanism drawn from Asian traditions,"[25] an idea that garnered as much support as it did controversy in China.[26] Tagore's travels to China in the 1920s have long occupied center stage in the history of modern China-India thought, eclipsing the lesser-known activities of Indian radicals in China at the time. The Bengali intellectual Manabendranath Roy, for instance, visited China in 1927 under the auspices of the Comintern. Roy had been influenced by radical German Marxists who, following Rosa Luxemburg, envisioned the colonies (and not the West, contra Marx) as leading the world to revolution and conceived of Chinese and Indians as forming a unitary revolutionary force.[27] Roy's visit to China proved transformative in his own political thought: what he saw as an "abortive revolution" in China (following the Guomindang's break from the USSR and its violent suppression of the communists) led him to articulate a more humanist approach to Indian independence, one that centered building solidarities across class divisions.[28] China also provided fertile ground for the activities of the Ghadar movement, comprised of an eclectic, transnational group of revolutionaries, united primarily in their action-oriented approach to Indian (and world) revolution.[29] In the 1910s, two Indian revolutionaries with Ghadar connections, Rashbehari Bose and Taraknath Das, coordinated Ghadar activities in China from Tokyo, disseminating revolutionary literature in China, purchasing weapons, and conveying arms and funds to India.[30] By the 1920s, the Ghadarites had established bases across China largely under the leadership of Daswandha Singh, who made an impassioned plea for solidarity in his 1925 speech, "Let China and India Unite for the Holy Cause," delivered in Beijing.[31] Singh called for India and China to "unite first, then . . . there will be stronger and firmer friendship between all Asia," supplementing Zhang Taiyan's pan-Asianism with a Ghadar-inflected call to arms against the colonizer.[32]

By the mid-twentieth century, China-India thought shaped not just imaginations of an autonomous modern state in both China and India, but also played a formative role in the actualization of these nation-states. The pan-Asian call to recover China and India's ancient connectedness as a strategy to dismantle Western supremacy evolved into the refrain of the postcolonial nation-states. In the late 1940s, as the newly formed People's Republic of China and Republic of India endeavored to establish diplomatic relations, the slogan "two thousand years of friendship"—proclaimed time and again by heads of state Zhou Enlai 周恩來 and Jawaharlal Nehru—harnessed a construct of China-India connectedness this time to bolster the young nation-states as they braved a new world. The notion of a connected history thus acquired an affective tenor as a signifier of "friendship" (or, in the rhetoric of the 1950s, of "brotherhood"), couching diplomatic relations within a narrative of long-standing solidarity, mutual exchange, and shared values, lest the less poetic narrative of a nation-state driven by its own strategic interests in asserting autonomy and consolidating borders betray too much in the poker game of Cold War–era politicking.

The narrative of "two thousand years of friendship" has served as a heuristic for thinking China and India together through the twentieth century and into the present day. Although born as a celebration of connectedness, the narrative—particularly in its cooptation by the mandates of diplomacy—now serves to erase more of the connected histories of China and India than it reveals, not least because it seeks out only those historical encounters that can be made to evince "friendship," omitting all else. Scholarly efforts over the last two decades have gone a long way toward exposing the mythology of the friendship narrative, exploring instead the full spectrum of China-India encounters and exchange, and offering a connected history that dismantles instead of bolsters the centrality and interests of the nation-states.[33] Such interventions extend what could be classified as a gesture of immanent critique in that they interrogate the object of criticism (here, the narrative of "two thousand years of friendship") according to its own logic (that of connection). As with the comparatist who combats the inequities of capital's expansionary drive to connect unevenly by seeking out more ethical, more humanist connection, an effort to critique a story of China-India connectedness by unearthing overlooked, newly discovered, or differently conceptualized connection unsettles the flawed master narrative but leaves unquestioned the internal mechanisms of its operation.

This is not a book of forgotten China-India connections told from new archives, although its texts—Chinese and Hindi literatures from the 1900s to the 1960s—have indeed yet to garner scholarly attention. This book takes as its central focus not China and India, but the discourses of comparison that shape the act of thinking China and India together, what I have referred to as the China-India comparative unit, a conceptual practice with a history of its own. This section has sketched segments of this history in order to demonstrate how intimately intertwined the China-India comparative unit remains to the philosophy of the modern state, and, in particular, to the formation of the nation-state in both China and India. The chapters of this book approach the China-India comparative unit from the perspective of those national boundaries that such comparative thought helped establish, borders erected and sustained as much upon visions of China-India oneness as on histories of fracture and division. Shifting focus away from the habitual frame of solidarity, this book studies the tenuous binds that bring the China-India comparative unit into view at the very moment of its own disintegration.

Languages of Exclusion

Scholarship in China-India studies often wrestles with the inaccuracy, artificiality, or anachronism of the terms "China" and "India" in accounting for both the long history of the interconnected regions and the variegated identities of the peoples that inhabit them, subjectivities that continue to be homogenized and suppressed by the nation-states in question. This book remains less concerned with what constituted "China" and "India" through the twentieth century than with how writers conceptualized these terms and engaged in practices of thinking the two together. In the texts I study, writers evoke the national categories of "China" and "India" through a variety of terms discussed in the chapters—in most cases, *Cīn* in Hindi and *Yìndù* 印度 in Chinese. Significantly, naming "India" in Mandarin Chinese carries its own distinct cultural and political attachments, just as "China" in Hindi evokes a set of associations and precedents markedly different from those in another Indian language. My focus on these two languages and their literary traditions in this book is informed by the histories of each in its particular national context: the ways in which discourses of exclusion found articulation in these languages through the early twentieth century as each came to occupy a position of relative dominance in forming and promoting ideas of the nation.

A brief word on these histories. The language identified as "Chinese" in the English-speaking world refers in most cases to the national language of China: Mandarin, known in China as *putonghua* 普通話, which literally means "common speech" but in fact designates a language largely derived from that spoken in Beijing. While Mandarin refers to a spoken language, "the hegemony of Mandarin has been made possible through its identification more or less with the written script, an identification that lends it a kind of permanence and authority not enjoyed by other Chinese speeches."[34] Mandarin is also known in China as *hanyu* 漢語 (literally, the language of the Han people), an appellation that reveals how closely the state's governance of ethnicity and that of language have remained tied to one another, wherein the language of a single ethnic group stands for a nation of fifty-six officially recognized ethnicities and a multiplicity of languages and topolects. The story of Hindi's rise to its current status as one of India's national languages similarly tells of language's role in crafting—and policing—ideas of the nation and national identity. In the late nineteenth century, anticolonial intellectuals endowed Hindi with a new national identity by combining the Devanāgarī script with Khari Boli, a regional dialect spoken in parts of north India. This effort initially sought to make British governance in India more inclusive by calling for the official use of Devanāgarī in administrative affairs. Asserting the representational validity of the Devanāgarī script, however, required developing a literary tradition and a national identity for the language, exercises that erected a division between Hindi and its "cultural other," Urdu, giving rise to linguistically based discourses of national and religious purity with enduring violent consequences.[35]

A comprehensive study of China-India comparative thought would need to account for literatures from China's varied linguistic and ethnic contexts as well as in multiple Indian languages. China-India comparison finds expression in many tongues and scripts: for instance, in Tibetan texts, by writers in Southeast Asia who cross between Sinitic and Dravidian languages, and in Indian literary cultures that carry very different leftist legacies to that of Hindi, such as Bengali and Malayalam. Here, I study a curated selection of Chinese and Hindi literatures (in the case of the former, some written in classical Chinese and others in the "vernacular" *baihua* 白話, a distinction discussed in chapter 1). These are the texts particularly relevant to this book's quest: of understanding how exclusionary national affiliations and resultant breakdowns of transnational relation become encoded in languages of dominance and registered in literature, and of exploring how comparative literary criticism can reopen and ethically handle literary expression seemingly set to disregard, reject, or, in the extreme, vilify national others.

States of Disconnect is a multilingual book, both in terms of its materials—the vast majority of the texts studied here are unavailable in translation—as well as its analysis, which inhabits simultaneously linguistically differentiated cultural spheres and historical periods. Multilingualism, a foundational tenet of comparative literature often considered a basic prerequisite for comparison, importantly stakes a stance against both the monolingualism of the nation-state model and the Anglocentrism of a globalized literary landscape. By reading texts in Chinese and Hindi, this book combats the inevitable myopia of monolingual China-India study and breaks with the colonial model of studying one or both in comparison with the West. At the same time, however, *States of Disconnect* unsettles several assumptions that underlie the use of multilingualism as a tool for comparison. In comparative literature, the study of two or more linguistically different literatures often signals, in and of itself, the transcending of national boundaries, a methodological crutch that dates to the discipline's emergence amid the creation of monolingual nations in Europe.[36] The very different contexts of language policy and plurality in China and India aside, this book engages in multilingual inquiry toward different ends, in order to study moments when such transcendence of the national remains out of reach or undesired. Furthermore, *States of Disconnect* questions expectations of parity or horizontality that readers may bring to a book that studies multiple non-Western literatures in their languages of origin. While reading texts in Chinese and Hindi goes some way toward undoing the linguistic and epistemic hegemony of the West, Chinese and Hindi articulations hold their own exclusions within, and particularly so in those texts under study here. As I discuss further in the book's conclusion, dethroning one center of power does not yield an equal playing field; doing so only calls for heightened vigilance toward the new centers that surface in its stead.

Relating Beyond "Relations"

The act of naming China and India carries further consequences. Whether inadvertently or by design, using the terms of the nation runs the risk of conducting academic inquiry in service of the nation-states wherein scholarship is put to national use. This collaboration (or collusion) between intellectual and national work proves all the more insidious when the nations in question seek to valorize certain forms of bilateral connectivity in order to bolster their own programs of violence and suppression. Conducting humanistic work on "China and India" risks enlisting the humanities in the service of the nation-state and its instruments of power even if the scholarship itself aims to dismantle national boundaries and poses comparison as the antidote to insular modes of thought. Disclaimers and rhetorical gestures no longer go far enough when the nations themselves hold a vested interest in championing comparison as a form of dominance. The "transnational" may no longer provide an attractive solution or easy justification for comparative academic inquiry when nations themselves endorse transnationalism as a means to expand their own spheres of influence and supremacy.[37]

A curious chart entitled "Periods of China-India Cultural Contacts" (figure 0.1) provides an instructive example. The chart makes regular appearances at the annual World Book Fair in New Delhi, most recently at the January 2020 iteration of the fair, when its theme centered on Chinese literature in commemoration of seventy years since the establishment of diplomatic relations between China and India. Intended for the one million people who reportedly visited the World Book Fair in 2020, the chart opened an exhibition displaying "over 2,000 years of cultural exchanges between China and India through photographs."[38] The chart features a line graph tracing the highs and lows of China and India's "cultural contacts" through differentiated periods labeled as follows: "Initial Stage (before 1st century)," "Development Period (1st–6th century)," "Golden Period (6th–10th century)," "Transition Period (10th–17th century)," "Low Ebb (17th century–1949)," and "New Era (1950–present)." The line graph rises and falls in accordance with the labels: a high peak during the "Golden Period," for example, gradually declines during the "Transition Period" before sharply falling into the "Low Ebb." The graph ends on an upward trajectory, the line promising to rise once again to the heights of the "Golden Period" and into a bright future of China-India cultural contact ahead.

The chart visually reproduces a system of periodization formulated by Jiang Jingkui 姜景奎, a professor of Indian studies at Peking University involved in creating the chart and curating the China-India exhibition at the World Book Fair. In his scholarship, Jiang has offered a sequence of seven

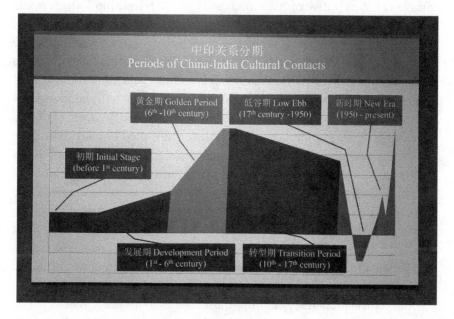

FIGURE 0.1 "Periods of China-India Cultural Contacts," World Book Fair, New Delhi, January 2020. Courtesy of Jiang Jingkui. Photo courtesy of Arunabh Ghosh.

stages that, he argues, capture the development and trendlines of exchanges between China and India over time.[39] Jiang puts forth his stages in opposition to prior systems of periodization that have long held sway in Chinese Indological scholarship, in the works of eminent scholars of India including Ji Xianlin 季羡林, Jin Kemu 金克木, and Xue Keqiao 薛克翘, all of whom chronicle the phases of China-India relations according to the Chinese dynastic periods.[40] Jiang calls for a new approach, one that takes Indian historical developments into equal consideration, breaking with the tendency to fold China-India relations into a China-centric history. Beyond reconceptualizing the periods themselves, Jiang's intervention calls for a larger shift in China-India studies away from studying one through the lens of the other, and toward the more ambitious task of grappling with the histories of both China and India simultaneously, constantly resisting the urge to enlist one side of the pairing in service of the other.[41]

As a corollary to China-India studies, the chart captures many of the exciting developments in this growing interdisciplinary field. In its portrayal of China-India relations as progressing through highs and lows, the chart disavows the narrative of "two thousand years of friendship," which would prefer to position the line graph at a perpetual, unchanging peak through history. Further, following Jiang, the chart gestures toward an expansive approach to China-India studies that strives to apprehend at once two objects of study, in both their particularities and totalities, and in rebellion against the tendency to relegate each to isolated realms of nationally defined disciplinary fields. Finally, the chart's exhibition at the popular World Book Fair in New Delhi, alongside bookstalls selling translated Chinese literature for Indian readers, signifies the immense interest in and market for all things China-India "on the ground," underscoring the fact that the practice of thinking China and India together is not the exclusive invention or domain of academic inquiry, as is often the case when the comparatist architects a particular pairing. Instead, the chart bespeaks the growth of China-India studies as an academic field in conjunction with, and in response to, the daily discourses of comparison already in circulation in both China and India.

And yet the propensity of China-India studies to find easy venues of resonance across and beyond the academy bears risks. Just as it celebrates the advances of the field, the chart also brings into view the thin line between China-India academic and national work, between public humanities and the discourses of erasure endemic to the nation-state. The chart conveys as much in what it explicitly states as in what it leaves unsaid. While its x-axis, for example, indicates a passage through time, the unlabeled y-axis remains open to interpretation. One reading could deduce from the y-axis the frequency of the "cultural contacts" that occurred during a given period, such that the peak of the "Golden Period" suggests the highest frequency of contact and vice-versa during the "Low Ebb." But the visual representation of the "Low Ebb" signifies much more than a decrease in frequency or intensity. Here, the line dips ominously below the x-axis, indicating a period of "negative" cultural contacts, before resurfacing into the "positive" realm. As the space below the x-axis thus becomes marked as "negative" in both quantitative and qualitative senses, the chart activates a slippage between numerical and emotive value. The "Low Ebb," roughly demarcating the period of Western and colonial presence and intervention in both China and India, becomes legible as a "negative" form of "cultural contact," in line with the postcolonial narrative of colonialism as tearing the otherwise friendly nations apart and pitting each against the other. Similarly designated as a "negative" fall, a brief "low" during the "New Era" unambiguously signifies the China-India war of 1962, when the two nations waged a short-lived war over territorial disputes. These "negative" moments remain unlabeled, yet the chart cleverly harnesses the visual medium of the Cartesian coordinate plane and its viewing conventions to endow what it presents as a disinterested, objective set of data with affective charge.

As a consequence of such rhetorical habits—of valorizing certain forms of "friendly" contact and glossing over other moments deemed problematic from the perspective of bilateral relations—humanistic work has tended to focus on the "highs" at the expense of the "lows." China-India literary studies have overwhelmingly centered the premodern period of translation and transmission under the auspices of Buddhism, and, in the modern period, the sole example that seems to combat the "negative" realities of colonialism: the reception of Tagore in Chinese literary circles of the 1920s.[42] Recent studies have called attention to the 1950s era of diplomacy as the heyday of positively valued relations such as "contact, cooperation, comparison, and competition."[43] Trained on such moments, those that the state designates as "friendly" connection, the humanistic eye filters out of view uncomfortable, "unfriendly" moments—colonial violence, the Tibet issue, contested borders, ongoing territorial disputes, to name a few—bracketing away all that is deemed inconvenient to the nation-states' geopolitical and security concerns. The alignment of China-India academic inquiry with the states' interests, be it inadvertently or by design, carries the grave consequence of perpetuating in scholarship the silences and erasures of nationally sanctioned narratives of "relations."

The notion of "relation" named in this book's subtitle stands in contrast to and in protest against the plural "relations," the latter designating the idiom of nation-states and its partnership with policy-based disciplines (such as international relations). I understand "literary relation" as a radical orientation toward an other—in the context of this book, toward a national other—made possible through engagement with literature, during which a nationally defined self is extended or changed by a relationship with the other.[44] *States of Disconnect* studies literary relation as a mode of thinking the self with the other that does not conform to the logic and demands of diplomacy, and that finds in the properties of literature ways of thinking the transnational beyond and outside the dominant state-sanctioned narrative of "relations." While the World Book Fair chart collapses "cultural contacts" into political relations (a conflation reiterated in its mistranslated title at the fair, which reads "China-India Relations" [*ZhongYin guanxi* 中印關係] in Chinese and "China-India Cultural Contacts" in English), I remain committed to the opposite gesture, of decoupling the two. In a sense, this book actively challenges being put to national use. Much of its historical content (the complicity of Indians under British employ in enacting colonial violence in China, the persecutions and censorship of Maoist political campaigns of the 1950s, and the border war of 1962) remains taboo or sensitive in state-sponsored arenas. In its insistence on delving into the dark side of China-India relations, this book resists its cooptation for national purposes at the same time as it studies practices of relating with national others according to the logics of literature in all its fictionalities and potentialities.

More broadly, the tendency to celebrate the "friendly" while papering over the "unfriendly" bespeaks a larger pattern of scholarly attention, one that assigns the study of friendly connection to the humanities and of friction and conflict to the political sciences. Transnational literary studies—and, more narrowly, the project of world literature—have remained largely preoccupied with accounts of affinity, solidarity, exchange, dialogue, collaboration, and so on. Such modes of analysis certainly provide crucial humanistic balance to the discourse of "tensions" that predominates the rhetoric of international relations. But what happens when we reorient our disciplinary lenses and reverse this division of intellectual labor? Can we counteract the prevalent discourse on antagonistic political relations not by furnishing instances of friendly connection, but by approaching such political relations themselves as matters of literary concern? In pursuit of such questions, *States of Disconnect* ventures into a critical space largely uncharted in literary studies, not just because this is the first book devoted to reading Chinese and Hindi literatures together, but, more important, because this book centers forms of transnational relation that have been deemed thorny or have been simply overlooked in comparative literary studies: the underbelly of politically proclaimed "friendship," the archival and embodied silences of cross-border dialogue, and forms of relation experienced in the absence of historical connectivity. By studying moments of political conflict and tension as they manifest in and shape literary form and practice, this book strives toward a literary understanding of transnationalism in crisis in order to develop hermeneutic strategies for grasping those facets of transnationalism that have tended to lie beyond humanistic reach.

States of Disconnect

The preceding sections have introduced disconnect as a crisis of transnationalism, the China-India comparative unit as the political and philosophical practice of thinking China and India together, and the concept of literary relation against the conventional "relations." I now address the final keyword in the title of this book: states. On its surface, "states" points to this book's interest in delving into moments when national categories crystallize (the unraveling of the China-India comparative unit) and in confronting head-on the resultant insularity of nationalist discourse. But beyond its literal manifestation as the nation-state, "states" describes the conditions of transnationalism in crisis a particular text inhabits and indexes.[45] This book conceptualizes three such states: friction, ellipsis, and contingency. Each defines a specific crisis of transnationalism—a historical moment when China-India connectivity is severed, interrupted, or rendered absent—that engenders particular patterns of literary practice, and that the literature in question explicitly seeks to make sense of.

Friction, ellipsis, and contingency function, in the first instance, to lay the contextual grounds from which the texts I read emerge and to supply the thematic focus of these texts. Studying these states of disconnect in literary form, however, reveals a further property. Expressions of violence, silence, and distance between China and India may appear antithetical to transnationalism, but when read as meditations on distinctly literary concerns—such as translation, signification, and interpretation—these texts yield vibrant possibilities for relation, for opening up the self to an ethical, transformative relationship with the national other. As will become clear throughout the book, the three states of disconnect at once register the mark of the nation's boundaries closing in and offer strategies for apprehending crises of transnational relation literarily, for discovering ways of relating transnationally that become discernable only through literary practice and criticism.

Together, friction, ellipsis, and contingency comprise what I hope to offer to comparative literature: an ethics of literary relation in the face of the breakdown of transnationalism. At the heart of this book lies an enduring motivation to find in literary practice, and, importantly, in literary criticism, ways to make sense of disconnect ethically, without forgoing a commitment to the nation's others and without reproducing either the exclusionary logic of the nation-state or the unequal systems of globalization. I return to this quest in the book's conclusion; for now, I briefly sketch the particularities of the three states, as those conditions and dispositions of thinking China and India together during the twentieth century to which this book attends and intervenes in, so as to aid the reader in identifying its workings in the chapters that follow. While the three states together hold and shape all five of the book's chapters, here I provisionally untangle each and identify those chapters most explicitly shaped by the presence of a given state.

Friction

The twentieth century holds important moments of collaboration, solidarity, and shared influence between China and India, moments that consolidate the China-India comparative unit; however, this period also witnessed tensions and the erosion of China-India unity, both in political registers and in cultural discourse. As I have suggested, the former instances have furnished the grounds for much of China-India humanistic scholarship, whereas the latter have often been assigned to the social and political sciences. This book sheds literary light on two such moments of friction, the elided "lows" in the New Delhi World Book Fair chart discussed above: colonial violence in the early twentieth century, when Chinese and Indians found themselves on opposing the colonizer/colonized divide, and the China-India border war of 1962. The fact that such moments have yet to garner critical attention in literary studies indicates an underlying assumption, particularly prevalent when reading non-Western texts, that because friction conventionally designates the breakdown of friendly political relations between nation-states, it also spells the absence of literary relation. Through novels, short stories, and poems that index China-India friction, I challenge this assumption, showing how the dialogic impulses of literary practice issue vectors of literary relation in the face of severed transnationalism. In so doing, I aim to redefine the notion of friction itself, away from its colloquial signification of obstacles to transnationalism, and toward its physical properties as the pregnant energy or generative heat emitted in an encounter between two chafing entities. Reading friction, thus, requires attention simultaneously to the conditions of political hostility and disintegration inscribed in the texts, and to the literary energy sparked during the clash: the reparative forms of world-making that the clash makes possible literarily.

Ellipsis

A significant "peak" in the World Book Fair chart's depiction of the twentieth century marks the 1950s, a now-fabled age of China-India "brotherhood" during which both nation-states enthusiastically looked to each other in crafting structures and models of modern statehood. I examine this era of China-India cultural diplomacy in order to interrogate the conceptual frames that have so far guided critical engagement with this period. Much of the interactions made possible by cultural diplomacy have been recorded, memorialized, and subsequently remembered under the sign of "dialogue," a metaphor literalized in photographs of state leaders and delegation members eagerly conversing with each other that often accompany archival records of transcribed speeches and interviews. In the context of cultural diplomacy conducted under the watchful eye of the nation-state, scripts of the words uttered and exchanged between the two parties gain heightened significance. The stakes are high, the potential resolution of thorny geopolitical issues hangs upon these words, and, as a result, the "dialogue" of cultural diplomacy, whether between China and India or more widely, remains necessarily subject to scrutiny, curation, and censorship, in ways both implicit and explicit. A turn instead to the ellipses of cultural diplomacy—words silenced, omitted, or illegible—opens up possibilities of relation beyond the official dialogue narrativized and edited by the nation-states. In texts of China-India cultural diplomacy, I attend to the elliptical as a repository of forms of literary relation that elude and remain unreadable in nationally sanctioned records of the period. Ellipsis grants access to moments when the machinery of cultural diplomacy malfunctions or breaks down; such moments reveal not the absence or failure of transnational relation but the limits of the nation-states' ability to overdetermine and exhaust ways to relate across national borders.

Contingency

Perhaps the most elusive of the three states, contingency brings into view literature's ability to play with ideas of past and future: to reopen a historically foreclosed past to the possibility that it could have happened otherwise, and to derail progression toward what may appear as an inevitable and predetermined future. To return a final time to the World Book Fair chart, contingency may be visualized for now as a counterpoint to the line graph's representation of a historical narrative of the China-India comparative unit. This book remains uninterested in replotting the highs and lows or in offering further plot points to such narratives; instead, through attention to contingency, I seek to reach those acts of thinking China-India together that frustrate the very idea of the past as a "plottable" series of events and that explore opportunities for transnational relation beyond cemented narratives of past events. My interest lies in literature's capacity to reopen the past to its full spectrum of potentiality. Additionally, beyond its narrative of the past, the World Book Fair chart also offers a vision of the future—the line graph soars toward its pinnacle, signaling happy times ahead—that functions as a telos of sorts, an eventual purpose in the service of which past events occur and for the fulfilment of which present events must endeavor. This chart is far from unique in its teleological narrative of the China-India comparative unit; in a sense, the act of pairing ideas of China and India throughout the twentieth century has always served as the means through which to pursue a predetermined end. The Chinese and Hindi texts of contingency studied in this book at once acknowledge and yet resist the lure of an inevitable future and, as such, diverge away from the preordained toward new, fictional horizons of possibility.

The states of disconnect sketched above play a twofold role in this book: each describes the conditions of transnationalism in crisis a given text emerges out of and intervenes in, and, at the same time, each activates the seeming opposite—the workings of specific forms of literary relation. In other words, friction, ellipsis, and contingency at once describe failures of transnationalism and, when examined literarily, offer new possibilities of transnational relation: what I articulate in the book's conclusion as an ethics. Importantly, each of the states exceeds its descriptive, contextual function and becomes a lively force for relation only when captured in literary form. What makes literature well suited to grapple with the breakdown of transnationalism ethically is its inherently dialogic character. Even when a Chinese short story, to cite an example from chapter 1, denigrates Indians as China's national enemies, or a Hindi poem, like those discussed in chapter 4, calls for unleashing militarized violence upon China, its very form as a literary text invites relation—most fundamentally, with the reader—despite the insularity of its content. By its very definitional premise, the literary text opens itself to readers and, therefore, to interpretation, at times despite its best efforts to predetermine its own horizons of meaning. Literature, then, apprehends the breakdown of transnational relation dialogically: what may appear on the surface as a rejection or disavowal of the other in fact holds within the relational forces of literary world-making, those particular qualities of literature that at once index and exceed the bounds of the real. Literature is by no means the only dialogic medium of cultural expression, but too often the study of literature foregrounds narratives of intention, historical circumstances of inception, and systematic paths of circulation—efforts that seek to understand a literary text by holding it in place rather than by celebrating its perpetual ungraspability. This book endeavors to restore to literature the full range of potentialities intrinsic to its dialogic character. My readings enact a constant negotiation between the contents of a text (expressions and themes of divisiveness) and its form, not least because I identify among literature's defining characteristics its drive to forge relation between and among writers and readers. Each chapter, therefore, registers a suspension between the opposing pulls of content and form, and, relatedly, of intention and interpretation. I find that a literary text's inherent dialogic character enables it to at once index a retreat from the transnational and conversely extend literary relation forged in the presence of and yet against the tides of political relations.

The Chapters

Although this book unfolds chronologically through the first half of the twentieth century, I do not aim to construct an exhaustive narrative of China-India literary interactions or exchange during this period. Several notable events that would comprise such a narrative—among them, Tagore's engagement with and reception in China from the 1920s onward, and the proliferation of Chinese translations and publications in India in the 1950s—do not feature centrally in this book, intentionally so for reasons outlined above. Instead, each of the chapters focuses on texts that actively position China and India together in states of disconnect, when the China-India pairing appears not as natural and celebrated but as strained and threatened, on the brink of dissolution.

The book begins in China at the turn of the twentieth century. Chapter 1, "Anatomy of Antagonism," reads a collection of Chinese poetry, short stories, and novels written between 1900 and the 1930s, largely products of Shanghai's semicolonial literary scene, that engage the much despised figure of the Indian policeman then stationed in Chinese treaty ports under British employ. In the Chinese literary imagination of the time, the figure of the Indian policeman came to signify the paradoxes of the Chinese colonial condition, wherein the enemy appeared in the guise of a fellow colonized being (the Indian) who perpetrated the violence of the colonizer (the British) upon China. Written in the experience of friction with the Indian figure, who appeared on the streets of Shanghai's International Settlement as both colonized and colonizer, brother and enemy, self and other, the Chinese texts articulate an antagonism at once founded upon intimacy and in expression of conflict. Each of the texts—from the enigmatic writer Yadong Pofo's 亞東破佛 little-known novel *Twin Souls* (*Shuang linghun* 雙靈魂, 1907) to Mao Dun's 茅盾 canonical *Rainbow* (*Hong* 虹, 1930)—engage in an exercise of thinking China and India together outside the tenets of pan-Asianism and its discourses of solidarity, extending a form of relation concerned not with connection but with repulsion. At the same time as it erodes friendly ties, this mode of thinking China and India proves generative, issuing an unexpected intersection between China's colonial condition and the concurrent late Qing and May Fourth literary debates that proved foundational to the formation of modern Chinese literature. The figure of the Indian policeman emerged as a literary vehicle through which seemingly peripheral writers and readers could participate in and reshape such debates on literary language, national consciousness, and revolutionary literature ongoing in elite literary circles of the time. The chapter tracks a transnational history of modern Chinese literature told antagonistically, from the perspective of the fraught lived experience of semicolonization and through sustained engagement with an unlikely and unwanted Indian interlocuter.

Chapter 2, "Revolution Redux," turns to India in the 1930s and to a collection of short stories by the Hindi poet-novelist Sachchidanand Hiranand Vatsyayan "Agyeya," written during his imprisonment for his involvement in anticolonial revolutionary activities. Set against the historical backdrop of 1910s China, these Hindi stories weave well-known figures such as Yuan Shikai, Sun Yatsen, and Liang Qichao into new fictional configurations, telling stories of staging revolution in China while treading the line between history and fantasy. Written in the 1930s, the stories bear the mark of an age in which Marxist narratives positioned China and India on a tandem march toward revolution. And yet, even as Indian Marxists championed revolutionary stirrings in China as heralding India's red dawn, for Agyeya imprisonment threw into question whether violent revolution, as opposed to a nonviolent Gandhian vision, truly afforded the best means to achieve independence in India. Written in the face of carceral confinement, Agyeya's stories enact layered gestures of breaking free: from the isolation of imprisonment, from the old order of things, and from the predetermination of a Marxist destiny that envisioned China and India together rising in revolution. China offers a landscape in which Agyeya's own revolutionary efforts can finally find realization, and yet, in the stories, the arrival of revolution seems to bring not jubilation, but a melancholic meditation on the costs of violence. Agyeya's stories thus contemplate unraveling the China-India pairing and unyoking the two through the seemingly contradictory act of writing China and India together. For Agyeya, the tenuous binds of the China-India pairing enable a literary exploration of the contingencies and the sacrifices of the revolutionary act, which come into view only once the inevitability of revolution—and of the China-India comparative unit—can no longer be taken for granted.

Chapter 3, "Dialogue and Its Discontents," studies the 1950s, the age of China-India brotherhood. Amid the flurry of state leaders and cultural delegates traveling to and fro, Chinese and Indian writers met in state-sponsored arenas to engage in dialogue, the foremost means of performing cultural diplomacy and consolidating bilateral relations. Such dialogue coincided temporally with the Maoist political campaigns of the mid-1950s, which brought new pressures to bear on the ideal of literary dialogue: during the Hundred Flowers Campaign of 1956, the party invited intellectuals and writers to air criticisms of the leadership, only to quickly rescind these literary freedoms during the Anti-Rightist campaign the following year. This chapter studies records of China-India cultural diplomacy unfolding upon this charged Chinese literary terrain, reading conference proceedings, reports, and travelogues by writers such as Lao She 老舍, Ye Junjian 葉君健, Mulk Raj Anand, and Ramdhari Singh "Dinkar" with an eye to the ellipsis, the fraught silences of both cultural diplomacy and political persecution. The chapter centers two scenes of poetic practice: an evening of poetry recitation held during the 1956 Asian Writers' Conference in New Delhi and recorded in poet Xiao San's 蕭三 memoirs, and the poet Dinkar's 1957 Hindi translation of a censored Chinese poem that he encountered during his visit to China at the height of the Anti-Rightist campaign. Both poetic scenes were made possible by the machinations of cultural diplomacy, and yet each remains illegible within the official records of diplomacy and confounds its nationalist logics. Disrupting both nation-states' agendas of how and why to put culture to national use, the two poetic scenes register the silences of cultural diplomacy while making possible an alternative, literary form of transnational relation. Such transnational literary relation thrives not in the performance of state-sponsored dialogue—the words carefully scripted, exchanged, and inscribed for preservation in the archival records—but in the capacity of the unsaid to bind dialogically in defiance of the tenets of diplomacy.

Chapter 4, "Word and World in Crisis," moves to 1962. In the winter of that year, as China and India waged war over contested territories, the Hindi literary scene witnessed an outpouring of writings denouncing the "Chinese invasion" into Indian territory and asserting independent India's spirit of patriotism. The outbreak of war brought to a decisive end the era of China-India diplomatic relations in the 1950s. This chapter examines a selection of Hindi literary texts written in the months immediately following the war, focusing on three moments of intertextuality in the pages of the popular Hindi magazine *Dharmayug*: a 1962 self-proclaimed "parody" of an earlier modernist poem on China-India brotherhood from the 1950s, mistranslations of Chinese poetry published in *Dharmayug* as evidence of China's "traits of treachery," and a short story entitled "New Madman's Diary," a satirical rewriting of the famous 1918 work by the Chinese writer Lu Xun. The texts engage with ideas of China as a brother turned enemy, mourning and denouncing the loss of a cultural ally now seen as a duplicitous traitor.

On the surface, and like much of the Hindi literature of 1962, the texts seem to offer little beyond racist, anti-China rhetoric and a virulent Indian nationalism that glorifies military might as a vehicle for national strength. And yet, even as these texts spell the end of brotherhood, reading friction between China and India caught in configurations of conflict ignites an energetic literary meditation on the faithfulness of the written word in a world suddenly turned untrustworthy. Through their intertextual traffic, the texts confront the ends of friendship with China by casting doubts on the fidelity of the sign and its claims of signification, and initiating a series of experiments with the fixity of literary meaning and the contingencies of interpretation. I show in this chapter how engaging hostilely with ideas of China afforded writers and readers a contemplation on literature's capacity to be read multiply in a literary climate that insisted on recruiting litera-ture narrowly in service of the nation's violence.

While the earlier chapters study texts that explicitly contemplate ideas of China and India together, chapter 5, "On Correspondence," turns to a case of China-India comparison that the writers in question did not anticipate but that has long captivated their readers and critics. The chapter examines the writings of Lu Xun and Premchand, two canonical writers whose paths never crossed, yet who are often paired as an exemplary comparison of Chi-nese and Hindi literatures. In the absence of historically evidenced interac-tion between the two, studies of Lu Xun and Premchand's works have tended to center a "similarities and differences" model of comparison. Such an approach aims to uncover points of aesthetic and political intersection between the writers; in contrast, I propose reading their lack of historical connection on its own terms by contending with Lu Xun's lifelong disdain for India and its literature while capturing his correspondence with Prem-chand, in both senses of the word as a resonance and a dialogic epistolary practice, metaphorically conceived. Exploring the historically unrealized potentialities of correspondence between Lu Xun and Premchand, this chap-ter reads each through the texts of the other, drawing out their fragmen-tary, dispersed, and mediated—but nevertheless dialogic—participation in what Lu Xun once termed "Mara" poetics, a literary spirit of revolt waged against the claustrophobic confines of conformity. The chapter puts into practice an exercise in reconceiving transnational relation as a project of literary world-making, in which correspondence across real, enforced barriers manifests not in loud proclamations of affinity but in the quiet workings of the trace that makes its presence known only as absence and in perpetual deferral.

While this book's introduction has discussed friction, ellipsis, and contingency as the conditions of transnationalism in crisis captured in the texts studied, in the conclusion, "A Comparatist's Guide to Disconnect," I draw out from these three states a schema for apprehending the relational potential disconnect attains in literary form. Reflecting on my readings in the preceding chapters, I show how an attunement to friction, ellipsis, and contingency can engender critical practices and ways of reading that open possibilities for relating transnationally when caught in disconnect, by inhabiting and experiencing its particular affordances through the medium of literature. The conclusion offers the three states of disconnect as hermeneutic strategies for contending with disconnect and finding in the seeming ends of transnationalism—amid declining globalized hyperconnectivity and rising national parochialism—an ethics of literary relation. As underscored in the conclusion, *States of Disconnect* ultimately offers humanistic tools for confronting the breakdown and failures of transnationalism while preserving its ethical commitment to opposing and exceeding national categories, thereby addressing the enduring yet timely question of how to compare in the face of disconnect.

ONE

Anatomy of Antagonism

The Indian Policeman in Chinese Literature

DURING THE EARLY decades of the twentieth century, Indian policemen were ubiquitous in China's foreign concessions, their presence marking the extraterritoriality of those areas under colonial governance. In Shanghai, the policemen served under the employ of the Shanghai Municipal Council (SMC) and were tasked with policing the International Settlement. They wielded the arms of the British empire and enforced colonial law on the streets of Shanghai's foreign enclaves. The Indian policemen thus epitomized the strange combination of cosmopolitanism and violence so characteristic of Shanghai's semicolonial landscape.

Indian policemen arrived in Shanghai via the machinations and circuits of the British empire. In the 1880s, following the perceived success of the Hong Kong Police Force's Sikh Branch, the British-dominated SMC moved to incorporate Indians into their own police force, the Shanghai Municipal Police (SMP). Formal recruiting of Indians into the SMP began in 1884, first locally from Shanghai's Indian population and later directly from Punjab, through the British Indian Army's recruitment channels.[1] The number of Indian policemen in the SMP reached three thousand at its peak, growing rapidly until British governance in Shanghai was officially dissolved in the wake of World War II, in 1943.[2] The Indians in Shanghai then gradually dispersed: some were posted in other parts of the British empire, some were repatriated to India, and others joined in Indian nationalist or Axis-led anti-British movements.[3]

The Indian policeman was brought to China as an executor of colonial violence. Nineteenth-century colonial theories of "martial races" had long cemented the mythology of the Sikh as biologically and culturally conditioned to excel at war.[4] Tales of the "Sikh warrior" circulated among the International Settlement's British residents and had informed the SMC's decision to employ Indians (many of whom had previously served in the British Indian Army) as guardians of Western economic interests and lifestyles in Shanghai against the ever-present threat of Chinese insurgency. Those in the International Settlement, Chinese and foreigner alike, regarded the Indian policeman as a loyal British subject who executed the colonizer's orders of violence; Shanghai's popular media often depicted the Indian policeman in a gesture of attack, beating up and mistreating the Chinese.[5] In the cultural imagination of colonial Shanghai, such portrayals functioned to fix the Indian policeman as the perpetrator of colonial violence and antagonist of the colonized Chinese.

This chapter studies the Indian policeman as a Chinese literary figure in a wealth of Chinese poems, short stories, and novels scattered among the profusion of Chinese journals and newspapers that circulated in Shanghai between 1900 and the 1930s. These texts engage the figure of the Indian policeman antagonistically, in expressions of hatred and hostility and often in scenes of violence. As such, Chinese texts of the Indian policeman stand in stark contrast to contemporaneous expressions of China-India friendship, for instance, in the discourses of pan-Asianism of the time. Consider, for example, the following call for a pan-Asian China-India alliance in the writings of the celebrated intellectual and revolutionary, Zhang Taiyan 章太炎 (1869–1936). In the 1907 charter for the Society for Asiatic Humanitarian Brotherhood (*Yazhou heqin hui* 亞洲和親會; also translated as Asian Solidarity Society) that he had famously founded while in Tokyo, Zhang Taiyan wrote: "We must unite the various clans and resuscitate old, but broken friendships. We must revitalize our Hinduism, Buddhism, Confucianism and Daoism and develop our compassion in order to squeeze out the evil Western superficial morality. . . . First India and China must unite to form a group. These two old countries of the East are huge and if they can be fortunate and obtain independence, they will form a shield for the rest of Asia."[6] Zhang Taiyan's vision of China and India joining forces to "squeeze out the evil Western" values that had infiltrated Asian societies under colonization, and of together forming a "shield for the rest of Asia," exemplifies the spirit of anticolonial solidarity that pan-Asianism aimed to engender. Such appeals resonated with and energized Chinese, Indian, Japanese and other anticolonial radicals gathered in Tokyo at the time, but on the streets of Shanghai, for those rooted in the daily experience of colonization, Indians appeared not as friendly allies but as the aggressors and perpetrators of colonial violence. While Zhang Taiyan called for repairing China-India "friendships" that had been "broken" under colonization, Chinese citizens subject to the Indian's policing confronted head-on the impossibility and undesirability of friendship with a figure who appeared as the colonizer in Indian guise. Chinese texts of the Indian policeman capture this dissonance, as in the following 1913 poem entitled "Mocking the Indian Policeman" by a poet who went by the name Diedie 喋喋 ("Chatterbox"):

> His face blurred like charcoal, bearded, all wrapped up in a red turban,
> Stupid like cattle, prodded along; he stands shamelessly before us.
> Such a tall, huge, strong man, yet, now his nation has fallen and he is only a slave,
> We should learn from his example, and immediately expose our own societal ignorance.[7]

The markedly divergent evocations of India in Zhang Taiyan's pan-Asianism and in texts of the Indian policeman, a figure often used (as in this poem) to typify India's complacent participation in the colonial project, underscore the vast divide between Chinese discourses on colonialism and those *of* colonialism, borne of the lived conditions of colonialism on the streets of China's semicolonies. Diedie's poem denounces the Indian policeman as a colonized "slave" (*nu* 奴) who, instead of rebelling against the binds of his own oppression, "shamelessly" (*buzhi xiu* 不知羞) inhabits a central role in furthering British colonization in China. Pan-Asianist calls for friendship with India seem entirely discordant with the anxieties of colonization heightened in everyday confrontations with this Indian proxy-colonizer. A 1934 photograph of the Indian policeman in Shanghai further captures these anxieties (figure 1.1); its caption reads, "The Indian policemen at every street junction: although they are leftover subjects of a colonized nation [*wangguo de yimin* 亡國的遺民], yet, they consider the Chinese people even lowlier than themselves."[8]

Denunciations of the Indian policeman functioned to deteriorate the China-India ties pan-Asians labored to forge, and yet, as I show in this

各馬路口的印度巡捕，可是在他們眼中，中國人是更渺小，更渺小的。遺民，雖然是亡國的

Policeman—*Indian.*

FIGURE 1.1 The Indian policeman in semicolonial China's treaty ports. "Ruci Shanghai" 如此上海 [Such is Shanghai], *Liangyou* 良友 89 (1934): 21.

chapter, expressing hostility toward the policeman in *literary* form made possible new forms of China-India relation—new ways of relating across the colonizer/colonized divide—that remain illegible under rhetorics of friendship or alliance, but that nonetheless bind together. Diedie's poem gestures toward this chapter's central concern: the intricate anatomy of antagonism as a relation that at once severs and binds, binding precisely in the moment of severance. Diedie renders the Indian policeman as a figure riddled with contradiction: he is at once intimidating and "stupid," "strong" yet weak, an agential subject passively subjected, a colonizer himself colonized. This critique of the policeman, moreover, quickly turns on itself: the concluding line unveils the poem's primary object of scrutiny as not the Indian other but the Chinese self who must take the Indian as a forewarning against colonization. In his ability to invoke and reflect the Chinese self, the Indian policeman blurs those Manichean distinctions between colonized and colonizer, self and other.

Upon closer examination, Diedie's poem reveals yet another interpretive layer. "Mocking the Indian Policeman" appeared in the *Comical Journal* (*huaji zazhi* 滑稽雜誌), a Suzhou journal printed in 1913–1914 and committed to publishing humorous materials in line with what Christopher Rea has termed the "age of irreverence" in modern Chinese popular culture.[9] A reader flipping through the journal would have read Diedie's seemingly heavy criticism of the "shameless" Indian policeman in a humorous, lighthearted tone. Humor enables the reader to momentarily disarm the Indian, stripping the policeman of his ability to victimize, framing him instead as the victim of ridicule. The poem's instruction to learn from the policeman's example provides another strategy for prevailing over the oppressor since the policeman becomes a means in service of enlightening the Chinese self. In this way, the poem beckons identification with the policeman in the same gesture as it enables the reader to imaginatively subvert the policeman's violence. Again, the poem exemplifies the self-effacing and power-inflected contradictory pulls of an antagonism apprehended in literary form. The poem, along with the trove of texts discussed in this chapter, demonstrates how everyday clashes between Indian and Chinese—the constant chafing of antagonists enmeshed in the web of colonial power dynamics—sparked Chinese literary engagements with ideas of India that at once explode notions of friendship and, at the other extreme, of enmity.

Beyond interrogating polar structures of transnational relation, this chapter also shows how Chinese texts of the Indian policeman played a formative role in shaping Chinese anticolonial discourse and literary modernity during times of historical transition. The first four decades of the twentieth century proved a crucial period in the development of modern Chinese literature, when normative ideas of the language, form, and uses of literature underwent rapid transformation in the quest to mold a literature best suited to herald China into modernity and nationhood. Literary histories of this period capture the vibrant debates that incited a wide variety of literary practice, from the search for modernity in late Qing fiction, to the New Culture movement of early Republican China, and competing visions of revolutionary literature in the 1930s. Throughout, the Indian policeman emerged as a literary vehicle through which seemingly peripheral writers and readers of popular literature could enter into debates ongoing in elite literary circles of the time, on asserting anticolonial national autonomy, vernacularizing literary language and form, and sparking the reader's revolutionary consciousness. As such, the Chinese literary figure of the Indian policeman articulates an unexpected intersection between the ontologies of China's colonization and the late Qing and early Republican literary discourses so foundational to modern Chinese literature. Texts of the Indian policeman imbue such discourses with the everyday anxieties of confronting colonization and reckoning with one's own position in its power-riddled operations. The story of the Indian policeman in Chinese literature, therefore, doubles as a story of modern Chinese literature's development viewed from the perspective of China's colonial experience. This chapter tracks a transnational history of modern Chinese literature told antagonistically, by centering the lived experience of semicolonization and through sustained engagement with an unlikely and unwanted Indian interlocuter.

India in Chinese Anticolonial Discourse

Zhang Taiyan's call for China and India to unite encapsulates one of two main strains of Chinese anticolonial discourse that centrally engaged ideas of India. The first, pan-Asian strain emerged at the turn of the twentieth century and found early articulation in the writings of Japanese intellectual Okakura Kakuzō, who envisioned a singular "Asia" made up of various mutually dependent components, together comprising an organism of sorts.[10] Okakura cast his vision of a single Asia in explicitly anticolonial terms, referring to Western encroachment in Asia as "the White Disaster" plaguing all of Asia, against which Asia must unite.[11] The concept of "Asia" as an anticolonial force quickly gained currency among Japanese, Chinese, Indian, Korean, Filipino, Burmese, and other intellectuals, who gathered in Tokyo and formed various associations to conceptualize Asia as one. Okakura's ideal of a united Asia, however, soon developed fissures. As early as 1905, when Japan's establishment of a protectorate over Korea foreshadowed Japanese expansionist aspirations in the rest of Asia, Chinese intellectuals grew wary of the idea of Asia as united under Japanese leadership. Already by 1907, Chinese intellectuals who had traveled to Japan in search of alternative paths toward China's modernization grew increasingly alarmed at Japan's expansionist ambitions in East Asia.[12] As a result, Chinese intellectuals—most notably, Zhang Taiyan—began to substitute their earlier hopes for a China-Japan partnership with new ideas for a China-India alliance.

Zhang Taiyan had immersed himself in the study of Buddhist texts prior to his arrival in Tokyo in 1906. By then, Zhang's interest in Buddhism had led him away from Western-centered discourse and toward a narrative of anti-imperial resistance based on ideas of Asian unity.[13] In Tokyo, Zhang met two Indian nationalist law students who visited him upon their arrival from America.[14] Zhang later wrote of the meeting as transformative: "I was completely overwhelmed by sadness after I had heard the Indian revolutionaries' bleak account of India's abysmal condition."[15] The men invited Zhang to participate in Indian anticolonial events taking place in Tokyo, and Zhang's growing association with the community of Indian nationalists in Tokyo further cemented his view of Japan as no longer a trusted Asian ally but a growing imperialist power that posed a threat greater than that of the Western powers.[16] Through Zhang's writings—in particular, the charter for the Society for Asiatic Humanitarian Brotherhood—pan-Asian thought grew to decenter Japan and instead foreground a China-India alliance. The society was disbanded some eighteen months after its establishment, yet the China-India pan-Asian alliance it inaugurated continued to hold sway in the decades to come.

The second strain of Chinese anticolonial discourse that engaged ideas of India can be termed the "front car" (*qianche* 前車) rhetoric. During the Hundred Days Reform (*wuxu bianfa* 戊戌變法) of 1898, a group of intellectuals and officials under the leadership of Kang Youwei 康有為 (1858–1927) attempted to implement institutional reforms within the structure of the Qing state. Amid growing threats of Western and Japanese encroachment on Chinese territory and resources, the reformers sought to strengthen the Qing state by better adapting it to the demands of a modernizing world while retaining the Qing emperor's political autonomy vis-à-vis the colonial powers. Their efforts came to an abrupt end with the Empress Dowager Cixi's suppression of the movement and expulsion of its proponents. Exiled intellectuals continued to debate from overseas the ideal path they hoped China would follow into modernity. Some looked to India as they considered possibilities for postdynastic Chinese state structures. In their writings, India functioned as a yardstick against which to assert both the imminence of China's colonization and the urgent necessity of fending off colonial invasion. China and India were commensurable enough, the narrative ran, for India's colonization to portend China's impending fall, but the two differed in one crucial respect: China could still avoid India's fate by learning from its example (as echoed in Diedie's poem) and implementing the necessary reforms, even if this entailed borrowing strategically from the West.

Kang Youwei's writings on India exemplify this narrative. In 1902, and while in exile in India, Kang published an essay on China's susceptibility to colonization. The essay responded to those scholars who, referring to the ongoing division of the Balkans and other Western regions, recommended provincialization or fragmentation as a viable option for China. Kang disagreed. India's colonization, he argued, stemmed precisely from the fragmented and internally combative nature of its many independent domains under Mughal rule, and such disunity had weakened its ability to mount a strong defense in the face of British colonization. A similar provincialization of China was sure to result in its colonization.

In order to persuade his reader to glean lessons from India, Kang had to first establish China and India as commensurate, a task he approached through a detailed comparison between the two. It would be a mistake, Kang argued, to apply Western theories to an Asian context; analogies to France and America necessarily fail to apply to China, given the fundamental contextual incompatibility between the West and Asia. In order to draw from another nation's model, Kang urged his reader to seek a nation with similar historical, geographical, political, and societal features as China, a nation with which China already shared a foundational sameness:

In comparison to China, is there any nation with a similar location in Asia, of a similar size, a similar ratio of coastal and landlocked territories, a similarly large-sized population; with as advanced an enlightenment, as ancient a civilization; with similar laws and customs, similarly soft-natured peoples; similarly invaded by Northerners, similarly unified, and with a similarly autocratic government?.... Fortunately, there is one nation ... that can act as our mirror, whose example we can learn from. It is close enough to our case, and unlike France and America, is not in an entirely different category from us.... This is none other than India.[17]

In the remainder of his lengthy essay, Kang expands on each of the categories listed above, enumerating the similarities between China and India in each aspect while drawing from a variety of historical sources and his personal experiences in India. He outlines India's Mughal history in detail, frequently pairing Mughal and Qing governance to highlight parallels and divergences between the two. Framing India as a "mirror" capable of revealing China's fate enables Kang to make a case for why China should avoid the path India seemed to have taken into colonization. Repeatedly, Kang warns his reader against inciting revolution in the name of internal divisions in China: "Revolution? [Provincial] Independence? That path is sure to lead to colonization and slavehood!. . . . If my compatriots do not want colonization, then do not follow the example of India's provincial revolution and independence."[18] Kang wanted China to diverge from India on the "railroad track" of history along which India figured as the "front car."

Unlike Zhang's call for China-India unity, the idea of sameness Kang Youwei articulated in his 1902 essay resists being collapsed into solidarity. Instead, Kang's sameness provides the necessary grounds upon which difference can become visible and, indeed, possible. Despite Kang's use of positivistic categories (e.g., size of land mass and population, geographical proximity) that seem to establish an all-encompassing, at times even simplistic, sameness between China and India, this sameness does not erase but enables difference. In Kang's writing, the China-India comparative unit is temporary and precarious. The binds that tie China and India together come into view only in the promise of their own dissolution. It is this antagonistic mood of thinking China and India together that informs the early texts of the Indian policeman. While ideas of pan-Asian solidarity have long occupied the center stage of China-India literary study, this chapter delves into the creative possibilities afforded by the figure of the Indian policeman to exceed idealistic proclamations of solidarity and explore instead the tenuous intimacies of thinking China and India together through the uneasy binds of a sameness undesired.

India was not the only colony that figured in Chinese intellectuals' debates on how best to resist colonization and retain national autonomy. Historian Rebecca Karl has shown that, in addition to India, early twentieth-century Chinese intellectuals closely monitored ongoing struggles and developments in the Philippines, South Africa, Poland, Egypt, Turkey, Vietnam, Manchuria, and a host of other sites in the colonial world.[19] Yet India stood apart in the Chinese cultural imagination of the time—a crucial point that has remained obscured in studies of late Qing transnationalism. The discursive centrality of India resulted in large part from the particular conditions of colonization in China, which brought Chinese and Indians face-to-face on the streets of China's foreign concessions from opposing sides of the colonizer/colonized divide.

Given the structure of colonial intervention in Chinese treaty ports, scholars have found it useful to analyze the distinct set of Chinese historical and cultural colonial categories under the rubric of semicolonialism. Shu-mei Shih, for example, has argued that the presence of pockets of extraterritoriality governed by multiple colonial powers—most prominently, Britain, Germany, France, Japan, Russia, and the United States—in cooperation and competition with each other engendered unique Chinese ideological, political, and cultural formations that do not align with experiences of formal colonialism (as in India).[20] In Shih's account, the mosaic of colonial enclaves produced a "fragmentary" or "diffused" colonial presence in China, resulting in an "ambivalence toward colonialism."[21] One factor in such ambivalence involved a bifurcated "split in the concept of the West" between an attractive, desirable metropolitan West and an undesirable colonial West. In addition, Shih argues, because Chinese "native culture" had been "deconstructed" by thinkers who sought to overthrow tradition in favor of modernity, an idea of "tradition" no longer existed as epistemologically distinct from the colonial realm and so could not serve unproblematically as a site of resistance. As a result, in colonial China, "it was difficult to target the enemy clearly," and "articulating resistance [proved] difficult."[22]

In this semicolonial landscape, the figure of the Indian policeman gains singular importance. On the streets of Shanghai, the West as colonizer remained largely invisible, obscured by the flashy and alluring signs of the metropolitan West. Instead, the Indian policeman, a daily oppressor of the Chinese in the International Settlement, fulfilled the role of the colonial enemy. His intimidating appearance—turban, long mustache and beard, large stature, baton in hand—made for an instantly identifiable and hypervisible sign of colonial jurisdiction and administration. And because he policed everyday crimes (such as traffic violations and petty thefts), the Indian policeman embodied the face and facet of colonial governance with which Chinese citizens had the most direct interaction. If, as Meng Yue has argued, colonial Shanghai embodied an "unruly" spirit as the playground of socially, politically, and legally ungovernable figures from bandits and prostitutes to anarchists, revolutionaries, and radicals, the Indian policeman stood as the antagonist of the very essence of Shanghai.[23]

Yet the Indian policeman inhabited the role of colonial enemy uncomfortably. Viewed at once as a proxy-colonizer and a colonized being himself, he sparked a form of resistance founded upon self-identification, infusing the discourse of Kang's tenuous China-India sameness with the realities and lived experiences of China's semicolonial condition. Given the popularity of the Indian policeman as the literary vehicle of choice in engaging ideas of colonialism, the Chinese colonial condition unexpectedly found its clearest literary articulation not in opposition to a (Western) colonizer but in mediation through a fellow (Indian) colonized being. By rendering the Indian policeman in literary form, writers explored an antagonistic mode of transnational thought that eschewed lofty assertions of pan-Asian solidarity, which seemed to find little resonance on the ground, while articulating a new idiom in which to express colonial anxieties and stage anticolonial protest.

The Concept of *wangguo nu*

A 1904 novel, *My People After Partition* (*Fenge hou zhi wuren* 分割後之吾人) by Xu Zhuodai 徐卓呆 (1880–1958), presents an early example of how Chinese literary engagements with colonialism inhered within depictions of the Indian policeman. Xu penned the novel during his days in Japan as a foreign student of physical education (1902–1905), some years before he burst onto the Shanghai cultural scene as the "Charlie Chaplin of the East."[24] *My People* was published serially in the popular journal *Jiangsu* 江蘇, printed in Tokyo by an association of overseas students from the eponymous province in China. The novel ranks as the first text Xu authored under the pen name Zhuodai, a tongue-in-cheek moniker simultaneously connoting greatness and stupidity.[25] The penname alludes to the farcical tone and sharp wit Xu would soon become well known for, and, indeed, *My People* bears signs of this literary style in its incipiency, marking Xu's transition from an overtly political literary persona into a master of comedy. The year before *My People*, Xu's novel *Tomorrow's Partition* (*Mingri zhi guafen* 明日之瓜分, 1903) appeared in the same journal under the penname Guazi 瓜子.[26] *Tomorrow's Partition* takes on the theme of confronting China's impending division by foreign powers, critiquing China's blind complacency in granting the colonizers entry and access. Expanding on the same theme, *My People* picks up where the earlier novel ends by imagining the aftermath of partition in a China already subjected to colonial rule.

My People opens with its protagonist Huang Shibiao 黄士表 (literally, "yellow scholarly model"), a Han Chinese from Jiangsu, reading news of China's dire circumstances following the invasion of the Eight-Nation Alliance (the foreign powers that sent troops to quell the Boxer Uprising of 1900). Huang Shibiao dozes off and is awoken by a tap on his shoulder. An old man named Huang Xuanchu 黃軒初 has appeared and offers to give Huang Shibiao a tour of the terrible sights of colonized China. The reader realizes that Huang Shibiao has "awoken" to a dystopic dream of China's future under colonization. The novel goes on to paint vivid scenes of the Chinese people's fate as colonized people living under the yoke of foreign rule.

In one such scene, Huang Shibiao and the old man are discussing the high colonial taxes and the common man's hardships when they happen upon a group of black-faced and turbaned Indian policemen marching to the orders of a British man. The old man explains that these are colonized Indians, "nothing but slaves."[27] Xu's characterization of the Indian policeman as a colonized slave evokes the concept of *wangguo nu* 亡國奴. By the end of the nineteenth century, *wangguo nu*—literally, "slave of the lost/vanquished nation"—had become a ubiquitous term to convey slavishness under colonization. The term *wangguo* pre-dates Western presence in China, its history extending back centuries, when it referred to a lost or conquered state during dynastic change.[28] In the context of late Qing discourse, *wangguo* immediately signified colonization, with the Indian policeman commonly figuring as the quintessential slave (*nu*), given his perceived complicity in carrying out the colonizer's dirty work in China.[29] As in Diedie's poem, writers quickly became accustomed to denouncing the Indian policeman as a colonized slave; the epithet *wangguo nu* fulfilled the dual purpose of expressing contempt for the Indian and the colonial apparatus he stood for while also asserting China's relative (albeit precarious) autonomy in the colonial world.

The *wangguo nu* concept emerges as a central preoccupation in *My People*. In order to depict a postpartition Chinese landscape, Xu effects a deeper, discursive transformation of the *wangguo nu* concept's system of reference. *My People* rewrites *wangguo nu* as capable not only of drawing a contrast between the colonized slave and still-autonomous Chinese, as in its popular usage, but also to articulate an equivalence between the two. Xu opens up the *wangguo nu*'s referential capacity by harnessing the figure of the Indian policeman, the exemplary colonized slave. In the novel's construction of a fallen China, depicting the Indian policeman proves a powerful literary strategy for positioning the Chinese subject not as separate from or in opposition to a colonized slave, but as a colonized slave himself.

To this end, Xu writes a series of interactions between Huang Shibiao and the Indian policeman, crafted to displace the idea of *wangguo nu* from the category of other and into that of self. A crucial scene unfolds in a teashop where Huang Shibiao and the old man retreat for a bite to eat. As they discuss the high price of food (again, a consequence of the inhumane taxes the British impose), an Indian man enters: "His stature was short and his face was yellow with a red cloth wrapped around his head. . . . Upon closer examination, he didn't look Indian at all." Confused, Huang Shibiao asks where the man is from and is surprised to learn that he is indeed Chinese. "Why are you dressed in this way?" Huang Shibiao asks. "Don't you know?" the man replies, "The British have ordered that our clothing must now change, we must dress like the Indians." Huang Shibiao is dumbstruck. Soon after, he leaves the tea shop to find a sea of people dressed like the Indian *wangguo nu*. This image of Indian policeman and Chinese subject as indistinguishable from each other literalizes Xu's resignification of *wangguo nu*. As this realization sinks in, Huang Shibiao declares, "I, Huang Shibiao, vow that one day I will finally take revenge on this great enemy."[30]

The notion of Chinese and Indian blending into one elicits terror, what Karl has termed the "terror of doubling" in her discussion of *My People*, "the immanence of Chinese as a 'lost people' evoked by the fearful plausibility of interchangeability of Chinese and Indians."[31] This is not a union of Chinese and Indian in solidarity, but neither does this gesture entail rupture or hostile estrangement. The hybrid image of a single body that appears both Chinese and Indian (here, yellow skin and Indian turban) realizes the intimacy of friction, a relation predicated upon contact. Closeness experienced on the most intimate of scales, that of the body, amplifies the terrifying nature of the encounter, thereby precipitating the novel's pedagogical imperative to jolt its reader out of the lull of complacency (as literalized in Huang Shibiao's vow of revenge). Huang Shibiao's—and the reader's—urge to resist this merging of Chinese and Indian further emphasizes the fleeting, strained quality of a China-India unity that finds expression as an object of rebellion, only in the imaginary dreamscape of a fictional text and only in the hope that this unity never ventures into the realm of the real. Echoing Kang Youwei's "front car" rhetoric, the hybrid *wangguo nu* furnishes a provisional China-India sameness necessary for arousing a desire for divergence.

My People takes its project—of refiguring *wangguo nu* to signify the Chinese self—a step further. The Indian *wangguo nu*'s enslavement granted him the power to oppress other colonized beings, making him complacent in his own colonization. A fallen China could not afford such passivity. To avoid this pitfall, Xu casts the colonized Chinese as even more enslaved than the lowly Indian. When Huang Shibiao first observes the marching policemen, he asks about the British officer standing behind them. The old man replies:

> "This is the Police Chief." Shibiao asked, "Why do they not appoint an Indian as the Chief?" The old man answered, "The reason is that they are Indians, they are a colonized people, nothing more than slaves. How could they be allowed to work in a position of authority? Ah! Indian people have lost their nation, yet they can hold a wooden baton and stand at the traffic junctions, wielding the power of the British, bullying, scaring, and ridiculing us. Although our compatriots are colonized, do not think that you can now bully others; you will still be bullied by others. At least Indians can still serve as the British's slavish beasts of burden. I'm afraid that our people cannot even be such slavish beasts." Upon hearing this, Shibiao couldn't help but cry.[32]

Here, the old man frames the colonized Chinese as oppressed not by the colonizer but by the colonizer's slave. The Chinese *wangguo nu*, then, becomes the slave of a slave. This theme recurs throughout, such as when Huang Shibiao witnesses two Indian policemen brutally kicking an elderly Chinese woman to the ground while wrongfully accusing her of causing a commotion.[33] The Chinese surpasses the Indian as the most wretched of the colonized people, further entrenching the Chinese subject within the concept of *wangguo nu*.

My People does not afford its reader the relief of awakening from Huang Shibiao's nightmare or witnessing his act of revenge. The novel ends abruptly after its first five chapters; the remaining parts never made it to print.[34] The novel's incompleteness leaves Huang Shibiao trapped in his nightmare, tasking the reader, instead, with the imperative of awakening. As the political potential of imagining oneness between the Chinese subject and Indian *wangguo nu* gained increased literary recognition, Xu's endeavor found completion in the various experiments with the Indian policeman that writers conducted in the years to come.

Twin Souls

In early March 1907, the popular Shanghai-based newspaper *Shenbao* 申報 issued an apology to its readers. *Shenbao* would no longer carry the novel that the newspaper had published in installments over the past week.[35] A new novel by the same writer would now take its place, a "bizarre and bewildering" tale entitled *Twin Souls* (*Shuang linghun* 雙靈魂). The novel would be written in an allegorical style, like that of Zhuangzi, with the aim of "awakening the nation's soul" (*huanxing guohun* 喚醒國魂).[36] As promised, the newspaper's 1907 spring issues published *Twin Souls* in twenty-four installments over the course of a month. The novel tells the story of an Indian policeman, Jing Erya 警爾亞 (literally, "police of Asia"), whose soul transfers into the body of a Chinese student, Huang Zuhan 黃祖漢 ("yellow descendent of the Han"). *Twin Souls* chronicles the adventures of its titular figure—a man whose body contains within it two souls, one Chinese and one Indian—each vying for dominance over the other.

The novel opens with Jing's death. One snowy night in Shanghai, in the course of a dramatic chase, Jing is shot by a gang of bandits. His body falls to the ground. Huang bumps into Jing at the precise moment of the latter's death, just as the soul is departing Jing's body. Huang experiences a jolt of fright and shock, a cold sensation washes over him. At this moment, unbeknownst to both Huang and Jing, Jing's Indian soul transfers into Huang's Chinese body. The Chinese and Indian souls remain unaware that they are now housed within a single body, and Jing never realizes that he has died. As the souls cyclically gain and cede control of Huang's body, the body (with a Chinese external appearance) alternates between acting out the life of an Indian policeman and that of a Chinese student. These fluctuations occur without warning, resulting in the following sorry scene in which this body bearing twin souls paces back and forth, one moment toward Jing's police station on a road bearing a "Western" name (Pike Road), and the next toward Huang's home on a road with a "native" Chinese name (Fuzhou Road):

> This one body, then, held two souls. Its consciousness had also split in two. Suddenly, for a moment, he would think of his name as Huang Zuhan. But the next moment, he would think he was Jing Erya. For a moment he would walk northwest, wanting to return to Pike Road. But the next second, he would suddenly start walking southeast, wanting to return to Fuzhou Road. And so, at this time, his thought and actions were chaotic, as though in a dream. He walked back and forth between the two ends of the bridge, like a butterfly caught in a spider's web, unable to escape.[37]

The twin-souled man remains trapped between the status of "foreigner" and "Chinese" in semicolonial Shanghai, a city that otherwise drew clear spatial and administrative demarcations between the areas under foreign jurisdiction and those under Chinese control. The twin-souled body frustrates such categories. In a series of comic incidents, for example, he salutes a passing British officer in English (much to the confusion of the general), while the next moment he frequents a local shop and orders breakfast in Chinese.

After several such episodes of confusion, Huang/Jing is admitted to a hospital in the International Settlement where a doctor finally diagnoses his twin-souled condition. The British doctor, however, fails to find a cure. Huang's desperate parents attempt a number of alternative methods to exorcise Jing's soul from Huang's body, including traditional Chinese medical remedies, folk shamanistic rituals, religious appeals, but to no avail. Finally, they take the twin-souled man to a "Universal Scientific Research Centre," where scientists from a host of Western nations descend upon him to offer various scientific solutions.

By the end of the novel, all attempts prove futile. Both Chinese traditional medicine and the Western natural sciences fail to cure Huang. An educationist by the name of Jili 基立 (meaning "foundational"), president of the research center, concludes that no external scientific cure can return to Huang autonomy over his body. For the Chinese soul to triumph, he must strengthen himself through self-education and thereby shield himself from Jing's onslaughts. If he does so, "it will not be difficult to cultivate [peizhi 培植] his Chinese soul and gradually defeat his Indian soul."[38]

Shenbao printed each installment of *Twin Souls* with the subtitle "allegorical fiction" (*yuyan xiaoshuo* 寓言小説), in line with the description of the novel in its initial advertisement. True to this description, the novel lends itself to a clear allegorical interpretation in which Jing's invasion and occupation of Huang's body stands for the foreign powers' colonial presence in China. This condition, the author argues, can only be rectified intrinsically through education and a self-motivated strengthening of a national consciousness, not by some externally enforceable cure borrowed from the West. Throughout, the novel provides explicit encouragement for its interpretation as a national allegory, voicing the familiar late Qing anxiety over China's increasingly colonized nature. In one such instance, when Jing's soul gains control over Huang's body, the narrative pauses, as is characteristic in late Qing fiction, to inject the following authorial aside: "I can see the daily diminishing of the nation's soul, while the foreign [*ke* 客] soul is increasingly aroused and flourishes. Alas!"[39]

The novel's rejection of Western science in favor of Chinese knowledge and ethics as providing a cure for the afflicted national soul finds further corroboration in the author's biographical details. Although *Twin Souls* appeared in *Shenbao* anonymously, the novel was later attributed to Peng Yu 彭俞 (1876–1946) under the pen name Yadong Pofo 亞東破佛.[40] Originally from Zhejiang province, Peng moved to Shanghai in 1906 where he published a series of novels and short fiction, including *Twin Souls*, while working at small printing houses to earn his living.[41] Around the age of forty, and on the recommendation of his friend the philosopher Ma Yifu 馬一浮 (1883–1967), Peng entered the Hupao temple near Hangzhou to study Buddhist and Daoist classics, eventually becoming a monk there. He reentered secular life in 1928 and resumed his literary career in Shanghai until his death.[42] Peng's interest in traditional Chinese forms of knowledge, which later led him to pursue a study of the classics as a monk, is evident in his literary practice in *Twin Souls*.

As a national allegory, *Twin Souls* fits comfortably with the newspaper *Shenbao*'s program. Founded in 1872 by the British merchant Ernest Major in Shanghai's International Settlement, the Chinese-language *Shenbao* modeled itself in opposition to the Qing court's official gazette, the main source of news at the time.[43] Unlike the gazette, which selectively conveyed voices of elites and those pieces of news officials deemed appropriate for dissemination, *Shenbao* prided itself as a vehicle for public opinion, debate, and entertainment in service of its "double agenda of general enlightenment and progressive change."[44] *Shenbao* described its mission in its inaugural issue as providing "the 'newest' and most 'up-to-date' knowledge, in order to 'renew the people.'"[45] Accordingly, *Twin Souls*'s publication in *Shenbao* would have amplified for readers the novel's express intention to "awaken the nation's soul" (as advertised in the initial announcement), with the invaded body's quest for autonomy unambiguously signaling the nation's plight under colonization.

Twin Souls performs its symbolic, allegorical function somewhat paradoxically, through an intensely material construction of and meditation on the site of the body. Take, for example, the novel's detailed explanation of how a single body can come to contain two souls. According to the canonical Chinese medical text *Huangdi neijing* 黃帝內經, the narrator explains, the soul resides within the liver. When a person suffers a fright, the gate to the soul's abode can suddenly open, whereupon the soul can escape from the liver, travel through the spine up to the brain, and exit the body through the "skull-gate" that has now also opened as a result of the fright.[46] The shock Huang experienced upon bumping into Jing caused the former's soul to fall out of his liver, but just as Huang's soul traveled toward the skull-gate, Jing's soul rushed in through it. At that moment, the chilly conditions of the snowy night (to which Huang's internal organs were now exposed, due to the opening in his skull) caused Huang's muscles to contract, closing the gate and trapping both Chinese and Indian souls within Huang's body. Both souls then followed the spinal path back to the liver and resided therein.[47] This minutely detailed and, according to the medical texts quoted, seemingly plausible explanation of the twin-souled condition literalizes the symbolic capacity of a protagonist who appears at once as an abstracted allegory and as a real, material being. In this way, the novel pulls the reader outward onto the conceptual scale of the nation at the same time as it draws the reader into the innards of the substantial body.

The allegorized nation's identity crisis under colonization similarly inheres within the site of the body as the twin-souled man struggles to recognize himself while under Jing's (the proxy-colonizer's) control. Forced to confront his body in a mirror, the man's confusion echoes the dissonance and disorientation of consolidating a national consciousness while under foreign rule:

The doctor asked his attendant to bring a mirror. He placed the mirror in front of Huang Zuhan. Huang peered in the mirror and was panic-stricken. He said, "I am Jing Erya! How could I have suddenly changed into a Chinese person? Ah! How can this be, how can this be?" The doctor said, "This body is not yours. Do you believe me now?" With great disbelief, Huang looked in the mirror again. After a while, he suddenly asked, now speaking in Chinese, "Why are you making me look in a mirror?"[48]

The souls struggle to come to terms with a body each feels alienated from. Huang is a stranger in his own body, while Jing, who later carefully examines the yellow color of his skin and newly shortened stature, encounters his body as belonging to someone else. Heightened attention to and detailed descriptions of the body's physical attributes and material specificity seem to contradict the novel's self-professed recommendation to read it symbolically. In heeding this direction, the readerly labor involved in resisting the lure of the literal and in constantly abstracting into allegory lies at the heart of the novel's educational ambition of cultivating the national soul as the only viable path to decolonization. Training the reader in abstraction inculcates a participation in the formation of a collective national consciousness; the novel thus performs its moral.

Shuttling its reader between the scales of the abstract and the concrete, the novel's anticolonial sensibility emerges as an aspirational yet embodied practice mediated through the lived experience of the ontological body. Since the Chinese body is reigned over by one soul at a time (usually by Huang's in the morning and Jing's in the afternoon), when Jing is dominant, the Chinese body performs the motions of a colonized British subject and experiences on a bodily register the conditions of the Indian's colonial oppression. In one scene, Huang/Jing is taken to the police station—ironically, the very police station where Jing used to work before his death. Jing holds control over the body at this point, but because he outwardly appears to be a Chinese man, another Indian policeman (Jing's former colleague) promptly throws him into a prison cell. Jing cries out to the policeman in an "Indian language" (yinyu 印語): ' "We have lost our nation, and our people have been stamped out! How can you not feel any compatriotism towards me and still imprison me?' The [British] inspector overheard him say this. Furious, he rushed into the cell and began beating [Jing] with a baton. Whenever British people hear the Indian policemen conversing in their local language, the

British at once start to beat them up, for they fear that this may spark [Indian] patriotism [*aiguo sixiang* 愛國思想]."[49]

This prison scene instigates a radical reordering of the conventional demarcations of colonizer/colonized in Shanghai that positioned the Indian proxy-colonizer and Chinese subject on opposing sides of the divide. Here, inhabiting a hybrid body allows both Chinese and Indian to experience the other's colonial condition, giving rise to an otherwise impossible realization of shared colonization. Furthermore, this realization occurs in the throes of layered conflict between Chinese and Indian: Huang and Jing compete to gain control over the Chinese body, the Indian prison guard unjustly imprisons the Chinese, the British inspector mistakenly beats the Chinese body while intending to punish the Indian. This tangled web of antagonistic relations unexpectedly enables the Chinese body to verbalize a position of sameness with the Indian policeman—he utters the Indian's words: we (*wobei* 我輩) have lost our nation, we are compatriots. The sound of these words incites the British inspector's ire. As he beats the prisoner, it is the Chinese body that receives the colonizer's abuse and endures the physical pain that, we are told, was meant to be inflicted on the Indian for his subversive use of the "Indian language." And just as Huang bears the British colonizer's violence, Jing, now imprisoned by his compatriot, is subject to the Indian policeman's exercise of power over the Chinese.

Later on, an interrogator interviews the prisoner, unaware that Huang's soul has regained control over the body. Confused by the conflicting answers he receives from the prisoner, who now claims to be a Chinese student, the interrogator raises his baton at Huang. Huang cries out, "You British are praised as the most civilized in the world, yet you use your power to punish and force people to submit to you!"[50] Here, Huang speaks Jing's protest: inverting the colonial logic of the white man's civilizing mission, he accuses the British of barbarism for perpetuating the violence that facilitates and bolsters their rule. Yet the possibility of solidarity between Chinese and Indian crumbles with the realization that Huang's vocalized combativeness with the British only underscores Jing's silence, a sign of the Indian *wangguo nu*'s slavishness and complacency. Huang's outcry performs Jing's rebellion at the same time as it highlights Jing's impotence in voicing his own protest. The experience of viscerally sharing in and bearing witness to the other's colonial subjugation makes possible a joint anticolonial critique animated by difference, one that positions Chinese and Indian as together opposing a shared colonizer in the same gesture as it rejects equation between the Chinese and Indian's colonial conditions.

Once the twin-souled man arrives at the research center, the novel shifts perceptibly in both tone and focus. While the first fifteen chapters tell the often comedic story of the twin-souled man's misfortunes, replete with episodes of mistaken identity and misguided cures, the remaining nine chapters at the research center are comprised of the scientists' lengthy speeches elaborating cures for the twin-souled condition based on Western scientific and medical discourses of the day ranging from hypnosis to optical physics.[51] Referring primarily to the second half of the novel, the eminent critic A Ying 阿英 (Qian Xingcun 錢杏邨, 1900–1977) evaluates the novel as an inferior work that exhibits the structure of a novel but lacks the descriptive content of one.[52] Indeed, the second half of Twin Souls seems to only loosely resemble the late Qing novel, given the move away from the event-driven earlier chapters to a discursive turn in the later chapters in which the plot fades into the background. The speeches transcribed in the novel's second half engage explicitly with ongoing late Qing debates on the applicability of Western methods for solving Chinese problems,[53] and anticipate post-1919 discussions on the validity of Western science (kexue 科學) versus Chinese metaphysics (xuanxue 玄學) in curing sociopolitical crises.[54] Injecting itself into these ongoing debates, Twin Souls rejects Western science in favor of traditional Chinese nonscientific and spiritual methods to cure the soul, a conclusion the Marxist A Ying deemed a failure.

A year after its publication in Shenbao, Twin Souls was reprinted in book form (see figure 1.2), and, significantly, A Ying evaluated the novel based on this later version. In its earlier iteration in the newspaper, Twin Souls ends with the statement that cultivating the Chinese soul will return to Huang autonomy over his body but provides no guidelines on how to undergo such cultivation. Published as a stand-alone book, Twin Souls now included an epilogue entitled "On Cultivating the Soul" (peizhi linghun shuo 培植靈魂說), also by Peng Yu but under a different pen name, Ruguan Heshang 儒冠和尚 ("Confucian scholar Buddhist monk"). The epilogue contains a treatise on the soul, structured as a series of quotations from a range of texts including the Confucian analects and Buddhist classics with each quotation followed by the author's commentary, foreshadowing

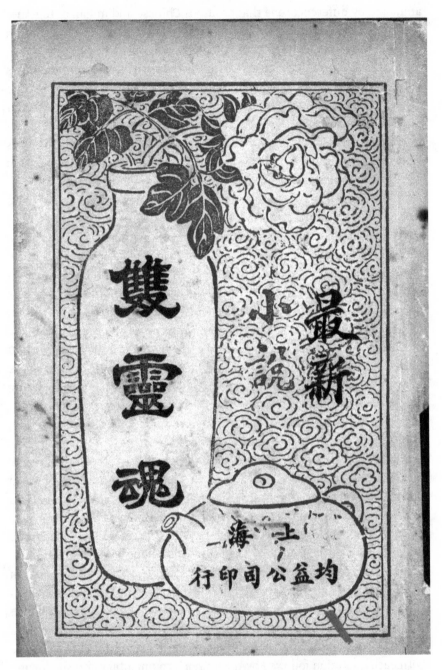

FIGURE 1.2 Cover of the 1909 republication of *Twin Souls* in book form. *Shuang Linghun* 雙靈魂 [Twin souls] (Shanghai: Junyi tushu gongsi, 1909), front cover.

Peng's entry into monkhood. Focusing on philosophical approaches to the soul, the treatise offers a counterpoint to the scientists' speeches at the research center and ends with endorsing the novel's approach to strengthening the soul by preserving "national essence" (*guocui* 國粹).[55] The epilogue frames *Twin Souls* along the lines of what David Wang has called the "involutionary" force of late Qing literature, a turning inward upon itself—in this case, introspectively, to traditional Chinese values—as a mode of newness and change that defies the teleological movement of Westernization in the name of modernization.[56]

The addition of an epilogue further underscores the tonal dissonance between the comedic initial chapters and the weighty, jargon-heavy second half. This disjointedness becomes heightened during a sustained reading of the book in a few sittings, as opposed to the more diffused rhythm of daily installments interspersed with the various other reading materials *Shenbao* offered in each issue. The heavier, more overtly pedagogical second half can lead the reader (as in A Ying's case) to identify this portion as more central to the novel and as best fulfilling its aim of "awakening the nation's soul"; such an awakening would enable the realization that Western learning and scientific methods cannot cure China's crisis of nationhood.

On the other hand, attention to *Twin Souls's* first, lighter half can tell a different story, as my reading suggests. At the research center, the narrative positions Chinese patient and Western cures in a binary relation that obscures the particularly non-Western, Indian characteristic of the ailment afflicting Huang. And yet it is precisely this Indian-ness that drives forward the novel's plot, with the Indian policeman's dual capacity to signify both colonizer and colonized offering a wealth of entertaining possibilities with which to stir the reader's imagination. As a literary device, the Indian policeman facilitates the novel's scalar navigation of the figurative and the visceral and thereby serves just as pedagogical a function as the novel's later chapters. The "awakening" enacted here is the formation of a national consciousness that comes into view neither wholly in opposition to a colonizer nor in complete solidarity with a fellow colonized being. The twinning of Indian and Chinese souls figures a national consciousness animated by a constant negotiation between selves and others, multiply conceived, born of suspension between the poles of sameness and difference, gravitating at once toward neither and both.

The Hongtou Asan

In the early decades of Republican China, the term *hongtou asan* 紅頭阿三 (literally "Red-head Asan") gained popularity as the preferred moniker for the Indian policeman, marking an ebbing and refiguring of the late Qing concept of *wangguo nu* and its attendant "front car" rhetoric. *Hongtou asan* was likely already in colloquial use (as *hongdou ase* in the Shanghai dialect), but increasingly appeared in print in the 1920s following May Fourth calls to vernacularize literary writing. Unlike *wangguo nu*, the mere utterance of which immediately communicated a denunciation of the policeman, taken on its own the term *hongtou asan* appeared neutral: *hongtou* visually marked the red turban the policemen wore as part of their uniforms, while *asan* remained semantically ambiguous. The uncertain origins of *asan* soon proved a popular topic of discussion in Shanghai's newspapers and journals, and possible definitions accompanied the term's increased frequency in print, endowing it with political and emotive heft.

Three possible explanations of *asan/ase* emerged as the most commonly cited, and in each case writers harnessed the search for etymological roots as a means to inflect the act of naming the Indian policeman with political resonance. The first theory suggested that *asan* derived from "Aye, sir"—a phrase that the policemen were often heard repeating to their British superiors. Linking *asan* to "Aye, sir" heightened the term's critical import: *asan* now evoked Shanghai's colonial power dynamics by depicting the Indian policeman as obsequiously obeying British orders.[57] A 1923 vignette outlines a second theory which traces *asan* to "Ah! Sir," presented as a common greeting in English. This explains, the vignette reads, why the Indian *asan* responds happily to a name otherwise reserved for monkeys. The policeman is not insulted, because *ase* sounds to him like "Ah! Sir," and so he thinks passersby are simply saying, "Hey, Mister!" to greet him. *Asan* proves an apt name, since, like the monkey (often featured in Shanghai's street performances), the Indian nods eagerly in his oblivion, unable to understand that he is the target of mockery.[58] A third explanation links *asan* to 第三 *disan* ("the third"), emphasizing the lowly rank the Indian policeman occupies in the British colonial hierarchy.[59] As these three possible etymologies of the term show, defining *asan* afforded writers an opportunity to fill the empty signifier with political charge and anticolonial critique.[60]

[54]

A 1927 short story entitled "Hongtou Asan" (*Hongtou Asan* 紅頭阿三) by Chen Kangtai 陳康泰, published in a Shanghai students' magazine, dramatizes the political and literary stakes of naming the policeman.[61] Written from the policeman's perspective, the story opens with his lament: ever since he arrived in China, all he hears are the sounds of people mocking him. He senses hatred from the rickshaw pullers and pedestrians on "N Street" in "S City" (Shanghai's Nanjing Street) when they shout *hongtou asan* at him, but struggles to understand what these four characters mean. One day, following an unpleasant incident with a rickshaw rider who yells "Get lost, *hongtou asan*," he has an epiphany. He cries out, "I understand now! You hateful Chinese, I understand now! You condemn me as a *wangguo nu*! But you shouldn't get too complacent. Soon you, too, will become a *hongtou asan*!"[62] Conjoining *hongtou asan* and *wangguo nu* revitalizes the late Qing discourse and mobilizes the latter term's capacity to enact a mirror-like function; the Indian's acknowledgment of his own colonization facilitates a warning of China's impending fall.

The story recalls this older rhetoric in order to critique it. The policeman's realization links the colloquial *hongtou asan*, a distinctly verbal utterance (indeed, the short story opens with the phrase between quotation marks, visually highlighting its orality), with the older, more literary formulation of *wangguo nu*. This conceptual maneuver alludes to the literary debates of the time on the appropriate linguistic register of literature. May Fourth debates crystallized the binary between the vernacular (*baihua* 白話) and classical (*wenyan* 文言) modes of writing, with proponents of "new literature" urging writers to break the shackles of tradition and modernize literature by writing in the vernacular. The Indian policeman's struggle to define himself unfolds in dialogue with this ongoing negotiation of literary identity in the Chinese cultural sphere, with the condemnation of *wangguo nu* evoking here both late Qing anticolonialism and May Fourth iconoclasm.

In depicting a first-person narrator in a foreign land who is plagued with a crisis of nationality, "Hongtou Asan" explicitly alludes to the archetype of the May Fourth antihero, a literary figure perhaps best exemplified in the writer Yu Dafu's 郁達夫 (1896–1945) now canonical novella "Sinking" (*Chenlun* 沉淪) published in 1921, some six years prior to "Hongtou Asan." "Sinking" tells of an unnamed Chinese protagonist in Japan, anguished by his own nation's impotence and weakness, qualities he comes to embody. In one scene, in a moment remarkably resonant with the Indian policeman's epiphany described above, Yu Dafu's protagonist confronts the disparaging terms that name him as a Chinese Other in Japan: "The Japanese look down upon Chinese just as we look down upon pigs and dogs. They call us Shina-jin, 'Chinamen,' a term more derogatory than 'knave' in Chinese."[63] Both the Indian policeman in "Hongtou Asan" and Yu Dafu's protagonist stand in a foreign land as the lone representatives of their nations, and each is tormented by and battles with the national inferiority those around him seem to attribute to him. And just as Yu Dafu's protagonist struggles to overcome such inferiority and longs for his nation to grow stronger, so does the policeman yearn for India to overthrow its colonizer. The policeman melodramatically grieves his weak nation: "My nation has been conquered and extinguished. Ah! Motherland, why don't you fight back? Because of your cowardice, your people are everywhere mistreated by others!"[64] His cries hold the echo of the protagonist's lament in "Sinking," who, at one point, condemns himself and his nation in the same breath: "You coward fellow. . . . Why did I come to Japan?. . . . Since you have come, it is a wonder that the Japanese treat you with contempt? China, O my China! Why don't you grow rich and strong? I cannot bear your shame in silence any longer."[65] In a final parallel, both texts end with an image of national estrangement, their protagonists poised on the shores of the foreign land and gazing longingly toward their motherlands, contemplating (and perhaps committing) suicide. Standing at the edge of the sea that lies between China and Japan, Yu Dafu's protagonist utters his final words: "O China, my China, you are the cause of my death!. . . . I wish you could become rich and strong soon! Many, many of your children are suffering."[66] "Hongtou Asan," too, leaves its protagonist weeping at the edge of Shanghai's Huangpu river, the channel by which the policemen arrived in China via ship. "Ah! Motherland," the policeman apostrophizes, "my vast yet weak and cowardly motherland, from today onward I forsake you! . . . I wish you all—my compatriots—oh, how I wish, one day soon, you could all wash away from your heads these three words: *wangguo nu.*" The policeman's voice drowns in sounds of the river.[67]

By marking itself as a pastiche of "Sinking," "Hongtou Asan" announces its participation in May Fourth discourses of the time: the Indian policeman curiously speaks in an idiom explicitly consonant with May Fourth appeals for China to shed off the vestiges of its past and to rise as a modern nation. Written in the vernacular *baihua* (another shared feature with "Sinking"), the story's depiction of the Indian policeman's grief and shame for his motherland's weakness immediately evokes the trope of "national humiliation" in May Fourth literature.[68] The famous protests on May 4, 1919, broke out in large part as a response to what students considered China's humiliation during the negotiation of the Treaty of Versailles, which awarded parts of China to Japan. This preoccupation with national humiliation grew into a larger literary concern with China's failure to modernize, resulting in a host of short stories with protagonists who personified China's perceived powerlessness and mourned the nation's failures. Such literary practice especially shaped the style of the Creation Society (*chuangzao she* 創造社), a literary group formed in 1921 of which Yu Dafu was a founding member. During its early years, the writings of the society excelled in depicting "a romantic hypertrophied . . . expansive, libidinous, and tormented self" in order to "enthrall and agitate a young generation increasingly frustrated by the reality of a fast disintegrating post-dynastic China."[69] By retrospectively positioning itself as among the writings of the early Creation Society, "Hongtou Asan" inscribes the Indian policeman in May Fourth discourse at the same time as it frames the Indian's anguish of colonization in terms familiar to the Chinese reader and legible within popular literary conventions of the time.[70] The story emphatically presents the Indian policeman as the object of Chinese hatred and yet beckons its reader into a relation of identification with this despised figure, replicating the intense pull of recognition so many of Yu Dafu's readers experienced in the pages of "Sinking."

I draw out these convergences between the largely forgotten "Hongtou Asan" and "Sinking," a widely read and critically acclaimed text, in order to demonstrate how the Indian policeman provided a literary vehicle through which a young, unknown writer like Chen Kangtai could enter into and participate in the discourses and practices of the literary elite. Just as Yadong Pofo's *Twin Souls* reshapes late Qing discourses on India and debates on the viability of Western solutions for Chinese problems, so does "Hongtou Asan" intervene in literary conventions of its time. By crafting an intertextual nexus with "Sinking" (a text deeply concerned with intertextuality itself, given its experiments with allusion and translation), Chen experiments with casting the *hongtou asan* as the May Fourth antihero.[71] This layering of literary tropes enables a doubled critique: on one hand, of the Indian figure as a pathetic product of his nation's failures, and, on the other, of the narrowly national preoccupations of the May Fourth protagonist who remains trapped within a blinkered obsession with his own nationality. Sharing in the May Fourth protagonist's national shame, the Indian policeman makes possible a moment of transnational relation that grows out of and yet disrupts nation-based literary conventions of the time.

May Thirtieth Literature

The spring months of 1925 witnessed strikes and protests against working conditions in Shanghai's foreign (largely Japanese) owned mills and factories. The death of a Chinese worker in mid-May further stoked the workers' anger and drew radical students to the International Settlement, where they delivered speeches and distributed pamphlets against foreign intervention in China. As students joined in the workers' protests, the express target of protest expanded beyond working conditions in foreign-owned factories to, more broadly, the "unjust nature of imperialism."[72] Unrest brewed beneath the surface of daily life in colonial Shanghai, finally erupting on May 30, when protestors gathered outside the International Settlement's Laozha 老閘 police station to demand the release of students who had been arrested shortly beforehand. Faced with a sea of angry but allegedly peaceful protestors, the foreign police (of the SMP) opened fire on the masses, fatally wounding several students and workers. Eyewitness reports of pools of blood spreading across the streets of Shanghai painted a horrifying image. Chinese newspapers largely held the Indian policemen responsible for the fatalities, accusing them of blindly carrying out unjust and inhumane British orders to brutalize and open fire on the unarmed protestors.

Over the following months, this massacre (can'an 惨案), as it came to be known in the Chinese public sphere, fueled a nationwide movement. The events of May 30 unleashed a new wave of Chinese hatred toward the already despised Indian policeman. As the perpetrator of bloodshed at Laozha, the Indian policeman came to symbolize the evils of foreign rule in China, and protestors often evoked the policeman as their object of dissent. Literary depictions of the May Thirtieth massacre invariably featured the Indian policeman violently containing the protests.[73] Ba Jin's 巴金 (1904–2005) novel *The Setting Sun* (*Siqu de taiyang* 死去的太陽, 1931), for instance, offers a detailed semifictional account of the protests: the protagonist Wu Yangqing witnesses a "massive Indian policeman grabbing his classmate by the collar," a Western policeman "viciously" beating up a student, and "a stream of fresh, red blood streaming down [the student's] face."[74] Such literary engagements helped keep alive the memory of the events on May 30, 1925, and the Indian policeman's role in the massacre, as the May Thirtieth movement (*wusa yundong* 五卅運動) grew into what scholars have characterized as the first organized mass movement explicitly against the intervention of foreign powers in China.[75]

May Thirtieth discourse took shape alongside the crisis of communist survival following the Guomindang's anticommunist purge in 1927. As Marxist theory permeated the literary sphere via the USSR and Japan, leftist writers (and the literary societies they were affiliated with) launched public debates on the definition and practice of "revolutionary literature." Shanghai's consecutive massacres—on May 30, 1925, and on April 12, 1927, when Jiang Jieshi (Chiang Kai-shek) ordered the killing of thousands in Shanghai—yoked together the Indian policeman with literary explorations of a communist revolutionary consciousness. As a result, the controversial figure of the Indian policeman offered leftist writers a literary site of contestation: in writing the Indian policeman, proponents of rival literary schools crafted their visions for the form revolutionary literature ought to take.

Two prominent figures in Shanghai's literary circles, Jiang Guangci 蔣光慈 (1901–1931) and Yang Cunren 楊邨人 (1901–1955), experimented with casting the Indian as a sympathetic comrade, writing against the dominant portrayal of the policeman as despicable and violent, and extending to him a Marxist-inflected notion of solidarity. In 1928, Jiang and Yang, together with other like-minded writers, founded the Sun Society (*taiyang she* 太陽社), a literary group closely aligned with the CCP that prioritized the utility of literature in realizing proletarian revolution.[76] Members of the society called for literary practice to break from aesthetic concerns and melancholic portrayals of tormented individuals (as in writings of the older May Fourth generation) and instead to empower the oppressed masses by sparking revolutionary consciousness and promoting the bright future revolution would bring.

Yang's story, entitled "Hongtou Asan" and published in 1930, tells of a Chinese man who visits the International Settlement courthouse (the Mixed Court) to observe the trial of his two revolutionary friends. In the courtroom, the narrator sits among a group of Indian policemen. As he awaits the turn of his friends' trial, the *hongtou asan* seated beside him whispers (in broken

English) "Do you come to see the school-boy?"[77] Taken aback, the narrator looks up to find an Indian policeman with "extremely kind and friendly eyes."[78] The two proceed to engage in a surreptitious conversation (again rendered in English):

"Yes, I come to see my friends. . . . Yesterday my friends . . . had not come back home. . . . So I come to see them. Do you know what was matter with them?"
"The school-boy is good, the policeman is bad!"
"Is the school-boy good?"
"Yes, school boy is good. You know we cannot go back home. The Englishman is bad. So very bad."[79]

The Indian policeman's expression of solidarity with the Chinese protestor (the "school-boy") and criticism of the colonizer have a profound impact on the narrator. He is "immediately moved by [the *hongtou asan*]. The pain of those weak peoples who are oppressed by the imperialists immediately [rises in] [his] heart, as though [he], too, is a *hongtou asan*."[80] The story ends on an optimistic note, with the narrator convinced that his encounter with the Indian policeman is proof that the colonized peoples, "[his] brothers, have all risen up."[81] Unlike earlier texts that fictionalized oneness with the Indian policeman in the hope that this similarity would not be actualized, and that China would avoid following India's path into colonization, in this May Thirtieth climate Yang explores the emancipatory potential of identifying with the Indian policeman and together striving for revolution. The image of the Chinese man as himself a *hongtou asan* issues a call to arms, not against but alongside the Indian.

Jiang's 1929 short story "Asan" appeared in the inaugural issue of *Pioneer* (*Tuohuangzhe* 拓荒者), the journal of the League of Left-Wing Writers founded in 1930 following a CCP-ordered truce between former rivals, Lu Xun and the Sun and Creation Societies.[82] Narrated from the Indian policeman's point of view, the story tells the tale of Asan, an Indian policeman, who ends up arrested by the British and put behind bars. In the days prior, Asan had arrested the student protestors who would gather in the International Settlement to distribute leaflets and chant slogans. Asan did not understand what the students were protesting or what "Bolshevik" meant, a term his British superiors often used to label the protestors as loathsome. One day, Asan dutifully arrested a student he caught distributing fliers, but as he hauled his prisoner away, the student said to him, "Friend, we are all oppressed people! We want China's liberation, and freedom for China's poor. Why do you oppose us? Is it that you have forgotten your motherland? We should unite." The student's words have an immediate effect on Asan: "A small wave began to stir in his mind: China's liberation . . . India . . . the British . . ."[83] He sets his prisoner free. As Asan realizes the connection between his own colonization and the student's call for Chinese revolution, Jiang constructs an expansive, collective form of revolutionary consciousness that redraws the lines of conflict, replacing the colonizer/colonized divide with one between the (capitalist) imperialists and the oppressed. The rearranged categories of class antagonism make possible new solidarities.

A British chief witnesses the exchange with the Chinese student and reprimands Asan. "You, too, are a Bolshevik," the chief says before throwing Asan behind bars. "Asan, having never understood what a Bolshevik is, and never dreaming that he could be called one, was now dragged into the jail like any other prisoner." As he thinks back to his mistreatment at the hands of the British, "he finally understood what Bolshevik means."[84] Demonstrating the power of literature to cultivate revolutionary consciousness in the most unlikely, antirevolutionary of figures, Jiang inverts the epiphany Yang's narrator undergoes; here, it is the *hongtou asan* who voices sameness with the Chinese protestor.

Jiang and Yang received caustic criticism for their favorable portrayals of the Indian policeman, likely due in equal parts to the widespread hatred for the policeman and the fragmentation of Shanghai's literary sphere into various camps. Critics accused such portrayals of attempting to recuperate the Indian policeman from his villainous role in the May Thirtieth Incident. In a highly satirical essay, one critic, Jin Xuan 錦軒, writes: "It appears that the *hongtou asan* has recently come into some good luck. Unbelievably, he has been praised by some benevolent Chinese heroes upholding justice. They say that, in the blink of an eye, the *hongtou asan* is capable of gaining awareness, of understanding, and of rising up."[85] Jin Xuan goes on to ridicule the absurdity of the instantaneous emotional transformations in the stories by Jiang and Yang, finding it ludicrous that the Indian policeman could be capable of expressing any political convictions. He concludes that if China is to rise up one day, it will not be due to such fanciful and unrealistic writing.

Intolerance towards the idea of the Indian policeman as an imagined comrade-in-arms meant that this literary figure continued to carry out an unfixable function in constant fluctuation. The Indian policeman could be neither wholly friend nor enemy; moments of antagonistic clash aesthetically generated both solidarity and rebellion. Mao Dun's 茅盾 (1896–1981) well-known novel *Rainbow* (*Hong* 虹, 1930) stages precisely such an encounter between the Indian policeman and its protagonist, Mei. The novel's dramatic climax depicts Mei participating in a students' protest (based on May Thirtieth). The previous night, Mei's group leader had instructed her to refrain from violence during the protests and to strictly follow orders of "nonresistance" (*wudikang* 無抵抗).[86] Not one to play by the rules, Mei feels restricted by these orders but decides to follow them for the sake of the larger cause. Entering into the protesting masses, Mei initially joins in the scripted chants. Then, suddenly, she comes face-to-face with an Indian policeman: "A massive Indian policeman blazed before her eyes. Like a demon, he charged towards her."[87] Mei bursts into a rage: ' "Nonresistance?" This word flashed through her mind. Immediately, with even more force, she roared out, 'People of China, come together! Let's attack these murderous bandits—Ah! You colonized slaves!' As though they were stones, she flung her last few words at the Indian policeman, who was now charging straight toward her."[88] Mei adamantly expresses—and, indeed, is able to express—her own political convictions only once she encounters the Indian policeman. Throughout the novel, Mei struggles to reconcile her romantic and political interests and repeatedly fails to construct a political identity as distinct from that of the men she admires.[89] But in the moment when she physically collides with the Indian policeman, she breaks free, violating the order of nonresistance. Mei hurls the insult of *wangguo nu* not only at the policeman, but also at the part of herself reflected in the Indian's subjugation; this self-image can manifest only in the clash with the policeman. Mei realizes that she, too, is a "colonized slave," and it is this split-second twinning of selves that enables her to voice her protest. No longer constrained by the orders or influence of others, she is now unrestrained and violent. Mei finally articulates a politics of her own.

In May Thirtieth discourse, the literary Indian policeman emerged as an active participant in the crafting of revolutionary literature, both in his ability to spark Chinese protest as the object of rebellion and in the promise that he could join in such outcry. Literary experiments with the Indian policeman illuminate a collaborative undertow, drawing the Chinese protestor and Indian policeman together in expressions of protest, precisely during a historical moment that marked the height of antagonism between Chinese and Indian actors in Shanghai.

The Gandhian Policeman

With a new revolutionary consciousness pervading the nation following the May Thirtieth movement, Chinese news sources increasingly covered independence movements unfolding across the colonial world. Through the 1920s, the Chinese print media—publications associated with communists and nationalists alike—reported on Gandhi's freedom movement underway in India, with intellectuals vigorously debating the merits and feasibility of Gandhi's revolutionary vision.[90] In March 1930, Chinese newspapers carried news of the "Dandi March," a two hundred and forty-mile march Gandhi led on foot in resistance to (or noncooperation with) the colonial Indian government's monopoly on salt production and the tax levied on salt. The Dandi March announced Gandhi's ability to mobilize thousands across class-based and other social divides, in open nonviolent rebellion against British rule and toward a common goal of *svarāj* (self-rule). News of such developments in India soon traveled to China, and Chinese journals and newspapers published numerous articles on and photographs of the Dandi March.[91]

Gandhi's growing presence in the Chinese literary sphere gave rise to a paradox: among the most popular Indian figures in literary discourse, on one extreme lay the Indian policeman as the ultimate colonized slave, and on the other was Gandhi, the harbinger of revolution and savior of the Indian people. This contrast comes to life in a political cartoon published in a 1931 issue of the journal *New Life* (*Xin shenghuo* 新生活), captioned "Hongtou Asan and Gandhi" (*Hongtou Asan yu Gandi* 紅頭阿三與甘地) (figure 1.3).[92] The cartoon depicts the two caricatured figures paired through a series of visual contrasts. The Indian policeman is dressed in the uniform of the British colonial police force, complete with his characteristic turban; Gandhi stands bare-chested, wearing only his signature cap and a roughly sketched *dhoti*. The policeman's large, corpulent stature dominates the image, his plump arms spread open, his belt barely containing his bulging stomach. Gandhi is skeletal: a sunken, wrinkled face, a thin torso outlined by ribs, bony shoulders and arms jutting out at odd angles as one frail hand grips a walking stick. This odd Indian couple—one figure colonized and passive and the other

FIGURE 1.3 "Hongtou Asan yu Gandi" 紅頭阿三與甘地 (Indian policeman and Gandhi). *Xin Shenghuo* 新生活 2 (1931): 10.

awakened and revolutionary—stand side by side as the two extreme poles of the concept of India as it then circulated in the Chinese literary sphere.

Beyond identifying the two figures in the caption, the journal provides no additional commentary on the cartoon.[93] The cartoon does, however, offer a series of helpful visual clues that convey a tone of comical irony. The Indian policeman, a ferocious perpetrator of violence, is shown here as laughable, unthreatening, and even doltish in his awkward, pigeon-toed stance. Gandhi is similarly drawn in a manner oppositional to popular images of the time that framed him as a formidable man marching forth, leading a nation to independence; here, he is feeble and pathetic. Stripped of their usual referents, the policeman and Gandhi reveal the farcical nature of India's struggle: an emaciated, half-naked man fights against British colonization, while the strong and capable policeman only reinforces it.

In critique of the kind of discourse the cartoon captures, of relegating the Indian policeman and Gandhi to two different, discordant ideas of India, some Chinese writers sought to reconcile the contrast by writing the Indian policeman as simultaneously deplorable and exemplary. A popular strategy to this end involved endowing the Indian policeman with a Gandhian revolutionary consciousness. Such a strategy had the added benefit of avoiding harsh criticism of the kind directed at Yang and Jiang. Writers could now circumvent explicitly expressing solidarity with the Indian and burdening the Chinese communist with the task of enlightening the policeman. The fictionalized Gandhian policeman avoided such unpopular literary trends while still achieving the intended effect of recuperating the policeman from his widespread disrepute and presenting him as a fellow colonized subject alongside the Chinese.

A 1930 short story, "Death of an Indian Policeman" (*Yinbu zhi si* 印捕之死) by Pan Jienong 潘子農 (1909–1993), features an Indian policeman named Gan Kexin 甘克辛, whose very name foreshadows the conceptual joining together of Gandhi and the policeman: the character *gan* comes from the Chinese transliteration of "Gandhi" (*Gandi* 甘地), and the character *xin* from the Chinese translation of "Singh," a common surname among the Indian policemen. Gan is stationed in "X City," based on Shanghai's International Settlement and described as a police state entirely under British control. One day, the British chief orders Gan to aid him in arresting X City's revolutionary Indians who have gathered to discuss Gandhi's Dandi March. Gan knows these revolutionary Indians well. They are members of a "National Salvation Association" (*jiuguo hui* 救國會), founded by the Indians of X City in support of Gandhi's anti-British movement. In the past, Gan had himself participated in the association, helping others evade arrest. This time, however, he has no choice but to arrest the association's members. Facing this predicament, "he experienced the extent of the British people's viciousness. It is not enough that they slaughter Indian people, . . . they make Indian people arrest their own innocent compatriots and revolutionary visionaries."[94]

Later, as Gan escorts two Indian revolutionaries to the police station, he experiences much internal turmoil. He knows that disobeying orders will result in punishment, even death. He compares the value of his own life with that of the revolutionary Indian youths he has arrested. Finally, with the cause of the nation in his heart, he sets his prisoners free. Just as expected, the British chief beats Gan bloody. Ultimately, Gan voices his confession in explicitly anticolonial terms. He cries out, "Ever since you British destroyed our peoples, not a day passes without us Indians having to live in an abyss of suffering. That is why our motherland's visionary and hero, Gandhi, leads our independence movement against all odds, in order to return glory to our ancient nation."[95] The next day, Gan commits suicide in his prison cell.

"Death of an Indian Policeman," along with other Chinese texts in the 1930s, imagines the Indian policeman as gaining a revolutionary consciousness and joining forces with independence movements underway in India.[96] On a historical register, the notion of Indian policemen as revolutionary anticolonials is no mere fantasy: Indian policemen were involved in Ghadar activities in Shanghai, as well as in the nationalist Indian Independence League and Indian National Army under the leadership of Subhas Chandra Bose.[97] That such nationalist activities, with violent missions for Indian independence from British rule, were in fact antithetical to Gandhi's nonviolent vision likely remained unknown to many Chinese writers and readers. The literary sphere instead allowed an otherwise impossible view of Indian nationalism, one in which the Indian policeman and Gandhi could stand side by side, united in the fight against the British.

Past Pan-Asianism

In addition to the Indian policeman and Gandhi, a third Indian figure who set off somewhat of a frenzy in the Chinese literary sphere of the 1920s and 1930s bears mention here: the Indian Nobel laureate Rabindranath Tagore. Much ink has been spilled on Tagore's contentious visit to China in 1924. At first, Tagore's arrival in China seemed a natural extension of a China-India pan-Asian alliance of the sort Zhang Taiyan had envisioned. In his introductory speech welcoming Tagore to China, Liang Qichao echoed this pan-Asian discourse, positioning Tagore as the actualization of China and India's eternal brotherhood and casting his visit as the latest iteration of this age-old familial relation: "At the time when most civilizations had not yet become active, [we] had already begun to study those problems which concern the whole of mankind. . . . India led the way for us. Indeed, India is our elder brother, and we are [India's] younger brother."[98] Tagore reiterated this message in the various lectures he delivered during his month-long tour of China, calling for China and India to unite "not through some mechanical method of organization, but through a spirit of true sympathy."[99]

Objections to Tagore brewed in the months before the poet's arrival in China, and, despite the best efforts of his hosts, protestors disrupted his talks. Chinese students, particularly those studying at Tsinghua University, organized boycotts and distributed dissenting handbills during Tagore's lectures. The pamphlets accused Tagore of endorsing a regressive view of civilization, spirituality, and antimaterialist humanism, ideologies that the students equated with passivity, inaction, and apathy.[100] The protests grew by the time Tagore arrived in Hankou, a treaty port with a sizeable British concession, where students demonstrated with placards bearing the slogans "We don't want philosophy, we want materialism" and "Go back, slave of the colonizer!" (evoking the *wangguo nu* epithet conventionally reserved for the policeman).[101] Prominent literary figures such as Mao Dun, Zhou Zuoren, and Lu Xun published articles opposing Tagore's lectures and poetry with varying degrees of hostility. Their objections were challenged by equally vocal proponents of Tagore's thought, including Zheng Zhenduo, Liang Shuming, and Xu Zhimo.[102]

The poet Xu Zhimo 徐志摩 (1897–1931), a close friend of Tagore's who had been instrumental in bringing the poet to China, had presciently anticipated that Tagore might be received as antirevolutionary, and that Chinese students would inevitably equate Tagore with the Indian policeman. In September 1923, Xu published an article in *Short Story Monthly* (*Xiaoshuo yuebao* 小說月報) entitled "Tagore Visits China" (*Taige'er lai hua* 泰戈爾來華) in an attempt to preempt such attacks. "We often think of India, Korea, and Poland together as examples of colonized nations," Xu wrote, adding in parenthesis, "([but] I think we have most misunderstood the Indian people . . . most people are under the misapprehension that the Indian people and those policemen on the streets are one and the same!)."[103] In this parenthetical inclusion, which appears as a fleeting and casual aside in the article, Xu enacts the crucial maneuver of decoupling Tagore and the Indian policeman; he separates the policeman from "the Indian people," leaving this category now open to redefinition. He then argues that while China may appear more free from the perspective of its political system, India displays a freedom of spirit (*jingshen de ziyou* 精神的自由). "India has achieved a rousing of spirit [*xinling huodong* 心靈活動]," Xu writes. "[Indians] have even given rise to a political leader with a religious nature—Gandhi. . . . It is only the names of Gandhi and Tagore that provide ironclad proof of the Indian people's continued survival."[104] Here, Gandhi and Tagore exemplify the spirit of the Indian people; the two together name the concept of "India." As a "religious" political leader, Gandhi becomes commensurable with Tagore's spiritualism; Tagore, in turn, gains a revolutionary cadence in his association with Gandhi. The Indian policeman, meanwhile, remains ejected out of and exiled from the idea of "India" that Xu Zhimo, Liang Qichao, and others promoting pan-Asian discourse carefully constructed.

And yet, as the texts discussed in this chapter suggest, the policeman embodied most immediately India's presence in both the material and literary grounds of China's colonial condition. For those closest to China's semi-colonization, for whom the violence and injustices of colonial rule proved no mere abstraction but constituted lived, everyday realities, it was the policeman, and not Tagore, who signified the salience and urgency of the task of engaging with ideas of India. In pan-Asian discourse, the exercise of thinking China and India together required bracketing away and erasing the policeman, lest he upset the romantic ideal of China and India as ancient brothers, together oppressed by the West. The texts discussed in this chapter share with the pan-Asianists an anticolonial imperative, but find within the figure of the Indian policeman himself possibilities for practicing a different form of transnational, comparative thought in order to express resistance. Such anticolonial expression emerges not from China-India solidarity (or "true sympathy," as Tagore put it)—indeed, such solidarity hardly resonated with those confronting the lived realities of colonization—but from a more tenuous and precarious intimacy conversely engendered in thinking China and India together as antagonists.

A final literary example illustrates the Indian policeman's literary capacity to expose and exceed the limits of pan-Asian discourse. A 1936 poem, "Ode to the Indian Asan" (*Gei Yindu Asan* 給印度阿三) by Bai Yun 白云, reads:

> On the streets of the flourishing International Settlement,
> At the closely watched doorways of the banks,
> At the bustling entrance of the many shops,
> We can see, we can see,
> Our armed Indian brother.
> Six feet tall; strong, robust limbs,
> A white turban wrapped around his head; black-faced, like soot,

You have become imperialism's obedient dog,
Roaming around all over Shanghai.[105]

Referring to the policeman sarcastically as "our armed Indian brother"
(*wuzhuang de Yindu xiongdi* 武裝的印度兄弟), Bai Yun at once activates and critiques the cliché of China-India fraternity. The Indian policeman stands
simultaneously as a "brother" and as "imperialism's obedient dog," evoking
the blurred self/other dynamic in an expression of intimacy inextricable
from enmity. The poem continues:

Ah! Indian Asan, you are but a guard dog of the world!
You silly, clueless creature, without embarrassment or shame!
For whom do you bear arms? For whom do you toil?
Whom do you work for, whom do you serve?
You lamentable, pitiful, last descendent of the Sakyamuni,
You have brought boundless scorn on all of Asia.
Ah! Indian Asan, you stupid man,
After all, at whose chest is your pistol aimed?[106]

The poem at once upholds and scorns pan-Asian narratives that laud India
as the font of Buddhist spiritualism. In the same breath, Bai Yun reviles the
Indian policeman for his present and reveres him for his past: "You lamentable, pitiful, last descendent of the Sakyamuni / You have brought boundless scorn on all of Asia." Finally, with a line that encapsulates the precarious binds of antagonism, the poem concludes by suggesting that in pointing
his gun at his Chinese victim, the Indian policeman only aims the weapon
at himself. In the image of the Indian policeman shooting a Chinese protestor who is revealed as none other than the Indian himself, opposing the
same enemy and striving toward a shared revolution, oneness between Chinese and Indian comes alive only in the moment of its death.

In China-India literary discourse, discussions on Tagore's lasting influence
in Chinese poetry and on his own deep interest in building China-India cultural ties continue to occupy center-stage. Such topics stand as exemplary
of a pan-Asian ideal of China-India literary relation, a relation drawn in the
spirit of unity, in recognition of "essential" characteristics (be it spiritual,
cultural, or historical) that China and India share, and in joint rebellion
against the West. Even when studies venture beyond Zhang Taiyan, Xu

Zhimo, Tagore and the other proponents of China-India pan-Asianism, much of China-India literary scholarship still evokes the sentiments characteristic of pan-Asian discourse, positioning China and India as cultural equals, together engaged in long-standing and harmonious cultural collaboration and exchange, and looking to each other in opposition to the West. In many ways, such a conception of China-India literary relation bespeaks the success of early twentieth-century pan-Asianists who labored to erase from the narrative of China-India brotherhood those power-inflected hierarchies endemic to all China-India cultural interactions, far beyond but especially characteristic of the colonial period. A casualty of pan-Asian idealism, the figure of the Indian policeman reveals those obscured dimensions of Chinese literary engagements with ideas of India that unfolded alongside and in defiance of pan-Asian discourse.

At the same time, the Chinese texts of the Indian policeman articulate a new idiom of anticolonial dialogics not founded upon easy proclamations of solidarity yet committed to anticolonial transnational thought. From these texts, a particular kind of transnational literary relation emerges: precarious, fleeting, in flux, characterized by the contradictory pulls of attraction and repulsion, at once luring the reader toward historical fixity and throwing her back into the contingencies of interpretation. This practice of comparison—of conceptualizing the Chinese self in an undesired yet intimate relation to an Indian other—resides at the heart of modern Chinese literature's development when viewed from the perspective of China's colonial condition. The potential and challenge of writing the Indian policeman in literary form enabled writers to play with the dominant discourses of their time, from the late Qing "front-car" rhetoric of India as a cautionary tale, to early Republican-era debates on vernacularizing literature, to preoccupations with revolutionary literature in the late 1920s and 1930s. At each historical juncture, writers harnessed the figure of the Indian policeman as a vehicle for entering into and imbuing these ongoing literary debates with the urgencies of lived colonial realities. Centering the figure of the Indian policeman thus writes the narrative of modern Chinese literature's development anew, as a story of anticolonial protest waged against and through an unwanted yet inextricable Indian presence.

TWO

Revolution Redux

Agyeya's China Stories

A DARK MORNING in Hankou. A crowd assembles in the square: men, women, children, some scattered soldiers. Murmurs of unrest spread through the crowd. A red glow appears over the horizon, and pillars of smoke rise in the distance. "There's our signal!" the soldiers cry out. For a while, the people gathered stir, their gazes fixed on the horizon burning crimson. Finally, the crowd ignites: "Revolution!" The clarion call resounds throughout the nation. Revolution, long awaited, has at last arrived in China.

This scene of the dawn of revolution in China appears, unexpectedly, in the Hindi short story "Cursed" (*Abhiśāpit*) by the poet-novelist Sachchidanand Hiranand Vatsyayan "Agyeya" (1911–1987). And, surprisingly still, this scene, tinted red in Marxist hue, does not evoke that quintessential communist revolution of 1949; Agyeya wrote "Cursed" in 1932, some seventeen years before communist victory in China. "Cursed" alludes instead to the Chinese revolution of 1911, which resulted in the collapse of the Qing dynasty, and with it the millennia-old system of dynastic rule. The story features characters bearing the names of prominent political figures of the time, recast here in new pseudofictional roles. Liang Qichao sheds his celebrated persona as a late Qing intellectual and reformer, donning instead the fictional guise of a spy who schemes to infiltrate Yuan Shikai's newly established monarchy in order to assassinate Yuan and instate the Guomindang, under Sun Yatsen's leadership, at the helm of a truly revolutionary order.

This fantastic itinerary, woven through with allusions to the 1911 revolution and its aftermath, unfolds in a landscape at once deeply historical and dizzyingly fictional.

Just as transliterations of Chinese names and places rendered in the Devanāgarī script stand out as strange imported words that interrupt the characteristically poetic flow of Agyeya's prose, so does Agyeya's "China" figure as at once jarringly foreign and hauntingly familiar. References to the by then well-known people, sites, and events of early republican China—the 1911 revolt against dynastic rule, the birth of the Guomindang with its republican vision, Yuan Shikai's suppression of the Guomindang and Sun Yatsen's retreat to Japan in 1913, Yuan's dissolution of the parliamentary system in favor of his own imperial ambitions in 1915, and the resultant growth of the anti-Yuan revolutionary movement in South China— all lend "Cursed" an uncanny air of familiarity. And yet, in the story, known events suddenly pivot, launching into unexpected trajectories and meeting imagined ends. Without warning, historical personages cast in predictable roles defy their destined paths, embarking on fictional adventures towards new fates. No sooner does the people's revolution, that ultimate telos of Marxist history, arrive, than any sense of historical certainty dissolves altogether.

This chapter studies the three short stories that comprise Agyeya's China-based oeuvre: "Cursed," "Unstained" (*Akalaṅk*, 1931), and "Hariti" (*Hāriti*, 1931). Agyeya penned his China stories as he reckoned with his own loss of faith in revolutionary violence to beget liberation in an Indian anticolonial landscape increasingly inclined toward nonviolent rebellion. Confronting the receding possibility of armed revolution in India, the China stories celebrate the potentialities of a history derailed, traversing the many detours off a road no longer leading toward a singular destination. By dwelling in a past already narrativized—the events of 1910s China had received much attention in Indian newspapers and politically active circles of the time— the stories reopen foreclosed past events to the whims of fictional reimagination. Agyeya's China stories thus conduct an experiment in thinking China and India together not through the logic of historical necessity, as two nations on a tandem march toward revolution, as leftist narratives of the time would have it, but through the play of contingency, a form of storytelling that revels in the capacity of historical uncertainty to conjure new horizons of possibility.

Worlds of Imprisonment

A crucial detail lies at the heart of the China stories: Agyeya wrote them while imprisoned in the Delhi and Multan jails between 1931 and 1934 for his involvement in anticolonial revolutionary activities. As a teenager, Agyeya joined the Hindustan Republican Socialist Association (HRSA), a revolutionary group originally formed in 1923 in reaction to mounting frustrations with Gandhi's insistence on a nonviolent path to Indian independence.[1] In contrast, the HRSA stated its primary goal as the establishment of "a Federated Republic of the United States of India by an organised and armed revolution."[2] The HRSA collected funds for its activities through banditry and looting, procured arms and ammunition through similar illegal channels, and, when arms became increasingly difficult to acquire and store, manufactured and detonated bombs targeted at disrupting the daily functioning of the British government in India. Most famously, in 1929, the HSRA member and celebrated revolutionary Bhagat Singh threw smoke bombs into an active session of the Indian Legislative Assembly along with copies of the HRSA's Red Pamphlet. The pamphlet began with the words of the "French anarchist martyr" August Vaillant—"it takes a loud voice to make the deaf hear"—and ended with "Long Live the Revolution," a translation of the HRSA's rousing call to action, *"Inqalāb zindābād."*[3]

In July 1930, members of the HRSA erected a bomb factory with funds obtained through a successful looting of the Gadodia Stores, a prominent market in Delhi. Yashpal, an HRSA member who would later become the foremost communist Hindi writer, spearheaded the operation, obtaining picric acid, gun cotton, nitroglycerine, and the other necessary supplies for manufacturing explosives. But the operation needed someone with the requisite scientific expertise in bomb-making. The HRSA network, communicating via telegrams, identified a student who had recently earned a bachelor of science degree from Forman College in Lahore and had achieved a rank of first in his class.[4] This young student, S. H. Vatsyayan, would soon come to be known as "the unknowable" (Agyeya).[5]

Agyeya had become acquainted with HRSA revolutionaries as a young student in Lahore during the late 1920s. His induction into the HRSA occurred during a plot to break out Bhagat Singh, who was then imprisoned in the Lahore Central Jail. Agyeya was tasked with driving the escape vehicle despite not knowing how to drive: "The order was that he should be able to drive within three days," and so he feverishly learned to do so.[6] The escape, scheduled for June 1, 1930, fell through at the last moment.[7] Soon after, Agyeya joined Yashpal at the bomb factory in Delhi, then operating under the guise of a soap factory named Himalaya Toilets. Yashpal narrates:

> In order to protect the bomb manufacture inside, we had to have some sort of cover on the outside. Since we needed a continuous supply of running water to wash the picric acid, we decided that our cover should be a soap factory.... Someone who knew chemistry could be very helpful in our preparations of picric acid. Sacchidanand Hiranand Vatsyayan was sent from Lahore for this purpose.... Vatsyayan made some jars of face cream and scented oils from books on cosmetics. We pasted labels with the factory's name on all the jars. We were men with aesthetic sensibilities—Vatsyayan and I. And we gave very artistic names to our products.[8]

At the factory, Agyeya was known only as "Scientist," his identity concealed even from his fellow HRSA members. When the police began to unravel the HRSA's Delhi schemes in late 1930, an arrested revolutionary-turned-informant, Kailashpati, provided the following description of the Scientist: "Age about 25 years, height about 5'-11," stout build, wheat complexion, full round face, light moustache cut at the ends, wore black framed spectacles."[9] Agyeya, in fact only nineteen at the time, was arrested on November 15, 1930, in Amritsar: "The police hauled me away in the middle of the night, like bandits, and made me a prisoner, and then ... after I had spoken to, and then yelled at, and then got beaten up by senior police officials—it seemed to me that my life was quickly coming to its end."[10] So began the term of three years and four months Agyeya spent in jail.

The Crown initially tried Agyeya's case in front of a Special Tribunal convened for the adjudication of what was termed the "Delhi Conspiracy Case." As part of the trial, Agyeya was made to participate in an "identification parade" before the informant Kailashpati, which he did with "a very truculent attitude," according to the superintendent of the police, making "various unreasonable demands before he would consent to attend."[11] Such refusal to cooperate with court proceedings ranked among the HRSA's tactics to continue their revolutionary activities from within jail. The arrested revolutionaries frequently frustrated the colonial government's workings by refusing to attend court dates and, while in court, breaking into revolutionary songs and sitting with their backs to the judge in a staged denial of the Crown's authority over them.[12] Due in large part to the revolutionaries' efforts to endlessly extend the trial, the Delhi Conspiracy Case was withdrawn in 1932. Agyeya was now retried under the Explosive Substances Act of 1908, and in 1933 he was sentenced to five years in jail. He promptly filed an appeal; on February 2, 1934, Justice Jai Lal wrote in his judgment, "In my opinion, the case against Vatsyayana fails . . . on account of the unreliability of the prosecution evidence. . . . I accept the appeal of Vatsyayana and acquit him."[13]

The vicissitudes of Agyeya's trials meant that, throughout the course of his imprisonment, he remained suspended in a state of precarity—neither wholly alive nor dead, caught in a life that seemed to be "quickly coming to its end"—uncertainty about his own future woven through with that of the nation. These twinned anxieties found expression in literary form. "As soon as I arrived in jail and was able to procure writing materials," Agyeya later wrote in his memoirs, "I did nothing other than spend three to four days, all day and all night, writing with a pencil in old, worn-out notebooks."[14] His contemplations on revolution and imprisonment took the form of short stories (including the China stories), a poetry collection later published as *Prison Days* with a foreword by Nehru, and the first drafts of his seminal tripartite novel, *Shekhar: A Life (Śekhar: Ek Jīvănī).*[15]

Frantic writing kindled a craving for reading: in an effort to sate his voracious appetite for reading materials, Agyeya maintained frequent correspondence with the eminent Hindi literary figures Jainendra Kumar and Maithilisharan Gupt, both of whom were well positioned, given their connections in publishing circles, to supply Agyeya with the latest books and magazines. At times, Agyeya sent them his own writings in the hope that these might find publication. Jainendra recommended several of Agyeya's stories to his close friend and mentor, Premchand, who was then editing the magazine *Awakening (Jāgaraṇ)*. Agyeya became an avid reader of the magazine during his imprisonment.[16] *Awakening* proved a crucial source of news on developments in India and abroad; in addition to regular news columns on international affairs, the magazine ran several in-depth features on political figures including, during Agyeya's time in jail, Lenin, Trotsky, Marx, Sun Yatsen, Stalin, Mussolini, and Hitler.[17] *Awakening*, along with the other magazines and books Agyeya had access to, served as fruitful reference materials for Agyeya's historically informed short stories.[18]

In his foreword to Agyeya's *Prison Days*, Nehru writes of political prisoners as leading "double lives—the life of prison, ordered and circumscribed, bolted and barred, and the free life of the spirit, with its dreams and visions, hopes and desires."[19] For Agyeya, the world's wide horizon of possibilities came into focus at the moment when his access to that larger world dimmed and his own life hung in the balance. Through his short stories, he launched on a literary journey to distant places in an attempt not to escape imprisonment but to experience it, to inhabit the "double," competing pulls of life and death, of wanderlust and confinement, of contingency and circumscription. Of the eighteen short stories Agyeya wrote while imprisoned, eight are set in various locations outside of India, in China, France, Russia, Greece, Turkey, and Cuba. In line with the three China stories, Agyeya crafts each as a politically charged literary space of revolution, the sites of fictionalized past events such as the Russian revolutions of 1905 and 1917, the Greco-Turkish wars of 1919–1922, the 1933 Cuban uprising against president Gerardo Machado, and the legacies of the French Revolution in 1920s Paris.[20] These short stories comprise Agyeya's earliest foray into literary practice.

On the Brink of Revolution

It may come as a matter of little surprise, given the Indian radical Left's preoccupation with China in the late 1920s, that of all the foreign landscapes Agyeya explores, he dwells longest in China; the three China stories form the largest subset of his jail stories set in a single location outside of India. Agyeya's sustained engagement with China echoes the affective attachments Indian radicals formed to China in the wake of the May Thirtieth Incident of 1925, when, as readers will recall from the previous chapter, Shanghai's colonial policemen (among them, Indian policemen under British employ) opened fire on protesting students and workers.

The incident and its resultant nationwide protests—collectively known as the May Thirtieth movement—proved of particular importance in international communist circles for two reasons. First, communists abroad viewed the movement as the first national rebellion in China specifically drawn along class lines. The initial protests in Shanghai had occurred in opposition to poor working conditions in Japanese-owned factories. As the movement expanded, China's laboring masses appeared at the frontlines of a class-based struggle against the capitalist owners of the means of production. The proletarian-led revolution Marx and Engels had anticipated now appeared imminent. Second, the May Thirtieth protests expanded from demanding better working conditions in foreign-owned factories to opposing foreign presence in China in toto. For the first time, protestors specifically targeted "imperialism" (*diguo zhuyi* 帝國主義) as China's express enemy; "it was one of the results of the May 30 Movements and the propaganda of the [GMD] and CCP that this hitherto unfamiliar word became known all over China."[21] The beginnings of a properly proletarian revolution as a means to defeat imperialism and colonialism, just as international networks of radical communists had envisioned, suddenly seemed achievable in China.[22]

The imminence of revolution in China foretold a communist path to independence in India. The Soviet Comintern predicted that China's May Thirtieth had sown seeds that would inevitably blossom in India; revolution would travel "via China to the Federal Republic of the United States of India."[23] On July 9, 1925, the chairman of the Comintern's executive committee proclaimed, "China has revolted today; tomorrow . . . India will rise. Shanghai, Hong Kong, Peking and Canton have revolted today; tomorrow Calcutta and Madras will rise."[24] Indian communist publications reiterated this conviction: the November 1926 issue of the leading Indian communist M. N. Roy's journal, *Masses of India*, ran a series of articles on May Thirtieth, arguing that if "the Kuomintang has been successful in uniting all revolutionary nationalists in the struggle against foreign imperialism . . . the same thing can be done by the Indian nationalist movement."[25] An air of excitement for the impending Chinese revolution pervaded radical Indian anticolonial discourse; China emerged as the foremost site of revolution's anticipated actualization.

Agyeya's China stories anachronistically transpose this revolutionary hope May Thirtieth had sparked onto the earlier Republican period of 1910s China. The China stories draw affectively on the valence of May Thirtieth China as the harbinger of revolution to reimagine an earlier moment; doing so opens historically foreclosed events once again to their potentialities, launching an investigation into the supposed inevitability of revolution. This literary experiment allows Agyeya to interrogate the promise of revolutionary violence in India—which, at the time, seemed to have borne little other than the imprisonment and death of the revolutionaries—in delivering radical societal transformation. Agyeya's attempt to displace revolution from its exalted position as the assured telos leads him on a quest to unravel the very notion of history as a linear progression toward a unitary goal.

Out of Joint

The scene of revolution's arrival in "Cursed," with which this chapter opens, exemplifies Agyeya's splicing together of the post–May Thirtieth vision of impending proletarian revolution with the established narrative of early Republican China. The second section of "Cursed" begins with the realization of that long-anticipated, elusive dream:

> Darkness spread over Hankou. . . . Far on the horizon, a dull red light began to glow, and from it, pillars of smoke arose. Heavy dark clouds filled the sky emitting an occasional roar, like that of a hungry tiger. No winds blew; the atmosphere was charged with the vibrations of a suppressed energy. The crowd of people anxiously looked toward the red light. The soldiers shouted, "There's our signal! Revolution! Revolution!" From the houses surrounding the square came cries of "Attack! Attack! Victory to the hungry people!"
>
> But the people? They were standing motionless—simply staring at the blood-signal with worried eyes. The entire weight [of that signal] was not yet able to enter into the frantic minds of the people. The clouds rumbled, the far-away crackle of fire was in the trembling air, soldiers were invoking revolution. But the people—the people stood still, stunned, like a burnt-out pyre, like an unconscious, dormant desire, like a mind plagued by paralysis, yet like a shapeless, helpless, nameless phantom, agitated by unrest. . . . Suddenly, their steely torpor broke; suddenly, an inner light blazed! Men awakened, women awakened, laborers awakened, civilians awakened. Suddenly, an entire slumbering nation awakened and roared "Revolution!"[26]

Revolution (*krānti*), a "phantom" (*prêt*), takes shape as at once palpable—in the "trembling," "vibrating" ominous air—and as distant, a glow on the horizon, as yet ungraspable, "shapeless" and "nameless." A single word, "Hankou," conjures the landscape of China, but, absent that lone reference, the sentences that follow depict an abstracted scene, transferable into any context. Similarly, the people figure here only in universal categories of

[78]

"men, women, laborers, and civilians," offering placeholders for the world's oppressed together awaiting the promised deliverance. Revolution's abstraction and transferability bespeaks its supposed inevitability, just as China's perceived march toward revolution had anticipated for observers of the May Thirtieth movement the same chain of events unfolding in India. This scene appears, at first, to subscribe to such a narrative.

But, unlike its position in the metanarrative of progressive history, revolution does not appear endlessly deferred, does not linger perpetually upon some future horizon; for a moment, revolution seems to arrive. The red glow on the horizon becomes intimately attainable, literally embodied in the people's ignited "inner light." And this arrival does not occur at the end of the story, as some final climax or culmination, but toward its beginning, out of place in a narrative that presents itself as a story about the dawn of revolution. Proceeding from the end, the story appears to unfold in reverse. Revolution arrives in a "time out of joint,"[27] doubly so, as a "phantom," or perhaps, a "specter"—"what seems to be out front, the future, comes back in advance: from the past, from the back"—and as an anachronism, defying the impulse to narrate history in order.[28] The phantom ontologized must confront its conditions of reality, the messy terrain upon which the logics of cause and effect collapse, revealing no legible chain of events from which to chart a trajectory toward a (now disjointed) end.

This revolution, the long-awaited climax depicted in heavy-handed ideological strokes that mark its Marxist impulse, quickly turns out not to be a victory at all, let alone a communist one. The air of abstraction dissolves into a barrage of specificities, inserting the disoriented reader into the thick of 1911 China. The scene zooms into a conversation among a group of men talking in hushed tones: "Comrades, we have called this session of the Guomindang today in order to make an important decision. As you know, Liang Qichao, upon whose erudition and good sense we had such hopes . . . has behaved inappropriately."[29] The conversation reveals that Liang, a member of the Guomindang seeking to appoint Sun Yatsen as China's new leader, has deceived the party and is rumored to have fled to Manchuria. His betrayal resulted in the "pillars of smoke" rising in the distance, which the reader now realizes signal not the people's victory but the revolutionaries' defeat. Far from heralding the dawn of revolution, the red glow in fact announces the violent suppression of the revolutionaries at the hands of Yuan Shikai's army, appointed by the Qing emperor to quell the rebellion. In stark contrast to its momentous arrival, the red glow abruptly dissipates: "A blast in the distance. That red light suddenly burst, scattering through the sky. For a moment, the sky filled with blazing red stars. Then darkness, the rumbling of clouds, commotion among the people."[30] Beginning in the end, from the aftermath of revolution's sighting in a historical moment that has already passed, "Cursed" dethrones revolution from its glorified position as the ultimate goal in the same gesture as it frees the past from its imposed fidelity to a narrativized chain of events that plot a predetermined course in revolution's own image.

The pattern repeats throughout the story: revolution's presence tantalizingly close, conjured into being by the anticipation of the expectant crowd that summons it, and yet never quite there in its asymptotic reticence. At one point, the story cuts to Peking and offers a meditation not on revolution's arrival but on its remains:

> Revolution is often compared to the deluge [*pralay*], the end of the world. But after revolution has burned bright, the way in which the entire nation becomes filled with wretched, broken lives, with uprooted ties, with the poor, grey-haired, starving, wounded, disappointed, heaps of human wreckage— how can this find comparison with deluge? That living sea of anguish: can the monolithic stillness of the world-ending deluge truly account for this?[31]

The scene narrates the aftermath of a revolution violently waged, bypassing revolution's event (the happening of the impossible) and skipping ahead to its wake. In its disjointed apparition, revolution's coming back from a future deferred makes possible a confrontation with its wreckage, a view foreclosed in a discourse that bestows to revolution the postponed promise of a better tomorrow. Disjointedness forces a reckoning between the transcendent and its unlikely grounds of existence. Glimpsed in retrospect, revolution begets not utopia but an apocalyptic "sea of anguish"; revolution marks not the "end," like the flood that decimates in a flash leaving stillness, but the provenance of a world that must bear revolution's violent legacy.

Unlike the hopeful crowd awaiting revolution's dawn at the beginning of the story, here the people of Peking wait in terror (*ātaṅk*): "a terror hung over Peking" as tales of Yuan Shikai's brutality, of towns and villages across China strung with the "the severed heads of slain revolutionaries" reaches Peking.[32]

As the people now await revolution with fear, the story enacts yet another inversion in the scene of revolution's arrival/aftermath; anticipation dissolves into its antonym: dread. Revolution thus unfolds in reverse both temporally and affectively, the bright dawn confronts in its mirror image a gruesome devastation.

Yet, even in its aftermath, revolution's spectral presence deceives. The following paragraph informs that "revolution's flames had not yet reached Peking. . . . Vanquished in Hankou, revolution had drifted toward Nanjing."[33] The aftermath reveals itself as a premonition, in turn the declaration of a future untold. The preceding scene of revolution's aftermath in Peking foretells a devastation "not yet" wrought, or perhaps already wrought by a revolution in the figure of the revenant. The narrative casts a backward glance forward, toward a foreshadowed future through the gaze of "the angel of history," transfixed upon the heaps of wreckage of that violent storm called progress.[34] As the people of Peking await China's true savior, Sun Yatsen, revolution remains furtively ungraspable, present only its nonpresence: "The people, in the feverish delirium of awaiting [Sun Yatsen], did not receive any reliable news" on his whereabouts as a barrage of headlines contradictorily announce Yuan's suppression of the revolutionaries and Sun Yatsen's arrival, leaving the people "confused, not knowing who to believe and who not to."[35] "Cursed" ends with an anticlimactic, retrospective announcement of revolution's eventual success: "This month in Canton, an independent democracy was established. At the beginning of June, Yuan died."[36] Revolution's event once again evades coming into view even as the story concludes by naming it.

Amid revolution's perpetual haunting, the central arc of "Cursed" follows two Chinese radicals—Liang Qichao and his (entirely fictional) sister Shai-Va—caught between Yuan and Sun's competing political factions as they navigate a tangled web of loyalty and betrayal, alliance and deception, in the underground world of revolutionary operations. Liang and Shai-Va, the story reveals, have in fact fled to Japan after wrongful accusations of betraying the Guomindang. Anxious to return to China to clear their names and turned away by Sun Yatsen (with whom Liang secretly meets in a Tokyo hideout), Liang and Shai-Va enlist as Japanese spies. The two, under their new aliases Kasheyi (Liang) and Leena (Shai-Va), are dispatched to China to pose as members of Yuan's inner circle. Meanwhile, Yuan has defeated the Guomindang in Hankou and established his fascist government in Peking with his right-hand man Tang Shao (an allusion to Tang Shaoyi 唐紹儀, the first premier of the Republic of China in 1912), who Yuan later discovers is in fact a covert Guomindang leader named Wusung, in league with Sun Yatsen.

Like the revolution that reveals itself as defeat and arrives only in its aftermath, each of the story's main characters—Liang/Kasheyi, Shai-Va/Leena, and Wusung/Tang Shao—straddle multiple, contradictory identities, fluctuating between both sides of the Yuan/Sun divide that forms the central axis of conflict in the story. As the characters navigate shifting grounds of allegiance, Agyeya's China takes shape as a world rife with uncertainty, in which even the most renowned of historical personages, whom the reader may vest with a degree of certainty, turn deceitful, revealing hidden identities. Consider, for example, the following scene in which Shai-Va/Leena sets out to confront Wusung/Tang Shao, her former love, who she believes has betrayed Sun Yatsen by joining Yuan's government. Wusung, in turn, believes that Shai-Va herself is the traitor:

In a yellow house in Peking, some ten–twelve men had gathered. Some were wearing Yuan Shikai's army uniform. Each had an expression of secrecy on his face, as though he were pondering a highly confidential matter.

One man, who appeared to be the leader of those gathered, said, "Friends! We must make a quick decision on this matter. He is learned and talented, we cannot disregard him."

One member said, "Tangshao, give us a practical solution!"

"What should our stance on national traitors be?"

"But what proof do we have of his treachery?

"I've known him for a long time . . . and his sister too . . . his sister . . ."

"What about his sister, Wusung?"

The door flew open with a bang. Everyone spun around—a beautiful young woman wearing a Chinese gown was standing there, her pistol pointed, her unblinking, piercing eyes blazing into Tang Shao.

Without shifting her stare from Tang Shao's face, she said again—this time in a scorn-filled voice, cutting like a blade's edge:

"What about his sister, Wusung?". . . .

Without hesitation, the woman [Shai-va] strode forward. Tang Shao led her to a door. Opening the door he said, "We are all armed. You cannot escape."

Stepping into the doorframe, the woman looked in: a man, approximately forty years of age stood within. . . . The woman took a closer look at the man, from head to foot.

Her limbs fell loose. The pistol dropped from her hand. Her voice breaking, she said, "Doctor Sun . . . Yat . . . Sen!"—and she dropped to the ground.[37]

A series of misrecognitions, dramatic reveals, and gasps of surprise endow this cinematic scene with a charged air of suspense. Leena dramatically barges into a secret meeting of Yuan's men. Tang Shao mirrors and outdoes that entrance when, mere sentences later, he discloses a second hidden room with Sun Yatsen within, unveiling his true allegiance to the Guomindang. In the span of a single page, the entire story pivots; a gathering of Yuan's men (dressed in Yuan's "army uniform") now unmasked as a meeting of the Guomindang under Sun's leadership. Shai-Va, herself disguised as a spy (Leena), who enters the scene armed with the knowledge of Tang Shao's true identity as Wusung, must suddenly confront her own position in the dark. And just as the deceitful revolution left the dizzied people "not knowing who to believe and who not to," the reader grapples with uncovering the characters' many layers of secrets.[38] Engrossed in untangling the story's complex fictional configurations, the reader scarcely notices her own grounds of historical certainty—faith in the idea that past events unfolded in a certain way and not otherwise—crumble away.

The profusion of historical allusions in "Cursed"—to landmark events of early Republican China and to figures such as Liang Qichao, Tang Shaoyi, Sun Yatsen, and Yuan Shikai, all of whom maintain vestiges of their "real" identities at the same time as they reveal themselves to be different than expected—frames the story as in need of decoding. On one hand, the careful historical engagement with China appears superfluous in a story that explicitly makes no claims to educate its reader about China or its 1911 revolution; as such, one critic dismisses "Cursed" as "cumbersome" and "weighed down" by the "intensity of details regarding the foreign backdrop, names, and [historical] events."[39] And yet the allusions appear to hold the key to making sense of the story, tempting the reader to parse "Cursed" for fact and fiction, to identify each allusion in order to separate the historical from the fictional. At the same time as it invites such analysis, "Cursed" constantly foils any attempt to apprehend it as a story foretold, as a totalizing narrative that conceives of the past as foreclosed and the future as inevitable. Countering the tendency among radical leftists who looked to China as the harbinger of communist revolution in India, Agyeya's China questions the assumptions underlying that deterministic logic, and, in so doing, the story defies the mandates of historical necessity.

On Violence

Against the impulse of circumscribed teleology, Agyeya's China stories assign the past to an open horizon of possibilities, keeping the past "suspended between occurrence and nonoccurrence," as "something that is not necessary or eternal, but something whose opposite could have happened in the very moment in which it happened."[40] In his literary terrain of China, a space particularly conducive to experiments with historical thought and its reimagination, Agyeya reenacts revolutionary violence of the kind the HRSA engaged in, making the act of violence happen differently in order to evaluate its range of possibility and viability.

"Unstained," the earliest of the three China stories, tells of Martin, a Guomindang soldier, whose reputation of undying loyalty to the revolution earns him the nickname "Unstained." The story opens with the Guomindang army ordering the residents of Martin's village to break the levees between their lands and the Yellow River, in order to flood their homes and prevent the advancing "enemy army" (Yuan Shikai's men) from gaining ground. Martin refuses to comply, much to the anger of Christabel (Martin's love) and the other villagers, who accuse him of treason and cowardice. But Martin, true to his reputation of loyalty, devises a secret plan. He returns to his estate with a mysterious load of materials:

Martin closed all the doors, picked up the spade and shovel from the corner of the room, and began to dig. When he had dug out a pretty big ditch in the middle of the room, he stood up and stretched, and then took both loads off the horses and placed them in the ditch. Then, he opened the bundle of something rope-like wrapped around his waist, and placed one end of it into the ditch. He proceeded to fill the ditch back up, and then dug a drain-like hole from the ditch to the window, and for a long way from the other side of the window, into which he pressed the rope. The rope ended approximately sixty yards from his house.

He left the end of the rope above ground and covered it up in a pile of dead leaves and sticks. He then returned home, closed the shutters, and sat completely lost in thought.[41]

Markers of secrecy and ambiguity in the scene—the unspecified "load" (*bojh*), the metaphoric descriptors "rope-like" (*rassī-sī*) and "drain-like" (*nālī-sī*)—contrast with the precision of Martin's deliberate actions. As the plan, devised by a violent revolutionary who, much like the HRSA "terrorists," is shunned by his community, concretizes, the story recalls an infamous bomb plot of 1929, later uncovered as a scheme of the HRSA. In December 1929, a year before Agyeya's imprisonment, members of the HRSA attempted to rig and detonate a bomb on a railway track outside Delhi upon which the vice-regal train, carrying the Viceroy and his wife, was due to pass. Detonating a remote, battery-operated bomb from afar proved an untested method for the HRSA members, who had so far only hurled handheld bombs at their targets. "Over 300 yards of flexible electric wire was buried under the earth by Yashpal [and others]. . . . The connections were tested . . . with the battery, and bombs were then buried under the track."[42] The next morning, as the train passed over the rigged portion of the tracks, Yashpal (who would later become Agyeya's partner at the soap factory) detonated the bomb, but he narrowly missed the Viceroy's compartment and succeeded only in damaging the restaurant car.[43] The train completed its journey and the Viceroy remained unharmed; the plot thus failed. The incident was widely reported as a "dastardly attempt on the life of the Viceroy," igniting "outrage" in London.[44] The Crown insisted that "British policy in India will not be deflected in the slightest by deeds of violence," while Indian leaders denounced the plot as "one of the most unfortunate incidents in this country."[45]

In "Unstained," the plot unfolds differently, this time not as the condemned violence of terrorists but as the careful plan of a misunderstood revolutionary. Moreover, Martin's plan enables the HRSA plot to find a different resolution. Following his arrest for his supposed disloyalty to the Guomindang, Martin's empty estate becomes a refuge for the enemy: "Today, the enemy-army has the run of Martin's estate. Today, seven hundred of the nation's enemy have found shelter and are hatching their plans of advancing further south."[46] The reader learns that, prior to his imprisonment, Martin had deputized a fellow revolutionary, Simon, to detonate the elaborate bomb rigged in the previous scene. Simon now stealthily approaches the periphery of Martin's house amid the enemy army's cheers of celebration, while Christabel observes the scene from a distance. Simon sets some grass on fire, and then "smoke [begins] to rise from the ground. After a while, a tiny 'hiss-hiss . . .' as though dynamite were burning."[47] Suddenly, Christabel feels an earthquake, an intense pressure; she closes her eyes and then "boom!"—a massive explosion.[48] In one fell swoop, seven hundred men of the enemy army burn. As Christabel regains her senses, Simon recuperates Martin from the charges of disloyalty: "Martin was a member of the secret association of the Guomindang," he explains, "before he was imprisoned, he had instructed me to set this wick on fire."[49] Against the backdrop of an annihilated enemy, Martin's heroism and sacrifice finally dawn on Christabel.

In Agyeya's China, where past events are consigned to the realm of possibility, the HRSA's acts of revolutionary violence can once again happen, this time to different ends, "as something whose opposite could have happened in the very moment in which it happened."[50] In this iteration, a formerly misaimed bomb hits its target, a failed plot finds success, the revolutionary emerges a hero. Armed revolution can be immanently palpable; the sensation of a victorious bombing viscerally felt. Revolutionary violence can finally—at last, and for the last time—burn bright.

Triumph's Tragedy

Agyeya's experiments with reimagining the past and deconstructing narratives of history suggest his preoccupation with the idea of contingency as a destabilizing yet emancipatory force, calling into question formerly held beliefs yet liberating in its capacity to bring into view differently possible worlds. "Revolutionaries, ultimately, are a breed of determinists," Agyeya once wrote; they have "a firm (but amorphous) faith in the scientific chain of cause-and-effect [kāryă-kāraṇ-paramparā]."[51] While in jail, Agyeya experienced a transformation away from such a "formula of destiny"; he found that "gradually the formulas of cause-and-effect disentangled themselves and began to come to hand."[52] A world no longer subject to the narrow demands of causality suffuses with uncertainty, operating according to the logic not of sequentiality but of disjointedness and contingency; history can unfold otherwise.

Put differently, Agyeya's preoccupation with contingency arose from and manifested in a crisis of political conviction. While in jail, as his lived conditions of circumscription found expression in his literary rebellion against determinism, he began to lose faith in revolutionary violence, questioning its capacity to deliver Indian independence. In search for "the answer to a question posed to oneself," as he described his jail writings, the stories reopen the potentiality of revolutionary violence in order to probe its potency.[53] "When I was released," Agyeya later wrote, "it wasn't that my enthusiasm for revolution had cooled off, but I had definitely left behind terrorism and underground movements. The use of violence had become marked by too many doubts."[54] The China stories capture the revolutionary's loss of faith with the method of armed revolution the HRSA had once envisioned.

Of Agyeya's three China stories, "Hariti" captures such disillusionment most poignantly. The story tells of its titular protagonist, a young girl devoted to serving Sun Yatsen's Canton army as a soldier and spy. As in the other China stories, "Hariti" paints a vivid picture of early twentieth-century China: "When she was six years old . . . her father was killed at the hands of German soldiers—blown up by the canons—because he was a member of a secret society called 'the Boxers.' After that, in the Boxer rebellion of 1900, when she was not yet eleven years of age, German and British soldiers burned her village to the ground. Men and women burned to death, and amongst them was Hariti's aged mother."[55] The story goes on to detail Hariti's narrow escape from the fire and her childhood on the banks of the Sikiang River (Xijiang), eking out a living in a community of poor, opium-addicted fishermen. Hariti eventually joins the Canton army as it prepares for the onslaught of Yuan Shikai's monarchist army steadily approaching from Manchuria. The story introduces the two armies as diametrically opposed to each other: "The Canton-army was comprised of volunteers; in Yuan Shikai's army, the soldiers earned wages. The Canton-army was motivated by the ideal of equality; Yuan Shikai's men were motivated by personal gain. The Canton-soldiers held the desire for democracy [prajātantră] in their hearts; Yuan Shikai's soldiers aimed to reestablish the weakened foundations of imperialism. The Canton-army fought for their beliefs, Yuan Shikai's fought for profit."[56] As a victim of the destruction imperial powers wrought in China during the Boxer Rebellion, Hariti remains intensely committed to the defeat of Yuan's imperialist army. She exemplifies each of the Canton army's values, particularly its call to cast aside "personal gain" for the sake of the greater cause and to strive toward "the ideal of equality."

For Hariti, the act of giving herself entirely to the cause manifests most explicitly in the erasure of her womanhood; she must live in the Canton army's encampments disguised as a man and must sacrifice her "womanly" desire to love: "She would wake up every morning, put on her men's uniform, and say a prayer to some omnipotent power: 'Give me steadfastness so I may pass the tests to come. I have remained denied of love . . . I do not have the right to love; I am a slave. I have no desires for fame—what fame can there be in slavery—but may I follow my path and not be misguided, may I remain worthy of my beliefs.' "[57] As in this daily ritual, the story calls attention to Hariti's revolutionary identity as antithetical to her femininity: her short hair, male uniform, and unbeatable physical prowess all serve as undesirable yet essential features of her masculine appearance.[58] Hariti's willingness to shed her womanhood entirely, the ultimate "personal" sacrifice necessary for the establishment of a radically different societal order, bears the marks of a communist revolutionary vision, which frames the individual's interests as perfectly aligned with the common interests of the collective. Yet Hariti's daily disavowal of her womanhood conveys a sense of loss— "I am a slave," she says—hinting at a schism between the individual and collective; here, the individual, although deeply committed to the greater cause, becomes oppressed by the very collective she champions. The story asks whether the revolutionary's victory truly promises her emancipation.

One day, the general of the Canton army entrusts Hariti, his most able soldier, with delivering a letter of the utmost importance. Hariti accepts this secret mission with her characteristic devotion and determination. She enlists her closest comrade, Kwanyin, along with a trusted group of men, and sets off on the treacherous journey. Along the way, the convoy encounters Yuan's army. A bitter battle of gunfire ensues. Kwanyin sacrifices himself so that Hariti may persevere onward. Eventually, narrowly escaping death, Hariti arrives at her destination and delivers the letter to its intended recipient, a woman named Diana Pei-fu.

But "Hariti" is not a story of victory. A successfully executed mission instead spells debilitating defeat and profound loss. Having lost those closest to her and risked her own life, Hariti finally delivers the letter to Diana

Pei-fu and watches her read it: "Diana took out the letter and opened it. Her face turned red, and her eyes lowered with embarrassment. She kissed the letter and whispered 'Beloved!' "[59] Hariti realizes that the entire mission had been not for the conveyance of an urgent message of revolutionary importance, but for a trivial love letter, the most egregious exercise of "personal gain" so antithetical to the revolutionary cause. An ugly truth dawns: Hariti's sacrifice of "the right to love" had ultimately enabled not the realization of liberation, but another woman's selfish exercise of that right, a deeper entrenchment of inequality.

As Hariti's belief in the revolution shatters, her entire being disintegrates: she dies on Diana's sofa with a look of deep disdain on her face. Ironically, only in her death, induced by revolution's betrayal, is Hariti's womanhood finally recognizable.[60] In the moment before her death—as "a smile glimmers on her face, a smile not of the peace of achieving success, nor of the pride of attaining victory, only a chilling smile of derision and scorn"—Hariti throws off her uniform in a final disavowal of her revolutionary identity. Diana exclaims, "But . . . but . . . you are a woman!," but it is too late, for Hariti is "no longer a woman," only a body of a departed soul.[61] Hariti's death brings a liberation of its own: she is no longer a revolutionary, but, in a moment of tragic triumph, casting off her revolutionary garb sets her true self free.

Agyeya's other China stories similarly end with triumph's tragedy, victory in revolution presaging the revolutionary's demise. "Cursed" ends with the revolution the story had initially promised—Sun Yatsen's army defeats Yuan Shikai—but the revolutionary meets a different fate. Kasheyi (Liang) storms Yuan's palace, fails in his attempt to assassinate Yuan, and turns his gun upon himself. Outside the palace, Yuan's men arrest Leena (Shai-Va) as she distributes anti-Yuan pamphlets. Kasheyi and Leena's original identities remain undiscovered, and the true revolutionaries, Liang and Shai-Va, are soon forgotten, cursed to eternal disrepute. In "Untainted," Christabel rushes to exonerate Martin once she learns of his true heroism, but she arrives upon Martin's scene of execution a moment too late, just as bullets pierce his body. In all three stories, the success of revolutionary violence (Sun Yatsen's eventual victory in "Cursed," Martin's bomb, Hariti's mission) meets only with the revolutionary's anticlimactic death; indeed, the stories eschew culmination altogether. Revolutionary violence reneges on its promise to deliver liberation.

In his 1975 introduction to the first published compilation of his short stories, Agyeya reflected on what he identified as the romantic idealism of his jail writings:

> In my first batch of short stories, there is a clear note of idealism. These are stories written by a revolutionary in support of revolution. Today, there are many revolutionaries who would consider idealism an insult . . . but the revolutionaries of that time were idealists and took pride in their idealism. If the idealism of that time betrays a glimpse of romance, then [this romance] is but a reflection of the reality of the time. There was a romantic innocence in terrorist movements and in idealist revolutionaries.[62]

In his China stories, Agyeya celebrates such idealism in the same gesture as he subjects it to scrutiny. In the open field of possibilities that demarcates the spatial poetics of Agyeya's China, the stories harness the power of "romantic innocence" to summon revolution into being, to make it present in an effort to lay bare the impossibility of that presence. In this sense, the China stories tell a tale of coming of age in colonial India that runs counter to the more typical trope of the freedom fighter whose political awakening results in his devotion to the cause, his heroic role in the fight for independence, and his eventual immortalization in his posthumous martyrdom. Agyeya's revolutionary traverses a quieter path: his mourning of the remains of a revolution past reveals its singularity as only one vision of transformation upon an infinite horizon of possibility. Agyeya described his quest for the different forms revolution could take as an expression of his enduring commitment to radical transformation: "The dreams I envisioned during that era of idealism were yet to be fulfilled. I considered the instruments [to achieve those dreams] unusable, but I did not consider the aim to be wrong."[63] Agyeya's China stories challenge its reader to think the "aim" of radical transformation beyond the confines of a revolution already charted, in the freedom of a blank page yet to be inscribed.

"But . . ."

Years after his release from jail, Agyeya launched a revolution of a different sort. With the publication in 1941 of the first volume of his novel *Shekhar*, drafted in jail, Agyeya became known as the "champion of high modernism in Hindi,"[64] and *Shekhar*, "a modernist classic" in its inauguration of a turn away from the outward-oriented motivations of social realism toward a new foregrounding of internal psychological, existential, and textual spaces.[65] In the late 1940s and 1950s, Agyeya edited the *Saptaks*, the anthologies of experimentalist poetry that would launch the New Poetry movement, an era of innovation in the Hindi literary sphere, with which poets like Shamsher and Machwe (to whom I return in chapter 4) would soon become associated. Agyeya's vast oeuvre—of fourteen poetry collections, six short story collections, four novels, and numerous other prose writings—stands as the hallmark of Hindi modernist experimentalism.[66]

The radical newness of Agyeya's practice elicited much disapproval from leftist and progressive writers, who often levied accusations of "elitist, aloof, and reactionary" at his works.[67] The Hindi critic Jaidev, for example, famously charged experimentalist writers with "co-opting . . . Western" modernist practices, an indication of their "loss of interest in common people and their ordinary culture . . . [exacerbating] the growing chasm between the 'elite' and the common culture."[68] More recently, critics have emphasized the poverty of the conventional opposition between social realist purposiveness on one hand and modernist aestheticism on the other, particularly in accounting for a figure like Agyeya, who fashioned himself as a practitioner of high modernism and yet self-identified variously as "Marxist" and "communist."[69] True to his pen name, bestowed upon him by Premchand while he was in jail, Agyeya's works remain unknowable, defying determinism and thriving as enigma.

For all the critical attention Agyeya's works have garnered, his jail stories remain curiously eclipsed.[70] A 2013 volume entitled *Agyeya: Stories from his Jail Days* (*jel ke dinoṁ kī kahānīyāṁ*) and edited by the leading Agyeya scholar Krishnadutt Paliwal, brought together for the first time the eighteen jail stories previously scattered among various publications. Paliwal's introductory essay provides a detailed account of Agyeya's revolutionary days but conspicuously refrains from offering analytic insights into the stories. Paliwal states his intent as "not to review the stories" but solely to contextualize them: "By collecting together all of Agyeya's jail stories, my desire is only that learned readers may undertake the profound journey of reading these stories together . . . and understand Agyeya's early state of mind within the correct context."[71] Paliwal's reticence to review proves indicative of the fact that these stories fared poorly in Hindi literary circles; the jail stories earn only parenthetical mention in the large body of Hindi-language scholarship on Agyeya. Agyeya himself did not discuss the stories at length in his many memoirs and interviews, passing by them almost apologetically, as though they remained unworthy of his retrospection. "There were several stories written with the revolutionary moments in different countries for material," Agyeya said in one interview primarily about *Shekhar*, "movements in Russia, in China, in Cuba, in Mexico, all [written] during that period [in jail]. Not all were good stories but . . ."[72] Seemingly unable or unwilling to defend his jail stories to a readership that largely rejected them, Agyeya's thought trailed off mid-sentence, and the interviewer moved on.

Perhaps Agyeya's China stories dwell most comfortably in ellipsis, in the "but . . . ," as Agyeya put it, disruptive yet connective, vivid yet elusive. The three stories disturb the coherence of Agyeya's oeuvre—he would go on to abandon, for example, the sustained experimentation with historical allusion so central to the fabric of the China stories—but at the same time they profess threads of affinity with all that would become marked by Agyeya's distinctive hand. The China stories take shape incidentally, through the coincidental confluence of three simultaneous phenomena (Agyeya's imprisonment, the shift in his political convictions, and the affective attachment Indian leftist discourse extended to China in the wake of May Thirtieth) while evoking a sense of monumentality, of historical heft. In 1956, Agyeya would sign, along with Dinkar, a statement against the participation of the Chinese delegation at the Asian Writers' Conference, discussed in the next chapter. In 1985, as China and India repaired severed relations following the war of 1962 (the subject of chapter 4), Agyeya would travel to China as part of a Sahitya Akademi delegation. The literary space of China that Agyeya crafted while in jail seems a product of its times, and yet its incessant deconstructive impulse unravels historicity. As the stories call for reimagining the form of a revolution at once prefigured and deferred, they put into motion that very urging for a different sort of radical transformation, sowing the seeds of a commitment to literary experimentation poised to take Hindi literature by storm.

Agyeya wrote his China stories during a time when writing revolution in China figured as a trope of sorts in the transnational scene of revolutionary imagery. One may think of Agyeya's 1930s China stories as part of a larger collection of texts—including Soviet writer Sergei Tretyakov's 1926 play *Roar*,

China! set against the Wanxian Incident of that year, Yokomitsu Riichi's Japanese novel *Shanghai* (1928–1931) that unfolds in Shanghai's International Settlement during the May Thirtieth Incident of 1925, and André Malraux's 1933 French novel *The Human Condition* set in Shanghai during the communist uprising and subsequent anticommunist purge of 1927—all of which similarly contemplate the possibilities and limits of revolution in a fictionalized yet historical landscape of China. Unlike these texts, however, Agyeya's China stories explore revolution in China in order to ultimately disavow revolutionary means altogether, and to facilitate a confrontation with the ruins and disillusionments of a revolution waged violently. As Marxist and communist narratives of the time positioned China and India on a tandem march toward revolution, Agyeya's China stories unravel the China-India pairing even as China furnishes the grounds upon which Agyeya grapples with the fate of revolution in India. The China stories mark Agyeya's turn away from violent revolutionary means and toward nonviolence as better suited to deliver India's independence, and, in so doing, erode the binds of the China-India comparative unit Marxist narratives of the time sought to construct.

Unpairing China and India, however, makes possible a form of literary relation that takes shape against the pulls of a history that progresses as foretold, toward a predetermined telos: that of proletarian revolution. Also unlike the texts listed above that engage ideas of revolution in China in a largely contemporaneous sense, Agyeya's China stories are set not in May Thirtieth China but in an earlier period immediately following the 1911 revolution against dynastic rule, a revolution deemed successful. Alluding to an already established historical narrative allows Agyeya to reopen historically foreclosed events to the play of contingency and to the potentialities of a history derailed and out of joint, off the unitary track of determinism. Subject to fictional reimagination, history can unfold otherwise. Revolution appears not as the long-anticipated climax, but as an elusive haunting that makes its presence known only in its marked absence, in the destruction and wreckage left in its wake. Written during his own imprisonment, Agyeya's disillusionment with China and India's twinned revolutionary destinies enables a literary critique of the limitations of historical determinism and a revelry in the capacity of the literary mind to break free, to find different paths toward liberation.

THREE

Dialogue and Its Discontents

1950s Cultural Diplomacy Untold

IN THE 1950S, heads of state Zhou Enlai and Jawaharlal Nehru set the nascent PRC and newly decolonized Republic of India on a hectic course of diplomatic relations. This was the age of China-India dialogue. The public performance of diplomatic relations most often took the form of dialogue conducted at international conferences and during the visits of dignitaries and delegations from friendship associations. In 1956 alone, to present a lengthy yet still partial calendar of diplomatic activities, a Chinese delegation visited India from January to March, an Indian delegation traveled to China in April, a Chinese football team played against Indians in June, an Indian agricultural team visited China in July and August, Indian parliamentary and military delegations visited Beijing in September, Zhou Enlai arrived in India in October for a twelve-day visit, and a Chinese women's delegation followed in November.[1]

Such activities comprise the program of cultural diplomacy undertaken by both nations in the early 1950s. A facet of foreign policy, cultural diplomacy designates a particular strategy wherein "orchestrated governmental intervention [channels] the flow of culture to advance national interests."[2] In the context of the emergent Cold War world, activities of cultural diplomacy proved an integral means through which the United States and USSR scrambled to extend and reinforce their spheres of influence.[3] But the two blocs were not alone in recognizing the importance of cultural production in furthering national interests and in harnessing its powers of persuasion to win over hearts and minds. Cultural diplomacy also organized engagement across the Third World. Indeed, the delegates at the Bandung Conference of 1955 explicitly identified "cultural cooperation" as "among the most powerful means of promoting understanding among nations," and much of the ensuing activity of cultural exchange occurred via official diplomatic channels.[4] Programs of cultural diplomacy in the Third World have been largely understood within frames of resistance: as an anticolonial call for the recently decolonized world to learn about each other anew through cultural engagement unmediated and unrestricted by the former colonial rulers, and as a nonaligned stance asserted against the new types of imperialisms and forms of domination taking shape under Cold War polarities.[5] If scholarly treatments of cultural diplomacy tend to "elide the fundamental institutional location of cultural diplomacy within the machinery of government and, therefore, the inevitable restrictions imposed on it in terms of the interests it is meant to serve," as recent critiques suggest, this elision particularly shapes understandings of cultural diplomacy conducted in the Third World.[6] Studies of the superpowers' activities of cultural diplomacy more fully attend to cultural diplomacy's "institutional location within the machinery of government" and its resultant "inevitable restrictions"; when referring to the Third World, by contrast, studies tend to strike an optimistic, even nostalgic, tone.

There is indeed much to celebrate about cultural diplomacy conducted under the banners of decolonization and nonalignment. China-India cultural diplomacy of the 1950s, for instance, made possible unprecedented forms of exchange, cooperation, and collaboration, opening alternative pathways toward modernity and nationhood in both China and India, and forging new vectors of socialist internationalisms and solidarities beyond the binary logic of the two-bloc Cold War world. When Chinese and Indian writers met in arenas of cultural diplomacy, they enthusiastically engaged in the diplomatically inflected activities they were tasked with: they exchanged books, commissioned translations, recalled and celebrated ancient literary ties, shared the current state of literary practice in each other's nations, and composed works proclaiming China-India friendship. For a brief period, Indian literature became widely accessible for Chinese readers, and vice versa, with many writers leaving a lasting impression long after diplomatic relations began to sour in the late 1950s.

Still, the very real expressions and gestures of friendship recorded in the archives of cultural diplomacy mask, by design, the inevitable dissonances of a cultural sphere put to diplomatic use. Cutting across bloc or partisan lines, dissonances run through the mantle of cultural diplomacy writ large: a conflation between "interest-driven governmental practice" and the "non-state actors" (artists, writers, intellectuals) tasked with furthering such interests, a collapsing of "national interest"—cultural diplomacy's top priority—and the rhetoric of "common interest," in which the benefits of sharing culture transnationally become articulated, and a contradiction between the state's goal of "channeling" culture and the indeterminate and unpredictable workings of culture that evade such control.[7] Founded upon dissonances and elisions, China-India cultural diplomacy embodied the competing forces of an enthusiastic outpouring of cultural expression heralding brotherhood rubbing up against both states' attempts to rein in and steer the cultural sphere towards predetermined diplomatic aims. Nehru, in an effort to maintain the nonaligned tenor of diplomacy with China, struggled to bring under state control the numerous unofficial India-China friendship associations that had a propensity to initiate their own unsanctioned dialogues with China, and to ensure the political neutrality of India's many visitors to China, some of whom managed to travel without the Indian government's approval.[8] On the other side, Chinese cultural diplomacy comprised a more well-oiled machine that trained Chinese delegates on how they were to interact with foreign counterparts and that carefully choreographed spectacles of New China for foreign consumption.[9] Both Chinese and Indian cultural delegates confronted the pressures of straddling dual identities as artists-turned-diplomats and of engaging in cultural practice under intense political scrutiny both at home and abroad.[10]

In the context of cultural diplomacy, dialogue figures at once as a means to an end, and as the end in and of itself. Chinese and Indian writers met in the 1950s in order to engage in dialogue on literature as a means of establishing diplomatic relations between the two nations, and yet the mere fact that the literary dialogue occurred confirmed the preexistence of those diplomatic relations. Instances of real dialogue between writers simultaneously facilitated and stood synecdochally for metaphorical dialogue between the nations. This conflation of actual with metaphorical dialogue magnified what the writers said to each other into matters of national and international consequence. Amid such high stakes, dialogue was necessarily circumspect, a careful curation of words that aimed to attest to communication having taken place without running the risk of divulging too much. Inevitable moments of discomfort, hesitance, and silence remain virtually undetectable in state-sanctioned records of cultural diplomacy, and yet any attentive study of such activities must venture to read beyond the words on the page and to parse editorial interventions in the construction of official narratives.

The mechanisms of cultural diplomacy further necessitated an easy equivalence between literary relation and diplomatic relations, so that the act of relating literarily corresponded entirely with diplomatic agendas. If the fact of the dialogue's having taken place proved sufficient for at once cultivating and announcing diplomatic relations, what of the content of dialogue? Does it matter that the writers spoke with each other primarily about literature and literary practice, as opposed to the kinds of topics heads of states or career diplomats discussed? An investigation of what it means to relate literarily requires breaking with the epistemological regime of cultural diplomacy, which recognizes literary relation as legible and consequential only as a corollary to statecraft and only when ventriloquized by international relations. A different understanding, explored in this chapter, locates literary relation in the ellipses of cultural diplomacy, in the exclusions and excesses of state-sanctioned literary dialogue.

This chapter studies China-India cultural diplomacy as it unfolded upon the fraught literary terrain of two successive Maoist political campaigns aimed at cultural expression: the Hundred Flowers campaign of 1956, during which the Communist Party invited writers to air criticisms of the leadership, and the Anti-Rightist campaign of 1957, when the party rescinded its offer of literary freedoms and instead launched large-scale persecutions and programs of censorship. The Hundred Flowers and Anti-Rightist campaigns not only regulated literary practice on a national scale, but, crucially, also manifested in and shaped the many transnational sites of China's cultural diplomacy, both at home and abroad. As a result, the texts that chronicle cultural diplomacy also tell of the unruliness of literary spaces twice subjected to political circumscription, regulated by the mandates of both cultural diplomacy and the campaigns.

In this chapter, the search for silences begins with a consideration of the audible: What forms of literary relation did the poetic practices of cultural diplomacy most readily bespeak? The chapter then attends to the ellipses of such a poetic landscape in two mirrored parts: the first follows a delegation of Chinese writers that visited India in December 1956, during the height of the Hundred Flowers campaign; the second narrates the travels of an Indian poet in China in late 1957, during the Anti-Rightist campaign. Each part culminates in a moment of poetic reckoning: a contemplation in poetic form of the ability of literary relation to thrive in the ellipses—the unsaid and uninscribed—and thereby bypass and exceed the constraints of political directives. These poetic scenes throw into sharp relief a dissonance between form and content, of the generic demands of top-down political directives rubbing against the fundamental irreducibility of poetic practice. Dwelling in this dissonance does not undercut or make less meaningful the sanctioned forms of contact and exchange that cultural diplomacy made possible; instead, the ellipses of literary dialogue brim with the potentialities of new kinds of literary relation that refuse to abide the state's directives.

Loud Relation

In the early 1950s, the union between the realms of culture and diplomacy manifested most audibly in a particular poetic genre: the friendship song.[11] Songs proclaiming China-India friendship rang out across China and India, during public performances and over radio broadcasts, enacting the anthemlike function of rousing emotional attachment and collective participation, all to intensify political affiliation. In China, the poet Yuan Shuipai 袁水拍 composed several such songs, including one entitled "China-India Friendship Song" (ZhongYin youhao ge 中印友好哥), written in June, 1955.[12] Yuan penned the song on the occasion of an Indian cultural delegation's visit to China that same month, which was commemorated in a booklet published by the Foreign Languages Press (FLP) in Beijing. The FLP was China's official press for those publications intended to circulate abroad.[13] The English-language booklet, titled The Indian Cultural Delegation in China, collects photographs of the activities the Indian delegates partook in while in China. One photograph captures Yuan reciting his China-India friendship songs. The caption reads: "At a friendly meeting between Chinese artists and writers and Indian artists at the International Club on June 16, the famous Chinese poet Yuan Shui-pai recites his two poems 'To India' and 'To the Indian Artists.'"[14] The

booklet later includes Yuan's "China-India Friendship Song" in English translation (here, under the English title "China-India Friendship").[15] It remains
unclear whether this poem was among those Yuan recited at the gathering,
but, significantly, the English translation printed in the commemorative
booklet appears to have been prepared *for* recitation. Note, for example, the
emphasis the unattributed translator (likely among those employed by the
FLP at the time) places upon syllabic symmetry and rhyme in the opening
and closing stanzas of this five-stanza poem:

> The Himalayas tower to reach the sky;
> On either side our two great countries lie;
> Good neighbours we, who travelled to and fro;
> Two thousand years of friendship we can show.
> . . .
>
> Through two great lands, from Delhi to Peking,
> Above the clouds the songs of friendship ring;
> For here a thousand million people stand,
> And will advance together hand in hand.[16]

The poem is certainly also rhythmic in Chinese, but Yuan extends a much
looser hand toward the rhyme scheme and number of syllables in each line.
In the FLP's English translation, each line consists of precisely ten syllables,
with two rhyming couplets comprising each stanza. In Chinese, the poem's
sonic features vary by stanza—in one, consecutive lines mirror each other;
in another, alternative lines share in length and rhyme. For comparison, a
more literal translation of the opening and closing stanzas, one that priori-
tizes content over rhythm, could read:

> The Himalayas tower high toward the sky,
> We live divided on the two sides of the mountains,
> We have had much contact as good neighbors,
> Two thousand years of China-India friendship!
> . . .
>
> From Delhi to Beijing,
> Songs of friendship ring out to the clouds,

From Beijing to Delhi,
A billion people advance hand in hand.[17]

Unlike such a translation, the FLP's English translation, with its palpable beat and rhythmic arrangement, asks to be read out loud, to be recited collectively. Moreover, by virtue of its translation into English, the FLP's translation presents itself for recitation in a markedly international setting, at once announcing and performing China-India friendship across the English-speaking world. The translation makes audible the marching beat of the "thousand million people . . . advanc[ing] together hand in hand" depicted in its closing lines, each step forward echoing the poem's steady rhythm. The translation's repetition of a consistent rhyme scheme throughout, wherein each line of a couplet mirrors the next, bespeaks the very event of Chinese and Indian writers meeting with each other, of the Chinese and Indian peoples "coupling," finding something of themselves in the other.

The scene of poetry recitation would soon become a characteristic feature of Cold War cultural diplomacy.[18] International writers' conferences and gatherings invariably featured poetry recitations: poets recited their works in the original language with translators present or with preprepared English translations distributed among the attendees. The act of making poetry audible held particular significance here. Vocalizing the sonic and aural features of a poem enabled it to become viscerally experienced in a communal environment, thereby amplifying its message and rousing a shared response from listeners. In a gathering of Chinese and Indian writers and artists, reciting the friendship song perfectly demonstrated the Bandung-era tenet of cultural exchange as a tool for building mutual understanding.

Yuan's poem, its likely recitation at the delegations' gathering, and its English translation in the FLP booklet (the officially sanctioned record of cultural diplomacy) all serve to make politically proclaimed "friendship" highly audible. By exceeding the Chinese poem in the tightness of its sonic features, the English translation amplifies the poem's message, ensuring that it serve its intended function—of declaring and performing China-India friendship—in every subsequent reading. The poem thus predetermines its own meaning, shielding itself against interpretation (any reader/listener, in any place, at any time, cannot but understand or experience the poem as it was intended) and drowning out other potential forms of literary relation. Against the loudness of friendship songs, this chapter asks for an attunement to the silences: to scenes of cultural exchange and poetic recitation that escape recording and commemoration, and to poets and poems forcibly silenced. These silences come alive in the mark of the ellipsis, an invitation for forging relation against the stated.

A Conference of Consequence

The abbreviated calendar of 1956 China-India diplomatic activity that this chapter opens with omits one momentous event that year: the Asian Writers' Conference held in New Delhi over six days, from December 23 to 28. The conference brought together some 300 writers from eighteen nations taken to comprise "Asia": India, China, Pakistan, East Pakistan, Ceylon, Nepal, Mongolia, North Korea, Japan, North Vietnam, South Vietnam, Cambodia, Burma, Indonesia, Iran, Syria, Egypt, and the Asian Republics of the USSR. Newspapers widely announced the "first ever conference of Asian writers," and the organizers framed the conference as the initial meeting of Asian intellectuals and writers now able to reestablish cultural ties after centuries of separation under Western domination.[19] The Chinese writers in attendance viewed their participation in the conference as "the first international activity Chinese writers carried out after the establishment of New China, and the first step Chinese literature took towards the world."[20] In fact, the Asian Writers' Conference served as the precursor and progenitor of the better-known Afro-Asian Writers' Conferences, now remembered as the foremost site of nonaligned literary exchange. Studies rarely acknowledge that the first Afro-Asian Writers' Conference in Tashkent in 1958 was conceived at and grew out of this 1956 conference in India.[21] Despite its unprecedented, historic occurrence, this Asian Writers' Conference has curiously remained forgotten, both in histories of China-India cultural diplomacy and those of the Bandung Conference and its many offshoots of Third World and Afro-Asian internationalisms.

Its collective forgetting speaks to a peculiar characteristic of the conference's legacy. Unlike the many other international conferences of its time—which established bureaus and committees to ensure subsequent iterations, and published proceedings and resolutions adopted by delegates—the Asian Writers' Conference did not aspire toward permanence. Instead, on the conference's final day, the delegates specifically voted to dissolve their collective. Newspapers reported on the delegates' conviction that "cultural exchange could be developed without a permanent organisation."[22] A committee of five was tasked with tying up loose ends after the conference closed, but delegates agreed that this committee would cease to exist after six months. There was some talk of "publishing the deliberations and papers and of preparing a report on the possibility and methods of promoting cultural exchanges between countries of Asia," but such publications either did not materialize or did not withstand the test of time.[23] Rather than inscribing their gathering in the annals, the conference chose a legacy that paradoxically aspired to remain fleeting and unrecorded.

The conference's insistence on ephemerality befuddled onlookers. During the months of preparations, commentators in India had hoped that the conference would take "practical" steps toward instituting "facilities for the study of Asian languages, . . . translations from one Asian language into another," or even "a magazine in each language to foster a deeper understanding among their people of the culture of other Asian countries."[24] Suggestions that the conference develop a common script so that Asian writers need not communicate in English, the colonizer's tongue, met with much excitement.[25] But the conference refused to produce any such tangible results; it ended not with the laying of grand plans, but with a simple promise between the writers of Asia "to keep in regular and constant touch with each other."[26] One journalist wrote, "It has been rather acidly remarked that a slender volume of literary criticism on aspects of Asian writing would be more enlightening than the six-day discourses at New Delhi."[27] The conference appeared inconsequential at best and, at worst, an outright failure.

Yet, it is precisely through its perceived inconsequentiality that the Asian Writers' Conference enacted a radical agenda, one that eluded the measures of consequence used to assess such conferences of international solidarity-building of the time. The utilitarian logic of Cold War cultural diplomacy required that literature be made to perform the work of international relations, that the literary text be read as meaningful only insofar as it fulfills the function of a political treaty.[28] For the delegates at Bandung, culture ultimately functioned as one among several tools for furthering their political ambitions and goals.

Recruiting culture in service of realpolitik was not a novel innovation at Bandung, even for the newly formed nations in attendance. In 1954, China and India famously signed the Panchsheel Treaty (also known as the Five Principles of Peaceful Coexistence), which set the two nascent nations on a path of cooperation and exchange. In the years preceding the Asian Writers' Conference, Chinese and Indian writers had met (as part of larger cultural delegations including artists, scientists, etc.) to engage in cultural dialogue and to establish diplomatic relations between the nations. The mechanisms of cultural diplomacy thus ensured that the act of relating culturally corresponded with diplomatic agendas. Yuan's poem "China-India Friendship," discussed above, explicitly alludes to the Panchsheel Treaty in its penultimate stanza:

Construction is the task we both proclaim,
And none shall turn us from our common aim;
Today we strive for peace with all our might,
Five Principles our countries' guiding light.[29]

Yuan's poem thus stands literally and synecdochally for the treaty it names in the line "Five Principles our countries' guiding light." Capturing the spirit of the treaty in poetic language, the poem boasts of the ability and commitment of literary practice to perform the treaty's function of "striving for peace" between China and India and of "advancing together" into the postcolonial world as equal, sovereign nations, "hand in hand." This collapsing of poem and treaty reveals a particular rubric of consequentiality, wherein the poem emerges as meaningful only in its capacity to at once consolidate and perform the precepts of diplomacy. As such, Yuan's poem epitomizes the epistemological regime of cultural diplomacy, which recognizes literary relation as legible and consequential only as a corollary to statecraft.

Yuan's poem presents a helpful foil for the Asian Writers' Conference as an example of the kind of literary practice in which the conference remained resolutely uninterested. Instead, it harnessed the structure of the diplomatic conference—indeed, it modeled itself closely after the Bandung Conference, complete with Western and Soviet writers and journalists invited as observers, as in Bandung—to launch, from within this familiar generic form, a markedly different experiment. This experiment sought to probe possibilities for literary relation that exceeded and remained unexhausted by the official agendas of the participating nations. Any results of such an experiment would necessary remain illegible, and therefore unrecordable, within the idiom of cultural diplomacy. The conference's ephemerality and perceived inconsequentiality thus speaks not to its failure but to its search for ways to relate literarily beyond and in defiance of the tenets of diplomacy.

Logistical Politics of the Nonpolitical

The Asian Writers' Conference was first conceived by the Indian writer Mulk Raj Anand (1905–2004) and the processes of planning the conference fell primarily under his charge. Inspired by the principle of cultural cooperation adopted at Bandung, Anand convinced Nehru of the need for a meeting of Asian writers with the argument that "the intellectuals of Asia had not met for more than a thousand years, after the last Buddhist Conference in the 6th Century A.D."[30] In the 1950s, Anand gained a reputation in China as one of India's foremost progressive writers. While in London in the 1930s, Anand had joined forces with a group of Indian writers to pen a manifesto that would come to found the All India Progressive Writers' Association, and in the following decades he remained intimately involved in the Progressive Writers' movement rapidly gaining steam in India. His novels and short stories, written as they were in English, circulated expeditiously, finding easy paths to translation into Chinese. Anand first visited China in 1951 as part of an unofficial Indian delegation, and returned in July 1956 on a mission, successfully executed, to solicit support for the Asian Writers' Conference among Chinese writers.[31] He quickly assembled a planning committee, which included the Chinese novelist and then the PRC's minister of culture Mao Dun (Shen Yanbing 沈雁冰). That summer, members of the planning committee traveled to India from across Asia to meet for preparatory meetings. Anand had already petitioned Nehru for financial support.[32] The conference thus grew, both in inspiration and in execution, from within state-led channels of cultural diplomacy.

As December neared, however, the conference seemed caught in an identity crisis. For all intents and purposes, it appeared to be taking shape in the image of cultural diplomacy, and yet the planning committee announced its intention to decouple the "cultural" from "diplomacy." The conference would concern itself with matters exclusively of literary bearing and "political issues would be scrupulously kept out of the agenda of the conference," the committee stated.[33] The conference's "nonpolitical" agenda would include the following five topics: the current situation of literature in Asia, the literary traditions of Asia, freedom and the writer, the writer and his craft, and cultural exchange.

Planning a nondiplomatic conference from within the logistical apparatus of cultural diplomacy proved a near-impossible task, its infeasibility only compounded by the Chinese delegation due to attend. In an effort to ensure equal representation of India's linguistic and ideological diversity, the Indian participants had been selected by a politically diverse group of writers in conversation with the Sahitya Akademi, India's newly established academy of letters. The Chinese delegation, by contrast, was state sanctioned, with members holding official posts in the CCP. Minister of culture Mao Dun would act as head of the delegation and Zhou Yang 周揚 (then the vice minister of the Propaganda Department) would serve as the delegation's deputy head. The delegation also included novelists Ye Shengtao 葉聖陶, then the vice minister of education, and Ye Junjian 葉君健, who oversaw the translations division of the Ministry of Culture, as well as other prominent members of the China Writers Association such as Lao She 老舍, Baren 巴人 (Wang Renshu 王任叔), poets Xiao San 蕭三 and Han Beiping 韓北屏, the Manchurian woman writer Bai Lang 白朗, and head of the Xinjiang writers' association Ziya 孜亚 (figure 3.1). The Asian Writers' Conference in New Delhi would mark the first literary delegation of this size composed exclusively of writers that China had sent abroad. But in India, where the concept of the writer-official remained lost in translation, the Chinese delegates appeared as state representatives thinly veiled in literary guise. The presence of an officially vetted and sanctioned Chinese delegation at a conference that promised to "keep politics out" seemed ludicrous.

On December 18, a mere five days before the conference's scheduled opening, controversy surrounding the Chinese delegation erupted within the planning committee. Newspapers ran articles with headlines that announced a "split" between Anand and his friend, the Urdu progressive writer Sajjad Zaheer on one side, and, on the other, the remaining five Indian members of the planning committee. Those against Anand, including poet Ramdhari Singh "Dinkar" (to whom this chapter later returns) and writers Jainendra Kumar and Agyeya, released a statement contending that "the conference is inspired and controlled by persons of a particular political persuasion, not

1956 年 12 月中国作家代表团摄于印度泰姬陵
左起：茅盾1、杨朔4、周扬7、叶君健8、叶圣陶9、老舍10、白朗11、萧三12、王任叔13、韩北屏16

FIGURE 3.1 The Chinese writers' delegation in India in December, 1956. The caption identifies some of the figures as follows: "From the left: 1. Mao Dun, 4. Yang Shuo, 7. Zhou Yang, 8. Yu Junjian, 9. Ye Shengtao, 10. Lao She, 11. Bai Lang, 12. Xiao San, 13. Wang Renshu, 16. Han Beiping." *Xin wenxue shiliao* 新文學史料 3 (1986): back cover. Courtesy of Renmin wenxue chubanshe 人民文學出版社.

all of whom are even writers."[34] The statement essentially accused Anand—himself of leftist "political persuasion," given his close association with the Progressive Writers Association—of pandering to the Chinese delegation (to which the accusation "not all of whom are even writers" obliquely refers), thereby furthering a communist agenda at the conference. The signatories of the statement took particular exception to the fact that Mao Dun had vetoed the Indian members' suggestion to invite "writers in the Chinese language who belonged to Hong Kong, Singapore and other areas outside the People's Republic of China," including the expatriate Chinese writer Lin Yutang.[35] The statement blindsided Anand, who "repeatedly denied that the conference was dominated by the Communists" and insisted that "he was not to blame if the Communist countries of Asia sent Communist writers to the conference."[36] Debate over the official status of the Chinese delegation underscored the politically charged logistical challenges of planning a self-avowedly nonpolitical conference in this age of cultural diplomacy, when the categories of "culture" and "diplomacy" remained intertwined and in flux. Against the odds, on December 23, 1956, the writers of Asia gathered to embark on six days of literary dialogue.

The Hundred Flowers Campaign

The planning committee could not have foreseen a critical event unfolding in China, one that fortuitously coincided with the Asian Writers' Conference and suddenly brought into the realm of possibility what may have otherwise remained an idealistic and even naïve aspiration for a nonpolitical writers' conference. In mid-1956, as the planning committee feuded over the ability of national delegations to set aside diplomatic agendas in their literary activities overseas, the CCP unexpectedly announced an easing of political intervention in literary production. In a reversal of the restrictive climate during the previous Hu Feng campaign of 1955, the party now issued the slogan "Let a hundred flowers bloom, let a hundred schools of thought contend" (*baihua qifang, baijia zhengming* 百花齊放, 百家爭鳴), inviting writers and intellectuals to openly debate, disagree, and experiment. "Letting a hundred flowers bloom, a hundred schools of thought contend means that we stand for freedom of independent thinking, of debate, of creative work," Lu Dingyi 陸定一, the director of the Propaganda Department, announced in his May 1956 speech, "freedom to criticize and freedom to express, maintain and reserve one's opinion on questions of art, literature, and scientific research."[37] Promoting such freedom of thought, the Hundred Flowers campaign aimed to elicit criticisms of the party and to encourage intellectual experimentation in service of self-improvement and social progress.

By the time the Chinese delegates to the Asian Writers' Conference boarded their flight to New Delhi (via Burma) on December 19, the Hundred Flowers campaign had gained steam. After a period of initial skepticism toward the party's promised tolerance, in the winter of 1956 writers enthusiastically took up the Hundred Flowers call to engage in constructive criticism of the party's policies and bureaucracy and to explore new creative possibilities beyond what many considered the prescribed and formulaic quality of much of post-1949 literary production. An air of openness and experimentation wafted through the Chinese literary sphere. In September 1956, for example, the writer Qin Zhaoyang 秦兆陽 called for writers to depart from a "dogmatic" adherence to Soviet-style socialist realism and instead to strive for an expansive mode of realism, capacious enough to hold experimentation and complexity within. "We should consider each author's individual qualities," Qin wrote; "we should not demand the same thing from all authors and all literary forms. We should help develop rather than hinder each author's individual creativity. We should use fewer administrative orders that interfere with literary creation."[38] Such critical essays and experimental literary works invited debate: buoyed by the party's commitment to celebrate difference, writers publicly evaluated fiction and poetry and engaged with their colleagues' takes on a range of literary issues.

Such was the Hundred Flowers spirit that traveled, along with the Chinese delegation, to the Asian Writers' Conference in India. The Chinese delegates could not have known then that the Hundred Flowers period would soon come to an abrupt end. In mid-1957, Mao delivered his famous speech, "On the Correct Handling of Contradictions Among the People," which drew a distinction between "fragrant flowers" and "poisonous weeds," the latter label condemning writings deemed "harmful to socialist transformation and socialist construction" and detrimental to "the leadership of the Communist Party."[39] The publication of Mao's speech in June 1957 inaugurated what came to be known as the Anti-Rightist campaign (*fanyou yundong* 反右運動), discussed later in this chapter. Those considered to have voiced criticisms under the Hundred Flowers banner were now labeled "Rightists," resulting in a large-scale persecution of intellectuals.

The Asian Writers' Conference thus overlapped with a short-lived period in which Chinese writers could openly join in debate, disagreement, difference, and dissent and, moreover, could do so with the party's blessing. Importantly, the Hundred Flowers campaign unfolded not only in China, but also abroad, through the concurrent programs of cultural diplomacy Chinese intellectuals and writers partook in that year. The campaign lent these programs an openness to forms of cultural production across international lines of political alignment. Moreover, the campaign eased the pressure on delegates to represent a unitary party line while abroad; indeed, expressions of dissent now had the dual capacity to at once bolster the official Hundred Flowers policy and conversely undercut the party's hold on its itinerant writers. For the Chinese delegates, the felicitous convergence of the Hundred

Flowers campaign and the Asian Writers' Conference made possible a practice of cultural diplomacy that could momentarily disentangle literary relation from the demands of diplomacy, in line with the conference organizers' vision. Contrary to the expectations of skeptics, who had feared that the Chinese delegation would treat the conference as an opportunity to conduct international relations, the Hundred Flowers campaign enabled Chinese writers to explore different, literary forms of relation.

To Bloom and Contend

On December 21, their first full day in New Delhi, the Chinese delegation paid a visit to Pan Zili 潘自力, then the Chinese ambassador to India. Pan apprised the Chinese writers of the controversy within the planning committee over the Chinese delegation's participation and political affiliation and warned the writers that they may meet with hostile Indian counterparts.[40] While a diplomat like Pan would have preferred that the Chinese writers steer clear, and even feign ignorance of, these disputes, the writers surprisingly harnessed the "split" in the planning committee as an opportunity to cast the conference in the idiom of the Hundred Flowers campaign. Soon after the delegation's return to China, Ye Junjian published a lengthy report (in eleven installments) entitled "On the Asian Writers' Conference" (*Yazhou zuojia huiyi qianhou* 亞洲作家會議前後) in *Wenhuibao* 文匯報. Such reports customarily boasted of China's cultural activities abroad in the most favorable terms possible; moments of tension and controversy would be culled out. Remarkably, instead of papering over the planning committee's disputes, Ye addresses these in his report and is able to do so because he frames the conflict—and, indeed, the entire conference—in the language of and as exemplifying the Hundred Flowers' spirit.[41] "On several issues, it was not necessarily the case that all opinions would be identical," Ye wrote; "therefore, during the course of the planning process, at times it was unavoidable to encounter twists and turns. . . . But through friendly consultation, all these issues achieved resolution. Although some have a difference of opinion, as writers of Asia, everyone has much in common."[42] Ye's characterization of the conference as a celebration of differences for the sake of unity evokes lines from Lu Dingyi's Hundred Flowers speech, in which Lu had emphasized the inevitable "points of agreement and points of difference" among the people, arguing that contention would "in the end strengthen unity."[43] Through this Hundred Flowers rhetoric of celebrating difference for the sake of unity, the Chinese delegation could reframe the disputes surrounding their attendance not as hostile but in line with the literary spirit of debate flowering at home. The Hundred Flowers campaign opened a discursive space in which the Chinese writers could embrace the Asian Writers' Conference's "nonpolitical" agenda without sidestepping moments of debate (as premier Zhou Enlai was inclined to do at the Bandung Conference) and, at the other extreme, without transplanting wholesale Cold War realpolitik onto literary grounds (as the Chinese delegation was accused of at the Afro-Asian Writers' Bureau following the Sino-Soviet split in 1966).

In Ye's report, the Asian Writers' Conference emerges as a transnational extension of the Hundred Flowers ethos. Ye depicts the discussion on the first item on the conference agenda, "the current situation of literature in Asia," as follows: "The various literatures all have their own particular historical conditions and national characteristics; when they were all reported on one after the other at the same conference, everyone couldn't help but sense the feeling of a 'hundred flowers blooming.' "[44] Again, summarizing a discussion on the challenges of writing in Urdu, Punjabi, and Bengali in a post-Partition Indian landscape, Ye writes, "Regardless of how complicated such problems are . . . all writers are striving to ensure that their languages blossom into resplendent literary flowers."[45] Such botanical imagery punctuates Ye's report, just as floral and seasonal metaphors—"blooming," "springtime," "gentle breeze," "mild rain"—permeated public discourse in the Hundred Flowers period.[46] Writing the conference in the linguistic register of the Hundred Flowers, Ye extended to this meeting of writers, ostensibly gathered under the auspices of cultural diplomacy, the Hundred Flowers axiom of a literary space relatively free of state intervention.

As anticipated, the third item on the agenda, "freedom and the writers," generated the most heated debate of all the conference sessions. The Marathi writer Gangadhar Gopal Gadgil controversially proclaimed that "there is no free or genuine art in communist nations."[47] C. Rajagopalachari, the Tamil writer and former chief minister then on a literary hiatus from his political career, delivered a forty-five-minute-long speech arguing that writers "must be free to write what we choose to write."[48] Rajagopalachari insisted that art "should be pursued for its own sake," and that "writers must be able to swim

against the current of public opinion." Amid cheers from several participants, he urged writers to "leave politics in a separate apartment." He went
on to clarify, "I do not want you to discard politics altogether. . . . By all
means, have politics. But in the Writers' Conference, we meet as writers, not
politicians."[49] Such comments elicited a wave of contention. Ye's report highlights several dissenting opinions, including the Burmese writer Thein Pe
Myint's response: "Yes, we demand freedom for us—but not for going
against the people, but for serving them. Our intellect must be free and our
thinking must be independent, but not for going against the people, but for
serving them, not for putting back the wheel of history, but for pushing it
forward."[50] Conceptualizing the conference within the Hundred Flowers
paradigm allowed Ye to capture dissent in his official report, in which the
differing imperatives for literary practice vigorously debated at the conference would otherwise have remained omitted in favor of flat portrayals of
friendship. Thein Pe Myint's response, at once promoting both the writer's
freedom and service to the people, offered a Marxist synthesis of the contradictory voices, fittingly enacting the Hundred Flowers aim of arriving
at unity through a championing of difference.

Framed by this Hundred Flowers commitment in Ye's report, the views
voiced by Rajagopalachari and Thein Pe Myint at once evoke and erode what
have been termed the Cold War "mythologies of modernism and realism,"
"an artificial dichotomy" between the "ideological and aesthetic systems
overseen by the USA and the USSR."[51] Rather than foisting all desires for
autonomy in artistic creativity under the umbrella of American modernism—
and, conversely, all calls for engaged literary practice under that of Soviet-
style realism—the dissenting opinions raised at the conference articulate the
writers' effort to forge their own literary collective, against delimited lines
of ideological affiliation. This effort found further resonance in the category
of "Asia" under which the writers met, one that was then still in the making
and did not align neatly with either the emerging idea of the "Third World"
or the related nomenclature of "Afro-Asia," by which this conference would
later become eclipsed.[52] As a meeting of the writers of Asia, the conference
sought to make space for writers "as writers" in defiance of the pressures of
instrumentalization descending upon them from all sides. The Hundred
Flowers commitment to contention as the basis for relation brought an alternative notion of literary relation to life: instead of proclaiming subscription to a single ideological camp and its political and aesthetic agenda (be it

modernism, realism, or even the "agnostic" use of both that would come to characterize Third World anticolonial expression), disagreements, a difference of literary commitments, and diverging views on the value of literature formed the grounds of meeting among these writers of Asia.[53]

Significantly, Ye's report does feature one omission: fellow delegate Lao She's response to Rajagopalachari, which was recorded in Indian newspaper coverage. Lao She perhaps took too enthusiastic an interpretation of the Hundred Flowers policy for Ye's careful reporting, but his comments explicitly articulate the particular Hundred Flowers-inflected characteristic of contention that formed the basis of literary relation at the conference:

> Mr. Lao Sheh said all the different schools of literature should be encouraged. "In this way," he added, "our writers, irrespective of their political affiliations, the 'schools' they belong to, or field they specialize in, whether they are veterans versed in traditional classical literature or young writers striking out boldly on new lines, all should blossom out brilliantly. Then, we shall have a literature, brilliant and beautiful as satin, infinitely rich in treatment and subject matter." Mr. Lao Sheh said a writer should be allowed to write what he likes. "Writers should," he said, "encourage and criticize one another. That promotes the cause of literature. Neither criticism nor counter-criticism should be muzzled."[54]

Lao She's response drew from his recently published essay, "Freedom and the Writer," in which he outlined a radical program for implementing the Hundred Flowers policy in literary production by calling for the writer's complete creative autonomy. "A writer should have perfect freedom to choose what he wants to write about," Lao She wrote; "it is accepted that socialist realism is a progressive way of writing, but does that mean that all other creative methods are no good? To my mind, no. . . . We should give our literary works an infinite variety, not cast it all in the same mold."[55] In quoting directly from this manifesto-of-sorts as he addressed the writers of Asia, Lao She widened the scale of the Hundred Flowers vision from a narrow national policy in the Chinese literary sphere to a normative ethos for literary practice in a politically circumscribed world. The Asian Writers' Conference and the Hundred Flowers campaign amplified each other; their convergence made possible an ethics of literary relation "irrespective of political affiliation," as Lao She put it.

In these ways, the Hundred Flowers policy allowed the Chinese writers to partake in the Asian Writers' Conference's radical experiment in carving out a literary space from within the structural confines of cultural diplomacy. Casting debates at the conference as an extension of the Hundred Flowers spirit enabled the writers to participate in a form of literary dialogue that confounded the logic of diplomacy. On the final day of the conference, the delegates approved statements declaring jointly held views on each of the agenda items. The statement on the topic of "freedom and the writer" noted that "there was no unanimity of opinion among the delegates . . . and that they expressed different, and at times, completely divergent views."[56] While this lack of consensus may be deemed a diplomatic failure, the conference's open declaration of its dissension bears the mark of a different achievement: the formation of literary relation that takes as its basis not proclamations of friendship or solidarity, but a commitment to together bloom and contend.

Poetics of Literary Relation

The work of relating literarily at the Asian Writers' Conference exceeded its formal structure, extending beyond the panels and roundtables into informal evenings spent reciting poetry. Prior to the conference, the delegations had received a missive from Anand requesting that the poets carry with them a few selections of their writings, to be recited at informal gatherings of the poets of Asia.[57] The poet Xiao San wrote of such gatherings, capturing those intimate moments elided in Ye's report and in media coverage of the conference. In a two-part memoir published in the poetry journal *Shikan* 詩刊 in March and April 1957, Xiao San describes the experience of meeting as poets through the medium of poetry.[58] Unlike Ye's report, which includes lengthy transcripts and summaries of the delegates' speeches and discussions, and the FLP booklet that commemorates Yuan's poem and its recitation, Xiao San's memoir does not endeavor to represent the gatherings by reproducing the lines of poetry shared. Instead, Xiao San foregrounds the embodied experience of listening together, of opening oneself to the affective force of poetic evocation. "What profoundly moved me," Xiao San writes, "was that as the poets recited their poetry, everyone watched and listened intently. . . . When they heard exquisite lines of poetry, the hall would fill with sounds of appreciation. . . . Their heads and bodies would sway, now to the left, now to the right, as though poetry fused together body and heart/mind [*shenxin dou bei shige ronghua le* 身心都被詩歌融化了]."[59] In this setting that recalls the responsive interplay between poet and audience typical of the Urdu *mushaira* tradition of poetry recitation, the act of relating literarily proves as visceral a task as it is intellectual, the "fusing together" of body and mind.[60]

Xiao San's memoirs suggest that what the Asian Writers' Conference achieved—the meeting of poets as poets and not diplomats, the experience of poetry as poetry and not treaty—necessarily defies being recorded (for instance, in that "slender volume of literary criticism on aspects of Asian writing" the journalist quoted earlier had sought) and thereby resists becoming instrumentalized in the construction of political alliance. Abjuring such criteria of durability and consequentiality, the Asian Writers' Conference insisted on locating literary relation temporally in the present, in that moment of dialogic bond between writers and readers (or audiences) formed during the act of reading or recitation. Xiao San's memoirs of the conference are precisely that: not a reproduction of the literary exchange performed, but "only a spur to memory, an encouragement of memory to become present," to use Peggy Phelan's words from a different context.[61] Read as the performance, in Phelan's sense, of transnational literary relation, the Asian Writers' Conference "plunges into visibility—in a maniacally charged present—and disappears into memory, into the realm of invisibility and the unconscious where it eludes regulation and control."[62] The conference's emphasis on the ephemeral present thus fulfills a dual function of self-preservation and disruption. By coming alive only as memory and not as record, the conference could "elude regulation and control" of the kind its continued existence would surely have elicited. At the same time, by insisting on the presentness of literary relation, the conference interrupted the smooth workings of Cold War–era cultural utilitarianism, which infiltrated activities of nonalignment as much as those of both blocs. The conference proposed, instead, a poetics and ethics of literary relation that rejected the demands of the Cold War realpolitik and refused the system of "cultural cooperation" fundamental to it.

The poetic scene Xiao San's memoir captures brings momentarily into view the ephemeral poetics of relation extended at the conference—the "fleeting, delicate shivers" of the "world's poetic force"—further underscoring the necessary ephemerality of the work the conference accomplished.[63] Delivering his closing remarks, the Urdu poet Faiz Ahmad Faiz recited lines from a poem he had composed during his visit to China earlier that year: "We met in such a way, we separated so, Faiz, that now / The mark that will be left on the heart is a flower, not a scar."[64] The couplet, quoted in Ye's report, serendipitously portrays the conference as one among a hundred flowers, an association Ye furthered by adding, "Indeed, over the course of the conference, although at times we argued until red in the face, that which is now left in our hearts is 'a flower.' "[65] Beyond its fitting imagery, the couplet captures precisely the "mark" (dāg) of the Asian Writers' Conference as not the impress of permanence but the delicate transience of a flower, momentarily caught in bloom.

Springtime, a ubiquitous seasonal metaphor for the Hundred Flowers period, soon came to an end. In January 1958, now in the throes of the Anti-Rightist campaign, Xiao San published a very different account of his time in India, this time positioning the Asian Writers' Conference squarely within the realpolitik Cold War world. The opening stanza of his poem "On Returning from India" (cong Yindu guilai 從印度歸來) reads:

The Delhi winter is not without sunshine,
Today, the conference hall is bright, as usual.
Prime Minister Nehru comes to meet the writers.
Everyone expresses gratitude and applauds his speech.[66]

Notably, Nehru's brief visit to the delegates at the end of the conference, which does not feature centrally in either Ye Junjian's report or Xiao San's memoir, now becomes the defining feature of the conference.[67] As the writers "express gratitude and applaud" Nehru's speech, Xiao San casts the politician, who stands here for the nation-state, as the agential force to whom the writers merely respond, effectively reversing the writers' adamant attempt to set their own agenda at the conference. Indeed, as the poem continues, the already marginal writers disappear entirely from view:

Nehru and Zhou Enlai, the two Premiers
Together welcome the New Year,
"Indians and Chinese are brothers!"

This slogan fills people's mouths, their hearts fill with affection.

. . .

Suddenly, a dark cloud spreads across the sky.
The sun over India,
And the hearts of the people,
All are covered in shadow:
At this very moment, "Eisenhower-ism" encroaches,
Some know not whether to laugh or to cry.

. . .

Although I could not fulfil my wish to travel to Cairo and shake hands with our
    Egyptian friends,[68]
I just cannot believe that the Middle East is a "vacuum."
Let's cast off this "Ike-Dulles-ism" that suffocates the people!
Let's read, instead, Mao Zedong's poems that illuminate the East red![69]

Absorbed into the jargon of international relations ("Eisenhower-ism," "Ike-Dulles-ism," "the Middle East is a 'vacuum,'" and so on), the radical form of literary relation that had once flickered at the Asian Writers' Conference died out, its impermanence further heightened by that of the short-lived Hundred Flowers campaign. And yet, in its very effacing, the conference fulfilled its desire to remain fleeting and unrecorded. Its significance lies not in the recovery of a lost fragment of history that can be slotted into existing narratives of 1950s China-India relations, Third World cultural internationalism, or Asian solidarity. Rather, the Asian Writers' Conference asks to be apprehended elliptically, as that which must remain uninscribed in the official records and incomprehensible under the logics of cultural diplomacy in the Cold War world.

The Anti-Rightist Campaign in Hindi

By mid-1957, a mere six months after the Asian Writers' Conference drew to a close, cultural diplomacy with India unfolded upon a dramatically altered Chinese literary terrain, now fraught with the heightened censorship, insecurity, and paranoia of the Anti-Rightist campaign. Beginning in June 1957, the party issued attacks on all those associated with the Hundred Flowers movement, including intellectuals, writers, editors of journals and newspapers, and student activists. Many were publicly denounced and expelled to rural areas and factories for labor reform. Estimates suggest that some four hundred thousand to seven hundred thousand intellectuals were purged during the Anti-Rightist campaign, a much greater figure than in previous campaigns.[70] Amid this turmoil, the Hindi poet Ramdhari Singh "Dinkar" (1908–1974), who had earlier served as a dissenting member of the 1956 conference's planning committee, traveled to China at the invitation of the Chinese Writers' Association.[71] Dinkar had emerged as a prominent poet in the 1930s after his early poems *Renukā* (1935) and *Kurukṣetr* (1943), the latter an adaptation of the *Mahābhārata*, earned him literary prizes and national recognition. Although his oeuvre consists predominantly of poetry, he was also a prolific essayist and prose writer. Most famously, his *Four Chapters of Culture* (*Saṃskṛti ke cār adhyay*), a sweeping history of the development of Indian culture over the course of a millennium, received the 1956 Sahitya Akademi Award, the foremost Indian literary accolade. By the 1960s, Dinkar came to be known as a "national poet" (*rāṣṭrakavī*) in recognition of his artful ability to harness older genres of epic and lyric poetry in service of the nation.[72] Like many of his contemporaries, Dinkar practiced poetry as an extension of his political convictions. In the 1950s, Dinkar was centrally involved in the promotion of Hindi as a national language through his participation in the Society for the Propagation of Nagari (*nāgārī pracāriṇī sabhā*) and the Hindi Literary Conference (*Hindī sāhityă sammelan*). Such organizations had historical roots in late nineteenth- and early twentieth-century language politics of anticolonial nationalism in the Indian subcontinent.[73] Following the adoption of Hindi as an official language of India in 1949, the members of such organizations, including Dinkar, set about developing dictionaries and compiling histories of Hindi literature, among other activities. The promotion of Hindi (over English) as a national language remained at the forefront of Dinkar's speeches and priorities during his travels in China.[74]

In the mid-century decades, innovations in poetic language and competing ideas of modernity gave rise to various schools of Hindi poetry and an attendant field of lively literary criticism. Dinkar's oeuvre of the time illuminates intersections among the various poetic camps. Dinkar's early works share formal characteristics with *Chāyāvād* (or shadow-ist) poetry, a movement known for its romanticism and mysticism and characterized by a high

Sanskritic linguistic register, a generic interest in the epic, and a turn away from earlier Braj metrical conventions toward newer Khari Boli meters.[75] Thematically, however, Dinkar's poetry, often described as revolutionary in tone and imagery, veered closer to the progressive writers' vision of purposeful art. Yet his artistic sensibilities did not align easily with the agenda of the Progressive Writers Association, which Dinkar found overly prescriptive in its leftist political commitment.[76] In the 1940s, Dinkar welcomed the emergence of experimentalist (*prayogvādī*) writing, championed by poets who eschewed the strict social realism of the progressive writers in favor of modernist experimentation with poetic form. Dinkar shared with the experimentalists their desire to critique the status quo, but opposed what he viewed as the overly Westernized nature of the resultant "New Poetry" (*nayī kavitā*).[77] Dinkar's position in the interstices of several schools of poetry rather than at the forefront of a single movement, coupled with his involvement in Hindi language politics, cast him as a politically conscious yet relatively uncontroversial nominee to serve as a national cultural representative, particularly during this tumultuous time in China.[78]

Dinkar arrived in Kunming on October 26, 1957, for what would be a twenty-four-day tour, with stops in Beijing, Tianjin, Nanjing, Shanghai, Hangzhou, and Guangzhou. A record of his travels appears in a collection of his travel writings entitled *My Travels* (*Merī yātraeṁ*) published in 1970, which provides a detailed account in Hindi of his time in China, a view of cultural diplomacy rubbing against the literary persecutions of the Anti-Rightist campaign.[79] Read with an eye to the unsaid, Dinkar's China travelogue captures the ellipses of China-India cultural diplomacy: the silences, fissures, and tensions that brewed beneath the surface of politically proclaimed friendship.

The Quest for Ai Qing

When distilled down to a timeline of Dinkar's daily activities in China, his travelogue reveals a generic itinerary, similar to that undertaken by most Indian cultural delegates visiting China in the 1950s. Dinkar toured the popular attractions in each of the cities he visited. He dined with his hosts: members of the Writers' Association, including Lao She (whom he had met at the Asian Writers' Conference) and Li Ji 李季, and officials from the Indian embassy. He visited Zhou Enlai (figure 3.2).[80] He recorded radio broadcasts,

FIGURE 3.2 Dinkar (center) with Zhou Enlai (left) and Li Ji (right) during his visit to China in late 1957. *Ramdhari Singh Dinkar Racănāvalī* [Collected works of Ramdhari Singh Dinkar], vol. 10 (New Delhi: Lokbharati Prakashan, 2011), front matter. Courtesy of Rajkamal Prakashan.

which aired in Beijing and Shanghai, delivered speeches on "Indian culture, literature, art, and politics" to university students, and participated in roundtable discussions with Chinese writers.[81] He attended cultural events showcasing Chinese opera, music, dance, and stage adaptations of Lao She's *Rickshaw Boy* (1937) and Kalidasa's *Śakuntalā*. He visited the sites of New

China—public parks, mills, factories—that foreign visitors were often taken to. At first glance, therefore, Dinkar's itinerary appears consistent with the narrative of state-sponsored cultural exchange.

Beyond a record of Dinkar's daily activities, however, the travelogue also contains lengthy sections of commentary and reflection written after Dinkar's return as he prepared the travelogue for publication. Most notable among these sections is a chapter entitled "The Rectification Campaign," which outlines Dinkar's understanding of the Hundred Flowers and Anti-Rightist campaigns. The mixture of diaristic and essayistic writing endows the travelogue with a dual cadence of immediacy and retrospect. Reading the travelogue with an eye to these shifting temporalities suggests an alternative narrative, one in which the timeline of Dinkar's visit to China extends beyond the dates of his arrival and departure, and the visit centers not on the rituals of cultural diplomacy, but on Dinkar's quest for the Chinese poet Ai Qing 艾青 (1910–1996).

Such an alternative narrative would begin earlier in 1957, with the publication of a volume, *Shell and Conch* (*Sīpī aur śaṅkh*), containing Dinkar's Hindi translations of foreign poetry (from English translations).[82] In the introduction, Dinkar frames the volume as an experiment in translation using a *Chāyāvādī* idiom to demonstrate the compatibility of *Chāyāvādī* Hindi (as opposed to what he considered a Westernized, "scientific" use of Hindi in "new poetry") with contemporary poems from around the world.[83] The volume includes seven Chinese poems, which Dinkar accessed through Robert Payne's translated volume *Contemporary Chinese Poetry* (1947), including two poems by Ai Qing, whom Payne introduces as "one of the greatest—perhaps the greatest—of living Chinese poets."[84] Dinkar repeats this designation in his travelogue, repeatedly referring to Ai Qing as "China's greatest poet."[85]

Dinkar hoped to meet Ai Qing in China. On his second day in Beijing, during a banquet thrown by the Writers' Association in his honor, Dinkar asked Lao She and others about Ai Qing. Dinkar narrates:

> Ai Qing is a communist and is perhaps China's greatest poet. . . . But when I was in China, Ai Qing was not in Beijing. He had criticized communism as flawed (*kharāb*) in its practical form. As punishment, he was sent to the countryside to perform manual labor and live among the masses, through which he could re-examine his thinking. Seeing the shocked look on my face [upon hearing this], the others began to talk among themselves. I then said that there was nothing

surprising about this. In India, too, Vinobaji [referring to Indian activist Vinoba Bhave] was now leading a labor movement.[86]

This uncomfortable interaction marks Dinkar's first glimpse of the disjuncture between the image of literary openness the party attempted to outwardly project, and the anxiety and insecurity that permeated the Chinese literary sphere during these early months of the Anti-Rightist campaign. This disjuncture manifests here through the uncomfortable murmurs elicited by Dinkar's reaction to news of Ai Qing's persecution. Dinkar's hasty attempt to fill that silence, by quickly glossing forced labor reform as commensurable with Vinoba Bhave's very different land donation (*bhudān*) movement, highlights a strategic use of comparison as a means to perform cultural diplomacy.[87] Although deployed as a strategy to assert sameness and smooth over tensions, Dinkar's impulse for comparison reveals here, and repeatedly in the travelogue, the silences and fissures that rend the grounds of political "friendship."

Despite the efforts of the Writers' Association members, the Anti-Rightist campaign proved too pervasive to be easily covered up. In addition to those who voiced antiparty criticism during the Hundred Flowers debates, the Anti-Rightist campaign also targeted literary figures apparently deemed dangerous for their influence on younger generations. Writer Ding Ling 丁玲, for example, became a central target despite having stayed out of the Hundred Flowers debates.[88] Due in part to Ding Ling's earlier propensity to challenge the party line, and in (larger) part to her long-standing clashes with CCP cultural official Zhou Yang, the party levied charges against Ding Ling and her associates, including Ai Qing.[89] One public denunciation stated, "Influenced by Ding Ling and her kind, a number of youth have taken the wrong path. They have refused Party leadership and supervision and have opposed the power of the Party group."[90] Like Ding Ling, Ai Qing had remained cautious during this period, with the exception of a few writings, including a series of allegorical fables published in 1956, which came under attack during the Anti-Rightist campaign.[91] Still, his persecution resulted largely from his association with Ding Ling and an older generation of left-wing writers, many of whom were labeled as "Rightists" for views expressed in the 1940s and exiled to remote areas in northeast and western China.[92]

In this tense atmosphere, thick with heightened surveillance, Dinkar's request to meet Ai Qing would have precipitated discomfort, even crisis, in the Writers' Association. In the travelogue, Dinkar reflects on such moments explicitly in the context of the Anti-Rightist campaign. He speculates, for example, on the reasons behind Ai Qing's persecution. In a statement that proves more indicative of Dinkar's impressions of China than of Ai Qing's views, Dinkar writes, "Perhaps the great poet Ai Qing also voiced his dissent. Perhaps he said: this communism foisted upon us, this is not what we had made sacrifices for. If this is communism, then we have no interest in this communism."[93] Throughout the travelogue, Dinkar voices support for the Hundred Flowers spirit, crediting Mao Zedong with the implementation of this policy of openness, while also criticizing the party for the unfounded attacks against Rightists.

As a national representative of India visiting China under the banner of friendly cultural exchange, Dinkar soon realized his unique position in the Chinese literary sphere. India's nonaligned status afforded him the freedom to take an independent stance and to voice his personal opinions on the Anti-Rightist campaign, a privilege unavailable to visitors from the USSR or the Eastern bloc. Further, as a visitor during a period of friendly diplomatic relations between China and India, Dinkar occupied a relatively secure position from which to raise provocative questions. And, given the officially sanctioned nature of his trip, Dinkar found himself with easy access to high-ranking Chinese literary officials of whom he could ask such discomforting questions.

Throughout his visit, Dinkar ruffled feathers by openly pursuing his quest to meet Ai Qing, later coupled with requests to also meet Ding Ling. "While in Beijing," he writes, "I repeatedly expressed my wish to meet with poet Ai Qing and Madam Ding Ling, by whatever means necessary. But I never got a straightforward response to this query."[94] Dinkar records several oblique responses he received: "Mr. Li Ji, a poet who often accompanied me, said that Ai Qing perhaps did not make any such statement [against communism]. His offence was not making such statements. In reality, after the revolution [of 1949], he had become soft. He had begun to fill his poems with anticommunist sentiment and he repeatedly proved that he did not maintain his belief in communism."[95] Dinkar also inquired after Ai Qing during conversations with Zang Kejia 臧克家 and He Qifang 何其芳 (whose poems Dinkar had also translated). On the topic of Ai Qing, Zang apparently only said that "Ai Qing was in the wrong," and that the writers "supported whatever actions were taken against him."[96] He Qifang had a more convoluted response:

"When the Director of the Institute of Literature, Mr. He Qifang, came to meet me, I asked him about Ai Qing and Ding Ling. Mr. Fang [sic] said, 'Ai Qing pursues relations with married women. He also wanted to be the Director of the Art Academy. But the Party did not like this. This is why Ai Qing became upset.' About Madam Ding Ling, he said only that 'right now, you should not try to meet her. She is very unhappy.' "[97] He Qifang was not alone in citing Ai Qing's supposed depravity as justification for his disappearance. One writer in Tianjin claimed that Ai Qing and Ding Ling "treat life as the domain of pleasure and do not concern themselves with our present struggle. This is why they are rightists."[98] For his part, Dinkar took these comments with a grain of salt. He recognized that "in order to oppose Ai Qing and Ding Ling, people would say whatever it took to denounce them and to show that the Party had taken appropriate measures to deal with them."[99] Thus, Dinkar warns his reader against the veracity of these comments, a caution further underscored by the fact that Dinkar's record of these conversations underwent processes of multilingual mediation from Chinese into English (via Dinkar's translator) and subsequently into Hindi.

Dinkar's quest for Ai Qing ultimately reveals itself not as a search for the poet himself—indeed, Dinkar understood the futility of such a task—but as a marker of Dinkar's disruptive presence in the Chinese literary sphere of late 1957. Records of terse conversations about and critical reflections on the Anti-Rightist campaign punctuate the travelogue, disrupting happier accounts of sightseeing and witnessing life in "New China" that comprise the majority of the text.[100] The quest for Ai Qing, which may have begun with Dinkar's personal interest in the poet, grew over the course of his visit into the pursuit of a larger aim: to articulate, and thereby make visible, the silences and absences of literary persecution. Dinkar's insistence on repeatedly evoking Ai Qing and Ding Ling despite the palpable discomfort this caused, discursively made the persecuted writers visible during a time when the state functioned to remove them (and their writings) from public view. By articulating in Hindi that which could not be uttered in Chinese, the travelogue binds Chinese and Indian literary spheres in a form of literary relation that runs counter to political intentions and directives. Some twenty years later, in the late 1970s, Ai Qing, Ding Ling, and others exiled during the Anti-Rightist campaign reentered the Chinese literary stage during the "Second Hundred Flowers" period following Mao's death. Dinkar's travelogue holds echoes of those twenty years of enforced silence.

Translating the Ellipsis

The final chapter of Dinkar's China travelogue, "The Story of a Poem" (*Ek kavitā ki kathā*), breaks structurally from the diaristic narrative of the preceding pages and shifts to a different story, that of a poem and its fate in the 1957 Chinese literary sphere. Dinkar centers Liu Shahe's 流沙河 "On Plants" (*Caomu pian* 草木篇, 1957), which he translates more literally as "Grass and Trees" (*ghās aur peṛ*). This final chapter provides a fitting culmination of Dinkar's quest to grasp the silences of the Anti-Rightist campaign.

Dinkar introduces Liu's poems as having "set off a storm in the [Chinese] literary world."[101] In January 1957, Liu's series of prose poems had appeared in the poetry journal *Star* (*xingxing* 星星). Harnessing the Hundred Flowers trend of writing satirically in botanical and seasonal metaphors, Liu's series consists of five short poems—"Poplar" (*baiyang* 白楊"), "Vine" (*teng* 藤), "Cactus" (*xianrenzhang* 仙人掌), "Plum" (*mei* 梅), and "Poisonous Mushroom" (*dujun* 毒菌)—each critiquing the political climate of the time through the image of the plant in its title. The following lines from "Plum," for example, depict the plum tree's refusal to bloom despite the arrival of spring:

> In the springtime
> when a hundred flowers lured the butterflies
> by the charm of their bewitching smiles,
> she was quietly married to the white
> snow of winter.[102]

The image, with its explicit reference to the Hundred Flowers campaign, evokes the skepticism writers initially felt toward the Hundred Flowers policy, with the plum tree signifying the writer's hesitation to voice antiparty criticism despite the directive to "bloom and contend." In the early months of 1957, the poems set off a profusion of criticism, both praise and opposition. By mid-1957, Liu became the subject of scathing denunciation, and reproval of the poems appeared in print.[103]

Dinkar first learned of the poems in Beijing: "After much scrutiny," he writes, "it was decided that the poem was very flawed indeed, so flawed that it should not have been published."[104] Dinkar narrates his efforts to procure an English translation of the poems. Much like the persecuted writers removed from public view, the poems had become difficult to access in

Chinese, let alone in English translation; the first published English translation appeared much later, in 1981.[105] Dinkar's persistence eventually paid off. He obtained an English translation covertly prepared for him by an unnamed Indian diplomat. Based on this English version, Dinkar launched an attempt to translate the very ellipses of the Chinese literary scene he bore witness to: he translated the poems into Hindi. The final chapter of his travelogue contains Liu's censured poems in this Hindi iteration.

For the most part, Dinkar's translation conveys the content of Liu's poems. Although aware that the poem's meaning far exceeds the words on the page, Dinkar does not provide guidelines for interpretation. The interpretation of the plum tree's refusal to bloom as signifying the writers' skepticism toward the party's new policy, for example, would have been lost on Dinkar's Hindi readership. In this sense, Dinkar's translation risks being viewed as unsuccessful: it fails to capture precisely that which makes Liu's poems meaningful.

However, by delinking the poems from their predetermined interpretation, Dinkar's translation keeps open in Hindi interpretive possibilities that were foreclosed in Chinese. What the poems leave unsaid through the indeterminacy of Liu's elusive symbolism had become in China the only thing that the poems could say. Dinkar's decontextualized translation brackets away the singular reading of the poems as voicing political commentary on the Hundred Flowers campaign. In so doing, the translation restores to the poems precisely what the party's directives aimed to rein in: the openness of a literary text to multiple interpretations and acts of reading as it journeys through the hands of readers, across time and space.

In lieu of a guide for interpretation, and as though critiquing that essential paratext that inevitably accompanied the publication of translations in Chinese journals of the time, Dinkar supplements his translation not with an explanation of what the poems mean, but with an invitation to engage in debate over poetic meaning. He does so by reproducing his own futile attempts to understand why the poems had proven so controversial: "I discussed the poem in every city I visited, and I realized that all Chinese writers and poets stood against this poem. And everyone seemed to make the same argument against it. I would ask the same question, and every writer would give me the same staid response."[106] Dinkar goes on to outline a hypothetical conversation as representative of the one he repeatedly had with Chinese writers:

"What is your opinion of the poem entitled 'Caomu pian'?"

"The ideas expressed in that poem are different from my own."

"So what? It seems only right that a poet would write a poem expressing ideas different than your own. I want to know whether this poem is good or bad."

"It is bad."

"Why so? I have read an English translation of the poem. Stylistically, the poem seems quite interesting."

"But a poem is not all style. It should also contain within it healthy sentiments. 'Caomu pian' is bad because it does not contain a vision for a hopeful future."

"So if a poet feels hopeless, what is he to do? Should only hopeful poems be written?"

"If a poet feels hopeless, then he should work. He should see present life up close and try to understand it. Today, life in China is full of hope. This poet has purposely forgotten to see this life."

"But what if a poet feels hopeless in love, what is the principle regarding this?"

"We are not against such poems, but this poem is not even about that."[107]

The conversation continues on the issue of hopefulness, with Dinkar arguing that poets are not obliged to write only of hope; they also write of despair. Dinkar's reconstructed conversation with the Chinese writers, who were understandably cautious during this fraught Anti-Rightist moment, captures the tensions and frustrations of a dialogue that leaves much unsaid. Yet its omissions mark moments of communicative possibility, articulating an ethical commitment to keeping open literary debate and an insistence on literature's capacity to be read multiply. The questions Dinkar raises do not focus on how Chinese readers interpret the poems or on whether Liu was rightly persecuted. Instead, Dinkar's concerns take on a transnational, even universal, bent: the criteria for judging poetry, the relationship between form and content, and the poet's thematic imperatives. In this way, the poems enter a new semantic field of interpretation, accruing layers of meaning and anticipating different terms of debate, as they journey beyond the discursive and linguistic scales of the nation.

Dinkar's travelogue proposes a reconceptualization of the premise of China-India cultural diplomacy as now holding within its operations the threat of frustrating its own logic. Literary relation emerges not in the act of dialogue—the pre-scripted words exchanged—but in the capacity of the elided to bind dialogically in defiance of the tenets of diplomacy. Dinkar's translation stands in contrast to the English translation of Yuan's poem with which this chapter opens: while the English "China-India Friendship" seeks to proclaim its unitary message as loudly as possible and to drown out all other potential forms of relation, the Hindi translation of "Caomu pian" registers the poem's silencing and silences without prescribing to them a singular meaning. A poem taken out of circulation in Chinese finds new paths in Hindi, joining Chinese and Hindi literary spheres in an exercise of reading, writing, translation, and interpretation unsanctioned by the nation-state.

In the age of China-India cultural diplomacy, when both states valorized dialogue as simultaneously performing and attesting to friendly political relations, the act of engaging in dialogue about literature often seemed synonymous with the work of establishing diplomatic international relations. Yet the records of cultural diplomacy hold the possibility to be read otherwise, with an eye to the exclusions and the excesses of state-sponsored dialogue. Borne as much of accident (its confluence with the Hundred Flowers campaign) as of design (Anand's idealistic vision), the Asian Writers' Conference of 1956 makes visible—through its invisibility in records of cultural diplomacy—a poetics of transnational literary relation that exceeds and disrupts the mandates of cultural diplomacy. Reading the conference literarily foregrounds its entwinement with the aesthetics of the Hundred Flowers campaign, aesthetics expressed in every iteration of the telltale floral and botanical imagery that punctuates Ye's depiction of the conference. Hundred Flowers aesthetics, brought to life at the conference, evince a commitment to contention and dissension, an acute sense of transience, and an intense and constant negotiation of what can and cannot be uttered. The conference calls attention to that which must remain absent from records—namely, a form of literary relation, captured elliptically in Xiao San's memoirs, that rebels against top-down demands placed by national agendas upon literary practice and experience.

Similarly preoccupied with the possibility of a literary relation that eschews its enforced equivalence with diplomatic relations, Dinkar's travelogue explores the potentialities of relating literarily not through proclamations of friendship, but during those frictional moments that spell the failures of diplomacy. Dinkar's China travelogue inscribes the literary tensions of the Anti-Rightist campaign, making present in Hindi those texts and writers rendered absent in Chinese. In Dinkar's translation, Liu's poems, overdetermined and fixed in meaning in the Chinese literary sphere, become reopened in Hindi to the interpretive contingencies of reading the poems anew in a different context and language, and with unbounded horizons of poetic meaning. These twinned scenes of poetic practice—recitations at the Asian Writers' Conference captured in Xiao San's memoirs, and Dinkar's translation of Liu's censured poems—call into question the nation-state's tendency to presume literature's utility in the work of international relations and to treat literature as a readily available and pliant resource that can be put toward predetermined ends.

FOUR

Word and World in Crisis

Hindi Texts of 1962

AS A MARKER of crisis in the history of China-India thought, perhaps no moment looms larger than 1962. That year, war broke out between China and India, bringing to a head territorial disputes over contested borders and rising tensions over Tibet.[1] The war marked the demise of diplomatic relations between China and India in the 1950s, ending the spirit of friendship that had heralded the entrance of the newly established nation-states onto the world stage. Under the 1950s banner of brotherhood, programs of cultural diplomacy (discussed in the preceding chapter) had facilitated much literary collaboration and exchange: a flurry of cultural delegations traveled to and fro, writers shared texts and practices, a wealth of translations enabled new modes of engagement and networks of influence, and presses established channels of distribution. The war formally ended all such literary activity.

In China, the end of cultural diplomacy resulted in the abrupt erasure of India from the literary sphere. By 1962, substantial literary engagements with India ceased to appear in print at least until the reestablishment of diplomatic relations in 1976. Expelled from the literary sphere, mentions of India now appeared in newspapers, in reports on the events of the war, in denunciations of India's interventions in Tibet and claims over Chinese territory, and on maps of the disputed border line. Engagements with India were thus transplanted from the realm of friendship (the literary journal) into that of fracture (the political arena of the official newspaper).[2]

In India, too, literary relations with China in their 1950s iteration came to an end. The war closed official channels of literary exchange; the sentiment of brotherhood quickly transformed into a collective sense of betrayal at the hands of a cultural ally, igniting outrage and mourning. But instead of erasing China's presence, Hindi literary sites—journals, writers' meets, presses—witnessed the opposite. 1962 ignited an explosion of Hindi literary engagements with China in a cacophony of poems, novels, short stories, plays, songs, literary criticism, editorials, jokes, and satire. The sheer volume of writing suggests that the literary emerged as a key medium for reckoning with the ends of China-India friendship.

This claim—that the war announced not the end but the continuation, and even intensification, of Indian writers' literary preoccupations with China—may seem controversial at first glance. After all, popular belief and China-India scholarship alike treat as virtually axiomatic the deeply entrenched notion that 1962 marks a caesura in the history of China-India cultural relations. The texts this chapter studies have fallen out of such histories, dismissed as superficial "anti-China rhetoric," for a variety of long-held assumptions that have functioned to privilege material connectivity and affective affinity in defining the kinds of literary relation worthy of study and commemoration. Extending critical attention to the Hindi texts of 1962 challenges such assumptions, revealing an archive of texts that position China and India together in states of disconnect.

This chapter focuses on such texts published in the popular Hindi weekly *Dharmayug*. In the 1950s, *Dharmayug* had grown into the most widely circulated Hindi magazine at the time.[3] Like other commercial Hindi digests in the postindependence era, *Dharmayug* catered to the growing middle class and boasted entertainment for every member of the family: the magazine's regular columns included writings on current events, Indian history and culture, scientific developments, sports, as well as sections devoted to women and children.[4] In 1960, under the editorship of the renowned Hindi writer Dharmavir Bharati, the magazine framed itself as offering content of intellectual, literary, and social value, providing the middle-class family with an informed view of India and the world while promoting Hindi as a national language. Bharati, who had already established himself as a litterateur, endowed the magazine with a distinctly literary sensibility, and *Dharmayug* soon gained a reputation as a respected literary forum, publishing both well-established writers and newcomers.[5]

Immediately following the outbreak of war on October 20, 1962, and for months after China declared a ceasefire on November 19, *Dharmayug's* pages brimmed with literary preoccupations with China and the war. From November 1962 to March 1963, the war infiltrated virtually every page of *Dharmayug's* issues: the front pages printed lengthy features on China, a profusion of war-related poetry and short stories comprised the bulk of the issues' literary content, and peppered throughout were political cartoons caricaturing Mao Zedong and Zhou Enlai and advertisements for donations to the recently established National Defence Fund. A new column entitled "Challenging the Chinese Dragon" (*Cīnī ajăgar ko cunautī*) regularly published nationalist poetry lauding the bravery of martyrs on the front lines, condemning China's treachery and stoking the nation's wrath. *Dharmayug* began advertising its writings on China prominently on the cover of each issue and promoted forthcoming war-related content to boost subscriptions. As such, *Dharmayug* stands as testament to both the outpouring of Hindi literary writing on the war and the voracious readerly appetite for engaging China in literary form fueled and sustained by such writing.

This chapter sifts through the many texts of 1962, centering a collection of Hindi literary engagement with China that revels in the creative potentialities of inhabiting the ends of diplomatic relations. The perceived betrayal of a brother turned traitor, the falsehood of a friendship that had been hailed by the highest leaders of the nation, precipitated a crisis of faith in the world and, at its fundamental core, in the word. The texts I read confront the ends of friendship with China by throwing into question the fidelity of the written word, casting doubts on its claims of signification. If an entire nation could be betrayed, a decade-long cultural ethos be misunderstood, could not the word, the text, deceive? As a battle over fixing the nation's territorial borders unfolded on the front lines, writers experimented with fixing the meaning of the word in a world that had suddenly become untrustworthy. Written upon upended and unstable grounds of meaning, these texts engage the trope of China's betrayal as a contemplation on the duplicity of the word (indeed, "betrayal" itself suggests at once the concealment of truth and its confession), and the binds and unboundedness of its interpretation.

A Poem and a Parody

The December 30, 1962, issue of *Dharmayug* carries a poem anonymously published under the initials "Pra. Ma." The opening stanzas read:

> I saw
> swelling over the horizon
> such a big dragon.
>
> Seeing this,
> I placed the sword
> of a solemn pledge
> upon its chest
> and vowed:
>
> This mighty snake in the sky's lair,
> until I crush it,
> I will not rest.[6]

The poem immediately announces itself as evoking the war. The image
of the dragon looming over the horizon invokes the trope of China casting
its expansionist gaze over India, an already clichéd gloss of the rhetoric in
which the Indian media had reported the presence of Chinese troops in
Indian territory (as designated by India's maps of its northeastern border).
The contested borderline—the mountainous lands of the Himalayan range
that figured in the Hindi literary imagination as a spiritual font, the origin
of the life-giving Ganges river, and the mythological abode of Lord Shiva—
features here as the elusive, glimmering line of the "horizon" (*kṣitij*), now
darkened by the mighty dragon. The hero raises his sword, echoing the
nationalist outcry the war had unleashed for India to shed its nonviolent
garb of anticolonial struggle and defend its hard-earned freedom with military might. Proclaiming a vow to fight for the nation, our hero embarks on
his quest to slay the dragon. The poem continues:

> And with this mighty message,
> like a messenger on the run—
> I ran:

Carrying the light of the four directions;
tied to my feet, the feathers of zeal
and the arrow of ceaseless speed.

And upon reaching there,
into the embrace of my loathed,
I thrust the sword.
And standing upon that border,
we were both numb, benumbed by fury.

An arrow—
like the signal of that eternal death
all-encompassing, like the four directions of the world,
steady, aimed at the target—
was about to be released at the dragon.[7]

As the hero rushes to the battleground, carried upon the wings of the
nation's "zeal," the ever-receding line of the horizon transforms into a concrete "border" (sīmā), a definite line on a map. For a moment, the hero and
the dragon seem to be poised at the brink of "embrace," but this flicker of
friendship soon reveals itself to be one of "fury" (roṣ). The dragon slayed, the
nation's border claimed, the poem ends with a declaration of victory:

(The difference between us
is the glow
of our great victory.)[8]

The parentheses deceptively frame this concluding stanza as a tangen-
tial aside, when in fact, the lines encapsulate the poem's central message:
that of India's victory over China. Although the Chinese troops had easily
overpowered the Indian army (and staked China's claim over the disputed
territories before Zhou Enlai ordered a ceasefire and retreat), the poem
recasts India's indisputable defeat in the 1962 war as a "great victory" (baṛī
vijay). By writing the war as a heroic quest, the poem preordains and ensures
the hero's victory; indeed, the generic structure of the quest allows for no
other outcome. Yet the parentheses also undercut the declarative force
of the lines contained within. The announcement of victory takes on a

speculative tone, compounded by the prospective temporality of the preceding line ("an arrow . . . was about to be released"). Victory seems imminent but as yet beyond grasp. The parentheses highlight the conjectural quality of a moral victory claimed in the face of material defeat. In this war begotten of China's duplicity and deceit, the poem insists, India emerges the true hero.

Read in this vein, the poem falls entirely in line with the wartime tenor of writing China in Hindi. Images of the treacherous dragon, the border in jeopardy, the heroic soldier bravely raising arms in defense of the nation, and India's moral victory appeared again and again in poems and short stories. Here was a formula based on platitudes that seemed only to heighten in import with every repetition. Such texts think China and India together perversely, inaugurating a mode of comparison conducted in the parochial, virulent, and exclusionary nationalist idiom of war.

The poem encourages such a nationalist reading, its publication in *Dharmayug* amidst a host of other such poems further framing it as a prototype of its kind. However, the reader detects a hint of irony. The poem was published under the title "A Parody: China" followed by a subtitle that simply states: "With Apologies to Mr. Shamsher." To clarify this elliptical allusion, *Dharmayug* published the poem alongside the text it references: a poem entitled "China" (*Cīn*) by Shamsher Bahadur Singh (1911–1993), originally published in 1959.[9] On the left margin of Shamsher's 1959 poem, running vertically down the edge of the stanzas, appears a string of Chinese characters spelling out "The People's Republic of China" (*Zhonghua renmin gonghe guo* 中華人民共和國) (figure 4.1). The poem reads in full as follows:

I saw
blooming on the horizon
such a big flower!

Seeing this,
I placed the sword
of a solemn pledge
upon my chest
and vowed:

That flower in the sky's parting,
until I kiss it,
I will not rest.

And with this mighty message,
like a messenger on the run—
I ran:

Carrying the light of the four directions,
tied to my feet, the feathers of ecstasy
and the arrow of ceaseless speed.

And upon reaching there,
I embraced my love
and standing upon that border,
we were both happy.

An arrow—
like the signal of eternal beauty,
all-encompassing, like the four directions of the world,
steady, aimed at the target—
was about to be released.

x x

(Within us
is the glow
of a great victory.)[10]

An acclaimed poet of the time, Shamsher had risen to prominence in the 1940s as the editor of the literary journals *Kahānī* (Story) and *Nayī Sāhitya* (New literature).[11] During his years of editorship, he fostered an interest in the progressive writers' movement, briefly joining the Communist Party of India in 1945, an experience he later reflected upon as "bringing to life the hazy societal ideals that had been swirling in [his] mind."[12] Yet, when his first published poems appeared in the 1950s, Shamsher entered the Hindi

FIGURE 4.1 Pr. Ma.'s "A Parody: China" (1962) printed in *Dharmayug* on the right of the page, alongside the poem it parodies—Shamsher's 1959 poem "China"—reproduced on the left. The Chinese characters that appear in the left margin accompanied Shamsher's poem in its original publication. Dharmayug; © Bennett, Coleman & Co. Ltd.

literary scene not as a progressivist (*pragativādī*) but as an experimentalist (*prayogvādī*), at the forefront of the incipient modernist school of "New Poetry" (*nayī kavitā*). The school had announced itself through the publication of an inaugural anthology, *Tār Saptak* (1943), as committed to experimentation, in rebellion against the socialist realism of the progressives and the ornamental dreaminess of the romanticists (*chāyāvādī*).[13] A selection of Shamsher's poems appeared in the second installment of the school's anthologies, *Dūsrā Saptak* (1951), marking his literary debut and cementing his position among the New Poets. Still, Shamsher's poetry appeared unperturbed by the seeming incongruence between progressivism and experimentalism, a contrast around which lines of debate had been drawn at the time. His poems took on an abstract form, even flirting with Marxist thought, albeit obliquely; in the words of one critic, "Progressivism was limited to the margins of Shamsher's poetry."[14] Shamsher foregrounded these margins in the preface to his poems in *Dūsrā Saptak*, describing his poetic vision in a distinctly Marxist-inflected tone. "Art is the true reflection of life," he wrote, "and today, metamorphosis quickly approaches the lives of all countries, because today is undeniably the age of revolution."[15]

Shamsher conceivably termed his zeitgeist "the age of revolution" with China on his mind. *Dūsrā Saptak* was published, incidentally, on the heels of a momentous event: the establishment of the People's Republic of China in 1949. Indian leftists celebrated New China, an achievement they viewed as heralding the realization of a long-awaited Marxist revolution. Shamsher's statement in *Dūsrā Saptak* captures the excited anticipation of transformation and change ("metamorphosis") glimpsed on the horizon. Although composed some years later in 1958, "China" recalls that joy of witnessing revolution coming into being.

Read as a tribute to the new nation named by the Chinese characters in its margin, Shamsher's "China" narrates the protagonist's flight to a beloved who appears on the horizon in the guise of a blooming flower, climaxing in their union as they lock in embrace. The poem visually performs this climax: the lines "I embraced my love / and standing upon that border / we were both happy" materialize on the page in the striking vision of Chinese characters printed alongside lines of Hindi poetry, the two bound together in a spectacle of poetic intimacy. The arrow in the penultimate stanza, of "eternal beauty" trembling in anticipation of its release, evokes the hopeful yet nervous anticipation of beholding a world on the brink of revolution. The poem ends with the warm afterglow of union in joint victory ("within us / is the glow / of a great victory"); the PRC had blossomed from shared dreams.

Pra. Ma.'s parody of "China" now takes on new meaning. Replacing only 20 of the poem's 126 words, the parody artfully transforms a romantic ode to a triumphant China into a condemnation of and triumph over it. Shamsher's opening stanza "I saw / blooming on the horizon / such a big flower" now reads as "I saw / swelling on the horizon / such a big dragon." The quiet satisfaction of uniting in victory becomes a declaration of absolute fracture: "The difference between us / is the glow / of our great victory." And just as Shamsher's poem visually enacts its embrace through its arrangement on the page, the parody stages its battle, poised in confrontation with the Chinese characters in Shamsher's and, given its adjoining placement on *Dharmayug*'s page, its own margins. The white space between the Chinese characters and Hindi poetry, once signifying the border upon which the lovers embrace, now marks the front lines of two nations at war.

The parody distorts Shamsher's "China" only to sustain it. The simple economy of the parody's poetic trick discloses layers of intertextual play within. In preserving the form, rhythm, and most of the words of Shamsher's poem, the parody pays its respects both to Shamsher's art and to his vision of a China-India union. Doing so reveals the illusory nature of Shamsher's beloved—how easily love (*prem*) can turn into loathing (*hiqārat*)—and chastises the naïveté of those who trusted a traitor. One set of clichés substitutes another: with a hint of humor, the parody's staid images of Indian nationalism replace and reprove the stereotypical Marxist obsession with and reverence for China. Pra. Ma.'s rewriting thus proves doubly parodic, its critique aimed at both the real "People's Republic of China" named on Shamsher's horizon turned front line as well as the discursive China imagined as a comrade. Pitting literal against figurative, the parody heightens the dissonance between the two.

The Fixity of Meaning

For regular readers of *Dharmayug*, the signature "Pra. Ma." may not have presented much of a mystery. These initials would have immediately invoked Prabhakar Machwe (1917–1991), a prominent literary figure of the time and a frequent contributor to *Dharmayug*. Machwe began his literary career in the late 1930s as an avid writer for Hindi and Marathi magazines. He made a name for himself through a vast oeuvre of poetry, short stories, novellas, and literary criticism, as well as a robust collection of translations between Hindi, Marathi, and English. A selection of his poems appeared in the above-mentioned experimentalist anthology *Tār Saptak* in 1943, and, like Shamsher, who identified as progressive while nonetheless eschewing the social realist tenets of progressivist literature, Machwe aligned himself politically on the left (he was attracted to both Marxism and Gandhism) while artistically identifying as an existentialist in those early days of his career.[16] In 1954, Machwe gained national prestige as the assistant secretary to the Sahitya Akademi, established in the same year with the aim of promoting both literary diversity (exchange between India's various languages) and unity (a consolidated view of "Indian literature"). While on a hiatus from the Sahitya Akademi in 1959, Machwe taught Indian literature as a visiting professor at the University of Wisconsin, Madison, where the American civil rights movement inspired him at the same time as the "deafening" drone of "constant anti-communist propaganda" chafed against him.[17] Machwe returned to India and the Sahitya Akademi in September 1961, about a year before China and India would go to war.

In the wake of the war, Machwe regularly published China-related writings in *Dharmayug*, stoking the literary obsession with China unfolding in the magazine's pages. For example, the December 2, 1962, issue carried Machwe's article entitled "Marathi Literary Conference in the Shadow of War," a report of the forty-fourth iteration of the conference held in Satara, Maharashtra, at which Machwe was among the some 1500 delegates in attendance. Machwe's report provides a glimpse into the literary crisis the war had instigated; several such writers' conferences convened in the early post-war months opened a space for heated debate on how literature ought to reckon with the violent ends of friendship with China. At the Marathi Literary Conference, Machwe writes, China formed a central preoccupation, from the presidential address by Maharashtra's then chief minister Yashwantrao Chavan, who urged writers not to abandon their pens during the nation's critical time of need, to public recitations of anti-China poetry. Machwe's sustained interest in the intersection between literature and the China war as evidenced in *Dharmayug* would make him a likely candidate for the poet behind "A Parody," an attribution further strengthened by Machwe's reputation as a renowned Hindi poet and his inclusion in the same hallowed pages of the *Saptaks* in which Shamsher made his literary debut (which would also explain the deferential apology to Shamsher at the opening of the parody).[18]

"A Parody" appeared in the same issue of *Dharmayug* as a second article by Machwe, this one attributed explicitly to him, entitled "Traits of Treachery in Modern Chinese Poetry" (*Ādhunik Cīnī Kavitā Mem Bheṛiyā-Vṛtti*). The article presents Machwe's "literal translations" (*akṣarśaḥ anuvād*) of Chinese poetry, via English translations, with the aim of exposing China's apparent long-standing hunger for war waged in order to sate its expansionist appetite. "The educated reader," Machwe writes in his brief preface to the translations, "need not be told that the Chinese 'use' poetry, too, as a weapon."[19] Translations of excerpts from ten poems follow, all of which elucidate, in Machwe's reading, the deep-seated Chinese conviction that "there will be no peace until the entire world comes under communist rule."[20] Machwe paints an image of Chinese poetry of the time as consumed with celebrations of war and proclamations of communist victory. One poem reads, "I know that when the red flag waves above the world / a new day will dawn"; another, "like a rock, our determination / will crash down upon the enemy with such heavy force / that the enemy will fall to his knees."[21] Machwe's translations appear to furnish all the proof necessary for China's treachery: friendship had been a farce all along, war had been inevitable.

Given how sharply such Chinese poems diverge in tone from those that circulated in India under the aegis of friendship, a reader may be inclined to question whether Machwe himself penned these poems so conveniently well suited to the now popular view of the Chinese as warmongers. Dispelling any such doubts, Machwe hastens to clarify that his poems are based upon a 1954 volume entitled *The People Speak Out*, a collection of English translations of Chinese poetry by Rewi Alley. Tracing the journey of these poems—from their Chinese inception into Alley's resolutely pro-China volume and then, unexpectedly, into *Dharmayug*'s pages abounding with anti-China sentiment—tells of the fate of literary meaning in a world bent on fixing interpretation only to confront the futility of such a task.

An infamous "friend of China," Alley (1897–1987) traveled to China from his native New Zealand in 1927 and remained there for an impressive sixty years—through the late Republican period, the Sino-Japanese War, the civil war between the communists and nationalists, the establishment of the PRC, the Great Leap Forward and Cultural Revolution, Mao's death, and the age of "reform and opening up" under Deng Xiaoping—until his death in Beijing in 1987.[22] Alley presents a rare instance of a foreigner permitted to remain in China during phases of large-scale upheaval, when the position of foreigners in China grew increasingly precarious and circumscribed.

Alley's time in China can be roughly categorized into three broad phases: those years spent predominantly in Shanghai (1927–1942), in Shandan, Gansu (1945–1951), and in Beijing (1952–1987). Initially involved in humanitarian efforts in semicolonial Shanghai, Alley joined the Chinese Industrial Cooperative movement (also known as *Gung ho* or *gonghe* 工合) during the Sino-Japanese War.[23] In the early 1940s, when it became difficult for the movement to maintain its political neutrality amid tensions between the nationalists and communists, Alley shifted his attention to the Shandan Baile School and moved to Gansu in 1945 to become its headmaster. The school, which had been established by British journalist George Hogg, espoused an alternative pedagogical program that emphasized both book learning and experiential skill. With the communist victory and founding of the PRC in 1949, the school came under suspicion, both for its foreign headmaster and because it did not subscribe to the education system now implemented in New China. Alley was faced with a decision: he could either return to New Zealand or remain in China under the terms of the Communist Party. Alley chose the latter and spent the remainder of his life in Beijing as a central feature of the party's propaganda and publicity efforts. He was afforded a lavish lifestyle and relative autonomy in exchange for regular publications in the English-language media on China's successes after liberation and the PRC's achievements. As a foreigner, Alley likely seemed a more reliable source of information on New China to those skeptical about official Chinese reports; the party capitalized on this, frequently requesting Alley to publish strategic books and articles, and, in the 1950s, a visit with Alley became a standard feature of foreign delegations' activities in China.

Occasionally trying his hand at poetry himself, Alley undertook various translations of Chinese poetry as part of his work as a propagandist for the PRC. Fluent in Chinese and an avid reader and collector of Chinese literature, he still enlisted the help of his Chinese friends to glance at his translations and offer corrections. Between 1952 and 1964, he published six volumes together containing hundreds of translations of both classical and contemporary poetry, from the *Book of Odes* (*Shijing* 詩經) and Tang dynasty masterpieces to folk songs and poetry of New China.[24] The wide temporal breadth of Alley's chosen works indicates his tendency to harness the past in service of the present: Alley often framed classical Chinese poems as repositories of evidence for the inherent revolutionary characteristics of the Chinese people, or as presenting the beginnings of a centuries-long struggle that would culminate in communist revolution.[25]

Following this pattern, *The People Speak Out* brings together eighty-nine poems, "some pre-liberation and some post-liberation poetry," under a loose theme of "protest against oppression and social injustice," topics that Alley reads Chinese poetry as having been preoccupied with since its earliest practice. "At no time in their long history," Alley writes in the preface, "have the Chinese people suffered meekly. Always has there been rebellion, always outspoken criticism."[26] While the volume includes a largely equal number of pre- and postliberation poems, the preface centers the poetry of New China as forming the impetus for and central focus of the volume:

> Since this great people have been released from the thralldom of the old society, poems of the people sing not only of the joy in entering the new day, but also of the desire for those things which will ensure the right to continue with peaceful construction; of things like the resistance against imperialist aggression, defence of national independence, protest against Japanese remilitarization and support for the cause of world peace. . . . It is hoped [the volume] will enable the English-speaking reader to understand more fully the new China that has emerged and which is rapidly establishing itself again as one of the main stabilizing forces in our world.[27]

Alley's careful framing of China as at once "rebellious" and a "stabilizing force in our world," committed to "peaceful construction" and "support for the cause of world peace," aligns well with China's foreign policy of the time. China had recently hosted the Asia-Pacific Peace Conference in Beijing in 1952, and in April 1955, a year after the publication of Alley's volume, Zhou Enlai had joined representatives of newly decolonized Asian and African nations at the Bandung Conference. Both conferences indicated the party's desire to present China as a leader in its own right, instead of as a satellite of the USSR, at the forefront of charting a new global order. Alley frames his translations as part of that same project.

Similarly, the collection of post-1949 poetry that Alley curates in the volume aligns with the official program of Chinese literature in practice at the time, which largely adopted the literary vision Mao Zedong had famously

set forth in 1942.[28] That year, Mao addressed a group of writers, intellectuals, and party cadres gathered at Yan'an through speeches that have since
come to be known as Mao's "Talks at the Yan'an Conference on Literature and Art." In these talks, Mao laid out a radical view of literary practice, breaking with the earlier conception (in the 1920s and 1930s) of literature as the consecrated products of artistic genius attributed to elite
writers. Instead, Mao called for literature to be guided by and produced for
the "workers, peasants, and soldiers," a phrase that recurs throughout the
talks as shorthand for the collective masses. Positioning the masses at
both the beginnings and ends of literary practice entailed taking inspiration
from the "budding forms" of popular art (what Mao identified as "wall
newspapers, murals, folk songs, folk tales, popular speech") and harnessing
such forms to produce literature that serves the interests of its readers, the
masses.[29]

Alley's translations in *The People Speak Out* exemplify this commitment to
the workers-peasants-soldiers and their budding forms of art. In brief foot-
notes, he identifies several of the poets he includes as factory workers in
Shanghai's mills, coal miners, and construction workers involved in infra-
structural projects such as ship- and dam-building. Alley includes translations of poems taken from wall newspapers, which he describes as "a few
selections from the great mass of village wall newspapers when the people,
following liberation, had the chance for the first time to publish openly what
was in their hearts."[30] Songs sung by soldiers marching into war, folk songs
of "minority peoples," and peasant's refrains all comprise Alley's canon of
poetry of New China, comfortably appearing alongside the occasional more
famous name (such as He Qifang 何其芳 and Ai Qing 艾青). In a radical departure from earlier volumes of Chinese poetry in English translation—
particularly Robert Payne's 1947 *Contemporary Chinese Poetry*, which follows
the "great poets" model—Alley presented to the English-speaking world
poetry by and for China's masses, selected according to standards for literary value set by New China, not the West.[31]

The People Speak Out was self-published by Alley in Beijing, and, given Alley's
standing in the PRC's publicity efforts, the volume would have found widespread distribution through the Foreign Languages Press (*waiwen chubanshe*
外文出版社; FLP) and the International Bookstore (*guoji shudian* 國際書店),
the PRC's main organs for the translation of texts and their dissemination abroad.[32] In the 1950s, the FLP's publications—such as the PRC's

English-language literary journal *Chinese Literature*, to which Machwe subscribed—had become easily available in India and Alley's translations likely reached Machwe via these circuits.[33]

The poems of New China fell into Machwe's hands having undergone multiple layers of fixity that determined the text's meaning and distilled its message into a unitary and imminently digestible form. At Yan'an, Mao's vision for literature called, in many words, for the obsolescence of interpretation. Writing the shared experience of the masses in order to serve collective interests required a hardy literature that could travel intact, its message immune to the interpretive whims of individual readers and varied contexts. Alley's translations aspire to replicate this principle. In order to prioritize capturing the poems' content and message, Alley takes creative liberties with form. In the preface to *The People Speak Out*, he writes: "The main purpose of these translations is to try and carry through the poet's idea into that kind of language which would enable the ordinary people of the English-speaking world to receive much of impact of the message given.... The usual devices of the poet to help him to give appeal to his song—rhyme and rhythm—have been abandoned in favour of clarity and simplicity."[34]

And still these poems—twice fixed, in Chinese and in English—appear in Hindi translation in an entirely new guise. Machwe reads *The People Speak Out* selectively, carefully translating and excerpting together only those lines that can be made to speak to China's expansionist ambitions. In Alley's translations, poetry of the war of resistance (the Sino-Japanese War) and the Korean War had functioned to elevate and bring into the folds of "Chinese literature" those joyful songs of the workers, peasants, and soldiers that had hitherto remained excluded. Transformed through Machwe's editing, these songs about the Japanese and Korean wars now depict exuberant Chinese troops eagerly marching into war with India.

Consider, for example, the following lines from Alley's translation of Ai Qing's "Welcome to 1953" (*Yingjie yi jiu wu san nian* 迎接一九五三年), written in celebration of China's victory at Shangganling during the Korean War: "Over the front line / lies a pall of smoke; and from there and the rock tunnels / come our men, eyes a little bloodshot."[35] Alley successfully conveys Ai Qing's depiction of the soldier's exhaustion while returning home from a hard-won battle, albeit in language that reads less elegantly than Ai Qing's verse.[36] Machwe renders these lines as follows: "Over the front line is a curtain of smoke / from the stone trenches our soldiers advance / red eyes gleaming."[37] Minor misreadings—the soldiers "advance" (baṛh) instead of returning home, their tired eyes now gleam red (lāl-lāl āṁkhen) as though with evil intent—have immense consequences. In another instance, Alley's translation of the line "only / when the red flag waves / can the new day be / surely born,"[38] which commemorates the establishment of the PRC, appears embellished in Machwe's rendition as "I know that when the red flag waves above the world / a new day will dawn," the addition of "above the world" (duniyā par) signaling expansionist desires.[39] A final example from Alley's translation of a soldier's song written "in the Eighth Route Army" during the war of resistance: the line "we shall nourish the flower / of victory, making it blossom / all over these barren hills" reads in Hindi as "we shall nourish the flowers of victory / which will blossom on those snowy hills."[40] Machwe's substitution of "barren" with "snowy" immediately signals the China-India war fought on the snowy peaks of the Himalayas; in India, the image of snowy peaks had become synonymous with the front lines at the time, so much so that the Himalayas had come to metonymize the war.

In one reading, Machwe's efforts can be understood as blatantly irresponsible mistranslation, the disingenuous manipulation of literature to fit a predetermined narrative. But reading Machwe's translations alongside "A Parody"—as readers of Dharmayug would surely have done, since the two appear only a few pages apart—enables a view of the two as engaged in a shared artistic experiment. In both, Machwe flexes his skills in replacing the fewest possible words to effect dramatic interpretive change. This literary sleight of hand enables a deeper contemplation on the interplay between interpretation and determination.

Shamsher's "China" presents a celebration of abstraction. In the words of one critic, "If the comments published with the poem and the Chinese characters on the margins are not mentioned, there is nothing of progressivism [or of China] left in the poem on its own."[41] Shamsher challenges his reader to make sense, through interpretation, of the relationship between the poem's substance and its marginalia. Machwe's parody of Shamsher's abstract poem demonstrates the fickle nature of the written word, drawing attention to how easily (in only twenty words!) the abstract can become the concrete, the inferred literalized.

In parallel and contrast, the translations enact an inverse traffic between interpretation and determination. Machwe's language game reopens the twice-fixed poems to interpretation, subjecting them to the very interpretative labor they were meant, under Mao's program, to dispense with. Machwe reads the poems anew, and, in so doing, he reveals the fragility of the "message" Alley labored to impart. In a final ironic twist, Machwe undoes the poems only to add yet another layer of fixity: under his hand, the poems of New China endure a third process of determination, now as evidence of China's "traits of treachery." While "A Parody" enacts determination at the cost of abstraction, the translations fix literary meaning only to reveal the futility of doing so.

Signs of Modernism

Shamsher's "China" includes an authorial note printed directly below the title. It reads: "The Chinese characters given in the margins denote the name of the Chinese nation: 'The People's Republic of China.' I have taken inspiration from the original meanings and evocations of these various characters, and have created this new form."[42] The practice of taking "inspiration from the original meanings and evocations" of Chinese characters in poetry immediately calls to mind Ezra Pound, the poet singularly responsible for bringing the Chinese written character into the canon of modernist poetry. Read alongside Pound, Shamsher's and Machwe's poems gain yet another shade of meaning. Shamsher's "China" transforms from a Marxist paean into a quintessential modernist experiment, and Machwe's parody throws into relief the fate of modernist indeterminacy in a literary climate grasping for fixity. Paired together, the poems recall the literary debates that unfolded in the wake of the 1962 war on the relationship between the literary text and the real world, between the word and its referent.

The New Poets, with whom both Shamsher and Machwe were associated, introduced to Hindi literature a self-avowedly modernist sensibility. While the New Poets varied in their experiments with aesthetics and form, their writings shared a commitment to free verse written in accessible Hindi (as opposed to the high Sanskritic register of romantic poetry) and a thematic preoccupation with the conditions of Indian modernity typified by the individual's fragmentation and estrangement from a sense of collective identity.[43] Shamsher cited T. S. Eliot and Ezra Pound among his main influences; "in terms of technique," he wrote in the preface to his poems in *Dūsrā Saptak*, "Pound has perhaps become my greatest model."[44] Shamsher aligned himself so closely with Eliot and Pound so as to qualify the "new-ness" of his New Poems: "My poetry can be considered new in . . . Hindi. But in English, their newness would be considered if not very old, then some-what old, or at the least, entirely familiar."[45]

Shamsher shared with Pound, "in terms of technique," an interest in the visual image. In his 1913 manifesto of sorts, "A Few Don'ts by an Imagiste," Pound had set forth, by admonition rather than affirmation, a poetic prac-tice dedicated to the "image," which he famously defined as "an intellectual and emotional complex in an instant of time."[46] Imagism in Pound's poetics aspired to do away with "superfluous words," ornament, meter, and other such conventions and called instead for visual immediacy, to instanta-neously impart an image to the "imaginative *eye* of the reader" in highly crafted and precise language.[47] Shamsher, who had received formal train-ing in the arts and espoused a penchant for abstract art, found inspiration in the Poundian image. "The medium I have chosen alongside poetry, inside poetry, is that of abstract painting," Shamsher once said. "I usually grasp things as a painting and try to transfer the first impression in words."[48] Gajanan Madhav Muktibodh, an acclaimed poet and Shamsher's contem-porary, wrote of Shamsher's poetry as a constant negotiation between the precepts of poetry and of abstract impressionist art: the painter "does his work in only a few strokes of the brush, entrusting the rest to the viewer's imagination. . . . [Shamsher] has stealthily instated into poetry the basic rules of impressionist art."[49] Although dismissing Pound's instruction to "go in fear of abstraction," Shamsher's practice of conveying a painting in words mirrors Pound's lifelong preoccupation with apprehending the visual poetically.

Pound famously found such poetic potential in the Chinese written char-acter, which he misread as capable of visually representing its referent. Unlike the English written word, which had an arbitrary and abstracted relationship to what it signified in the real world, Pound understood the Chinese character as meaning what it showed (and showing what it meant). The Chinese character thus made feasible a direct and instantaneous mode of communication. Pound first encountered the Chinese character through Ernest Fenollosa's manuscripts on Chinese and Japanese language and art, which elaborated a theory of the Chinese character as visually evoking its real-world equivalent, thereby collapsing the distance between signifier and signified.[50] Pound edited and published Fenollosa's essay under the title "The Chinese Written Character as a Medium for Poetry: An Ars Poetica," first in 1918 in multiple installments, and then in 1936 as a book.[51] Even prior to reading Fenollosa, Pound had sought a visually immediate form of poetry; now he upheld the Chinese character as affording such possibilities and thereby providing a model for imagist poetry. Although he began studying the Chinese language only in 1936, his oeuvre reveals a longer, sustained captivation with Chinese language and poetry: beyond imagistic references in *The Cantos* (1930–1969), Pound famously—or, rather, infamously—"translated" classical Chinese poetry (his *Cathay* appeared in 1915), the *Shijing*, and the Confucian analects.[52]

The Chinese characters in the margins of Shamsher's poem now emerge as akin to Pound's project of rendering Chinese characters in poetic form. The characters that name the Chinese nation feature in Shamsher's poem as at once denoting the object of the poem's tribute and as sources of ideogrammic inspiration. "China" originally appeared in Shamsher's first poetry collection, *Some Poems*, published in 1959, eight years after his poetic debut in *Dūsrā Saptak* (figure 4.2).[53] Initially penned in 1958, "China" underwent subsequent revisions and rewritings over the course of a year and a half as Shamsher prepared the manuscript for publication.[54] The poem's brevity and immediacy seems at odds with Shamsher's long labor over it. But this extended meditation betrays a careful intentionality and multiple reworkings of the poem's 126 words and of their arrangement on the page beneath the title and authorial note, indented away from the edge of the page to accommodate the adjacent Chinese characters. The Chinese characters, each of which adjoins a single stanza, appear larger in scale than the Hindi words, with one character exhausting the space of the several lines that comprise the stanza's margin.[55] In this expanded scale, the characters' individual constituent strokes become accentuated and discernable—"a few strokes of the artist's brush"—while the adjacent poem signals a "transfer into words," as Shamsher put it, of the characters' meaning visually derived.

In his preface to the volume in which "China" first appeared, Shamsher provides the following disclaimer: "In any case, it should not be assumed that I know the Chinese language even a little bit! But this is a different matter."[56] Like the young Pound, Shamsher did not have firsthand knowledge of the Chinese language despite his statement that the poem draws upon "the original meanings and evocations" of the characters. In place of Fenollosa, who had mediated Pound's knowledge of the Chinese language, Shamsher

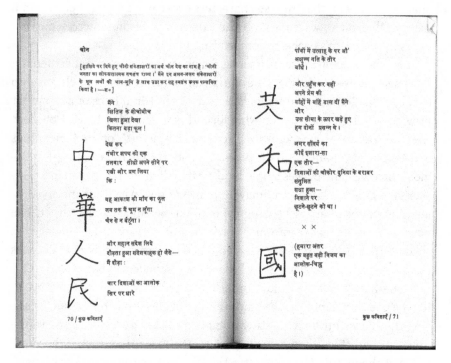

FIGURE 4.2 Shamsher's "China" as it first appeared in his poetry collection *Some Poems* (1959). *Kuch Kavitāeṁ va Kuch aur Kavitāeṁ* [Some poems and some more poems] (New Delhi: Radhakrishna Prakashan, 1984), 70–71. Courtesy of Rajkamal Prakashan.

encountered the Chinese characters via the flows of cultural diplomacy. He likely learned of and copied the characters from one of the many Chinese publications that had flooded the Indian literary marketplace in the 1950s. Whereas Pound has long been criticized for his ahistorical appropriation of the Chinese language with no regard for its actual properties and functions in China, Shamsher not only names the "real" China but does so with a historically specific set of characters (not merely "China," *Zhongguo* 中國, but the "People's Republic of China" *Zhonghua renmin gonghe guo* 中華人民共和國,) that acknowledge the PRC's establishment as well as the context of exchange that afforded him access to those characters. In Pound's readings of Chinese language and poetry, China passively recedes to the background; Pound constructs a conception of "China," informed by the legacies of orientalist discourse, to serve his own poetic agenda. In

Shamsher's poem, the Chinese characters evoke not a myth of China but a reality—that of New China—and the characters become active participants in the poem's processes of meaning-making.

Shamsher's poem presents itself as a cipher: the poem's arrangement on the page invites decoding. The authorial note promises a relationship between the Chinese characters and its adjacent Hindi lines of poetry, but provides no clarity or clues on what form this relationship takes. How does the "inspiration" Shamsher draws from the characters' "original meanings and evocations" manifest in the poem? Perhaps the character *zhong* 中 (middle), which visually evokes a line dividing in half, finds resonance in Shamsher's image of the horizon, or maybe Shamsher saw in *he* 和 (connoting conjunction or togetherness) the figure of an arrow aimed at its target. The poem seduces its reader into such conjecture and "translation." Engaged in this interpretive work, the distracted reader in fact unknowingly decodes the poem, not by discovering any hidden correspondences between the Chinese characters and the Hindi words, but by practicing and thereby revealing the poem's meaning as the search and struggle for meaning itself. By setting the reader off on a frantic attempt to relate the Hindi words to the Chinese characters, the poem encourages the reader to traverse the white space of the margin that separates the two, just as the "messenger" races toward the border to embrace his beloved. The poem unveils the identity of the messenger as the reader, and the contents of his message as the reader's interpretive work that forges literary relation between Hindi and Chinese, India and the PRC. The poem's meaning is thus precisely its image, the strokes on the page: Chinese and Hindi, side by side, the white space between them opening a space of interpretation and relation, of the reader-messenger's quest for meaning.

True to form, Machwe's parody plays with the poem's image. On *Dharma-yug*'s page, the parody appears beside Shamsher's "China," encouraging the reader's eye to flit between the two in an attempt to identify which of Shamsher's words the parody modifies. The "apparition" (as Pound would have put it) of the two poems vying for the reader's attention visually enacts the debates that had erupted in Hindi literary circles upon the outbreak of war. On one side, writers called for literature to reassert the nation's sovereignty by writing literature of and for the nation, exalting the nation's glory and arousing the reader's patriotism. On the other side, writers resisted a predetermination of the shape literature ought to take, arguing, instead, for the openness of the literary word and text. Reading Machwe and Shamsher side by side visually performs such debates.

A writers' meet held by the Sahitya Akademi in late 1962 witnessed just one example of these debates. The meet brought together writers from across India together on the subject of "Creative Writing in the Present Crisis," a prompt the writers interpreted variously as descriptive (an evaluation of present-day literature) and normative (the form creative writing should presently take). Much of the discussion centered on the effusive literary response to the war, a "creative upsurge" during which some "thirteen thousand songs were composed . . . in Hindi alone [and] the wave bands of the All India Radio [were] rent with patriotic songs, plays, features, and stories," not to speak of the print media.[57] Lines of debate emerged around the perceived value of these works and whether writers deemed them worthy of emulation. Syed Abdul Malik argued that, "for the time being, [writers] had to forget the niceties of literary formulae and artistic standards. . . . The brutal [Chinese] aggression posed before the writers a new problem. It was not the problem of creating 'literature' as such, it was a question of existence or annihilation."[58] Malik echoed several other writers' speeches in his assertion that if "our writings fall short of literary standards, it is not to be regretted. The national consciousness and patriotic fervour will . . . amply compensate for the deficiencies of literary formalities and academic requirements." A Kashmiri writer, J. L. Kaul, extended this line of thought to its logical end: "All that was written was not and could not be great art . . . this has been called propaganda. Why not? . . . All art is, in a sense, propaganda."[59]

Offering counterpoints, others called for the writer's freedom to "create literature as such." Jayakanta Mishra contended that writers "do not and cannot—and indeed, need not—respond uniformly or mechanically in any particular way dictated by anybody. . . . You cannot stop a creative genius from creating an escapist poetry as much as a realistic poetry—it is not possible to lay down any fixed lines of creative activity."[60] The most sustained discussion on the writer's freedom came from Mulk Raj Anand (who, in 1956, had spearheaded the Asian Writers' Conference discussed in the preceding chapter): "To a writer no possession is dearer than freedom," he said. "I suggest that this freedom to create from the compulsions of our consciences . . . from our integral vision, can only flourish in a society where 'the hundred flowers' are allowed to flourish."[61] Anand's evocation of the "hundred flowers" recalls the earlier era of China-India literary relation during the 1950s, when the trope of "hundred flowers" enabled writers to exceed the political limitations of cultural diplomacy.[62] Anand strategically uses this distinctly Chinese phrase to appeal to a humanism that exceeds the nation-state. "We are Tagore's universal men," he says, summoning another figure of China-India closeness. "Our fraternity is not exclusively with the writers of our country, but also with ... writers of the world."[63] Ultimately, however, the voices calling for writing to serve the Indian people and nation drowned out Mishra's and Anand's appeals for literary autonomy.

Amid such reevaluations of the writer's imperatives, the experimentalist writing that had flourished in the *Saptaks* of the 1950s suffered, eventually petering out. The New Poets had already come under attack for emulating Western poetics and abstracting poetry away from reality. In the wake of the war and the attendant crisis of meaning, there appeared to be little patience and appetite for words that did not explicitly say what they meant. Machwe's parody satirizes the call for delimiting the writer's task and the meaning of literature. Replacing Shamsher's artful abstract imagery with barefaced nationalist clichés, the parody elicits the reader's judgment on whether "artistic standards" matter in this crisis and whether the meanings of literary words ought to be fixed. In so doing, the parody appoints the reader as a participant in the literary debates that too often centered on writers without much consideration of the work and joy of reading.

A Mad World

While Machwe's parody calls into question the meaning of the word, a second parody probes the search for meaning in an upended world. "New Madman's Diary" by the Hindi humorist and satirist Harishankar Parsai (1924–1995) appeared in *Dharmayug*'s February 24, 1963, issue.[64] The title immediately invokes Lu Xun's canonical Chinese short story, "A Madman's Diary" (狂人日記 *Kuangren riji*), an allusion made explicit in Parsai's subtitle, "(With Gratitude to Lu Xun)," and an authorial note at the top of the page that reads in full as follows:[65]

The Chinese writer Lu Xun was Premchand's contemporary. Like Premchand, Lu Xun also portrays in his works the downtrodden and oppressed peoples of his country. Lu Xun has a famous short story—"A Madman's Diary." The story presents the autobiographical notes of a man who has fallen prey to a phobia, which makes him believe that "they are all my enemies, they are all after me and want to eat me up." The story is a piercing satire of the cannibalistic systems of society. The story ends with the madman's exclamation: "for the past four thousand years, we have been eating human meat. But the children haven't acquired a taste for it yet. Save the children!" Over the past days, I often thought of this story by Lu Xun. On the basis of this story, I have written China's new madman's diary.[66]

Lu Xun's short story, published in the journal New Youth (Xin qingnian 新青年) in 1918, tells of a madman through entries taken from his diary. In his diary, the madman writes of his realization, gained during his madness, that those around him are cannibals plotting to eat him, and that the practice of cannibalism has been passed down through generations for thousands of years. As Parsai notes, the story ends with the iconic exclamation "Save the children," an expression of the madman's final attempt to spark an awakening to society's moral depravity, and a final glimmer of hope for a new future.

Formally, Lu Xun's story is comprised of two sections. The story opens with a brief preface, written in classical Chinese (wenyanwen 文言文), in which a first-person narrator describes how the diary of a man suffering from a "persecution complex" came into his possession.[67] The preface notes that the madman has since recovered and taken up an official bureaucratic post, and excerpts from his diary have been edited and published by the narrator in hopes that they be of use to medical research. The diary entries follow, written in vernacular Chinese (baihua 白話), presented as a series of numbered and undated blocks of text.

Much of the readings of Lu Xun's "Diary" has hinged on the relationship between the preface and the diary entries. The linguistic contrast between the classical preface and vernacular entries corresponds to debates underway during the iconoclastic New Culture and May Fourth movements (discussed in chapter 1), circles in which the journal New Youth carried much influence. Students and intellectuals, Lu Xun among them, had called for writers to no longer use classical Chinese, the traditional literary idiom, and instead to write in the vernacular, urging literature to cast off the chains of tradition and to strive toward a modern national consciousness. In "Diary," the two literary registers have accordingly been read as designating the realms of tradition and modernity. While on first reading the madman's diary may indeed appear as paranoia and delusion, the entries written in vernacular Chinese mark "madness" conversely as the voice of enlightenment and modernity. The plea to "save the children" similarly resonates with the radical agenda (and title) of New Youth as a vehicle for cultural transformation. Yet, whatever hope this ending presents quickly dissipates with the reader's realization that, as stated in the preface, the madman has reintegrated into the very systems of oppression he exposed and decried during his "illness." The story thus effects a circular movement in which the madman awakens to society's moral depravity only for his outcry to be dismissed as the ramblings of a madman and for him to eventually become reabsorbed (or consumed) by that against which he rebelled.

Parsai's "New Madman's Diary" presents a humorous take on Lu Xun's story. Parsai omits the preface, replicating only the undated diary entries, and casts a Chinese madman as his protagonist who quickly reveals himself to be Mao Zedong. The entries begin, as in Lu Xun's "Diary," with the madman contemplating the moon—"the moon is bright tonight," both madmen write—in a scene that sets into motion a recurrent contrast between light and darkness, enlightenment and madness, at the same time as it confuses the distinction between the two. The madmen are at once illuminated in moonlight and shrouded in darkness, enlightened figures trapped within narratives that insist on their madness. In repeating Lu Xun's opening line, Parsai brings into his story Lu Xun's central question: What is madness and what is truth?

Parsai's madman appears as a delusional and paranoid Mao, his madness feeding and fed by the insanity of the Cold War world around him: "The moon is a bomb, aimed at me by the imperialists," the madman writes in his opening entry. "I will blow up the moon, I will blow up each star. They are all satellites, satellites of the imperialists." The madman then recalls frantically uprooting flowers in a garden earlier that day: "I don't like flowers. Yes, 10–12 years ago I had said, let a hundred flowers bloom. I was mad then. No, a hundred flowers will not bloom. Only one flower will bloom—a big, yellow flower."[68] "Imperialists," "satellites," "hundred flowers": Dharmayug's reader, accustomed to perusing literary works printed alongside news reports of Cold War developments, would have read such jargon as embedding the story within the current state of the world. The allusion to the "hundred flowers" held particular import for Indian readers, as in Anand's

speech above, in recalling the 1950s. Referring to this bygone era, the madman assigns madness to the past and provides the reader with evidence of
his current lucidity. From the reader's perspective, the events the madman
predicts indeed seem to have borne out in the real world: in the wake of the
war, it appeared as though the "hundred flowers" spirit that had promised
the peaceful, thriving coexistence of competing schools of thought and ways
of life had never bloomed, and "a big yellow flower" of Chinese supremacy
and expansionism threatened to take its place. From the outset, Parsai's
madman declares himself as cured ("I was mad then") and professes to speak
to truth.

The madman's diary unfolds as a collection of encounters, ranging from
the humorous to the bizarre, with a cast of characters who recall the elder
brother, the doctor, and the villagers of Lu Xun's story. In Parsai's rewriting,
these characters appear as the leaders of various nations: India as a "friend,"
Russia as the "big brother," "Asia and Africa" as insignificant irritants. During visits from each of these characters, the madman portrays himself as
almighty, possessing limitless power with ambitions to rule the world, but
this façade only compensates for his obsession with what he realizes is the
singular guiding principle of the world—"eat or be eaten" (*khāo, nahīṁ to khā
lie jāoge*)—a truth that only he can see. Throughout the story, he attempts to
alert the other leaders to this fact while suspecting that they may be plotting against him. The only way to save himself, he insists, is by eating the
others before they can get to him.

One entry, for example, narrates the madman's meeting with an Indian.
"The Indian came again today," the entry begins. "What was that look in his
eye? That look frightened me. He was looking at me with friendship in
his eyes. He must want to eat me. Whenever one wants to eat someone, he
approaches his prey with friendship in his eyes. . . . No, I will not fall for this
deception." In another entry: "Some foreigners came to meet me from Asian
and African nations. . . . 'Only those who can eat the others will survive,' I
said. . . . They became frightened. Little did they know that I am more afraid
than them!" In the meeting with the Russian ("He considers himself my big
brother and guide," the madman scoffs), the Russian attempts to counsel the
madman only to be rebuked. The story leaves the madman trapped in and
consumed by his worldview of survival of the fittest: "This has been going
on for four thousand years. They will eat me the moment they get the chance
to. My only hope for survival is to eat them first. . . . Our children have not

yet tasted human flesh; this is their weakness. Teach the children to eat human flesh!"[69]

The paranoia and the delusions of a megalomaniac speak the truth—and madness—of national existence in a world consumed by the lure of power. In a post-1962 climate, alternative modes of national identity, like nonalignment and neutrality, seemed misguided and unfeasible ("I don't believe in neutrality," the madman writes). Casting Mao as a madman condemns China's perceived duplicity, but Parsai's critique probes further and spares no one. The story ridicules each of the nations it depicts: the "Indian" (Nehru) is self-aggrandizing and "arrogant" ("He considers himself my equal," the madman writes; "someday, I will set him right!"); the "African and Asian" leaders are naïve and easily intimated by the madman's might (he "speaks for seventy crore people"); and the madman has a falling out with the Russian (Krushchev) who seems concerned only with complacently preserving "world peace" and appeasing the "imperialists."[70] Casting a wide net over its objects of critique, the story presents itself not merely as a commentary on the China-India war, but as a larger indictment of the current state of the world.

The story's parodic lens extends beyond individual nations to the entire system and operation of international relations. One scene, for instance, exposes the empty performativity of cultural diplomacy. In it, the madman threatens the Africans and Asians one moment and the next successfully distracts them with songs of friendship: "With great excitement, they began singing the songs of friendship with me. Then we danced. They are quite gullible. They completely forgot about my threatening words. . . . An intoxication with friendship descended over them."[71] In this untrustworthy world, with nations engrossed in a chess game of epic proportions and consequences, "eat or be eaten" proves as much a madman's delusion as a fundamental truth about the madness of the Cold War.

In the months following the war, the search for answers—for what caused the war, what led to India's defeat, who to blame—consumed the Indian news media. Amid *Dharmayug*'s pages, filled with political analyses and dissections of international relations, Parsai's "Diary" urges a reckoning with the madness of searching for rational answers in an irrational world. The story parodies the attempt to understand China's inner workings by purporting to provide precisely that which so many sought: access to Mao's innermost mind, a firsthand, behind-the-scenes exposé of international politicking.

And yet, through its fictional frame, parodic register, and dark humor, the story explicitly demands, in direct defiance of discourse on the war, *not* to be taken seriously. The story's insistence on dwelling within the realm of madness finds corroboration in Parsai's omission of Lu Xun's preface, which functions in the Chinese story to bracket the madman away from the narrator's reality and to limit madness to the pages of the diary. Parsai's "Diary" offers no such containment of the text's madness, no distinction between madness and the real world. Instead, as the story reveals the search for meaning itself as a mad endeavor, the reader himself emerges a madman, now recruited into and trapped within the realm of madness, forever engaged in the senseless task of making sense of the war.

Unexpectedly, in a literary climate that denounced all things Chinese, the authorial note with which the story opens makes no effort to veil Parsai's evident admiration for Lu Xun, a sentiment echoed in the story's subtitle expressing "gratitude to Lu Xun." By introducing his reader to Lu Xun via Premchand, Parsai urges to extend to Lu Xun the high esteem and respect readers reserved for Premchand over all other Hindi writers.[72] Lu Xun appears here not as a representative Chinese writer, as he so often did in translation, but rather as part of an international coalition of like-minded writers, akin to the "fraternity" of "writers of the world" Anand had called for at the Sahitya Akademi writers meet. Amid the nationalist outpouring and condemnation of China, Parsai's mind lingered on Lu Xun ("Over the past days, I often thought of this story") and the potential of his "Diary" to speak to India's current crisis. Under Parsai's pen, "Diary" hints at the possibility of China and India bound in a literary relation that refuses to adhere to the rules of international relations, joining forces instead to reveal the madness of living by such rules.

The script of a 1966 play features on its cover the outline of a map of India with a sketch of Nehru superimposed upon it, his eyes downcast. A smirking Zhou Enlai creeps out of the Himalayas and peers over the northeastern border, a dagger in hand poised at Nehru's back. The play takes this scene as its title, *Backstabbing Neighbor* (*Dhokebāj paṛosī*), literalizing the refrain that continues to capture the collective memory of the 1962 war in India. A quintessential 1962 text, the play brings together classic tropes of the time: the usual cast of leaders (e.g., Nehru, Zhou, Mao, the Dalai Lama, the president of India Rajendra Prasad) dramatized together with literary tropes that had become ubiquitous in the many enactments and depictions of the war, such as brave soldiers on the border front, Chinese spies who eventually see the folly of their ways, and leftist intellectuals in mourning who must reform their romantic notions of China. The play stages conversations between leaders conducted behind closed doors, battle on the front lines, and the wakening of the Indian people's patriotism. In the preface, the author writes that "it is necessary today to take the Indian people toward the Himalayas and to bring about a fundamental change in their thought."[73] In other words, the play aims to harness the pedagogical capacity of literature to convey the "true" circumstances of the war, thereby awakening the Indian people from the "intoxication" (*naśā*) of friendship with China. Much of the Hindi literature of 1962 follows this program.

The texts this chapter studies similarly grapple with betrayal and the loss of faith in a world suddenly turned untrustworthy. But, unlike *Backstabbing Neighbor* and the genre of works it exemplifies, which ascribe to literature a fixity and fidelity to its claims of representation, Machwe (via Shamsher) and Parsai throw into question the ability of literature to faithfully represent the world, and of the word to correspond to a single, predetermined referent. The pages of *Dharmayug* facilitate such literary experiments on the search for meaning and the potentialities of interpretation; the magazine's pages open the texts to the contingencies of reading fact and fiction side by side, sustaining a traffic between and contemplation on the two modes of thought. The ends of friendship inaugurate a form of literary relation with China that thrives in the uncertainty of a world thrown into crisis, with no easy resolution in sight.

FIVE

On Correspondence
Lu Xun and Premchand

THE TASK OF comparing Chinese and Hindi literatures presents as among its most evident objects of inquiry the pairing together of two writers: Lu Xun and Premchand. Widely considered the progenitors of modern Chinese and Hindi literatures, respectively, Lu Xun and Premchand seem to lend themselves naturally to comparison. The two led uncannily parallel lives. Born in 1880, Premchand was a year older than Lu Xun; they died days apart in 1936. Both quickly acquired towering presences in their literary spheres. In the 1930s, both held leadership positions in and delivered the inaugural addresses to their respective Leagues of Left-Wing Writers (in India, the All-India Progressive Writers' Association).[1] Their literary practice similarly bears striking resonance. Each has been credited with vernacularizing literature: Lu Xun, for his championing of *baihua,* and Premchand, for his pioneering use of Khari Boli Hindi. Their writings sparked the rise of Chinese and Hindi progressive literature, sustained by a moral conviction both espoused in literature's capacity and responsibility to effect social change. Their oeuvres abound with aesthetic and ideological similarities, as extant scholarship on this topic has assiduously catalogued.[2]

If Lu Xun and Premchand appear ideally suited for comparison, the question of how to go about conducting this comparison presents a conundrum. Lu Xun and Premchand never met and, given constraints on circulation and translation, could not have read each other. Accordingly, one approach could entail plotting resonances and dissonances between their life and works, exemplifying a practice that seeks to connect distant texts by identifying common denominators and aesthetic and contextual intersections. Such a project would, however, confront a charge comparatists have long faced, of imposing upon disparate texts an externally derived normative standard of measure, thereby posing equivalences that only perpetuate structures of inequity and dominance.[3] A study seeking to compare Lu Xun and Premchand's practices of social realism, for instance, would inescapably require posing at the outset some model of "social realism," perhaps of Soviet origins, reifying the now invalidated notion of social realism as a unitary genre and obscuring Lu Xun and Premchand's own vastly varied experiments with capturing life in literary form. An attempt to avoid such dangers may lead the critic to begin with the texts themselves, by highlighting resonant particularities of their writings, such as, to cite a common topic of study, their shared interest in depicting peasants and rural life.[4] Still, such efforts would fall prey to "an epistemological instrumentalism built into metaphoric thought as a form of analogy."[5] In other words, the literary figure of the peasant would invariably function as an abstracted metaphor that establishes equivalency between Lu Xun and Premchand through analogy; "the image exists to serve the concept" as opposed to being read in and of itself.[6]

The specific case of Lu Xun and Premchand poses a further challenge to the imperative of comparison. Lu Xun held a lifelong contempt for India and remained outspoken in his criticism of Indian literature. He famously termed India "a shadow nation" (*yingguo* 影國), as this chapter goes on to discuss, for what he perceived as India's cultural decline from its heights of civilizational glory in ancient times, and its apparent failure to stage literary rebellion against colonization. In Lu Xun's writings, India features as silent, stagnant, and passive, that from which China should distance and differentiate itself. Lu Xun actively sought out, translated, and publicly reflected upon literatures of the world. Premchand, although well read and widely informed, tended to turn his literary gaze inward so as to scrutinize India's inherent systems of injustice and inhumanity from within.[7] In light of Lu Xun's disdain for India and Premchand's seeming disinterest in China, the critic's foisting them together risks being disingenuous and antithetical to the two writers' own writing and commitments.

Comparison notoriously decontextualizes, dehistoricizes, deterritorializes; why then compare Lu Xun and Premchand at all? In the 1950s, the translators who first made Lu Xun available in Hindi and Premchand in Chinese introduced each in the image of the other—Premchand as "the Lu Xun of India" and Lu Xun as the "Premchand of China"—casting each as the other's mediator and referent.[8] This pattern of designation, one that continues to hold sway, captures something of the experience of reading Lu Xun in India and Premchand in China: for those familiar with Premchand, for instance, reading Lu Xun elicited a powerful and revelatory sense of self-identification. So, in a 1956 speech delivered in Beijing, Premchand's close friend and frequent interlocuter, the Hindi writer Jainendra declared, "Ah Q is a character we have seen in India."[9] The task of comparing Lu Xun and Premchand, then, arises from and responds to the reader's intuitive sense of commensurability, even camaraderie, between the two. For generations of readers, the Lu Xun-Premchand pairing requires no justification, it simply exists, an immediate and experiential truth.

This chapter takes up the challenge of reading Lu Xun and Premchand comparatively. The two writers offer a case of comparison that seems self-evident and inevitable, and yet the act of actually conducting that comparison frustrates any easy response to the questions of how to compare, and why. The pairing should work, yet somehow it doesn't quite. This conundrum reveals how deeply our ability to think the transnational remains predicated upon paradigms of circulation and connectivity, paradigms that this case puts to the test. The challenge of comparing Lu Xun and Premchand reveals a crisis of transnationalism in its most extreme instantiation: How do we think the transnational in the absence of any evidence of, or even desire for, relation? Confronted with these absences, critics have tended to offer comparison as a reparative cure, as supplying that which is deemed missing. There is no material evidence tying the writers to each other, so we search for other historically documented links between the two—for instance, via the posthumous translations and reception of their works.[10] Alternatively, we craft aesthetic connection as a corrective to the writers' lived conditions of separation. In a previous iteration of this chapter, I envisioned an "unspoken dialogue" between the two, but that conceptualization reaches for the metaphor of dialogue to compensate for its lack, to bridge distance, fill gaps, and pave the missing pathways along which the transfer of meaning can occur.[11] Such strategies seem only to paper over disconnect, and, in so doing, they circumvent—instead of reckon with—the particular challenges of reading Lu Xun and Premchand together.

Here, I embark on an effort not to read dialogue as remediating disconnect, but to read disconnect dialogically. The former approach strives to resolve disconnect, whereas the latter takes disconnect as the necessary conditions that give rise to specific forms of dialogic relation, articulating an exercise in reading comparatively not in spite of but because of, through, and in the constant presence of disconnect. The lack of any historically evidenced connection between Lu Xun and Premchand issues an invitation to contemplate the bounds of historicist thought itself in shaping literary relation. While my readings remain grounded in the historicist impulse to contextualize—indeed, this chapter weaves through the specificities of both writers' literary spheres and interlocuters, of positioning individual texts in relation to their oeuvres, and of their contemporaneous yet differed inhabitance of the colonial world—I draw out such particularities not in order to establish causal links but to reckon with the failure of causality in accounting for how and why to read Lu Xun and Premchand together in the first place. Rather than erasing disconnect, I propose to dwell in it, amid the contingencies that thrive at the limits of historicism and its requisite demands of causality.

I locate such interpretive possibilities, of reading disconnect dialogically, in the idea of correspondence. As an approach to comparison, correspondence first names the readerly intuition of affinity between Lu Xun and Premchand: the powerful sense that one resonates with—or corresponds to—the other, the irresistible pull of tracking similarities that so many readers have pleasured in. I take the salience of this sense of correspondence as a point of departure and add to it the act of corresponding, the epistolary logic enacted in the practice of exchanging letters, of maintaining a correspondence.[12] Activating the epistolary workings of correspondence articulates a dialogic relation borne of and founded upon disconnect, a logic of exchange that can only occur in the face of separation, that contends with the fragmentary, dispersed, mediated, and always incomplete and interrupted quality of reading another's words in a different time and place. In this sense, reading Lu Xun and Premchand's correspondence makes sense of their mutual resonance through an exploration of literary exchange conducted indirectly, in fragments and in mediation, of words and ideas passing through the hands of dispersed writers and readers, of the vagaries of networks enabling, hindering, and transforming the passage of texts, and of the ability of all this chaos to make present a dialogic relation that comes into view only in the absence of causality, immediacy, and direct communication.

A Shadow Nation

"Poets are those who stir up people's hearts," the twenty-six year-old Lu Xun declared in his 1908 essay "On the Power of Mara Poetry" (*Moluo shili shuo* 摩羅詩力說).[13] Two years earlier, Lu Xun had forsaken his medical career in pursuit of a literary one and had joined the community of Chinese intellectuals in late Meiji Tokyo as they debated China's tumultuous path toward the imminent 1911 Revolution. In "Mara Poetry," Lu Xun defines the "Mara poet"—a term that would soon prove formative of both his own literary career and of modern Chinese literary thought—as one "determined to enact rebellion," whose "shout makes those who hear it rise up."[14] Lu Xun introduces his reader to lineages of Mara poetry by tracing the life and works of Byron (Lu Xun's exemplary Mara poet), Shelley, Pushkin, Lermontov, and a selection of Polish and Hungarian poets, all of whom practice, in Lu Xun's reading, a "radical poetics" of revolutionary romanticism.[15] Chinese poets must similarly aspire to incite and "disturb," to "wield arms" as the "warriors of the spirit" and rebel against conformity.[16] Lu Xun endows Mara poetry with the power to spark literary revolution and inaugurate a "national rebirth" (*guoren zhi xinsheng* 國人之新生).[17]

An early expression of Lu Xun's literary thought, "Mara Poetry" sows the seeds of ideas that Lu Xun would go on to wrestle with throughout his literary career. One such idea was Lu Xun's enduring disdain for India. "Mara Poetry" opens with a description of the "ancient imagination" of the world's great civilizations. This ancient imagination produced a wealth of poetry "whose voice travelled through time to enter people's hearts," spreading across the ancient world.[18] There came a time, however, when, "gradually, the culture [of such civilizations] declined, the fortune of the race was exhausted, the voice of the people no longer rang out, their glory no longer shone."[19] "All of them," Lu Xun writes of the transition of ancient civilizations into modern nations, "were reputable at the outset of history, they launched the dawn of culture, but today they have turned into shadow nations. . . . Of those that my countrymen have most commonly heard of, there is none like India."[20]

Lu Xun lists the glories of the ancient Indian civilization: the Vedas that rank among the world's greatest works, the splendid epics of the *Mahābhārata* and the *Rāmāyan*, and the poet and dramatist Kalidasa who received Goethe's unequivocal praise. But, despite these masterpieces, "the race lost its powers, its culture also wiped out, its once great voice gradually no longer rang forth from its people's souls."[21] Lu Xun briefly discusses Israel, Persia, and Egypt as examples of other "shadow nations" before concluding that, among these other nations that stem from ancient civilizations, India alone "seems to be in the depths of profound silence, utterly motionless."[22]

India, the quintessential "shadow nation" for Lu Xun, lurks at the edges of his literary thought, never featuring centrally in his fictional or essayistic writings and only making several fleeting appearances in the guise of a silent shadow. During his studies in Japan, for example, Lu Xun translated and published a collection of short stories in collaboration with his brother Zhou Zuoren. They included writings from Russia, Eastern Europe, England, America, and France, among other literatures.[23] Reflecting on this anthology in a later essay, Lu Xun described his search for "works of revolutionary outcry" as leading him to writings from Eastern Europe, because, although he "enthusiastically sought out such writings from India and Egypt, [he] was unable to find any."[24] Nobel laureate Rabindranath Tagore's visit to China in 1924 only further cemented Lu Xun's disregard for Indian literature. In the Chinese intellectual climate of the time, Lu Xun was not alone in finding Tagore's references to Eastern spirituality too retrogressive and apolitical, his critique of the materialist West as inducive of passivity, and the entourage of Chinese poets who championed his works too obsequious.[25]

Lu Xun charged Tagore with deepening India's silence and further sealing the exclusion of Indian literature from the revolutionary world-literary stage. In 1925, the literary supplement to the *Beijing News Supplement* (*Jingbao fukan* 京報副刊) invited distinguished literary figures to submit their lists of "Essential Books for Youths" (*qingnian bidu shu* 青年必讀書). The daily column published the responses of such figures as Hu Shi and Zhou Zuoren, both of whom recommended a combination of Chinese classical texts and Western writers ranging from Plato to Cervantes.[26] Lu Xun's polemical response appeared in the February 21 issue, some nine months after Tagore's sojourn in China. He declined to suggest specific titles, opting instead to include the following note: "When I read Chinese books, I always feel as though I am descending into quietude, like I am departing from real life; [but when I] read literature of foreign nations—with the exception of India—I always feel connected with life, I feel the urge to *do* something."[27] For Lu Xun, Tagore's works joined the ranks of the other "great" Indian texts, like the spiritual Vedas and epics, which promoted only passivity during an age in sore need of restlessness and action. Two years later, Lu Xun delivered a speech in Hong Kong entitled "Silent China" (*wusheng de Zhongguo* 無聲的中國) in which he once again relegated India to the shadowy realm of silence. "Speak out boldly, advance bravely," Lu Xun admonished the Chinese youth. "Let us try to think of those peoples who are now voiceless. . . . In India, other than Tagore's, is there any other voice?"[28]

As is characteristic of Lu Xun's writing, the polarizing rhetorical thrust of his language remains constantly softened by the complexity of his artistic practice, a practice that conversely favors untenable binaries and blurred distinctions. In "Mara Poetry," Lu Xun initially appears to draw a stark distinction between the old, degenerated "shadow nations" and the new, desirable Mara poets, but soon contrasts between "ancient" and "new," silent and audible, flicker and ultimately disappear.[29] India's "silence" in fact issues lasting echoes throughout the essay. Lu Xun admits to having "borrowed from India" the word "Mara," meaning "the devil, Europeans call this 'Satan'. . . . Now it defines those among all the poets who are determined to enact rebellion."[30] Following his dismissal of India's "ancient imagination," Lu Xun borrows from it the very word that comes to define his notion of poetic resistance.[31] The distance Lu Xun purports to carve out between the ancient and the new collapses into a relation of intimacy.

Silence in Lu Xun's writing seldom denotes emptiness or death, featuring instead as a "tremulous and vibrating" force, ever threatening to splinter and burst into life.[32] Reading such a lively silence at work endows the shadow nation with generative potential. Just as Lu Xun's Sanskritic articulation of an exemplary "Mara" poetics undercuts his pejorative depiction of India, his repeated insistence on India's dark silence serves to illuminate those Indian writings he sought but never found, the Indian texts in circulatory routes that never crossed Lu Xun's path. A prolific literary energy, "tremulous and vibrating," draws Lu Xun into dialogic relation with India, marking the subterranean unfolding of a necessarily impossible correspondence.

Mara Fables

"Other than Tagore's, is there any voice in India?" This question raises an issue central to Lu Xun's view of Indian literature: that of access. Calling for the standardization of vernacular Chinese as the national language, Lu Xun evoked in his "Silent China" speech the metaphor of "loose sand" (*sansha* 散沙) to describe the state of the Chinese people, whose "suffering is no longer interconnected" because writers "speak in the language of ancient times, a language that people do not understand and cannot hear. . . . We no longer need to . . . learn to speak the ancient language of dead people, we should speak the modern language of the living," Lu Xun suggests. "We should use the easy-to-understand vernacular."[33] In its ability to supersede regional and class divides, the vernacular allows the Chinese people to no longer live the scattered existence of "loose sand." In other words, the vernacular affords access: Chinese writers can access a wider audience through their practice, Chinese readers can access "each other's suffering," the Chinese people can access the "language of today" and "give clear expression to [their] thoughts and feelings," and, in so doing, gain access to the world, for only by using the vernacular can the Chinese people "live in the world, alongside the people of the world."[34]

Much like "loose sand," the Chinese and the non-Anglophone Indian literary spheres of the time faced insurmountable linguistic barriers and therefore remained scattered and separate, "oblivious to each other's suffering." During the early decades of the twentieth century, Chinese writers remained largely dependent on English translations of Indian writings to gain access to India's linguistically diverse literatures. As Lu Xun himself noted, however, "when foreigners translate, they do so with ulterior motives."[35] For the Indian Mara writers Lu Xun sought, evading the censors of the paranoid early twentieth-century British government presented a task that proved challenging enough; to reach British and international readerships through English translation was neither a priority nor perhaps even desirable for writers like Premchand. The British government of India aimed to stifle, not propagate, precisely those anticolonial writings Lu Xun expected to find Indian writers engaged in. Unsurprisingly, part of Lu Xun's skepticism towards Tagore emerged from Tagore's popularity in the West and his ability to have gained the official seal of Western approval: the Nobel Prize in Literature and translation into English (and consequently into Chinese).

By contrast, Lu Xun himself famously declined the invitation to be considered for the Nobel Prize.[36] Lu Xun's question "Is there any voice in India?" articulates the irony of access in the colonial world, wherein those voices that espouse Mara qualities become subject to the very suppression and silence that Mara writers rebel against. Read as part of Lu Xun's larger contemplation on the politics of access, therefore, "Is there any voice in India?" questions not the existence of Mara writers in India, but, rather, the audibility of such voices given the colonial power dynamics at play in each instance of publishing, translation, and circulation.

Other than those of Tagore, the Indian writings that did enter into the Chinese literary sphere did not overtly expound Mara qualities and so did not attract Lu Xun's attention. A large group of stories collectively titled *Indian Fables* (*Yindu yuyan* 印度寓言) gained wide circulation among Chinese readers in 1924. Translated by Zheng Zhenduo 鄭振鐸 under the pen name Xidi 西諦, the *Indian Fables* initially appeared in the pages of the popular literary journal *Short Story Monthly* (*Xiaoshuo yuebao* 小說月報) and were later anthologized in an illustrated book published in 1925, with a second, expanded edition appearing in 1931. Zheng's translated stories recall the Indian *Panchatantra* (Five treatises) fables, an ancient text dated to the second century BC.[37]

An important figure in the post-May Fourth Chinese literary scene, Zheng cofounded the Literary Research Association, an influential literary society among writers associated with the New Literature movement.[38] By 1923, Zheng had replaced his close friend Mao Dun as the editor of *Short Story Monthly* and would go on to produce an extensive collection of fiction, poetry, translations, commentaries, and literary histories. Zheng was at the forefront of the New Literature movement that called for Chinese literature "to light the flame of revolution," but he also remained committed to those "genres that for centuries had been . . . slighted as 'vulgar' . . . [Zheng] convincingly showed his readers . . . the originality and ingenuousness typical of folk art."[39] In disagreement with his New Literature contemporaries, Zheng believed in cultivating, rather than severing, China's historical relationship with India given what he emphasized as the lasting influence of Indian Buddhism on Chinese literature. "Without the marriage between China and India," Zheng wrote in 1932, "without the import of Buddhist literature into China, the development of medieval Chinese literature would have occurred under completely different circumstances."[40] Along with his

Indian Fables, Zheng was also responsible for early Chinese translations of Tagore's poetry, several articles defending the poet-novelist's revolutionary thought, and Tagore's first Chinese biography published in 1926. Years later in 1954, Zheng would lead a Chinese delegation on a visit to India during the short-lived era of China-India cultural diplomacy (discussed in chapter 3).[41]

In his preface to the first publication of his translated *Indian Fables* in 1924, Zheng cites the source of the stories as a curious eponymous volume "collected and translated by P. V. Ramaswami Raju," published in London in 1887.[42] Little is known about Raju outside of the short biography included on the title page of his *Indian Fables*, which describes Raju as "of the Inner Temple, Barrister-at-law; Tamil and Telugu Lecturer at University College, London; and late Telugu Lecturer at Oxford."[43] The volume likely fell into Zheng's hands either at the Beijing YMCA library he frequented as a student, or through his peers returning to China from Japan, where, as Zheng notes in his preface, *Indian Fables* was used as a textbook to teach schoolchildren English.[44] Raju's stories (and Zheng's translations) follow a familiar format—stories with titles like "The Fox and the Crabs" and "The Snake and the Parrot" tell of a conflict between two or three main characters (animal, human, or anthropomorphized objects) and end with a distinct epimythium, a concluding "moral" stated at the end of the story.

Late nineteenth-century Europe witnessed the publication of a host of similar volumes carrying "tales from the East." The editors of these books typically claim to have transcribed and translated ancient stories from some "native" Indian oral source, usually a maid or ayah.[45] Raju's book differs from those of the more anthropologically minded collectors of Eastern folk stories in two central ways. First, Raju introduces his fables as primarily instructive not of the Eastern character or people, but, rather, as the source of Western literature: "The East is the original abode of much of the Fable and Romance that have formed the heirloom of this world. . . . When Aesop gave his immortal collection of Fables to the world, he might have derived the bulk of his material from an Eastern source."[46] Second, as an Indian himself, Raju framed himself as a "native," lending an air of authenticity to the collection irrespective of the credibility of his sources. Indeed, Raju remains vague about the sources of his stories. He does not name the *Panchatantra* or any other textual or oral tradition, claiming instead that the volume "is the outcome of continued research during a number of years. . . . Of [the stories] a few have long had a standing in the literature of India, though in a slightly different garb. The rest may be said to have been derived from original sources."[47] The preceding year, Raju published a different volume of fables, *The Tales of the Sixty Mandarins* (1886), containing a collection of fantastical "Eastern" fable-like stories of his own invention.[48] Given Raju's penchant as a fabulist, he likely exercised a free hand and creative license (the "different garb" of the stories) in *Indian Fables*.

Zheng's translation erases Raju's authorial hand and does not consider the implications of the volume's publication in London, which hints at how the book likely helped sate the colonial metropole's voracious appetite for the fabulous East. Instead, Zheng presents Raju's stories as authentic, ancient Indian fables, and even intersperses Raju's stories with others from a Chinese Buddhist text of Indian origins, *The Book of Hundred Parables* (*baiyu jing* 百喻經). In various prefaces to the fables in *Short Story Monthly* and the translated volumes, Zheng contextualizes the stories within the genre of fables, crediting India with the origins of the genre and contrasting the "fable" (*yuyan* 寓言) with the different but related genres of "parable" (*biyu* 比喻) and "myth" (*shenhua* 神話). Of the three genres, Zheng argues, only the fable necessarily fulfills the didactic function of conveying a moral (*jiaoxun* 教訓) and therefore "speaks the truths of the human world."[49]

In one sense, Zheng's interest in Indian fables reflects a larger preoccupation of the New Literature movement with folk culture and the origins of folklore.[50] Beyond such efforts to bring the common folk into the folds of literary production, Zheng's writings also evince an interest in the fable's capacity to effect awakening and, as such, to enact a subversive function. Zheng was drawn to the fable's ability to "conceal" its teaching in the words and actions of its characters, so that "the reader obtains the moral without seeing the teacher standing before him" and can therefore realize and "correct the error of his own ways."[51] Fables "are perceptive and lovely, yet many hold within deeply satirical meanings," Zheng wrote, "although they were written many ages ago, yet, they seem as though they were created for the people of today."[52]

Upon the world-literary terrain of the colonial era, the fable acquired a uniquely mobile quality, its outwardly benign, apolitical mien granting it the ability to travel great distances and appeal to varied readerships on both sides of the colonizer/colonized divide. As they passed through the hands of Raju's enterprising authorship, British readers enthralled by the fabulous East, students in Japan learning English via seemingly neutral, approachable texts, and eventually into the Chinese literary sphere, the Indian fables transformed from orientalist artifacts telling timeless tales into stories "created for the people of today," bearing specific political resonance and holding the potential to incite.[53] The fable's wide accessibility has much to do with the particular affordances of its form. On its face, the fable appears to predetermine its own interpretation, the epimythium appended to its end fixing the story's meaning and offering the reader prescribed instruction on exactly how to understand the story. It is precisely this presumed stability, that the fable allows only a singular, universal reading, regardless of the specificities of the time and place of its composition and consumption, that casts the fable as innocuous enough to gain easy circulation in a world-literary climate hypersensitive to the risky potentiality of texts to yield politically rousing interpretations. And yet tracking the fable's itinerary in the colonial world reveals the deceptiveness of its self-proclaimed fixity. The fable's predilection for the fantastic and its disinterest in the tenets of realism—the dominant genre of choice for revolutionary and anticolonial writing of the day—enable it to rebel against its own didacticism, conversely endowing it with the capacity to be read multiply. In the guise of a harmless, minor story, the fable holds the potential to furnish the ideal literary grounds for cultivating Mara poetics and initiating incendiary innovation of the kind Lu Xun had called for.

The Mara potential of the fable makes possible a correspondence—an affinity that takes shape according to the epistolary logic of a figurative exchange conducted in the absence of connectivity, in fragments and in mediation—between Lu Xun and Premchand, for both writers returned to experiments with the fable throughout their literary careers, repeatedly reconsidering the affordances of the fabular form at the same time as they outwardly promoted a practice of less fantastical and more "realistic" writing.[54] In its rare ability to straddle the dual registers of universal and particular, ancient and new, silent and audible, fantastic and real, the fable, under Lu Xun and Premchand's pens, emerges unexpectedly as the exemplary Mara form, capable at once of "stirring up" the contextually rooted reader and of the achieving the world-literary status Lu Xun had envisioned in his transnational and translational conceptualization of Mara poetics. In what follows, this chapter delves into Lu Xun and Premchand's experiments with and explorations of the Mara capacity of the fable, modeling a practice of reading Lu Xun and Premchand together that reopens the by now overdetermined interpretive horizons of their individual works, bringing to light previously isolated and inaccessible realms of the Chinese and Indian literary spheres, and returning to Mara poetics—commonly understood as a uniquely Chinese formulation—the worldly dimension Lu Xun had once envisioned.

The Last Drop of Blood

In 1908, as Lu Xun wrote "Mara Poetry" in Tokyo, Dhanpat Rai, who the world would come to know as Premchand, published his first short story collection, *Dirge of the Nation* (*Soz-e-vatan*), under the pen name Nawab Rai. At the time, the young writer held a government position as a subdeputy inspector of schools in the United Provinces of British India.[55] Soon after the publication of *Dirge*, the explicit patriotic fervor expressed in the stories brought Rai to the attention of the censors. The local authorities convened an investigation into the authorship of *Dirge*, and since Rai was unable to disown his writing, he had no choice but to confess to his crime of sedition.[56] "You should be happy that you work in the service of the British government," the collector apparently smirked. "If these were Mughal times, you'd have your hands chopped off for spreading such insurrection."[57] The local authorities ordered that all extant copies of *Dirge* be burned, and that Rai's future writings be subject to official approval.[58] Not one to so easily succumb, Rai adopted a new pen name—Premchand—and embarked on a new literary career, publishing some three hundred short stories, twelve novels, and numerous translations and essays that would lay the foundations of modern Urdu and Hindi literatures.

Dirge contains five short stories, each an experiment in inflecting fiction with a political consciousness and nationalist message. As a whole, the collection explores expressions of familial, romantic, and patriotic love. Characters face challenges that call for prioritizing one kind of love over the others, only to realize that love for the nation subsumes and surpasses all other forms of love. Several of the stories read as fantastical and timeless tales, featuring wars waged against invaders to return the rightful people to power. In one such mythic story, "Sheikh Makhmoor," a country (*mulk*) named Jannatnishan (literally, "paradise-like") falls into the hands of unjust rulers. As an army gathers to return the rightful heir to the throne, the rebel

soldiers declare, "We will throw down the gauntlet in the face of our enemies! We will make our blood flow out like water for the sake of our dear
Jannatnishan."⁵⁹ Premchand's charges of sedition arose from such episodes
that draw implicit parallels between the invasion of fictional lands and
India's colonization and promote rebellion as a means to achieve freedom.

The most fable-like story in *Dirge* and Premchand's earliest short story,
"The Most Valuable Jewel in the World" (*Duniyā kā sabse anmol ratn*), exemplifies the collection's thematic concern with the intersecting emotive
threads of love and patriotism. The story follows the quest of its hero Dilfigar (literally, "wounded heart"), the true suitor of the princess Dilfareb
("trickster of the heart"). Dilfareb presents him with a challenge: "If you are
indeed my true love, go and bring back to my court the most valuable thing
in the world."⁶⁰ Dilfigar sets out on his quest and, after much searching, happens upon a scene of execution. As a criminal sentenced to death embraces
his son for the final time, tears spill out of his eyes. Dilfigar carries a tear-
drop back to Dilfareb who praises his attempt, but the tear, she says, is not
the most valuable thing in the world. A despondent Dilfigar sets out once
more. He travels "from east to west, from north to south, how many forests
and deserts he scanned, at times sleeping on the peaks of snowy mountains,
at times wandering in frightful valleys, but nowhere could he find the thing
he sought."⁶¹ Then, in a passage I return to below, he chances upon a scene
of sati and presents the ashes to Dilfareb, only to be turned away again. Dilfigar resumes his quest, this time contemplating conceding failure. An old
man suddenly appears and provides guidance: "In the East, there is a country named 'Hindustan' [India], go there and you will find what you seek."⁶²
India, Dilfigar soon discovers, is a horrifying, bloody battlefield littered with
the corpses of soldiers. "I am the son of India," the last living soldier tells
him. "Today, we have lost the nation of our fathers and grandfathers, and
now we are nation-less [*bevatan*]. . . . Why should I stay alive just to be a slave
in my own nation?"⁶³ The soldier dies with the words "Victory to Mother
India" on his lips. Dilfigar takes the soldier's last drop of blood to his princess. Finally, Dilfareb accepts him and presents him with a tablet upon which
are inscribed the following words in golden letters: "The last drop of blood
shed in the defense of the nation is the most valuable thing in the world."⁶⁴

Critics have categorized "The Most Valuable Jewel" as belonging to the
dāstān genre, a close relative of the fable.⁶⁵ Of Persian origin, the *dāstān*
typically features marvelous adventures, heroic quests, and romantic

encounters.[66] Like other literary traditions with oral roots, the *dāstān* "relied on the imaginative appeal of fantasy—enhanced by the opium preparations which both narrator and listeners customarily drank."[67] *Dāstān* stories characteristically unfold with a formulaic repetition of episodes and a cast of archetypical characters (e.g., the hero, the heroine, fairies who come to aid of humans). In this formal sense, Dilfigar and his quest fit comfortably within this generic landscape.

However, "The Most Valuable Jewel" consistently pushes against the generic conventions of the *dāstān*. A defining feature of the *dāstān* is that it concludes with a stasis: the hero overcomes all obstacles and "achieves his goal, he reaches a secure and happy state in which all his desires have been fulfilled, and further hazards are not to be expected."[68] Significantly, "The Most Valuable Jewel" concludes not with the "happily ever after" of hero and heroine, but with the words "The last drop of blood shed in the defense of the nation is the most valuable thing in the world." As the golden inscription on Dilfareb's tablet, this sentence initially appears structurally integrated into the body of the story: the narrative simply "reads out" the words inscribed on an object that doubles as a physical, eternal manifestation of the ephemeral drop of blood, and as a symbol of the union between Dilfigar and Dilfareb. On the page, however, this inscription appears indented away and as visually separate from the story, resembling a classic fable-like epimythium.[69] With the inclusion of this concluding line, Premchand's *dāstān* no longer serves the purpose of mere entertainment or opium-fueled flights of fancy; instead, Premchand borrows from the fable's conventions to inject the story with pedagogical intent, plainly appending the story's moral to its conclusion and thereby endowing it with an instructive function. Departing from the *dāstān*, "The Most Valuable Jewel" fulfills the didactic criterion Zheng deemed essential to the fable.

Premchand's epimythium deliberately disrupts the stasis achieved in Dilfareb's eventual acceptance of Dilfigar. Contrary to the fulfillment and satisfaction conveyed in the final encounter between the two, the moral differs dramatically in tone, evoking discontent, violence, and sacrifice. The image of the last drop of blood recalls the bloody scene Dilfigar had encountered in India: "A barren field where countless dead and dying bodies lay exposed. . . . The entire field had turned red with blood. Dilfigar's heart trembled. . . . The groans of the dying, their sobs, their prolonged deaths. . . . Never before had Dilfigar witnessed such a horrifying scene."[70] Read as a moral to be imbibed, the inscription calls for the actualization of this fictional scene, one in which patriots shed every last drop of blood in defense of the nation. As horrifying a scene as the moral conjures, the true "sons of India" must fight until the end, no longer content to live as "nation-less slaves" in their own land.

In this way, the moral of the story exceeds its didactic purpose. Despite the visual clues that mark the story's final line as a "moral," the sentence in fact presents an urgent call to arms. The conclusion of the story does not provide the narrative totality and complete resolution of "happily ever after"; instead, the moral opens up a field of restlessness, indefinitely postponing the story's true conclusion and bestowing readers with the responsibility of writing it. The classic epimythium tends to look backward at the fable in summarizing or reiterating the moralistic stance conveyed and in doing so brings the narrative full circle. Premchand's concluding sentence points toward the unwritten future—the impending real battle waged by the true sons of India in defense of their nation—thereby enacting a radical break in the narrative circle. The eulogy for the last drop of blood inscribed upon Dilfareb's tablet reveals itself as a prophecy, one so threatening and foreseeable that the British government thought the extreme measure of burning hundreds of copies of the story appropriate if only to keep readers from hearing Premchand's call.

In addition to its rousing message, "The Most Valuable Jewel" also practices Lu Xun's Mara poetics in its violent tenor. Throughout his "Mara Poetry," Lu Xun argues that Mara poets are those with a "willingness to kill," who "take up arms and shed blood. . . . If there are none [willing to] shed blood in front of the people, that is a disaster [for the people]."[71] Jon Kowallis reads such moments in "Mara Poetry" as expressing Lu Xun's belief in the efficacy of violent rebellion, suggesting that although Lu Xun "longed for peaceful resolutions of conflict, he realized that to require the oppressed and exploited to rely only on peaceful means of protest, while reserving violence as the monopoly of the state . . . [could] ultimately lead to greater cycles of violence" and only further perpetuate existing societal imbalances.[72] Significantly, "the last drop of blood shed in the defense of the nation" makes no promises of victory, emphasizing instead the bloodshed of a violent and righteous battle. Premchand's placement of the battlefield scene as the final and most poignant episode in Dilfigar's quest, the only one that gains Dilfareb's wholehearted acceptance of Dilfigar, further strengthens the story's sanction of violent means for national liberation, enabling the narrative to issue a forceful call to arms. Later in their careers, both Lu Xun and Premchand espoused changing evaluations on the role of violence in effecting change. At this early juncture in their literary lives, however, their writings draw a thin line between a literal and a figurative wielding of the pen and sword.

The Sati's Ashes

The battlefield scene and the inscription on the tablet may not have comprised the only components of "The Most Valuable Jewel" that the censors deemed seditious. Equally inflammatory, a scene depicting the controversial practice of sati lies at the heart of the story. During the second episode of his quest, Dilfigar happens upon the following scene:

> A pyre built of sandalwood, and on top of it, sits a young woman wearing her wedding finery and the sixteen adornments. Her dear husband's head lies upon her thigh. Thousands have gathered, and they rain flowers [on the woman]. Suddenly, a flame leaps alive from the pyre. The sati's face comes aglow with a light of purity. The pure flames embrace her, and in the blink of an eye, that flower-like body turns into a pile of ashes. The loving wife had sacrificed herself to her beloved. The last flame of the two lovers' true, pure, and immortal love blew out.[73]

Critics largely agree that the treatment of women in Premchand's works indicates his progressive attitude toward social reform, albeit with some ambivalences.[74] As a whole, Premchand's oeuvre expresses a continued and liberal involvement with the changing societal views toward women in early twentieth-century India. Francesca Orsini identifies "Premchand's critique of patriarchy [as] beyond dispute," for "it is only with Premchand that we have in Hindi and Urdu literature a sense that women make up half of society, and that they are as varied in character and social position as men."[75] In numerous short stories and novels, through a variety of female characters including wives, mothers, widows, and both low-caste and elite women, Premchand wrestles with the "nationalist valorization of Indian woman as emblem of self-sacrifice and service," the "domestic cruelty" of the patriarchal family, and the agency of women in producing "desired change in their homes."[76] Premchand's own relationships similarly evince his lifelong advocacy for women. After his first marriage dissolved, Premchand agreed to a second marriage upon his family's urging, but only on the condition that he would marry a widow, since he himself had been married before.[77] In 1905, he married a child widow, Shivrani Devi, expressing his stance in support of widow remarriage, then considered taboo. Given Premchand's sensitivity to women's issues and his progressive stance, the scene of sati in "The Most Valuable Jewel," especially his highly romanticized portrayal of self-immolation as the "flower-like body turning into ash," appears incongruent.[78]

Premchand's scene of sati is perhaps better understood in the context of the early nineteenth-century debates between British officials and Indian intellectuals surrounding the British abolition of sati in 1829. Lata Mani has argued that although British officials claimed to oppose sati because of its "cruelty or barbarity," concern for the treatment of women in fact played a minor role in the debates.[79] Instead, widow self-immolation became "the occasion for struggle over the divergent priorities of [British] officials and the indigenous male elite," mainly concerning the definition of "tradition."[80] For the British, the act of sati placed in contention two foundational tenets of the colonial civilizing mission in India: the aim of rescuing the uncivilized from their own savagery on one hand, and the policy of noninterference in native customs and religion on the other.[81] The decision to regulate sati hinged on whether the practice was in fact a "religious tradition," an issue the British approached through a convoluted process that essentially invented "a scriptural sanction and a [textual] religious tradition . . . for a practice which had been diverse, variable, and uneven."[82] On the other side, both "progressive" Indian intellectual elites supporting abolition and "conservatives" opposing criminalization mirrored the British in grounding their arguments in interpretations of the scriptures. As a result, "the women who burned were neither the subjects nor the objects of concern in the debates. . . . They were, rather, the ground for a complex and competing set of struggles over Indian society and definitions of Hindu tradition."[83]

The rhetorical tendency to treat sati as the grounds upon which to debate Indian tradition (instead of the sati—literally the "good wife"—herself) gained an afterlife in Chinese intellectual circles, most commonly in response to Tagore's writings. In his famous 1918 essay entitled "Humane Literature" (*Ren de wenxue* 人的文學), Zhou Zuoren calls for a New Literature that "affirms human life" and takes "human morality as its basis."[84] "Forcing people to commit suicide is exactly what constitutes inhuman morality," Zhou writes. "Such writings are therefore not humane literature."[85] In his discussion of Tagore, Zhou's critique of "inhuman morality" collapses into a critique of Indian tradition: "Another case is the Indian poet Tagore, who in his novels continuously sings the praises of Eastern thought. In one story he records the life of a widow and describes her 'sati of the heart.'" By "sati of the heart," Zhou refers not to Tagore's view of the practice of sati, but to his treatment of the widow as a sati, denoting her lifelong devotion to her husband. Positing sati as the death knell of "free choice," Zhou argues that if one "from free choice binds oneself in love to another . . . this indeed might be called a matter of morality. . . . An act brought about under pressure of despotic traditional societal rules and rituals is an altogether different matter." Zhou concludes his discussion of sati by alluding to a common accusation leveled against Tagore: "Those who expound 'Easternization' may consider it a valuable national characteristic, whereas in fact it is merely the evil fruit of an unnatural custom."[86] As Mani has shown, Indian elites' arguments against the abolition of sati had little to do with the practice of sati in itself and had more to do with protecting from colonial intervention the "private" sphere of tradition (considered separate from the public sphere of civil society, which was already subject to colonial rule). Zhou interprets this line of argumentation instead as Indian nationalists' subscription to a despotic tradition in the guise of a "national characteristic," and their consequent endorsement of "evil" and "unnatural" customs. Zhou would likely have read Premchand's depiction of sati in a similar vein.

In 1921, Lu Xun also charged Indians (and Tagore) with glorifying sati and thereby betraying their complicity in their own colonization: "As for Indians, they do not feel any distress towards their [own enslavement], they do not strive to live a humane life. Instead, they are furious at those who ban 'sati.' Therefore, even if there were no enemy [colonizer], [Indians] would still be 'lowly slaves' within the cage."[87] Lu Xun shifts the blame for India's colonization away from the British ("those who ban sati") and onto Indian tradition, suggesting that the latter functions as the true perpetrator of India's enslavement. Lu Xun included these thoughts in a postscript to his translation of the Russian writer Vasili Eroshenko's short story "A Narrow Cage," to which the phrase "lowly slaves within the cage" alludes. The postscript ends with a comparison between Eroshenko and Tagore: "I love this childlike, blind Russian poet Eroshenko indeed far more than the Nobel Prize recipient, Indian poet-saint Tagore, who only praises the 'sati' of other countries."[88] In line with the nineteenth-century sati debates in India, Lu Xun employs the word "sati" as a euphemism for the same objects of Zhou's critique—"Eastern" "despotic" tradition.

Lu Xun deemed a distinction between Eroshenko and Tagore especially necessary in light of a central scene in "A Narrow Cage," one depicting an act of sati. Lu Xun likely anticipated that Eroshenko's depiction of "sati," a word that by this time Chinese writers used as synonymous with India's degeneration, would expose the writer to the same criticism Tagore's works had received. Lu Xun translated Eroshenko into Chinese in order to champion the latter's writings, particularly his children's stories, many of which took the form of fairy tales and fables. The postscript to "A Narrow Cage," therefore, attempts to defend Eroshenko's depiction of sati. Preempting any equation between Tagore and Eroshenko, Lu Xun differentiates Eroshenko's position from Tagore's as not in "praise" of but in protest against sati and, by extension, the binds of Indian tradition. A closer look at the scene of sati in "A Narrow Cage," however, paints a far more ambiguous picture of Eroshenko's politics as expressed in the story.

Born in Russia in 1890, Eroshenko lost his vision as a child and later enrolled in the Moscow School of the Blind, where he developed the stirrings of an anti-imperialist, radical politics. By 1909, Eroshenko's involvement with the World Esperanto Association took him to London and Tokyo. 1917 brought the October Revolution, and Eroshenko traveled to Calcutta, India, in hopes of returning to Russia from there. British authorities, however, suspected him of collusion with the Bolsheviks and expelled him on the basis of sedition. He returned to Tokyo in 1919, where he befriended Lu Xun and was embraced by Chinese leftist intellectuals "as an emblem of intellectual adventure and new political possibilities."[89] During this time, Eroshenko wrote "A Narrow Cage" in Japanese (in which he had become fluent), with the "thoughts and outrage [he experienced] while in India . . . drifting" through his mind.[90] Eroshenko apparently once said to Lu Xun, "This story was written using blood and tears."[91]

"A Narrow Cage" is set in India and casts a tiger as its protagonist. In the opening scene, the tiger lies languishing inside a cage in a zoo, lamenting his captivity. Suddenly, he opens his eyes to find himself in a forest. He joyfully realizes that his captivity in the narrow cage had been but a nightmare. A series of episodes follows, each depicting the tiger's failed attempts to free those around him from their captivity. In one such episode, the tiger watches as the king's new bride is carried into the palace, as though entering a cage of her own. The tiger breaks into the palace in an attempt to free the queen, but mistakenly kills the king in a scuffle. The young queen is now a widow.

The scene of sati ensues. Concealed in the shadows of the forest, the tiger watches the king's funerary procession as a group of "Brahmins" and their "slaves" lead the queen onto the pyre alongside the king's coffin. Ready to pounce to the queen's rescue, the tiger observes her despair. Suddenly, troops break onto the scene and a "white man [waves] a strange slip of paper in the air, [issues] some sort of order, [escorts] the deer-like woman down from the pyre, and [folds] her into an embrace."[92] The scene suggests that the queen and the "white man" are involved in a romantic relationship. Later that night, the tiger watches as the queen returns to the forest alone wracked with guilt for evading sati at the hands of the white man; she cries out that she has forsaken her nation and plunges a dagger into her breast.

Contrary to Lu Xun's promotion of Eroshenko as an anti-imperialist, in "A Narrow Cage" Eroshenko replicates several aspects of the colonial discourse on sati. Most strikingly, Eroshenko's scene rehearses the sentence Gayatri Chakravorty Spivak famously posits as a summary of the history of the Hindu widow's repression: "White men are saving brown women from brown men."[93] This sentence represents the colonial creation of a discourse on the self-immolating widow that functions simultaneously to constitute and silence her. Following such a formulation, Eroshenko's "brown men" (the Brahmins) are characteristically conniving; the "white man" is gallant, heroically brandishing both the moralistic law (the piece of paper) and the widow's true love; the "brown woman" emerges as the ultimate victim in need of rescuing ("deer-like"), through the gaze of the tiger and the white man alike. For Spivak, such a discourse functions to mark the widow's "place of 'disappearance' with something other than silence and nonexistence, a violent aporia between subject and object status."[94] At the moment of her death, Eroshenko's widow inhabits precisely such an aporia: her exercise of "agency" is founded paradoxically on the utter lack of agency she is afforded in the scene, as demonstrated in her ultimate "choice" of a "voluntary" suicide instead of the forced sati. Before she stabs herself, the widow explicitly voices her eternal lack of choice. She laments the various parties she has wronged in being "saved" from committing sati by the white man—the gods, the Brahmins, even India—and, as such, she exemplifies Spivak's subaltern woman as one violently shuttled between the palimpsestic brinks of her repression.

In Lu Xun's reading, Eroshenko's sati exposes the intrinsic complacency and resultant enslavement of the Indian people, even in the absence of a colonizer; Lu Xun frames sati as a figment of precolonial, traditional India, a marker of India's backwardness and complicity in its own enslavement. Bringing Spivak to bear on Eroshenko reveals that this supposed "exposure" only reproduces the colonial discourse on sati. In other words, it is hardly surprising that Lu Xun finds no evidence of Indian rebellion in "A Narrow Cage," for what Lu Xun reads as Eroshenko's critique of the Indian colonial condition in fact only reenacts British epistemic colonization, a process that necessarily quashes rebellion and strives to render resistance silent.

Eroshenko's treatment of sati—refracted through Lu Xun's translation and endorsement—offers a mirror, reflective but inversely so, through which to reread Premchand. Premchand's scene of sati begins to articulate the critique Lu Xun sought (though perhaps not in Lu Xun's preferred terms), a critique of the representational strategies used to depict sati in colonial discourse. Contrary to Eroshenko's portrayal, Premchand's scene of sati exhibits a relative brevity and lack of theatricality. Indeed, Premchand devotes only a few sentences to the entire event and includes none of the dramatics surrounding the burning, such as Eroshenko's details of the pyre's construction, the widow's placement atop it, the setting of fire, plot twists, rescues, and so on. In fact, Premchand carefully erases the need for additional characters (white men, brown men) in the scene—the fire leaps alive as though of its own accord (*khud-b-khud*), the undifferentiated and silent crowd simply spectates. Amid the profusion of debating voices that constituted the colonial discourse on sati, and the many chaotic and clumsy processes that attempted to adjudicate the practice, Premchand's writes the act of sati as quiet and fleeting. The practice of sati, no longer the grounds for debate over Indian tradition, becomes centrally about the sati (good wife) as a symbol for love and devotion, a symbol Dilfigar sought to bring back to Dilfareb.

Premchand's scene of sati expresses a concern neither for the realistic details of actual burnings, nor for "rescuing" the widow or undoing her layers of repression; such concerns are not dismissed but bracketed. The fabular air of "The Most Valuable Jewel" allows Premchand to circumvent the thorny task of capturing a "real" scene of sati or of expressing an ethical stance toward it. On one hand, Premchand's romanticized equation of idealized devotion with the self-immolating widow cements the story within discourses of Hindu patriarchy, and yet the story's disinterest in the tenets of realism reframes its concern as not with the sati herself but with the representational strategies used to depict her. As such, "The Most Valuable Jewel" could be read as posing a challenge to the colonialist discourse of representing sati, a discourse that Eroshenko partakes in. In the large collection of British eyewitness accounts describing the practice, most share "cardinal moments" such as the British narrator's "attempts at dissuasion [of the widow]; [his] observation of the practices that preceded the burning; the setting alight of the pyre and destruction of the widow."[95] The accounts often detail successful "rescues," the women "being woken from their misguided reverie primarily by European dissuasion and the shock of physical pain, whereupon they are saved by their (usually Western) protectors."[96] Ultimately, sati appears in such accounts as the ultimate spectacle, evoking "the twin compulsions of horror and fascination."[97] Free from the surrounding chatter of competing interests, Premchand's sati unfolds in markedly straightforward and nonritualistic terms. Dilfigar observes the sati not as spectacle, in neither horror nor fascination, but as a quiet and poignant symbol of the eternal love that drives his quest.

Premchand's discursive rebellion against colonial strategies of representation unfolds in conjunction with his generic exploration of the Mara capabilities of the *dāstān* and fable. The fantastical and wondrous elements of the story allow the scene of sati a distance from realistic and material concerns with the practice, allowing the sati to occur in symbolic defiance of its official abolition. Still, while this literary persistence of sati may have contributed to the authorities' interpretation of the story as seditious, Premchand's careful placement of the scene as second (and not final) within the formulaic *dāstān* structure deemphasizes sati as a prescribed form of rebellion. After the flame of immortal love blows out, Dilfigar gathers a handful of ashes and rushes back to Dilfareb, this time convinced of his success. He presents the ashes to Dilfareb and narrates the scene to her "in words capable of melting one's heart."[98] Initially speechless, Dilfareb slowly responds, "Undoubtedly, these ashes you have brought me, which have the power to turn iron into gold, are among the world's most valuable things. From the bottom of my heart, I thank you for this precious gift. But there is something in the world even more valuable."[99] Dilfigar must set out once more. Dilfareb's gentle rejection of the ashes underscores the story's message:

the epimythium calls for readers to enact their rebellion against the colonizers through a different kind of violent sacrifice, one that must be staged on the battlefield.

Premchand devoted much of his later career to accomplishing what remains incomplete in "The Most Valuable Jewel"—namely, a critique of the Indian nationalist tendency to treat the woman as the inanimate grounds upon which to define and defend the autonomy and perceived purity of Hindu tradition. His later works stage a rebellion, articulated in the idiom of realism, against the many inequalities and hierarchies of Indian society. This early story, however, identifies British colonization squarely as the target of its critique. In its scene of sati, the story stages its anticolonial protest on two fronts: it disavows the representational practices of the colonial discourse on sati (the strategies used to depict sati in late nineteenth-century British eyewitness accounts, reiterated in Eroshenko's story), and it enacts literary disobedience in its symbolic disregard of the British legal ban on sati. Even at its most conservative, the story's subversive aesthetics and inflammatory message inaugurate its entrance into the realm of Mara poetics.

Outcry

Lu Xun's translation of Eroshenko's "A Narrow Cage" catapulted the story into an "instant sensation" among its newfound Chinese readership: "The phrase 'a narrow cage' quickly entered into wide circulation as a figure for the stifling traditional culture and oppressive familial arrangements by which the rebellious [Chinese] youth of the era felt themselves afflicted."[100] As an example of this new Chinese iteration of the "narrow cage," Andrew Jones cites Ba Jin's 1931 novel *Family* (*Jia* 家), a story about "May Fourth intellectuals freeing themselves from the stultifying confines of a provincial gentry family," in which Ba Jin appropriates the narrow cage as "a kenning and a key for the thematic thrust of the novel as a whole."[101] In this way, "a narrow cage" circulated in the Chinese literary sphere as shorthand for captivity, suffocation, and oppression, carrying within it traces of its earlier articulation in Eroshenko's story as an allegory for the layers of repression endemic to the colonial condition.

Eroshenko's continued influence in the works of May Fourth writers gains heightened significance in light of his deep association with Lu Xun. Jones has persuasively argued against the conception of Lu Xun as a singular figure with a stable authorial identity. The stability of Lu Xun's authorial identity comes into question particularly in light of his friendship with Eroshenko, since Lu Xun "simultaneously authors and is authored by Eroshenko in the act of translating him"; Lu Xun's writings may therefore be better understood as presenting "a composite voice constructed through myriad processes of creative citation."[102] The image of "the narrow cage" might offer one such case of "creative citation," Jones suggests, in its "prefiguring of Lu Xun's parable . . . about another sort of cage": that of the iron house.[103]

In December 1922, a year after he published his translation of "A Narrow Cage," Lu Xun wrote a preface to his first short story collection, Outcry (Nahan 吶喊, also translated as A Call to Arms). In this autobiographical preface, Lu Xun describes the current predicament facing Chinese writers through the following parable:

> Imagine an iron house, without any windows, impossible to destroy, and inside there lie many people sleeping soundly—it will not be long before they all suffocate to death. They enter death during their sleep, without the pain and sorrow of [realizing] this impending death. Now, if you rise up and shout out, jolting awake the relatively lighter sleepers, you would cause these unlucky few the inconsolable suffering of their inevitable death. And yet, even if just a few rise up, you cannot say for sure that there is absolutely no hope of breaking down the iron house.[104]

A popular topic of study, this metaphor raises questions that continue to intrigue Lu Xun's readers. What constitutes the iron house? Who are the people sleeping within, and what distinguishes the lighter sleepers from the deeper ones? Who is the figure faced with the predicament of staying silent or crying out? Can the iron house be destroyed, and what would its alternative look like? As close to a century of scholarship on the iron house reveals, Lu Xun provides no easy or fixed answers to these questions, and deliberately so.

Interpretive lineages tend to decipher Lu Xun's parable in some combination of three reading practices: the iron house as symbolic of traditional, Confucian Chinese societal constraints that the May Fourth intellectuals rebelled against; the iron house as expressive of Lu Xun's own inner psyche or of his political stance toward the writer's duty; and the iron house as a literary mechanism encoded within his writings, providing a guide for disentangling motifs and tensions such as old/new, silence/outcry, light/darkness, and loner/crowd in his short stories.[105] Approaching the parable from a different perspective, Jones questions Lu Xun's choice of imagery, since "iron houses as such were neither a common nor practicable type of residential building in China . . . nor is it an image that evokes or retains an organic connection to what we think of as 'traditional China.'"[106] Jones highlights the "semantic ambiguity" of the term "iron house" (*tiewu* 鐵屋, which could also be translated as "iron room," "iron chamber," or "cell") and reads Lu Xun's parable alongside scenes of figures sleeping in cells with iron doors in Edward Bellamy's *Looking Backward: 2000–1987*, Jules Verne's *Twenty Thousand Leagues Under the Sea*, and, importantly, Eroshenko's "A Narrow Cage."

To Lu Xun's iron house and Eroshenko's narrow cage, I add Premchand in a practice of anticolonial poetics concerned with allegorizing captivity, poetics that bind the three writers through the workings not of citation but of contingency. A striking image of Premchand's own "narrow cage" appears in his 1924 short story "A Tale of Two Bullocks" (*Do bailoṁ kī kathā*). Reading this story alongside Lu Xun and Eroshenko reveals interpretative possibilities that remain obscured when the story is approached in isolation, positioned exclusively in the context of Premchand's oeuvre and taken as exemplary of his interest in writing for children, as is most often the case.[107] From its initial guise as an entertaining children's story, "A Tale"—in its correspondence with Lu Xun's "iron house" via Eroshenko's "narrow cage"— emerges as a dark and twisted story narrated in the *dāstān*'s fabular idiom of the episodic quest, one that stages literary rebellion in the same gesture as it reflexively questions the capacity of the fable to bring that rebellion into fruition.

"A Tale" tells of Heera and Moti, two bullocks who develop a close friendship working together on their owner Jhuri's farm. One day, Jhuri decides to send the bullocks away to a relative's farm. Unwilling to forfeit their happy lives under Jhuri's ownership, Heera and Moti, who communicate with each other in a "silent language," decide to escape and return home. The remainder of the story unfolds episodically, following the adventures of the two bullocks as they overcome a series of obstacles on their journey home.

In one episode, Heera and Moti find themselves held captive within an enclosure (*bāṛe*) alongside other stray farm animals: "Some water buffalo, some goats, some horses, some donkeys; none saw any way out, and so they all lay on the floor like corpses."[108] As he observes the sorry state of the other animals, "a flame of rebellion blazes alive in Heera's heart."[109] He begins to ram the walls of the enclosure with his horns in an attempt to break through. A watchman catches Heera in the act and ties him up with a thick rope. Encouraging Moti to continue striking the walls, Heera says, "This [captivity] is no different than dying. If the walls are broken, just think of how many animals would be saved. So many of our brothers are captive here."[110] For the sake of the others, Moti redoubles his efforts. Finally, the walls crumble.

Faced with the sudden prospect of freedom, some of the other animals scamper away, others saunter out, confused and disoriented, until only the donkeys remain. The donkeys insist that they are safer inside the enclosure: "What if we are caught again?" and "We are scared, we'll just stay here," they protest.[111] Moti's attempts to convince the donkeys of the value of freedom fall only on deaf ears; he eventually resorts to forcibly driving the donkeys out with his horns. Unable to break the thick rope binding Heera and unwilling to leave his friend, Moti remains captive in the now open enclosure, and the two together await the punishment they are sure to receive at daybreak.

Most fable-like of Premchand's later works, "A Tale" conveys through fantastical characters and a lighthearted tone a dark story of bondage and the fight for freedom. The scene narrates a series of events that would ring familiar to Lu Xun's reader—Heera's "flame of rebellion" (*vidroh kī jvālā*) in the face of captivity, the predicament the bullocks face as they consider whether to sacrifice their own freedom if only to awaken their "brothers" who lie lifeless and oblivious in imprisonment, the bullocks' attempt to break down the walls of their captivity, their eventual self-sacrifice—painting the story with the parabolic strokes of Lu Xun's iron house. Explicitly inviting an allegoric reading, Premchand prefaces "A Tale" with a contemplation of India's colonial condition. The story opens with an introductory passage in which Premchand likens donkeys and bullocks to different kinds of colonized subjects. The donkey, Premchand writes, endures all injustice without fighting back: "A donkey expressing anger has never been seen or heard. Hit the poor fellow as much as you want . . . but you will never see a shadow of discontent flicker on his face."[112] The donkey's pathetic behavior mirrors that of the colonized Indian. Referring to Indians living in Africa, Premchand accuses the Indian of insisting on suffering in silence, much like the donkey: "Maybe if they [Indians] learned to fight back [literally, "answered bricks with stones"], then perhaps they would be considered civilized." In contrast to the subservient donkey, the bullock is known to "fight back," "rebel," and "express its discontent through a variety of methods."[113] The bullock represents those qualities the donkey (and the Indian he stands for) must strive to acquire.

In light of this preface, the interaction between the two bullocks and the donkeys in the enclosure acquires new meaning. If the donkeys embody the current complacency of the Indian populace toward its own captivity, the bullocks, like the wakened speaker in Lu Xun's iron house, attempt to enlighten and instill a rebellious spirit in these "deep sleepers." While the bullocks stage their protest against their captor, the donkeys ironically protest against their liberators, ventriloquizing the passivity of the colonized Indians in Premchand's preface ("We'll just stay here"). Physically pushing the donkeys into freedom against their will becomes the bullocks' only recourse.

The two bullocks' confrontation with the donkeys recalls the tiger in Eroshenko's "A Narrow Cage," who attempts to set free a captive flock of sheep. As the tiger romps through the forest and surrounding meadows, reveling in his newfound freedom, he happens upon an enclosure holding sheep within. The enclosure evokes memories of the tiger's prior captivity. "He [pounces] as fast as an arrow, his roar more frightening than thunder. . . . The sturdy posts [of the fence] topple one-by-one. . . . Within a couple of moments, a [wide] gap had opened in the fence. . . . You sheep! Dear brothers and sisters. Go out into a world of freedom. Come out of your cage," the tiger entreats, "but the sheep, scared out of their wits, could merely cower together motionlessly in one corner." The tiger grows angry: "Slave of humankind! Lowly slaves! You don't want your freedom?"[114] He lifts each sheep out into freedom, only to find them running back into the enclosure.

Jones studies this scene as an example of what he terms "misprision," the problem of language in the story: "the incommensurability between different languages and codes" of the tiger's "thought-world" and those of the human world he lives in.[115] When the tiger shouts out "slave of humankind" at the sheep, he "fails to realize that his discourse has sounded in the ears of the sheep only as an unintelligible roar."[116] The tiger misinterprets the sheep's inability to understand his language at the same time as he correctly interprets their preference, in the face of a roaring tiger, "to stay within the confines of their own mind-forged manacles."[117]

In "A Tale," the bullocks exhibit not misprision but its inverse: the ability to travel strategically between linguistic codes in order to address their desired audience. They are capable of understanding both human communication and that of various animals. Their private "silent language," sometimes also referred to as "symbolic language" (saṅketik bhāṣā), remains unintelligible to the human world, allowing them to plot coordinated attacks under the surveillance of humans. At the same time, their language affords them complete access to communication in the animal world, mapping the lines between human and animal worlds onto those of captor/captive. Still, language proves insufficient and ineffective. Just as the tiger must resort to physically lifting the sheep out of the enclosure, so must Moti forcibly drive the donkeys out toward their freedom. In both cases, freedom appears unachievable within the confines of mere language. As in Lu Xun's iron house parable, in which the lone figure considers whether his "shouting out," his outcry, can deliver enlightenment, both Premchand and Eroshenko dwell on the relationship between language—the discursive—and action, calling into question the ability of the story itself to break out of its own fantastic universe and into the realm of the real.

Further underscoring the futility of language in destroying the iron walls of captivity, both "A Tale" and "A Narrow Cage" end with the revelation of an unbreakable narrative cycle. The bullocks return home to Jhuri, their giddy joy of being back "at home" tempered by the reader's realization that the freedom the bullocks had sought meant only a return to their original state of captivity on Jhuri's farm. The bullocks simply pass through the hands of various owners in an unending cycle of captivity, never to achieve the freedom they had fought for at the enclosure. The tiger, too, remains trapped within an oppressively cyclical narrative. After the queen commits suicide, the tiger awakens to find himself back in his "narrow cage" at the zoo, where his story had begun. His adventures in the forest had been but a dream, and both the tiger and the reader remain imprisoned "in the very impasse with which [the story] began. . . . The narrative itself becomes a narrow cage."[118]

When inflected with the interpretive possibilities its correspondence with "A Narrow Cage" affords, "A Tale" ventures a response to the question Lu Xun poses in his parable: Is it right to cry out? Premchand suggests that the figure inside the iron house, the only figure aware of its captive state, has no choice but to cry out. The linguistic break between the human and animal worlds in "A Tale" positions the bullocks in a relation of radical sameness with other animals. The bullocks, therefore, have a responsibility to free their captive "brothers," even in light of their own inability to escape (suffocation, for Lu Xun). Ever the idealist, Premchand also echoes Lu Xun's suggestion that the outcry provides "hope" for the iron house's eventual destruction. By the end of the story, the bullocks no longer represent the figure within the iron house: they are no longer aware of their own state of captivity as Jhuri's beasts of burden. In an unexpected turn of events, it is the donkeys, absent from the pages of the story after their exit from the enclosure, who now possess the power to enlighten. Ejected out of the binds of the oppressively cyclical narrative, the unknown fate of the donkeys holds the possibility of their freedom and a hope for rebellion unfolding elsewhere, this time in response to a donkey's outcry.

Both Lu Xun and Premchand died before the literary revolutions they envisioned could be fully realized, and before their paths could cross, as they surely would have, in the 1950s. The impending rebellion their Mara poetics inaugurated remains forever postponed in their writings. For now, reading Lu Xun and Premchand together, and doing so while actively reflecting on the methodological challenges posed by this comparison, can offer insights for grappling with a world rife with divisions and barriers to access, wherein the national other remains out of reach. Rather than dismiss or retrospectively rectify Lu Xun's express disdain for India and Indian literature, this chapter has modeled a reading practice that seeks to understand his appraisal on its own terms. Reading Lu Xun's disregard for India—expressed mostly as fleeting derisions peppered throughout his oeuvre—requires a shift away from framing such mentions as negligible, minor matters of Lu Xun's personal opinion on India literature (a gesture based on a further fallacy that takes Tagore's writings to stand for "Indian literature") and instead asks for an orientation toward the historical conditions that necessitated Lu Xun's evaluation. In doing so, this chapter has attempted to apprehend the unraveling of the China-India comparative unit Lu Xun called for as a productive lens through which to rethink what it means to relate transnationally in a circumscribed and divisive world.

The literary spheres Lu Xun and Premchand—as well as their mediators, Zheng Zhenduo and Eroshenko—inhabited were bounded and shaped by both colonial intervention and national preoccupations. Colonial oversight restricted access to texts (Premchand's censored *Dirge of the Nation*) and movements of people (Eroshenko's expulsion from India), and both Lu Xun

and Premchand called for strengthening an inward-looking national literature as a vital means for staging anticolonial protest. And yet the impossibility of a historically evidenced link between Lu Xun and Premchand makes
possible the play of contingency, giving rise to a field of dialogic relation,
traced in this chapter, borne of accident, chance encounters, and unpredictable crossings that lie beyond the realm of the real. Raju's book of fables,
seemingly innocuous stories of the fabulous East, travels swiftly along
colonial circuits to Zheng, who reads these tales conversely as holding the
subversive potential of Lu Xun's Mara poetics. Zheng's reading of the fabular form prompts a turn to Premchand's experiments with Mara fables in
his earliest short story, "The Most Valuable Jewel in the World," a text that
remained beyond Lu Xun's reach but whose presence figures as an absence
in Zheng's writing on Indian fables. "The Most Valuable Jewel," in turn, points
toward Eroshenko's fable-like "A Narrow Cage," a story Eroshenko wrote with
thoughts of India on his mind and that Lu Xun read as offering a more radical vision of India than that of Tagore's. As an impossible intertext to "A Narrow Cage," "The Most Valuable Jewel" exposes and extends the limits of
Eroshenko's work through its dismantling of colonial representational strategies of India (embodied by the sati). Under Lu Xun's hand, "A Narrow Cage"
(and by extension, the missing trace of Premchand's critique) transforms
into his famed "iron house" metaphor, widely understood as a symbol not
only of Lu Xun's writings, but of May Fourth China. And, finally, freeing the
iron house metaphor from the constraints of national allegory, Premchand's
"A Tale of Two Bullocks" joins in and reshapes Lu Xun's image (in collaboration with Eroshenko), articulating a nationally unbound literary spirit of
revolt waged against the claustrophobic confines of conformity and returning to Mara poetics its transnational resonance.

   This itinerary unfolds neither through a charting of dialogue, which
would denote an ease of cross-border communication and an erasure of the
very real barriers that separated Lu Xun and Premchand, nor through proclamations of affinity, which would require bracketing away Lu Xun's explicit
disdain for Indian literature and Premchand's implicit lack of interest in the
comparison. Instead, I have suggested that this dialogic itinerary may be
better understood as correspondence between Lu Xun and Premchand, an
analytic practice that acknowledges the readerly intuition of resonance and
makes sense of this through an imagined epistolary exchange conducted in
fragments, in mediation, in the absence of causality, and in the open

horizons of contingency. What results is an exercise in literary world-making: an attempt to apprehend the totality of the world according to the particular logic and relational capacity of literature, a totality conjured in the face of disconnect that is remade anew with every act of reading and interpretation.

Conclusion

A Comparatist's Guide to Disconnect

STATES OF DISCONNECT takes as its point of departure moments of comparison in practice, in texts that actively think ideas of China and India together. In each instance, the exercise of comparison functions not to champion or unequivocally uphold the China-India comparative unit, but rather to throw into question the basis of the pairing and to reckon with its precarity, impossibility, or undesirability. The practice of comparison at work here is markedly self-effacing, posed conversely, and conducted in contemplation of its own limits. Comparison serves as both the object and vehicle of critique, for only by thinking ideas of China and India together can one unravel, splinter, and ultimately remake the comparative unit.

Each of the chapters opens with an instance of China-India comparison conducted as a means to disavow it: the Chinese texts discussed in chapter 1 engage the figure of the Indian policeman—and, through him, ideas of colonized India—as an unwanted antagonist whose presence (and that of a subjugated India) must be expelled from the Chinese nation and psyche. Agyeya's China stories explored in chapter 2 transpose visions of an Indian anticolonial revolution onto a Chinese landscape, and yet Agyeya does so in order to deconstruct the China-India pairing in Marxist discourse of the 1930s and to reckon with the possibility that India's path to liberation may diverge from China's march to revolution. In chapter 3, the literary figures discussed participate in the 1950s era of China-India "brotherhood," but in so doing expose the failures, erasures, and circumscriptions of that friendship, borne of a cultural sphere subjected to the nations' agendas and demands. The Hindi texts of 1962 examined in chapter 4 engage ideas of China only to denounce it as a traitor and to mourn the ends of a China-India alliance in the postcolonial world. And chapter 5 stems from Lu Xun's express disdain for India's literature, which he understands as passive and silent, complicit in India's colonization and incapable of issuing a call to arms, therefore lying outside the folds of his revolutionary Mara poetics.

Beginning from the ends of comparison, each chapter can be read as a reflection on transnationalism. The disintegration of the China-India comparative unit brings into sharp relief moments when national borders crystallize and nationalized forms of thought gain predominance, impeding the cross-border transfer of ideas and eroding ethical ways of relating across national divides. What is the fate of transnationalism when the hardening of national borders—and, consequently, the supremacy of nationally bound discursive categories, the blockage of transnational traffic and mobility, and the rise of expressions of hostility and antagonism—encroach upon and fragment ideals of the world as an interconnected totality? If forging transnational relation involves a process of self-definition that takes the national other as a constituent component of the self, so that the self is only fully realized in the encounter with this other, what happens to transnational relation when that national other is vilified or rejected, or remains out of reach? In taking up these questions, the chapters conduct an archeology of the present. Reading texts of disconnect from the early and mid-twentieth century, I find, can make discernable and enable a reckoning with a present crisis—namely, the inability of our globalized habits of thought to fully apprehend an insular world.

My hope for this book is ultimately a practical one: to offer readers conceptual tools for conducting comparison under hostile circumstances and to do so by confronting head-on barriers and threats to the work and ethos of comparison, rather than turning away from these obstacles toward nostalgic recreations of friendlier, better connected literary configurations and more radical pasts. I locate possibilities for such literary practice in what I have called "states of disconnect." In the introduction, I outlined three "states of disconnect"—friction, ellipsis, and contingency—and described these as doubly meaningful. I discussed each state, first, as naming conditions of transnationalism in crisis—in other words, as the contextual grounds of historical moments that unsettle entrenched patterns of thinking the transnational. Political friction between China and India (colonial violence and the 1962 border war), the ellipsed silences of China-India cultural diplomacy carried out against the Maoist political campaigns of the 1950s, and contingent acts of thinking China and India together in the absence of direct contact (Lu Xun at the turn of the century and Agyeya in the 1930s): these moments comprise states of disconnect, understood in the first instance as the fraught conditions of rising insularity and immobility. From conditions of friction, ellipsis, and contingency emerge the texts studied in this book.

Beyond this descriptive function, the three states of disconnect activate a second layer of meaning. Not only do conditions of friction, ellipsis, and contingency set the contextual stage, but, in the literary texts I read, these conditions become reflexively thematized, cast as matters of literary concern. The three states of disconnect thus take on new meaning as designating forms of literary practice and criticism, thereby making possible a literary understanding of a hostile and stalled world. In such an understanding lies the potentiality for ethical ways to relate with national others under restrictive circumstances and without recourse to globalized crutches of reparative connection. Considering the texts that comprise this book's archive makes clear that apprehending disconnect requires its own analytic tools. As I have argued, disconnect cannot simply be grasped in inverse, as the antonym of connection; instead, disconnect gives rise to its own particular logics of relation. The challenge lies in finding ethical ways to relate, in recognition of and yet against the narrowness and aversion that may have pervaded dominant discourse, public opinion, or even a text's stated intention. I offer friction, ellipsis, and contingency as the beginnings of a critical vocabulary for grasping this relational potential of disconnect. All three are woven through and grow out of texts discussed in each of the book's chapters. In the sections below, I recall moments from the chapters when a particular state comes to the fore and highlight instances of entanglement so as to theorize each as a fulcrum for comparison. While my readings of friction, ellipsis, and contingency are grounded in the case of China and India, I offer this vocabulary as exceeding the particularities of the case, as tools for conducting comparison in the face of disconnect as it becomes a characteristic feature of our contemporary world.

Friction

In the physical world, friction names the force that resists motion when two surfaces rub against each other, even as it is necessary for sustaining motion. Given its close ties to motion, friction has served as an apt theoretical metaphor in studies of globalization and mobility largely rooted in the social sciences. Responding to the rise of globalized paradigms of cultural analysis in the 1990s (what has been termed "flow thinking," stemming from anthropologist Arjun Appadurai's influential "global flows"), a mobility turn in the early 2000s sought to disrupt ideas of the world "as awash in fluidities" by turning instead to "blockages, coagulations, and assemblages . . . that congeal in space and social life."[1] In this context, friction calls attention to "the way in which people, things and ideas are slowed down or stopped," at times in aid of centers of power, such as when friction is "deliberately used to stop or slow down the mobilities of those who threaten established forms of power."[2] Friction here reveals the myth of visions of globalization as an unimpeded flow of capital, goods, and ideas that purports to connect the globe in a celebratory unity. Bringing this critique into the realm of ideas, Anna Tsing writes of friction as the "sticky" encounter between universals and particulars in a world of global connection.[3] Globalization sets universals (e.g., forms of capital, science, and social justice) in motion, but, for Tsing, "universal claims do not actually make everything everywhere the same"; instead, through friction, universals encounter particular historical conjunctures and "become practically effective."[4] Friction, therefore, is "the grip of worldly encounter," the "awkward, unequal, unstable, and creative" force through which universal aspirations are yearned for and remade in particular times and places.[5] Against the backdrop of a globalized world, friction reminds us of the uneven and unexpected manner in which global connections are forged, despite and in the face of programmatic predictions of globalized integration.

Such theories of friction help make sense of a connected and mobile world. But what of a fractured and stalled world, one that rises from the ruins of wrecked dreams of global connection? Friction now takes on an altered disciplinary tenor. When expectations of global connectivity rub against assertions of hostile and insular nationalisms, friction serves as a master trope of sorts in identifying severed connections and deteriorated relations between nation-states. This is a familiar, colloquial usage of the word, as in media coverage, for instance, that in recent years has announced much friction between China and India leading up to and in the wake of deadly incidents along the heavily militarized, contested border. This now commonplace understanding of friction stems from the disciplinary idiom of International Relations (IR), wherein friction loosely denotes tensions between nation-states—or, as the eminent IR theorist Hedley Bull put it (in the Cold War jargon of the 1970s), "misunderstanding or misinterpretation by the great powers of one another's words and actions."[6] Bull's definition of friction, which he articulates in the course of enumerating the functions of diplomacy, neatly lays out the underlying associations that inform our everyday understanding and figurative use of the word. He writes:

> A fourth function of diplomacy is minimisation of the effects of friction in international relations. Friction is the chafing or rubbing together of things in proximity. Given the juxtaposition of different political communities, each with its own values, preoccupations, prejudices and sensibilities, friction in international relations is always present, even between states and nations that perceive a wide area of common interests and whose relations are close and amicable. Such friction is a constant source of international tension and discord that may be unrelated to the "true" interests of the parties concerns.[7]

Bull's definition seizes on the moment of "chafing or rubbing," an intimate motion predicated upon closeness ("things in proximity") that conversely spells the erosion of that closeness ("tension or discord"). In Bull's conception of international society, friction is ever-present yet manageable, "minimizable," through effective diplomacy. Furthermore, friction is negatively charged: it stands in contrast to "common interests" and "relations that are close and amicable," resulting from moments of "misunderstanding or misinterpretation" that obscure the "truth," an inevitable yet undesirable by-product of difference (the "juxtaposition" of different "values, preoccupations, prejudices and sensibilities") in need of being reined in. If left unchecked, friction threatens to erupt into war, the ultimate dissolution of world order.

In the absence of globalized connection, traces of this IR notion of friction as negative, undesirable, and requiring regulation via diplomacy often underlie the priorities of transnational humanistic scholarship, leading to a critical pattern that can echo the rhetoric of diplomacy in the guise of humanistic inquiry. The humanities often seem to fulfill the role that Bull attributed to diplomacy of smoothing over the divisiveness of nationalized discursive categories, here through narratives of aesthetic affinity, shared practices, creative exchange, and so on. In both cases, stories of friendship seek to minimize friction. This pattern is especially heightened in studies of non-Western or South-South comparison. Our humanistic critical faculties for studying the "unfriendly" remains better attuned to the histories and legacies of colonialism and empire, wherein the "juxtaposition of difference" falls vertically along the lines of oppressor/oppressed or epistemological center and marginalized periphery. In contrast, when we draw axes of comparison unrouted or unmediated via the West and its centers of conceptual and political governance, we more readily default to frames of horizontality, similarity, and solidarity.

My readings of texts that think China and India together under conditions of violence and war aim to resist the easy tendency toward horizontality. Chinese texts of the Indian policeman studied in chapter 1 articulate the shock of experiencing colonial violence perpetrated not along cleanly demarcated, vertical lines of colonizer/colonized but at the hands of a fellow colonized figure who appears in the guise of a colonizer, an entangled complex of power pithily evoked in the poet Bai Yun's paradoxical image of "our armed Indian brother" (*wuzhuang de Yindu xiongdi* 武裝的印度兄弟).[8] Capturing the image of the Indian policeman in Chinese literary form—and, some decades later, of China as a traitorous aggressor in a Hindi literary idiom (chapter 4)—registers the dissolution of expectations of horizontality and a search for ways to relate beyond such linearities, precisely during moments of violent conflict when lines of separation can become cemented.

Friction thus offers a way to "stay with the trouble," to dwell in the discomfort of antagonistic literary expression without rushing to repair and smoothen.[9] Extending friction's theoretical itinerary into comparative literary study, I understand the term as knotting several threads of its prior conceptualizations: at once a distancing or severing of relations ("tensions or discord" in the IR sense) and the closeness of a fraught encounter (the uncomfortable rubbing together of "things in proximity"), at once destructive of one order yet generative of new energies emitted during the clash. Rather than positing friction as the destruction of closeness, my readings emphasize the affective dimension of a desire for repulsion that arises from sustained, intimate chafing: "a surging, a rubbing . . . bodies literally affecting one another and generating intensities," in Kathleen Stewart's words.[10] Friction's ability to "generate intensities" (in a physical sense, the heat and light emitted when two sticks rub against each other) features in Tsing's account as holding a disruptive potential, for sites of friction can make possible "new arrangements of cultural and power."[11] Along these lines, reading friction literarily in this book has entailed capturing and giving shape to the creative energy—the new horizons of meaning—sparked when antagonists rub up against each other, each resisting the other at the same time as the two remain bound together in conflict. The chapters of this book have suggested that reconceptualizing friction as a literary force calls for reckoning with the forms of intimacy that run through every distancing gesture, and the capacity of the clash to spark new and unexpected possibilities of meaning-making.

As discussed in chapter 1, Yadong Pofo's 1907 novel *Twin Souls* thematizes these contradictory pulls of friction. The Indian soul manifests as a colonizer, an unwanted presence that "invades" the Chinese body and must be expelled through a nationalized strengthening of the Chinese soul. And yet, even as the Chinese and Indian souls confront each other as antagonists, their cohabitation of the most intimate of spaces, the body, actualizes the intimacy of a frictional clash founded upon on sustained contact. Dwelling together in one body enables the Chinese soul to share in the Indian's experience of colonization at the hands of the British, making possible a Chinese view of colonization perceived through Indian eyes.

Beyond *Twin Souls*, the chapter shows how daily clashes with the Indian policeman in Shanghai gave rise to a lively collection of literature through the late Qing and early Republican eras, a formative period in the development of modern Chinese literature. As debates on the shape modern Chinese literature ought to take unfolded in elite literary circles of the time, the figure of the Indian policeman offered a vehicle through which marginal writers and readers (those most immediately confronting the lived experience of China's colonial condition) could enter into, participate, and reshape dominant literary discourses of the time. Literary engagements with the Indian policeman injected into pervasive national literary currents—on vernacularizing literature, crafting the May Fourth antihero, and debating the imperatives of revolutionary literature—the everyday paradoxes and anxieties of colonization. Reading China-India friction literarily generates new horizons of meaning: the literary Indian policeman reveals an alternative history of modern Chinese literature told from the perspective of China's colonial experience, one in which expressions of hostility and hatred toward the Indian prove just as foundational to ideas of Chinese literary modernity as the better-documented, "friendlier" accounts of influence and exchange often evoked through figures such as Tagore.

While chapter 1 examines China-India friction as it manifests in Chinese literature, chapter 4 approaches a similar set of questions through readings of Hindi literature, written in the wake of the China-India war of 1962 waged over the drawing of national borders. The chapter grapples with how to make sense of antagonistic literary expression that explicitly rejects transnationalism, what in this context is conventionally dismissed as anti-China rhetoric or nationalist propaganda. Staying with the uncomfortable rhetoric of *Dharmayug's* postwar pages, the chapter parses the affective dimensions of the war in India: mourning the loss of China-India "brotherhood," anger toward a cultural ally now perceived as a traitor and invader, and anxiety borne of the profound uncertainty the war effected over the still newly independent India's present and future standing on the international stage. Captured in literary form, the severing of relations with China in fact gains relational potential, wherein a hostile but nevertheless sustained literary engagement with ideas of China only further embeds China within Hindi literary thought and practice of the time, intimately and productively, precisely during a moment characterized by calls for China's removal from the Indian literary psyche. Even as Machwe—through his parody of Shamsher's "China" and his mistranslations of Chinese poetry—endeavors to claim India's moral victory over a treacherous China, his intertextual poetic experiments spark a meditation on the malleability of meaning, throwing into question the faithfulness of the written word in a world suddenly turned untrustworthy. Whereas Machwe grapples with the word and its meaning, Parsai's rewriting of Lu Xun's "Madman's Diary" reveals the senselessness of the search for meaning in a world fundamentally characterized by the madness of Cold War politicking. These distinctly modernist anxieties on the perpetual instability and inaccessibility of meaning are precisely what make the Hindi texts of 1962 meaningful: the modernist unsettling of rigid sites of meaning functions to undermine and rebel against the calls, resounding across India at the time, for unambiguously patriotic literature that champions the nation's military might. Reading these texts as literary friction allows us to confront head-on the outpouring of rage and hatred toward

China (instead of papering over these in favor of friendlier sentiment) and to mine the relational potential such expression can hold when captured in literary form.

These chapters together model an attunement of critical attention toward what non-Western or South-South transnationalism often keeps out of view, offering ways to read texts that think the transnational hostilely. The critical work needed to make sense of such texts requires an exploration of the literary properties of friction. Doing so makes it possible to grasp the intimacy that holds in shape configurations of conflict and the literary energy emitted in its potential to disrupt established orders and pose new possibilities. Friction no longer denotes the deterioration of transnationalism; instead, friction can now function to dismantle nationally restricted categories of thought and to harness the world-making capacities of literature.

Ellipsis

Ellipsis, the mark of omission, inscribes the trace of the nonverbal, words that remain unexchanged and yet express meaning in their very absence. Ellipses index silence, hesitation, pause—all the failings of a dialogue that holds as its apotheosis communication achieved via direct and uninterrupted verbal exchange. Ellipses refuse this premise, making possible instead the communicative potential of the unspoken and unspeakable, from momentary lapses of the linguistic to the depths of circumscription and enforced silence. The ellipsis inscribes disconnect: the breakdown of transnationalism that manifests in the realm of communication as failed dialogue, the syntactic separation of clauses that confounds an easy transfer of meaning. Read literally, however, the typographic rendering of successive dots conjures at once a chasm, the untraversable space left in the wake of splintered bridges, and a rhythm, a pulsing forth of the potential for literary relation. The ellipsis invites interpretation, binding writer and reader together in the pleasures of literary engagement: "It is a mark through which the interpretative act is explicitly handed over to another . . . who has to complete or somehow comprehend the missing text. The ellipsis is a written acknowledgement of the interactive dynamic of communicative acts."[12] In this way, ellipsis opens a contemplation on dialogics against the grain of dialogue. It enacts a form of relation beyond the confines of scripted dialogue and thrives in the capacity of interpretation to always keep meaning open, undetermined, and in flux.

The mark of silence has been understood as constitutive of meaning in ways both hegemonic and subversive. For Pierre Macherey, silence provides the necessary grounds for speech and gives speech its form: "What is important in the work is what it does not say. This is not the same as the careless notation 'what it refuses to say' . . . But rather than this, what the work *cannot say* is important, because there the elaboration of the utterance is acted out, in a sort of journey to silence."[13] Silence here demarcates the workings of ideology, taken in the Althusserian sense as the formless and participatory means through which the state ensures its domination. Confronting what the text cannot say through a reading of its silences can dismantle ideology's "false totality" by exposing its presence in the text and establishing "the existence of its limits."[14] Gayatri Chakravorty Spivak draws upon Macherey in her work on subaltern silence as exemplifying epistemic violence, but, in Spivak's account, silence cannot be read or undone, as Macherey would have it. Instead, any attempt to retrieve the subaltern from the silences of "imperialist epistemic, social, and disciplinary inscription" only enacts further violence, for how can the subaltern, "which is itself defined as a difference from the elite," be represented or known by those against whom she is defined and at the same time retain her fundamental difference?[15] While, for Spivak, silence marks the perpetual and irreparable collusion between representation and repression, Édouard Glissant understands the Other's silence as resistance, what he calls "opacity," a protest against the "reductive" force of transparency.[16] Rather than clamor to "understand" the other, a process that takes as its basis "the requirement for transparency," Glissant calls for the "right to opacity," to remain inaccessible and therefore irreducible.[17] Silence, thus, registers opacity as resistance: an effort not to lay bare and "grasp" difference (to make it one's own and thereby erase difference), but to recognize its presence as an actively asserted absence that frustrates our pursuit of transparency and exposes the hubris of the drive to "understand."[18] What Macherey dismisses as a "careless notation"—silence as refusal—Glissant takes up as the site of protest and empowerment.

Ellipsis, as I conceive of it, takes shape alongside these conceptions of the force of silence. My readings in chapter 3 linger in the ellipses of cultural diplomacy, an instrument of the state and ideology's playground, wherein the state shapes a "culture" in its own image by recruiting artists as participants in its ideological systems. This is the 1950s era of China-India "brotherhood," and yet reading the silences of cultural diplomacy remind us again of the relational capacity of disconnect, for it is only when cultural diplomacy begins to malfunction—when a confrontation with the limits of ideology begin to dismantle its false totality—that murmurs of literary relation become fleetingly perceptible. The fortuitous convergence of the Asian Writers' Conference of 1956 with the concurrent Hundred Flowers campaign in China made possible a literary practice that took shape in the form of cultural diplomacy while simultaneously dismantling its founding premise, that culture can be put to national use, from within. The conference remains illegible, a failure, within the nation's rubric of consequentiality, and is "silent," in Spivak's sense, in national records of Bandung or Third World internationalisms. Such discourses would necessarily inscribe the conference within political relations and Cold War politicking. Yet those elliptical, ephemeral moments, such as the informal evenings of poetry recitation that the writers' partook in, forge literary relation: a transformative and open gesture toward the other through the logics of literature. Dinkar's Hindi translation of Liu Shahe's censured poem constitutes another act of extending such literary relation. During Dinkar's 1957 visit to China at the height of the Anti-Rightist campaign, literary relation thrived not in the "friendly" activities of cultural diplomacy (sightseeing, speeches, interviews, gift exchanges), but in his confrontation with the ellipsed, the tensions and silences, of a circumscribed literary sphere. Liu Shahe's poem remains "opaque"—Dinkar is unable to quite grasp why a poem ostensibly about plants has proven so controversial—and, still, grappling with this opacity without rendering the poem transparent endows the poem an unlikely afterlife as the poem journeys into the Hindi literary sphere, beyond the reach of the state's determinations and once again open to interpretation.

In this book, the elliptical marks its presence in moments of dialogue (here, conducted under the auspices of cultural diplomacy) and draws attention to the disruptive potential of silences, tensions, the unsaid and unspeakable, that necessarily comprise dialogue. In claustrophobic spaces that register the state's delimiting hold, where national priorities prescribe how to communicate with others, ellipsis opens breathing room. This is an assertion of the political power of literary practice against the capitalized Politics (a distinction the delegates at the Asian Writers' Conference sought to activate in their calls for a "nonpolitical" conference), a kind of power that maintains its force through its resistance to transcription or articulation. Ellipsis underscores those aspects of literary practice that are not, that cannot be, written down: the infinitely variable ways in which a text becomes meaningful in the world through the unpredictable vagaries of interpretation. The ellipsis keeps open this in-between space, between a text and its canonized commentary that authors and authorizes its meaning singularly.

My conceptualization of ellipsis as marking generative gaps in the traffic of meaning joins in efforts within comparative literature to eke out spaces between the things compared, in rejection of frames of equivalence. Natalie Melas locates this critical gesture in the idea of "incommensurability," a term that pries apart the "basis for comparison" (the space that comparables "have in common," in which "previously separated objects [come] into comparison") and the "ground of equivalence," the measure or standard against which the objects become compared.[19] Against a comparison that relies on commensuration—a tautology of erasure wherein objects become compared because they seem similar, and they seem similar because they have been compared—Melas seeks to bring texts "into relation over a ground of comparison that is in common but not unified."[20] Melas's caution against standards of measure in comparison (the norm) ultimately seeks to move comparative literature's methods toward "postcolonial comparison," an analytic practice that attends to the ways in which postcolonial cultures come into contact and forge communities and collectivities in defiance of a singular standard of comparison and in a concerted effort to overthrow the "assimilatory tendency" of colonial knowledge and governance.[21] Melas's incommensurability resonates with the critique of equivalence Emily Apter levels at the project of world literature (narrowly defined as the institutionalized disciplinary construct), in which she identifies a problematic "reflexive endorsement of cultural equivalence and substitutability."[22] For Apter, world literature's assimilatory drive stems from its particular treatment of translation, given that efforts to anthologize and curricularize the literatures of the world are often premised upon an untroubled "translatability assumption."[23] In this guise, world literature positions the translator (whose authorial role is often reduced to a single signature) as "cultural universalizer, evangelizer of transcultural understanding."[24] Apter proposes instead attention to the "speed bumps" that world literature tends to zoom over, what she terms "untranslatability."[25] Untranslatability is not the impossibility of translation, but is rather an understanding of world literature viewed through "the lens of what impedes translation, through incommen-surability, nonequivalence, the history of violent erasure, carried-over silences and nonwords, or the effects of nontranslation."[26]

With theories of comparison that reject frames of equivalence, ellipsis shares a commitment to disrupting totalizing mechanisms of cultural anal-ysis through an insistence on difference, those knots of meaning upon which unified systems of knowing stumble and become derailed, that refuse disentanglement and remain unknowable in the face of pressures or expec-tations of transparency. Ellipsis also extends this critique in two directions. First, the totalizing system incommensurability stands against corresponds with the history and legacies of colonial conquest that uphold and impose "the sovereign authority of a single perspective."[27] By rejecting that single perspective, a postcolonial standpoint yields relationality between postco-lonial "cultures that come into constant contact without a unifying stan-dard, thus engaging in ubiquitous processes of comparison that are no lon-ger bound to commensuration."[28] Beyond the hegemonic, singular colonial perspective and its present-day manifestations, ellipsis exposes how encoun-ters between postcolonial cultures can also become subjected to "the sov-ereign authority of a single perspective"—that of the nation-state—and attendant demands of "commensuration," often articulated in the language of national solidarity. The Asian Writers' Conference exemplifies the desire across the emergent Third World of the time for the formerly colonized nations to learn of and from each other's cultures on their own terms. But even though this desire stakes an emancipatory, anticolonial stance, its ful-filment in officially sanctioned arenas of nation-building necessarily holds silences and omissions within. Ellipsis cautions against too romantic a view of postcolonial literary relation and brings into view the "unifying stan-dards" that may order comparison even in rejection of the colonial hege-mon's epistemological control.

Second, just as the ellipsis bears the mark of imposed demands of com-mensuration, it importantly invites reading and interpretation as active acts of meaning making: the ellipsis is ultimately generative, and multiply so. Ideas of untranslatability have tended to emphasize a radical "non-carry-over" or withholding of meaning, echoing Glissant's "right to opacity."[29] Withholding on the part of the translator—for instance, the refusal to trans-late terms that resist systems of knowing legible in global English—can pose an important challenge to the "reading posture of all-knowingness adopted by Western anglophone readers."[30] Strategies such as "subtractive reading and resistant translation" can be harnessed as a "tactic of withholding translation deployed against the predominance of global English."[31] Such strategies function to mark the limits of the epistemically powerful by forcing a confrontation with concepts and ways of life that are understandable only in their un-understandability. Read as an untranslatable, the Hindi translation of Liu's poem enacts this critical gesture of withholding meaning, but, unlike the untranslatable, this encounter with noncomprehension does not force an interpretative impasse. Instead, the ellipsis invites meaning-making as an ethical strategy of transformative collaboration against the nationalized policing of interpretative borders conducted via assertions of hegemonic "original" or "correct" ways of reading. I understand Dinkar's "failure" to communicate what Liu's poem intended to say as freeing the poem from its predetermined and authorized meaning in Chinese and inviting new readings, new interpretations in Hindi. By wresting the poem from a singular meaning, the Hindi translation opens up the poem to multiplicity, issuing invitations for interpretation conducted in the recognition of the communicative act every literary text opens with its reader, wherein the traffic of meaning is uneven and variable, dotted with ellipses.

Contingency

At several junctures, this book has contemplated the capacity of contingency to call the logics of causality and inevitability into question. On one hand, contingency seems synonymous with the causal: the contingent is dependent on that which came before and caused its occurrence. Contingency weaves a narrative of history that proceeds in its very unfolding instead of in accordance with a transcendent law or teleological drive.[32] On the other hand, contingency brings into view the arbitrariness of the very causality it names, the realization that any given moment "could have been otherwise."[33] The continuous connectivity afforded by causality splinters into a reckoning with the play of randomness and chance as the only "essential thing" about human existence.[34] As such, contingency lays bare the constructedness of all forms of inevitability—fate, telos, or, indeed, narrative itself—enabling an imagination of the disconnected. In a secular world in which history provides no assurances of emancipation, "contingency is a question of suffering,"[35] an often incapacitating and debilitating reminder of the utterly untamable, "accidental character" of life.[36] And yet this realization affords a liberation of its own. Poised at the edges of a moment that can both be and not be, contingency celebrates potentiality, a state of being "suspended between occurrence and nonoccurrence" in contemplation of the infinite possibilities held within a single blink.[37] Contingency revels in the open horizons of potentiality: the diversion of linear narrative into an endless "luminous spiral of the possible," the "becoming possible once again" of that consigned to impossibility, the re-calling of necessity into question.[38]

Agyeya's China stories discussed in chapter 2 embark on precisely such an exploration of the liberation contingency affords. Imprisoned in the early 1930s for his revolutionary activities as the young "scientist" of the HRSA, Agyeya's time in jail led him on a literary quest for freedom. His meditations on breaking free remained closely intertwined with his dreams for the nation's liberation, for which he had sacrificed his own freedom and—given the likelihood that he would be hanged, as was the case with his fellow revolutionary, Bhagat Singh—possibly his life. Agyeya's jail writings capture the many layers of this search for liberation. Most immediately, his short stories inscribe literary journeys to faraway lands undertaken from the confinement of a jail cell. Writing of revolution in China enables a further gesture of breaking free: in the wake of China's May Thirtieth movement, Indian communists, buoyed by Soviet optimism, announced the recent events in China as harbingers of India's impending revolution. China and India seemed to be marching together toward the long-awaited revolution. Apparently on the brink of revolution, China signified for Agyeya a literary landscape in which the violent revolutionary methods of the HRSA could finally find fruition. And so, in Agyeya's China, the HRSA's failed bomb plot occurs otherwise. There, the bomb explodes, eviscerating its intended target. The plot's failure in India is opened up to contingency: a historically foreclosed event confronts the possibility that it could have happened otherwise. But, at the same time as Agyeya's China evokes the euphoria of revolutionary success, the stories bespeak Agyeya's own growing doubts about the ability of violent revolutionary means to deliver India's independence. Amid celebratory proclamations of China and India's tandem march toward a revolution preordained, Agyeya's China stories diverge off the path of a history foretold and resist the pulls of necessity. The stories think China and India together in an attempt to decouple the two, to confront the destruction and wreckage of a revolution waged violently. Agyeya's experiments with contingency make possible a form of storytelling that harnesses historical uncertainty to conjure new horizons of possibility, marking Agyeya's own turn away from his conviction in violent revolutionary methods and toward a nonviolent, Gandhian vision for India's freedom.

While Agyeya's stories often strike a melancholic note, reading contingency can also arouse the subjunctive mood of comparison, a hopeful taking up of the invitation literature extends to its readers: to take pleasure in interpretation so as to keep open a text's many possibilities of meaning, and to wander alongside a text down the many potential paths of its unpredictable movements in the world far beyond grounds of inception and intention. Attending to a text's contingencies does not simply prioritize the reader's whims over the writer's labors, for we could think of contingency, alongside David Wellbery, as woven into the text from the very beginning: "Contingencies do not merely come to language from the outside but rather are effective, as it were, from the beginning, within the individual utterance. By virtue of this fact . . . the utterance can become an event, the site of the emergence of the new."[39] Contingency, therefore, captures the ability of the text to reveal itself as event, to offer "new," unforeseen meaning despite the illusion of "narrative programicity"[40]: "My text returns to me in a different context, and thus with a different meaning . . . something I cannot foresee."[41] Literary attunement to contingency shares with historicist and sociological literary approaches a fidelity to the particularities of text and context, yet it exceeds such approaches by giving equal weight to both the actualized and the unpredictable and unrealized potential. Contingency signifies a form a relation borne not of foreclosed instances of historical connectivity nor of the linear logics of causality and necessity, but of reopening the past—and the text—once again to a full spectrum of potentialities.

I experiment with such an approach to comparison in my readings of Lu Xun and Premchand in chapter 5, which exemplifies the intersection of all three axes of disconnect: friction, ellipsis, and contingency. The chapter takes as its point of departure moments of friction: the generative potential of Lu Xun's express disdain for India and its literature to make possible a new, contingent literary relation between Lu Xun and Premchand. Resisting the temptation to craft "dialogue" between the two writers (the "similarities and differences" approach to comparison), the chapter traces their correspondence, a metaphorical epistolary exchange—fragmented, mediated, and conducted in the face of distance, borders, and other barriers to direct communication—that captures the ways in which their writings "speak" to each other elliptically, through the dialogic capacity of the unsaid. Such correspondence occurs through the logic of contingency, which, in the absence of historically evidenced links between Lu Xun and Premchand, opens a field of literary relation borne of chance encounters and unpredictable crossings beyond the realm of the real. The chapter offers a version of Lu Xun and Premchand that readers may find unfamiliar; indeed, it overlooks their most canonical writings in favor of their (often lesser-known) experiments with a nonrealist literary form—the fable. The fable at once furnishes the textual basis for Lu Xun and Premchand's correspondence (through stories that, via Zheng and Eroshenko, enact Mara poetics) and informs my practice of reading, for here I borrow from the fable its commitment to exceeding the bounds of the real and its steadfast celebration of the fictional. Reading Lu Xun and Premchand through the play of contingency enables a *literary* vision of the world—a totality conjured from the contingencies of imagination and interpretation.

My conceptualization of contingency as a guide for comparison arises from and gives shape to the unexpected and unpredictable workings of both friction and ellipsis. As I have discussed, I read friction as the productive literary energy emitted during the antagonistic clash and uncomfortable chafing of oppositional forces, an energy that is capable of generating new, unexpected intimacies disruptive of established orders. This understanding of friction as powerful in its unpredictability draws from Tsing's attention to "the unexpected and unstable aspects of global interaction" and the "contingency of encounters" between universals and sites of particularity.[42] Similarly, in remaining unarticulated and untranscribed, the ellipsis opens texts to unpredictable, unexpected, and unintended horizons of meaning. I envision the ellipsis as a site of meaning-making that binds writers, readers, and critics in a joint literary act of forging relation against predetermined, singular, and enforced scripts of interpretation and interaction. I position contingency, alongside friction and ellipsis, as sharing an interest in the ability of the unforeseeable to remain unmanageable, thereby troubling and breaking through regimes of certainty.

That said, reading for the contingent does simply not collapse all intention and structure into total randomness. That extent of dissolution nears meaninglessness and induces an analytic paralysis of its own. In contrast, I understand contingency more precisely as entwined with ideas of historical time and historicized pasts; reading for the contingent thus attends to literary experiments with historicism. Agyeya's China stories conduct such an experiment. By dramatically fictionalizing the well-known lives of eminent Chinese historical figures (Liang Qichao and Sun Yatsen among them), Agyeya stages a contemplation on the confines of a fixed narrative of the past that casts the future as foretold. From a teleological historical narrative that rationalizes anticolonial struggle as conducted in anticipation of revolution's ultimately arrival, Agyeya wrests free open, untold futures for India, futures still in the making, still poised at the edges of potentiality. In his stories, revolution does not mark a celebratory climax at the end of the narrative; instead, revolution arrives in its nonarrival, ellipsed from the narrative of its own telling and perceptible only in the ruins and wreckage of its aftermath. If historicism is the taming of contingency in the crafting of past narratives, Agyeya rewrites the past viewed from the perspective of contingency set free and, in so doing, unyokes narrative from remaining beholden to a looming predetermined ending.

My readings of Lu Xun and Premchand endeavor to glean from Agyeya's quest—for a past untold and a future unforeseen—a practice of comparison conducted through the workings of contingency. As a critical tool, reading for contingency disrupts an understanding of literature "as a symbolic expression of social relations," wherein the literary "is merely a relay of social forces, a medium for refracting them."[43] Whereas sociological approaches can risk limiting the literary text's force to its roles as a reflection of social relations or a repository of historical events, reading for contingency recognizes literature's potential as a lively agent of change, making possible imaginations of pasts beyond historicist narratives and bringing into view otherwise foreclosed futures. Rather than allowing for literary meaning to be predetermined elsewhere, in the disciplinary realms and idioms of history or sociology, reading for contingency beckons the literary-critical work necessary for apprehending the full force of the fictional, and for doing so ethically, in service of relation. As a fulcrum for comparison, contingency draws attention to unrealized vectors of relation, nonencounters that "could have been otherwise," that become perceptible specifically through literary ways of being in the world. Lu Xun and Premchand offer one such example of writers whose correspondence stems, in the impossibility of crossed historical paths, from the recurrent readerly experience shared by generations of their readers of finding traces of one in the texts of the other. Contingency nurtures this literary intuition in its ability to disturb authorized bases of comparison. Seeking out comparison beyond the historicist impulse—which tends to recognize as valid only historically evidenced instances of exchange and genealogies of influence—can conjure an imagination of relation beyond the systems of circulation that have historically determined connection. When those systems malfunction and break down, reviving past potentialities of literary relation formed in the face of nonoccurrence can open hostile and insular presents to unexpected others and can help summon more inclusive futures.

Toward an Ethics of Transnational Literary Relation

Friction, ellipsis, and contingency together offer a critical vocabulary, and concrete hermeneutic strategies, for making sense of states of disconnect. Each registers a strain upon our ability to think the transnational, when relating ethically with national others becomes severed, interrupted, or rendered absent. This book reads such moments as reflexively and explicitly thematized in literary form. In taking up literary expressions of transnational hostility, tension, and disavowal, this book hopes to cultivate an ethical drive to combat the breakdown of transnational relation by explicitly turning toward moments conventionally deemed antithetical to relation. Such a gesture invites a critical reflection on the kinds of narratives we have grown accustomed to valorizing in transnational humanistic study and, in the process, those we risk turning a blind eye to. While happier stories of collaboration, solidarity, and connected pasts can help shift emphasis away from the vitriolic rhetoric of present-day nationalisms, the temptation to turn away in fact leaves the object of critique standing, unexamined and uninterrogated. If the task of comparison is ultimately to strive for ethical relation, this book calls for a concerted taking up and unmaking of the impossibility and undesirability of relating with others as a crucial step toward that imperative.

This book has also strived to make a case for the indispensability of literary work. I hope to have clarified the crucial value of the literary in both facing the inadequacies and failures of globalization, and combatting the growing tendency of national parochialism to overdetermine being in the world. A world-literary ethic involves not just reading literature from around the world, and not just reading the world as it appears in literature, two strategies that currently organize the project of world literature. These grander ambitions would be enriched by this book's modest proposal to return to the basics in a sense, to *reading* literature, self-consciously engaging in interpretation, and to reading *literature*, recognizing that which differentiates this kind of text from others. *Reading* invokes the humility of acknowledging the limits of the scholarly eye, the inevitable distance between authorial and critical intention; of recognizing literary criticism as interpretation, no more or less "correct" than the many other acts of interpretation that mark a text's presence in the world. And reading *literature* asks for a constant attunement to form and practice, the acts of writing and reading through which this particular kind of text at once interacts with and is irreducible to either the archival document (the record) or the diplomatic treatise (the treaty). Can we reconceive of the task of the world-literary critic as less to render a text "transparent" and more to take up literature's invitation to make meaning in ways that engender an ethical relation with the other? Doing so may allow us to bring into view a totality—the world—according to the contingencies of literature, and to grant the literary its full potential as a lively and disruptive world-making force, capable of forging transnational relation when none seems at hand.

Acknowledgments

IT TOOK A world in lockdown for me to learn that writing need not be a solitary activity. Writing with Paola Iovene, Juliane Noth, and Catherine Stuer made the isolating work of turning ideas into words part of a shared daily rhythm. I thank them for showing up for my writing every day, and for their wisdom and honesty in moments of struggle. Countless conversations with Paola helped hazy thoughts find clarity, and she read my writing with her characteristic patience and thoughtfulness. I am also grateful to Tom Kelly for reading every page of this book, some several times, and for nudging my writing and thinking down paths I would not have otherwise explored.

States of Disconnect grew from my doctoral dissertation. I thank the members of my committee—Haun Saussy, Ulrike Stark, and Paola—for seeing in inchoate versions of this work seeds of potential, and for their invaluable guidance. Also at the University of Chicago, I thank Dipesh Chakrabarty, Tamara Chin, Leela Gandhi, Françoise Meltzer, and Judith Zeitlin for shaping my thinking within and beyond the classroom. For their camaraderie and friendship, I thank the members of my cohort: Chloe Blackshear, Megan Macklin, Nic Wong, and particularly Mollie McFee, who was a steadfast source of support, laughter, and sage advice through the writing and publishing process. I had the good fortune of spending my final year in Chicago amid the vibrant intellectual community of the Franke Institute for the

Humanities. I am grateful to all the 2016–2017 Franke Fellows for sharing their inspirational writing and engaging with mine.

This book finds deeper roots still in the undergraduate thesis I wrote at Vassar College. At Vassar, Martha Kaplan nurtured my academic interests and ambitions with unparalleled care. I thank also Michael Joyce, Amitava Kumar, and Yu Zhou for their genuine commitment to teaching, in the most wholesome sense, the benefits of which I continue to reap.

I am grateful for the members of the Department of Comparative Literature at Queen Mary University of London. Will McMorran, Kasia Mika, Angus Nicholls, Leonard Olschner, Shital Pravinchandra, Galin Tihanov, and Kiera Vaclavik each serves as a role model of warm collegiality and commitment to comparison in all its intellectual and practical forms. I thank my department in particular for supporting my absences, and for making it possible for me devote long stretches of time over the last five years to this book. I am also appreciative of the members of the Queen Mary Postcolonial Seminar and South Asia Forum, and especially Chris Moffat for his comments on a version of chapter 3. I have explored parts of this book alongside my students; I thank them for their openness to new texts and ways of thinking.

The Harvard University Asia Center and Center for Global Asia (CGA) at New York University Shanghai granted me time away from teaching and administrative duties, valuable access to research resources, and logistical and financial support crucial to this book's publication. At Harvard, I thank the Asia Center staff and community, and Taia Cheng for her research assistance. My thanks also to Ma Xiaohe at the Harvard-Yenching Library, who helped track down rare sources and permissions. The CGA faculty and staff made it possible for me to spend time in China during a period of seemingly insurmountable restrictions on travel and welcomed me into their jovial and lively community. I feel incredibly fortunate to have brought this book to completion in Shanghai, where my research began in many ways.

I have learned much from colleagues with whom brief meetings at various conferences and panels grew into meaningful collaborations and lasting friendships. Tansen Sen has supported my work in ways impossible to enumerate; for now, my thanks to him for reading several portions of this book, for generously sharing sources, and for his guidance through the many stages of book-writing. My research has benefited greatly from conversations and collaborations with fellow China-India scholars: Prasenjit Duara, Cao Yin, Arunabh Ghosh, Gal Gvili, Yan Jia, Viren Murthy, Madhavi Thampi, Brian

Tsui, Anand Yang, and Zhang Ke. What began as a common interest in China-India work blossomed into a firm friendship with Krista Van Fleit. I thank Krista for sharing in the everydays of work and life, and for her insightful comments on drafts. I am grateful to all those who engaged with my work during workshops and talks, and in the course of editing special issues and volumes: Magalí Armillas-Tiseyra, Barnali Chanda, Anup Grewal, Hala Halim, Satoru Hashimoto, Margaret Hillenbrand, Anne Garland Mahler, Shuang Shen, Sarah Townsend, and Nicolai Volland. Jennifer Wenzel and Harish Trivedi's generous thoughts on earlier chapter drafts guided my thinking through several subsequent versions.

I am immensely thankful to those who read this manuscript in its entirety. Andrea Bachner, Francesca Orsini, Karen Thornber, and David Wang endured the manuscript when it was still in the making, offering formative feedback and encouragement during a crucial stage of its development. Laura Brueck, Sangeeta Ray, and Wang Pu reviewed the manuscript with rigor; their constructive comments greatly improved the book.

This book has lived in many homes. Friends in China—Chen Xuefeng, Du Wei, Elizabeth Knup, Arthur Kroeber, and Li Jing—made research over long stays possible and pleasurable. In India, S. Padmanabhan lent me his vast knowledge of Hindi literature at the Sahitya Akademi, and Dr. Shreebhagwan Pandey guided me tirelessly through enigmatic texts. Several early research trips were funded by the Committee on Southern Asian Studies and Center for East Asian Studies at UChicago, and the UChicago Centers in Beijing and New Delhi provided indispensable logistical support.

I thank Christine Dunbar, Christian Winting, and Susan Pensak at Columbia University Press for expertly ushering this book to publication, and Emily Shelton for her careful copyediting. Parts of this book have been published earlier: a version of chapter 1 appeared in Tansen Sen and Brian Tsui, eds., *Beyond Pan-Asianism: Connecting China and India, 1840s–1960s* (New Delhi: Oxford University Press, 2021); and portions of chapter 3 were published as "A Poetics of the Writers' Conference: Literary Relation in the Cold War World" in *Comparative Literature Studies* 58, no. 3; and "Ellipses of Cultural Diplomacy: The 1957 Chinese Literary Sphere in Hindi" in *Journal of World Literature* 4, no. 4. I thank the presses and journals for allowing me to reprint this work. I also thank Dai Mengfei, Xiao Zhifei, Shripati Ankolekar, Ashok Maheshwari, and Alind Maheshwari for their help with obtaining image permissions.

For taking me as I am and standing with me still, I thank Susannah Kroeber, Mrinalini Ramesh, Anandi Rao, Shweta Sharma, Fiona Shen-Bayh, Siddharth Sigtia, Bhargav Thakur, and Mudit Trivedi. Finally, I am deeply grateful for my family. It is due to their resolute belief in the inherent value of intellectual work that an academic path has always felt like my calling. My aunts Archana and Ranjana Mangalagiri and sister Ankur Nanda unconditionally supported my work across great distances. Sutirtha and Aparajita Bhattacharya have embraced me as their own. This book owes its existence to them all, and particularly to my mother, Anjana Mangalagiri, whose strength and accomplishments through adversity afforded me a transnational childhood and ignited in me the spark of comparison. Shouvik Bhattacharya unquestioningly put me, and this book, above all else. He read each of its many versions—from term papers to proofs and the hundreds of drafts in between—with deep intellect and precision. Every day with Shouvik has made me a better reader, writer, and thinker. I thank him.

Notes

Introduction

1. Pheng Cheah, *What Is a World? On Postcolonial Literature as World Literature* (Durham, NC: Duke University Press, 2016), 1–45. Cheah uses the term "new world literature" to designate the revival of world literature debates in comparative literature in the early 2000s. This period marked an intensification of neoliberal globalization and a parallel "delegitimation of the humanities in universities and public consciousness" (27). "New world literature" is marked by comparative literature's preoccupation at the time with both theorizing its entanglement in the forces of contemporary globalization and articulating literature's relevance to global existence.
2. For a history of China-India comparative thought from the first millennium into the twentieth century, see Adhira Mangalagiri and Tansen Sen, "Introduction: Methods in China-India Studies," *International Journal of Asian Studies* 19, no. 2 (2022): 169–85.
3. Quoted from the subtitle of Sheldon Pollock and Benjamin Elman, eds., *What China and India Once Were: The Pasts That May Shape the Global Future* (New York: Columbia University Press, 2018).
4. Alessio Mattana, "The Allure of Synthesis: Science and the Literary in Comparative and World Literature," *Comparative Critical Studies* 17, no. 3 (2020): 351–72.
5. David Damrosch, Haun Saussy, and Jacob Edmond, "Trying to Make It Real: An Exchange Between Haun Saussy and David Damrosch," *Comparative Literature Studies* 53, no. 4 (2016): 660–93.
6. Hutcheson Macaulay Posnett, *Comparative Literature* (New York: D. Appleton, 1892), v.
7. René Wellek, "The Crisis of Comparative Literature," in *The Princeton Sourcebook in Comparative Literature: From the European Enlightenment to the Global Present*, ed.

David Damrosch, Natalie Melas, and Mbongiseni Buthelezi (Princeton, NJ: Princeton University Press, 2009), 165.

8. Hugo Meltzl, "Present Tasks of Comparative Literature," in *The Princeton Sourcebook in Comparative Literature: From the European Enlightenment to the Global Present*, ed. David Damrosch, Natalie Melas, and Mbongiseni Buthelezi (Princeton, NJ: Princeton University Press, 2009), 46.

9. Wellek, "Crisis of Comparative Literature," 165–66.

10. Emily Apter, "Comparative Exile: Competing Margins in the History of Comparative Literature," in *Comparative Literature in the Age of Multiculturalism*, ed. Charles Bernheimer (Baltimore, MD: Johns Hopkins University Press, 1995), 86, 90.

11. *Comparative Literature in the Age of Multiculturalism* and *Comparative Literature in an Age of Globalization* are, respectively, the titles of the 1995 and 2006 State of the Discipline Reports of the American Comparative Literature Association.

12. Karl Marx and Friedrich Engels, *The Communist Manifesto: With Selections from the Eighteenth Brumaire of Louis Bonaparte and Capital*, ed. Samuel Beer (New York: Appleton-Century-Crofts, 1955), 13–14.

13. Cheah, *What Is a World?*, 28.

14. Cheah, 28.

15. Cheah, 28.

16. G. W. F. Hegel, *Philosophy of History*, trans. J. Sibree (New York: P. F. Collier, 1905), 176–77.

17. Hegel, *Philosophy*, 165, 76.

18. Hegel, 230.

19. For a sustained discussion of Hegel's "Orient," see Teshale Tibebu, *Hegel and the Third World: The Making of Eurocentrism in World History* (Syracuse, NY: Syracuse University Press, 2010). A critique of Hegel's technique of comparison, specifically in relation to China and India, can be found in Pollock and Elman, *What China and India Once Were*, 11–24. Additional meditations on conducting China-India comparison can be found in Prasenjit Duara and Elizabeth Perry, eds., *Beyond Regimes: China and India Compared* (Cambridge, MA: Harvard University Asia Center, 2018); and Peter Van der veer, *The Value of Comparison* (Durham, NC: Duke University of Press, 2016).

20. Hegel, *Philosophy*, 70.

21. On late-Qing engagements with the colonized world, see Rebecca Karl, *Staging the World: Chinese Nationalism at the Turn of the Twentieth Century* (Durham, NC: Duke University Press, 2002).

22. Liang Qichao 梁啟超, "Yindu yu Zhongguo wenhua zhi qinshu de guanxi" 印度與中國文化之親屬的關係 [The kindred relation of Indian and Chinese culture], *Chenbao fukan* 晨报副刊 (May 3, 1924): 1–3.

23. Okakura Kakuzō, *The Awakening of Japan* (New York: Century, 1904).

24. Yuan Cai, "Zhang Taiyan and the Asiatic Humanitarian Brotherhood, 1907," in *Pan-Asianism: A Documentary History, Volume 1: 1850–1920*, ed. Sven Saaler and Christopher Szpilman (Lanham: Rowman & Littlefield, 2011), 183.

25. Prasenjit Duara, "Asia Redux: Conceptualizing a Region for Our Times," *Journal of Asian Studies* 69, no. 4 (2010): 972.

26. Stephen Hay, *Asian Ideas of East and West: Tagore and His Critics in Japan, China, and India* (Cambridge, MA: Harvard University Press, 1970).

27. Kris Manjapra, *Age of Entanglement: German and Indian Intellectuals Across Empire* (Cambridge, MA: Harvard University Press, 2014), 174.

28. Kris Manjapra, *M. N. Roy: Marxism and Colonial Cosmopolitanism* (New Delhi: Routledge, 2010), 84.

29. Maia Ramnath, *Haj to Utopia: How the Ghadar Movement Charted Global Radicalism and Attempted to Overthrow the British Empire* (Berkeley: University of California Press, 2011), 2.

30. B. R. Deepak, "Revolutionary Activities of the Ghadar Party in China," *China Report* 35, no. 4 (1999): 439–56.

31. A transcription and Chinese translation of the speech appeared in the July 13, 1925, issue of the *Beijing News Supplement* (*Jingbao fukan* 京報副刊).

32. Daswandha Singh, "Let China and India Unite for the Holy Cause," *Jingbao Fukan* 京報副刊 206 (1925): 8.

33. See, for example, Tansen Sen, *India, China, and the World: A Connected History* (Lanham, MD: Rowman & Littlefield, 2017). The following article provides an overview of the field of China-India studies: Tansen Sen, "The Emergence, Development, and Current State of China-India Studies," *Journal of Asian Studies* 80, no. 2 (2021): 363–87.

34. Rey Chow, "On Chineseness as a Theoretical Problem," in *Sinophone Studies: A Critical Reader*, ed. Shu-mei Shih, Chien-Hsin Tsai, and Brian Bernards (New York: Columbia University Press, 2013), 47.

35. Harish Trivedi, "The Progress of Hindi, Part 2: Hindi and the Nation," in *Literary Cultures in History: Reconstructions from South Asia*, ed. Sheldon Pollock (Berkeley: University of California Press, 2003), 960.

36. For a critique of multilingualism's uses in comparative literature, see Rey Chow, "The Old/New Question of Comparison in Literary Studies: A Post-European Perspective," *ELH* 71, no. 2 (2004): 289–311.

37. The Belt and Road Initiative, for example, has made available large pots of government funding for transnational academic work on those regions of interest to the initiative.

38. "China-India Photo Exhibit, Major Attraction at New Delhi Book Fair," *China Daily*, January 7, 2020, https://global.chinadaily.com.cn/a/202001/07/WS5e13f027a310cf3e35582e8a_2.html (accessed May 3, 2022).

39. Jiang Jingkui 姜景奎, "Lun ZhongYin guanxi de fenqi wenti." 論中印關係的分期問題 [On the periodization of Sino-Indian relations], *Journal of Guangdong University of Foreign Studies* 23, no. 3 (2012): 5–10. Jiang's periods largely map on to the World Book Fair chart, with some discrepancies in the final stages. His periods run as follows: an initial period (before the first century), development period (first to sixth centuries), golden period (sixth to thirteenth centuries), transition period (early thirteenth to mid-seventeenth centuries), period of decline (mid-seventeenth century to early twentieth century), exploratory period (early twentieth century to 1988), and the new era (1988 to the present).

40. Ji Xianlin's periodization, for example, runs as follows: Origins (pre-Han), Active Period (post-Han to Three Kingdoms), Heyday (Jin, Northern and Southern

dynasties, Sui, and Tang), Decline (Song and Yuan), Resurgence (Ming), Great Transformation (late Ming to early Qing), Trickle (Qing, *jindai, xiandai*). See Ji Xianlin 季羨林, *ZhongYin wenhua jiaoliu shi* 中印文化交流史 [A history of Sino-Indian cultural exchanges] (Beijing: Zhongguo shehui kexue chubanshe, 2007).

41. Such an approach stands in contrast to Chen Kuan-hsing's proposal to use "India as Method," wherein, as opposed to Europe or the West, India serves as a "reference point" (*canzhao* 参照) through which China can gain a better understanding of itself. See Chen Kuan-hsing 陳光興, "Zuowei fangfa de Yindu" 作為方法的印度 [India as method], *Dushu* 讀書 12 (2010): 10–15.

42. For two recent representative examples of English-language scholarship, see John Kieschnick and Meir Shahar, eds., *India in the Chinese Imagination: Myth, Religion, and Thought* (Philadelphia: University of Pennsylvania Press, 2014); and Gal Gvili, "Pan-Asian Poetics: Tagore and the Interpersonal in May Fourth New Poetry," *Journal of Asian Studies* 77, no. 1 (2018): 181–203.

43. Arunabh Ghosh, "Before 1962: The Case for 1950s China-India History," *Journal of Asian Studies* 76, no. 3 (2017): 697.

44. This conception of "relation" draws from the writings of Édouard Glissant, to whom I return in the conclusion.

45. For an instructive contemplation on the meanings of "state," see Judith Butler and Gayatri Chakravorty Spivak, *Who Sings the Nation-State?* (Calcutta: Seagull, 2007), especially 1–11. Butler writes, "How do we understand those sets of conditions and dispositions that account for the 'state we are in' (which could, after all, be a state of mind) from the 'state' we are in when and if we hold rights of citizenship or when the state functions as the provisional domicile for our work? If we pause for a moment on the meaning of 'states' as the 'conditions in which we find ourselves,' then it seems we reference the moment of writing itself or perhaps even a certain condition of being upset, out of sorts: what kind of state are we in when we start to think about the state?" (2–3). These questions inform my thinking here.

1. Anatomy of Antagonism

1. In this chapter, I use the term "Indian policeman"—instead of "Sikh policeman"—to name the central figure under discussion, in line with the terminology most commonly used in Chinese media and accounts of the time, which primarily use the term "Indian policeman" (*Yindu xunbu* 印度巡捕) to refer to the men. The tendency to group the policemen under the blanket term "Sikh" finds origins in colonial administrative and epistemological practices. In the nineteenth century, "Sikh" in British colonial discourse emerged as a category constructed by colonial ideologies of martial races in order to further instrumental purposes of defending and policing the empire. Although a common term in colonial British parlance, "Sikh policeman" more accurately identifies not the men themselves (many of whom, in any event, did not belong to what the British defined as the Sikh community in Punjab) but rather a

mythic colonial construct used strategically to homogenize a variegated group of people into what was considered a "martial species." On the colonial construct of "Sikh," see Tony Ballantyne, *Between Colonialism and Diaspora: Sikh Cultural Formations in an Imperial World* (Durham, NC: Duke University Press, 2006), 34–85; and Richard Fox, *Lions of the Punjab: Culture in the Making* (Berkeley: University of California Press, 1985), 3.

2. Isabella Jackson, "The Raj on Nanjing Road: Sikh Policemen in Treaty-Port Shanghai," *Modern Asian Studies* 46, no. 6 (2012): 1672–704.

3. For a fuller historical account of the SMP's Indian force, see Cao Yin, *From Policemen to Revolutionaries: A Sikh Diaspora in Global Shanghai* (Leiden: Brill, 2017).

4. On the construction of the Sikh as a "martial race" see Heather Streets, *Martial Races: The Military, Race, and Masculinity in British Imperial Culture, 1857–1914* (Manchester: Manchester University Press); and Gavin Rand and Kim Wagner, "Recruiting the 'Martial Races': Identities and Military Service in Colonial India," *Patterns of Prejudice* 46, nos. 3–4 (2012): 232–54.

5. For a discussion of the iconography of the Indian policeman in popular culture, see Liu Yongguang 劉永廣, "Zhimin chiru yu wenhua xixue: 'hongtou Asan' xingxiang de suzao yu chuanbo" 殖民恥辱與文化戲謔: '紅頭阿三' 形象的塑造與傳播 [Colonial shame and cultural irony: the portrayal and circulation of the image of Red-head Asan], *Lishi Jiaoxue* 歷史教學 12 (2018): 20–30.

6. Translated and quoted in Viren Murthy, "Rethinking Pan-Asianism through Zhang Taiyan: India as Method," in *Beyond Pan-Asianism: Connecting China and India, 1840s–1960s*, ed. Tansen Sen and Brian Tsui (New Delhi: Oxford University Press, 2021), 110–11.

7. Diedie 喋喋, "Chao Yindu xunbu" 嘲印度巡捕 [Mocking the Indian policeman], *Huaji Shici* 滑稽詩詞 2 (1913): 34.

8. Chen Jiazhen 陳嘉震 and Ouyang Pu 歐陽璞, "Ruci Shanghai" 如此上海 [Such is Shanghai], *Liangyou* 良友 89 (1934): 21.

9. Christopher Rea, *The Age of Irreverence: A New History of Laughter in China* (Berkeley: University of California Press, 2015).

10. Inaga Shigemi, "Okakura Kakuzō and India: The Trajectory of Modern National Consciousness and Pan-Asian Ideology Across Borders," *Review of Japanese Culture and Society*, no. 24 (2012): 41.

11. Okakura Kakuzō, *The Awakening of Japan* (New York: Century, 1904), 95.

12. Yuan Cai, "Zhang Taiyan and the Asiatic Humanitarian Brotherhood, 1907," in *Pan-Asianism: A Documentary History, Volume 1: 1850–1920*, ed. Sven Saaler and Christopher Szpilman (Lanham: Rowman & Littlefield, 2011), 181.

13. Viren Murthy, *The Political Philosophy of Zhang Taiyan: The Resistance of Consciousness* (Leiden: Brill, 2011), 79.

14. Zhang renders their names in Chinese as Luobohan 逻钵罕 and Baoshen 保什. B. R. Deepak has conjectured that "Baoshen" may be Surendra Mohan Bose. The men communicated in Japanese, since Baoshen was fluent in the language. See B. R. Deepak, *India-China Relations in the First Half of the Twentieth Century* (New Delhi: APH, 2001), 40; and Murthy, "Rethinking Pan-Asianism," 112–15.

15. Quoted in Cai, "Zhang Taiyan," 179.

16. One such event was a meeting held on April 20, 1907, commemorating Shivaji, a seventeenth-century Maratha king who famously led an uprising against the Mughal emperor Aurangzeb. For further details on the Shivaji Commemoration, see Rebecca Karl, *Staging the World: Chinese Nationalism at the Turn of the Twentieth Century* (Durham, NC: Duke University Press, 2002), 168–74. For Zhang Taiyan's report of the meeting, see Zhang Taiyan 章太炎, "Ji Yindu Xipoqi wang jinian-hui shi" 記印度西婆耆王紀念會事 [A report on the meeting commemorating the Indian king Shivaji], *Minbao* 民報 13 (1907): 19–26.

17. Kang Youwei 康有為, "Yu tongxue zhuzi Liang Qichao deng lun Yindu wangguo youyu ge sheng zili shu" 與同學諸子梁啟超等論印度亡國由於各省自立書 [A letter to fellow scholar Liang Qichao and others on India's colonization due to the independence of its provinces], in *Kang Youwei quanji* 康有為全集, ed. Jiang Yihua 姜義華 and Zhang Ronghua 張榮華 (Beijing: Zhongguo renmin daxue chuban-she, [1902]) 1998, 334.

18. Kang, "Yu tongxue," 335.

19. Karl, *Staging the World*, 16.

20. Shu-mei Shih, *The Lure of the Modern: Writing Modernism in Semicolonial China, 1917–1937* (Berkeley: University of California, 2001).

21. Shih, *Lure of the Modern*, 36–37.

22. Shih arguably makes too easy a distinction here between "formal" and "semi" colonization. Many of her claims about semicolonialism, such as the lack of an "untainted and untroubled sanctuary" of "native culture" that could serve as the "unquestioned locus of resistance," holds true for the many forms antico-lonial resistance took throughout the colonized world, even in those regions Shih labels as "formal" for having a "uniform colonial infrastructure." Simi-larly, Shih's claim that a bifurcated cultural attitude to the West—as an oppres-sor to be criticized and a modernizing force to be emulated—is unique to Chi-nese semicolonization remains unpersuasive. Generalizations about the structures of colonialism aside, her compelling analysis of the particular cul-tural formations in colonial China remains instructive. Shih, 36–37.

23. Yue Meng, *Shanghai and the Edges of Empires* (Minneapolis: University of Minne-sota Press, 2006).

24. Christopher Rea, "Introduction: 'Charlie Chaplin of the East,' Xu Zhuodai," in *China's Chaplin: Comic Stories and Farces by Xu Zhuodai* (Ithaca, NY: Cornell Univer-sity East Asia Program, 2019), 1–29. On Xu's understudied writings published during his time in Japan, see Chen Linghong 陳凌虹, "Xu Zhuodai liu Ri jingli ji zaoqi chuangzuo huodong kao" 徐卓呆留日經歷及早期創作活動考 [Xu Zhuodai's experiences in Japan and early works], *Zhongguo xiandai wenxue yanjiu congkan* 中國現代文學研究叢刊 11 (2016): 60–69.

25. On Xu Zhuodai's pen names, see Rea, "Introduction," 10–11.

26. This earlier pen name, literally "melon seeds," could also be read as "son of China," since *guafen* 瓜分 or "cutting up the melon," alluded to in the novel's title, was a common metaphor for the colonial powers' intention to carve up China like a melon. On the *guafen* metaphor, see Rudolf Wagner, " 'Dividing Up the [Chinese] Melon': The Fate of a Transcultural Metaphor in the Formation of National Myth," *Transcultural Studies* 8, no. 1 (2017): 9–122.

27. Xu Zhuodai 徐卓呆, "Fenge hou zhi wuren" 分割後之吾人 [My people after partition], *Jiangsu* 江蘇 8–10 (1904): 8.134.

28. Rebecca Karl, "'Slavery,' Citizenship, and Gender in Late Qing China's Global Context," in *Rethinking the 1898 Reform Period: Political and Cultural Change in Late Qing China*, ed. Rebecca Karl and Peter Zarrow (Cambridge, MA: Harvard University Asia Center, 2002), 217.

29. In late Qing discourse, the Indian's slavishness was perhaps surpassed only by "black slaves" (*heinu* 黑奴). See Karl, *Staging the World*, 120–24.

30. Xu, "Fenge hou," 9–10.235.

31. Karl, *Staging the World*, 159–63.

32. Xu, "Fenge hou," 8.134.

33. Xu, 9–10.244.

34. Incomplete novels were not uncommon in the late Qing literary sphere. Writers' enthusiasm to get new stories into print often left old ones unfinished. The serial format of long-form fiction, published over several journal or newspaper issues, added another layer of unpredictability and inconsistency. On reading late Qing fictional incompleteness constructively, see Lorenzo Andolfatto, *Hundred Days' Literature: Chinese Utopian Fiction at the End of Empire, 1902–1910* (Leiden: Brill, 2019), 55–82.

35. This novel was *The Female Knight-Errant of Qixia* (*Qixia nüxia* 棲霞女俠), also by Peng Yu (the author of *Twin Souls*), apparently a translation of a work attributed to a Japanese writer, Iwatani Ranken 巖谷蘭軒. Serialization of the novel was discontinued in *Shenbao* because it had since been published in book form.

36. "Benbao fuyin" 本報附印 [Printed in this newspaper], *Shenbao* 申報, March 11, 1907.

37. Yadong Pofo 亞東破佛, "Yuyan xiaoshuo shuang linghun" 寓言小說雙靈魂 [Twin souls: an allegorical story], *Shenbao* 申報, March 12–April 6, 1907, 3.19.

38. Yadong Pofo, "Yuyan xiaoshuo," 24.18.

39. Yadong Pofo, 24.18.

40. Although the characters *pofo* 破佛 may suggest anti-Buddhist sentiment (if understood literally as "destroying the Buddha"), the pen name is better interpreted when *po* is taken in its less common usage to connote exposition or revelation. In this sense, *pofo* may be better translated along the lines of "exposing the truth of the Buddha."

41. Some scholars have categorized *Twin Souls* as among the works Peng is said to have translated from Japanese, but this seems unlikely for at least two reasons. First, scholars disagree on whether Peng was proficient enough in Japanese to be able to translate. See Fu Jianzhou 付建舟, "Wan Qing Zhe ji zuojia Yadong Pofo shengping zhushu kao" 晚清浙籍作家亞東破佛生平著述考 [The life and writings of Yadong Pofo, a Zhejiang writer in the late Qing dynasty], *Suzhou jiaoyu xueyuan xuebao* 蘇州教育學院學報 33, no. 5 (2016): 14. Second, I have found no record of which Japanese source text *Twin Souls* could conceivably be a translation of, and it is difficult to see how a novel steeped in late Qing discourses of Chinese national autonomy could have been translated from Japanese.

42. Snippets of Peng's life as a monk appear in the diaries of Feng Zikai 豐子愷 (1898–1975) and Li Shutong 李叔同 (1880–1942), who overlapped with Peng at Hupao.

For biographical accounts of Peng, see Fu Jianzhou, "Wan Qing Zhe ji"; Liu Delong 劉德隆, "Shuang linghun" 雙靈魂 [Twin souls], *Ming-Qing xiaoshuo yanjiu* 明清小說研究 2 (1996): 231–35; Peng Changqing 彭长卿, "Yadong Pofo zhuanlue" 亞東破佛傳略 [A biography of Yadong Pofo], *Qingmo xiaoshuo yanjiu* 清末小說研究 5 (1981): 26–39.

43. Barbara Mittler, *A Newspaper for China? Power, Identity, and Change in Shanghai's News Media, 1872-1912* (Cambridge, MA: Harvard University Asia Center, 2004), 3.

44. Mittler, *Newspaper for China?*, 18.

45. Quoted in Mittler, 14.

46. Such movements of the soul within the body would not have been entirely foreign to the reader. According to Chinese folk medical beliefs, a fright can cause body-soul dissociation with involuntary "soul-loss" occurring as a common ailment. Stevan Harrell, "The Concept of Soul in Chinese Folk Religion," *Journal of Asian Studies* 38, no. 3 (1979): 519–28.

47. Yadong Pofo, "Yuyan xiaoshuo," 2.18.

48. Yadong Pofo, 9.18.

49. Yadong Pofo, 4.19.

50. Yadong Pofo, 5.19.

51. Such scientific approaches are in line with late Qing science fiction explorations of the idea that problems of the soul could be cured through Western scientific techniques. See Luan Weiping 欒偉平 "Jindai kexue xiaoshuo yu linghun: You 'Xin Faluo xiansheng tan' shuo kaiqu" 近代科學小說與靈魂——由《新法螺先生譚》說開去 [Early modern fiction and the soul: starting from *New Tales of Mr. Braggadocio*], *Zhongguo xiandai wenxue yanjiu congkan* 中國現代文學研究叢刊 3 (2006): 46–60.

52. A Ying 阿英, *Xiaoshuo xiantan* 小說閒談 [Casual discussions on fiction] (Shanghai: Gudian wenxue chubanshe, 1958), 95. A Ying is one of the few critics to have published a sustained discussion of *Twin Souls*.

53. This debate was famously articulated in terms of the substance-function or *tiyong* 體用 concept, captured in the phrase *zhongxue weiti, xixue weiyong* 中學為體, 西學為用, meaning "Chinese learning as substance/essence, Western learning for function/application." Proponents of Westernization pushed the concept as a method for using Western learning in a utilitarian way while preserving Chinese essence. See Joseph Levenson, *Confucian China and its Modern Fate: A Trilogy*, vol. 1 (Berkeley: University of California Press, 1968), 59–78.

54. On the *kexue/xuanxue* debates, see Wang Hui, "Discursive Community and the Genealogy of Scientific Categories," in *Everyday Modernity in China*, ed. Madeleine Yue Dong and Joshua Goldstein (Seattle: University of Washington Press, 2006), 80–120.

55. The concept of "national essence" took on new significance in the 1900s, marking a school of thought that promoted the revitalization of Chinese cultural heritage as paving the path to modernity. See Tze-ki Hon, "National Essence, National Learning, and Culture: Historical Writings in Guocui Xuebao, Xueheng, and Guoxue Jikan," *Historiography East and West* 1, no. 2 (2003): 242–86.

56. David Der-wei Wang, *Fin-de-Siècle Splendor: Repressed Modernities of Late Qing Fiction, 1849-1911* (Stanford, CA: Stanford University Press, 1997), 33–36.

57. Shi Jiu 拾玖, "Hongtou Asan kao" 紅頭阿三考 [On Hongtou Asan], *Shenbao* 申報, August 24, 1935, 5.
58. Cheng Guan 澄觀, "Yindu Asan mingcheng zhi youlai" 印度阿三名稱之由來 [The reason behind the Indian Asan's name], *Hongguang* 宏光 5 (1923): 61.
59. "Hongtou Asan yu lacheren" 紅頭阿三與拉車人 [Hongtou Asan and the rickshaw puller], *Shiyong Yingwen banyuekan* 實用英文半月刊 2, no. 4 (1937): 49.
60. Attempts to define the *hongtou asan* etymologically were accompanied by an ethnographic interest in the Indian policeman. One article entitled "The Beautification Methods of the Indian Asan" decodes the odd physical appearance of the Indian policeman through a series of photographs that explain, step by step, the process through which Sikh men tend their hair and tie their turbans. See "Yindu Asan meirongshu" 印度阿三美容術 [The beautification methods of the Indian Asan], *Shijie Huabao* 世界畫報 3, no. 5 (1941): 32–33. Although appearing to provide objective, disinterested information, a politicized undertone pervades the article, such as when the Sikh bangle or *kaṛā* (an important religious ornament for Sikhs) is described as the policeman's shackle, a symbol of his subservience to his colonial master.
61. The story is published in the Shanghai Nanyang Advanced Business School's student association magazine.
62. Chen Kangtai 陳康泰, "Hongtou Asan" 紅頭阿三 [Hongtou Asan], *Nanyang gaoji shangye xuexiao xueshenghui jikan* 南洋高級商業學校學生會季刊 1 (1927): 40.
63. Translated in Yu Dafu 郁達夫, "Sinking," in *The Columbia Anthology of Modern Chinese Literature*, ed. Joseph Lau and Howard Goldblatt (New York: Columbia University Press, 2007), 51–52.
64. Chen, "Hongtou Asan," 40.
65. Yu, "Sinking," 35.
66. Yu, 55.
67. Chen, "Hongtou Asan," 41.
68. For a foundational (and controversial) discussion of this trope, see C. T. Hsia, "Obsession with China: The Moral Burden of Modern Chinese Literature," in *A History of Modern Chinese Fiction* (Bloomington: Indiana University Press, 1999), 533–54.
69. Xiaobing Tang and Michel Hockx, "The Creation Society (1921–1930)," in *Literary Societies of Republican China*, ed. Kirk Denton and Michel Hockx (Plymouth: Rowman & Littlefield, 2008), 107.
70. Interestingly, "Hongtou Asan" appeared in the same year that Yu Dafu publicly announced his withdrawal from the Creation Society, suggesting that the short story could have been written as a tribute to the writer.
71. On intertextuality in Yu Dafu's writing, see Valerie Levan, "The Meaning of Foreign Text in Yu Dafu's *Sinking* Collection," *Modern Chinese Literature and Culture* 24, no. 1 (2012): 48–87.
72. Jeffrey Wasserstrom, *Student Protests in Twentieth-Century China: The View from Shanghai* (Stanford, CA: Stanford University Press, 1991), 63.
73. Daniel Fried, "A Bloody Absence: Communist Narratology and the Literature of May Thirtieth," *Chinese Literature: Essays, Articles, Reviews* 26 (2004): 23–53.

74. Ba Jin 巴金, *Siqu de taiyang* 死去的太陽 [The setting sun] (Shanghai: Kaiming shudian, 1931), 6–9.

75. On the May Thirtieth movement, see Nicholas Clifford, *Spoilt Children of Empire: Westerners in Shanghai and the Chinese Revolution of the 1920s* (Hanover: University Press of New England, 1976); Hung-Ting Ku, "Urban Mass Movement: The May Thirtieth Movement in Shanghai," *Modern Asian Studies* 13, no. 2 (1979); Richard Rigby, *The May 30 Movement: Events and Themes* (Canberra: Australian National University Press, 1980); and Wasserstrom, *Student Protests*, 95–124.

76. The Sun Society was an offshoot of the Creation Society. Although both were comprised of leftist writers and both promoted the practice of revolutionary literature, the writers in Sun Society were cardholding members of CCP and developed close ties with the Party. See Tang and Hockx, "Creation Society," 103–36.

77. Yang Cunren 楊邨人, "Hongtou Asan" 紅頭阿三 [Hongtou Asan], *Dazhong wenyi* 大眾文藝 2, no. 3 (1930): 12.

78. Yang, "Hongtou Asan," 13.

79. Yang, 13.

80. Yang, 14.

81. Yang, 15.

82. Jiang's story is included in Harold Isaacs's *Straw Sandals*, a collection of Chinese short stories (1918–1933) curated by Isaacs in conversation with Lu Xun and Mao Dun and published much later in 1974. Referring to his correspondence with Lu Xun on whether to include Jiang's story in the collection, Isaacs notes: "In one of his letters about this collection, Lu Hsun, who was on record as having scant regard for this writer and, indeed, the whole type he represented [likely referring to members of the Creation and Sun Societies], indicated indifference as to which of his stories might be used, but no objection to including him." See Harold Isaacs, ed., *Straw Sandals: Chinese Short Stories, 1918-1933* (Cambridge, MA: MIT Press, 1974), lx. Isaacs mistranslated "Asan" as "Hassan," endowing the Indian policeman with an individualized (and unlikely) name. This has the effect of reframing the story as narrating an extraordinary incident concerning a single policeman, whereas the anonymity of "Asan" in fact enables Jiang to center a collective revolutionary consciousness shared among the colonized and oppressed.

83. Jiang Guangci 蔣光慈, "Asan" 阿三 [Asan], *Tuohuangzhe* 拓荒者 1, no. 1 (1930): 59–60.

84. Jiang, "Asan," 61.

85. Jin Xuan 錦軒, "Hongtou Asan" 紅頭阿三 [Hongtou Asan], *Qianfeng zhoubao* 前鋒週報 6 (1930): 46.

86. Mao Dun 茅盾, *Hong* 虹 [Rainbow] (Shanghai: Kaiming shudian, 1930), 224.

87. Mao Dun, *Hong*, 265.

88. Mao Dun, 265.

89. For an instructive close reading of *Rainbow*, see Rey Chow, *Woman and Chinese Modernity: The Politics of Reading Between West and East* (Minneapolis: University of Minnesota Press, 1991), 103–7.

90. For a discussion of "Gandhi fever" in the Chinese media, see Wang Ruliang 王汝良, *Zhongguo wenxue zhong de Yindu xingxiang yanjiu* 中國文學中的印度形象研究 [The image of India in Chinese literature] (Beijing: Zhonghua shuju, 2018), 149–68.

91. See, for example, "Gandi kang Ying yundong" 甘地抗英運動 [Gandhi's anti-British movement], *Guowen zhoubao* 國文週報 7, no. 20. (1930): 8–9; and "Yindu zhi fan Ying yundong" 印度之反英運動 [India's anti-British movement], *Dongfang zazhi* 東方雜誌 27, no. 8 (1930): 1–3.

92. *New Life* ranked as a relatively minor and short-lived journal, publishing twenty-one issues during its ten-month run from April 1931 to January 1932. Although bearing the same name, the journal pre-dates Chiang Kai-shek's "New Life Movement" 新生活運動 inaugurated in 1934, when Chiang called for a militarized Chinese nation, disciplined through a resurgence of Confucian values. A cursory study of the journal reveals no direct relation to what later emerged as the New Life Movement.

93. "Indian Policeman and Gandhi" appears as an independent image without reference to the articles in the issue; as such, the issue provides little context for the cartoon beyond the journal's general interest in those concerns facing Chinese residents of Shanghai's International Settlement (increased traffic congestion caused by trams, for example). Such decontextualized cartoons frequently appear in the pages of *New Life*. "Indian Policeman and Gandhi," along with the other cartoons in different issues, bears the signature "Xie man" 謝曼. Additional cartoons by the same artist include scenes from life in Shanghai and its International Settlement.

94. Pan Jienong 潘子農, "Yinbu zhi si" 印捕之死 [Death of an Indian policeman], *Kaizhan* 開戰 5 (1930): 38.

95. Pan, "Yinbu zhi si," 45.

96. To give another example, "From Gandhi to Nehru," published in a youth magazine in 1937, similarly attempts to reconcile the politics of the Indian policeman stationed in Shanghai with the competing philosophies of Gandhi's noncooperation movement and Nehru's socialist approach to Indian independence. Framed as a dialogue between two Indian policemen, the story reads as a pedagogical endeavor to teach its young readers about the current political landscape of India. The story ends with the protagonist, an Indian policeman stationed in China, resolving to quit his job and return to India to join the independence movement. See He Zou 何奏, "You Gandi dao Nihelu: Yige Yindu xunbu de gushi" 由甘地到尼赫魯：一個印度巡捕的故事 [From Gandhi to Nehru: the story of an Indian policeman], *Xin shaonian* 新少年 3, no. 9 (1937): 58.

97. Cao, *From Policemen to Revolutionaries*, 140–62.

98. Liang Qichao 梁啟超, "Yindu yu Zhongguo wenhua zhi qinshu de guanxi" 印度與中國文化之親屬的關係 [The kindred relation of Indian and Chinese culture], *Chenbao fukan* 晨报副刊 (May 3, 1924): 1.

99. Quoted in Stephen Hay, *Asian Ideas of East and West: Tagore and His Critics in Japan, China, and India* (Cambridge, MA: Harvard University Press, 1970),158.

100. Hay, *Asian Ideas*, 171.

101. Hay, 181.

102. Hay, 204.
103. Xu Zhimo, "Taige'er lai hua" 泰戈爾來華 [Tagore visits China], *Xiaoshuo yuebao* 小說月報 14, no. 9 (1923): 2.
104. Xu, "Taige'er lai hua," 2.
105. Bai Yun 白云, "Gei Yindu Asan" 給印度阿三 [Ode to the Indian Asan], *Shidai zhishi* 時代知識 1, no. 7 (1936): 43.
106. Bai Yun, "Gei Yindu Asan," 44.

2. Revolution Redux

1. Originally founded by Sachindranath Sanyal under the name HRA, "S" (Socialist) was appended in 1928 by Bhagat Singh. On the HRSA and Bhagat Singh, see Kaushalya Devi Dublish, *Revolutionaries and Their Activities in Northern India* (Delhi: BR, 1982); and Chris Moffat, *India's Revolutionary Inheritance: Politics and the Promise of Bhagat Singh* (Cambridge: Cambridge University Press, 2019).
2. Dublish, *Revolutionaries*, 178.
3. The full text of the pamphlet is available in Dublish, *Revolutionaries*, 200–201.
4. "S. H. Vatsyayan: A Chronology," *Mahfil* 2, no. 1 (1965): 1–2.
5. Agyeya famously received his penname from Premchand, who published Agyeya's first short story under the pen name, since any publications during Agyeya's imprisonment could only be authored anonymously. For the story of how Agyeya received his pen name, see Krishnadutt Paliwal, "Agyeya: Jel Jīvan kī Manobhūmikā" [Agyeya: The state of mind of imprisonment] in *Agyeya: Jel ke Dinoṁ kī Kahānīyāṁ* [Agyeya: stories from his jail days], ed. Krishnadutt Paliwal (New Delhi: Vani, 2013), 22–23.
6. Paliwal, "Agyeya," 13.
7. Bhavan Singh Rana, *Chandra Shekhar Azad: An Immortal Revolutionary of India*, trans. Brij Bhushan Paliwal (Delhi: Diamond, 2004), 87–92.
8. Yashpal, *Yashpal Looks Back: Selections from an Autobiography*, trans. Corinne Friend (New Delhi: Vikas, 1981), 155.
9. Statement of Kailashpatti an import in the Delhi Conspiracy Case, 1931, File No. 11/15/1931, National Archives of India, Home Department Political.
10. Agyeya, "Author's Introduction," in *Shekhar: A Life* (Gurgaon: Penguin Random House India, 2018), xi. Translation is Shingavi and Dalmia's.
11. General Reports on the Progress of the Delhi Conspiracy Case, 1930, File No. F-4-13 1930, National Archives of India, Home Department Political.
12. Paliwal, "Agyeya," 13.
13. Question in the Legislative Assembly, File No. 7.22/37/35 1935, National Archives of India, Home Department Political.
14. Paliwal, "Agyeya," 21.
15. Only the first two volumes of *Shekhar* were published in 1941 and 1943, respectively. On *Shekhar*, see Nikhil Govind, "Agyeya: Enmeshments of Revolutionary Subjectivity," in *Love and Freedom: The Revolutionary in the Hindi Novel* (New Delhi: Routledge, 2014), 109–33; Angelika Malinar, "The Artist as Autobiographer:

Sekhar Ek Jivani," in *Narrative Strategies: Essays on South Asian Literature and Film*, ed. Vasudha Dalmia and Theo Damsteegt (New Delhi: Oxford University Press, 1998), 229–42; Simona Sawhney, "The Mark of the Political in *Shekhar Ek Jivani*," in *Hindi Modernism: Rethinking Agyeya and his Times*, ed. Vasudha Dalmia (Berkeley: University of California, 2012), 41–58; and Snehal Shingavi, "Agyeya's Unfinished Revolution: Sexual and Social Freedom in Shekhar: Ek Jivani," *South Asia: Journal of South Asian Studies* 39, no. 3 (2016): 577–91.

16. Agyeya, *Smr̥ti–lekh* [Memoirs] (New Delhi: National, 1996), 45.

17. *Awakening*'s regular columns included news items from across the globe ("News Compilation," *samācār saṅkalan*), essays on current social conditions in India, short stories and poems, women's affairs, and in-depth discussions on international affairs.

18. In addition to frequent updates on the ongoing Chinese civil war in its news column, *Awakening* published a series of full-length articles on China between 1931 and 1934 (the years of Agyeya's imprisonment), including "The Tragic Story of Chinese Women" (October 1932), "China's Political Condition" (April 1933), "The Spread of Fascism in China" (May 1933), and "China's Savior: Dr. Sun Yat-sen" (September 1933). Premchand, ed., *Jāgaraṇ* [Awakening], vols. 1.1–2.52 (1932–1934).

19. Jawaharlal Nehru, "Foreword," in *Prison Days and Other Poems* (Benares: Saraswati, 1946), 5.

20. While in jail, Agyeya wrote a total of eighteen short stories. Ten of these are set in India. Of the eight others, three are set in China, two in Russia ("The Meeting," 1931; "Greater than Reason," 1932), one in Greece/Turkey ("On the Path to Ankara," 1933), one in Cuba ("The Curse of Cassandra," 1933), and one in France ("The Path Not Taken," 1931). For an overview of the stories, see Theo Damsteegt, "Violence in the Age of Gandhi—Ajneya's Early Short Stories," *Studien Zur Indologie und Iranistik* 11–12 (1986): 312–13.

21. Richard Rigby, *The May 30 Movement: Events and Themes* (Canberra: Australian National University Press, 1980), 113.

22. This understanding of the May Thirtieth Movement's larger significance appears, for example, in M. N. Roy, *Revolution and Counter-Revolution in China* (Calcutta: Renaissance, 1946), 353–67.

23. David Petrie, *Communism in India, 1924–1927*, ed. Mahadevaprasad Saha (Calcutta: Editions Indian, 1972), 187.

24. Petrie, *Communism in India*, 188.

25. Petrie, 197. Although the official, internationally recognized Communist Party of India, of which Roy was a founding member, remained wary of associating with "terrorist" organizations such as the HRSA, members of the HRSA, well read in international affairs, would have kept abreast of the party's publications.

26. Agyeya, *Agyeya Racănāvalī* [Collected works of Agyeya], ed. Krishnadutt Paliwal, vol. 3 (New Delhi: Bharatiya Gyanpith, 2011), 355–56.

27. Jacques Derrida, *Specters of Marx: The State of Debt, the Work of Mourning, and the New International* (New York: Routledge, 1994). Derrida takes the phrase from Shakespeare's *Hamlet*.

28. Derrida, *Specters of Marx*, 10.

29. Agyeya, *Agyeya Racănāvalī*, 356.

30. Agyeya, 357.

31. Agyeya, 362.

32. Agyeya, 362.

33. Agyeya, 362.

34. Walter Benjamin, *Illuminations* (New York: Schocken, 1969), 257–58.

35. Agyeya, *Agyeya Racănāvalī*, 362.

36. Agyeya, 373.

37. Agyeya, 365–66.

38. Agyeya, 362.

39. Suresh Chandra Pandey, *Agyeya: Sāhityă Vimarś* [Agyeya: literary discussions] (New Delhi: Naman, 2010), 183.

40. Duns Scotus quoted in Giorgio Agamben, *Potentialities: Collected Essays in Philosophy* (Stanford, CA: Stanford University Press, 1999), 262.

41. Agyeya, *Agyeya Racănāvalī*, 82–83.

42. Dublish, *Revolutionaries*, 87.

43. Dublish, 88.

44. "Message to King," *Times of India*, December 24, 1929, 11.

45. "Message to King."

46. Agyeya, *Agyeya Racănāvalī*, 87.

47. Agyeya, 88.

48. Agyeya, 88.

49. Agyeya, 89.

50. Duns Scotus quoted in Agamben, *Potentialities*, 262.

51. Agyeya, "Author's Introduction," xii–iii.

52. Agyeya, xii–iii.

53. Paliwal, "Agyeya," 21.

54. Agyeya, *Agyeya Racănāvalī*, 20.

55. Agyeya, 64.

56. Agyeya, 65.

57. Agyeya, 66. Hariti's sacrifice of the "right to love," a sign of her sacrificing her womanhood, becomes further amplified given her name, which alludes to an eponymous Buddhist deity known as the "Goddess of Motherly Love." On Hariti in Buddhist lore, see Miranda Shaw, "Hariti: Goddess of Motherly Love," in *Buddhist Goddesses of India* (Princeton, NJ: Princeton University Press, 2006), 110–42. Buddhist texts depict Hariti as "the epitome of maternal grace, a serene and benevolent matron, surrounded by children and cradling an infant at her breast" (110). In Buddhist lore, Hariti apparently transformed from an ogress who devoured children into a follower of the Buddha and beacon of maternal love. Agyeya's "Hariti" inverts this transformation, depicting instead an orphan, deprived of maternal love, who replaces that lost love with her devotion to the revolutionary army, a devotion that costs her her femininity. The Buddhist allusions evoked in Agyeya's naming of Hariti (and her comrade Kwanyin, named after the well-known eponymous Chinese goddess of Buddhist origins,

Guanyin) recalls the narrative of China and India's ancient connectedness while rewriting that link in the idiom of revolution.

58. As a woman who assumes a male identity in order to don the soldier's uniform and wield arms, Hariti resonates with the Chinese folk heroine Mulan, who similarly disguises herself as a man to fight in the army. The earliest records of the story date to the twelfth century, with subsequent versions appearing in the sixteenth-century (most famously in Xu Wei's play *The Female Mulan Joins the Army in Place of Her Father* 雌木蘭替父從軍) and again in nineteenth-century late Qing renditions. While I have not found evidence of Agyeya's familiarity with this story, Hariti makes for an apt comparison with Mulan and other Chinese female figures with male attributes, such as the trope of the female knight-errant (*nüxia*). Studies include: Shiamin Kwa and Wilt Idema, eds., *Mulan: Five Versions of a Classic Chinese Legend with Related Texts* (Indianapolis: Hackett, 2010); and Roland Alternburger, *The Sword and the Needle: The Female Knight-Errant (xia) in Traditional Chinese Narrative* (Bern: Peter Lang, 2009).

59. Agyeya, *Agyeya Racănăvalī*, 77.

60. In his characterization of Hariti as a woman revolutionary, Agyeya echoes a central concern for many Hindi writers of the time. In the early twentieth century, nationalist debates on the "woman's question" led to the development of a Hindi literary trope centered on the concept of *sevā* (service). Traditionally denoting one's relationship with a deity or a guru in the nineteenth century, *sevā* took on new shades of meaning in the twentieth century, now associated with service to society (*samāj-sevā*) and to the nation (*deś-sevā*). On the discourse of *sevā* and the women's question, see Partha Chatterjee, "The Nationalist Resolution of the Women's Question," in *Recasting Women: Essays in Colonial History*, ed. Kumkum Sangari and Sudesh Vaid (New Brunswick, NJ: Rutgers University Press, 1989), 233–53; Shobna Nijhawan, *Women and Girls in the Hindi Public Sphere* (New Delhi: Oxford University Press, 2012); and Francesca Orsini, "Domesticity and Beyond," *South Asia Research* 19, no. 2 (1999): 137–60.

61. Agyeya, *Agyeya Racănăvalī*, 77.

62. Agyeya, 19.

63. Agyeya, 21.

64. E. V. Ramakrishnan, *Making It New: Modernism in Malayalam, Marathi, and Hindi Poetry* (Shimla: Indian Institute of Advanced Study, 1995), 29.

65. Harish Trivedi, "Agyeya and His Shekhar: The Second Greatest Novel in Hindi?," *Indian Literature* 55, no. 1 (2011): 82.

66. On Agyeya's modernism, see Vasudha Dalmia, ed., *Hindi Modernism: Rethinking Agyeya and His Times* (Berkeley: University of California, 2012).

67. Shingavi, "Agyeya's Unfinished Revolution," 578.

68. Jaidev, *The Culture of Pastiche: Existential Aestheticism in the Contemporary Hindi Novel* (Shimla: Indian Institute of Advanced Study, 1993), 15.

69. Harish Trivedi, *Colonial Transactions: English Literature in India* (Manchester: Manchester University Press, 1993), 72.

70. Theo Damsteegt's scholarship (cited above) stands as perhaps the only English-language study of Agyeya's jail stories. Damsteegt also discusses "Hariti" in

Theo Damsteegt, "Violent Heroines: Ajneya and Violence—Revisted," in *Violence Denied: Violence, Non-violence, and the Rationalization of Violence in South Asian Cultural History*, ed. Jan Houben and Karel Kooij (Leiden: Brill, 1999), 341–72.

71. Paliwal, "Agyeya," 26.

72. Sharat Kumar and Geeti Sen, "Interview with Ajneya (S. H. Vatsyayan)," *India International Centre Quarterly* 10, no. 4 (1983): 39.

3. Dialogue and Its Discontents

1. For a growing chronology of China-India activities in the 1950s, see Arunabh Ghosh, "1950s China-India Chronology," 2017, https://histecon.fas.harvard.edu /chinaindia1950/ (accessed May 3, 2022).

2. Ien Ang, Yudhishthir Raj Isar, and Phillip Mar, "Cultural Diplomacy: Beyond the National Interest?," *International Journal of Cultural Policy* 21, no. 4 (2015): 371.

3. On the United States' CIA-funded cultural operations in Europe and parts of the Third World, see Frances Stonor Saunders, *The Cultural Cold War: The CIA and the World of Arts and Letters* (New York: New Press, 2000). For an account of Soviet engagements with literature and film of the Third World, see Rossen Djagalov, *From Internationalism to Postcolonialism: Literature and Cinema Between the Second and Third Worlds* (Montreal: McGill-Queen's University Press, 2020).

4. "Final Communiqué of the Asian-African Conference of Bandung (24 April 1955)," in *Asia-Africa Speak from Bandung*, ed. Ministry of Foreign Affairs of the Republic of Indonesia (Djakarta: Ministry of Foreign Affairs, 1955), 163.

5. For an example of the latter framework, see Monica Popescu, *At Penpoint: African Literatures, Postcolonial Studies, and the Cold War* (Durham, NC: Duke University Press, 2020).

6. Ang, Isar, and Mar, "Cultural Diplomacy," 370.

7. Ang, Isar, and Mar, 365, 370.

8. In 1951, for example, an "unofficial" Indian delegation traveled to China without the Indian government's explicit approval. See Adhira Mangalagiri, "The Culture of Cultural Diplomacy: China and India, 1947–1952," *China and Asia: A Journal in Historical Studies* 3 (2021): 202–16.

9. Julia Lovell has written about what she terms "China's international hospitality machine." Her analysis of the practice of inviting "foreign guests" (*waibin* 外宾) between 1949 and 1976 reveals an elaborate system of state control in producing "officially micromanaged foreign visits to Maoist China." Julia Lovell, "The Uses of Foreigners in Mao-Era China: 'Techniques of Hospitality' and International Image-Building in the People's Republic, 1949–1976," *Transactions of the RHS* 25 (2015): 154, 144.

10. For recent studies of China's Cold War–era cultural diplomacy in the Third World, see Yang Wang, "Envisioning the Third World: Modern Art and Diplomacy in Maoist China," *ARTMargins* 8, no. 2 (2019): 31–54; Emily Wilcox, "Performing Bandung: China's Dance Diplomacy with India, Indonesia, and Burma, 1953–1962," *Inter-Asia Cultural Studies* 18, no. 4 (2017): 518–539; and

Duncan M. Yoon, "'Our Forces Have Redoubled': World Literature, Postcolonialism, and the Afro-Asian Writers' Bureau," *Cambridge Journal of Postcolonial Literary Inquiry* 2, no. 2 (2015): 233–52.

11. For an account of some of these songs, see the section on "The Friendship Song" in Tansen Sen, "The Materiality of Friendship: Kongfuzi as a Source for China-India Interactions During the 1950s (Part I)," March 11, 2022, https://storymaps .arcgis.com/stories/20b8d81ad58a4146ba24d1e0a832183c (accessed May 3, 2022).

12. Yuan's poem "China-India Friendship Song" (*ZhongYin youhao ge* 中印友好哥) was later published in the following poetry collection: Yuan Shuipai 袁水拍, *Gesong he zuzhou* 歌頌和詛咒 [Praises and curses] (Beijing: Zuojia chubanshe, 1959), 74–75. Yuan wrote three additional poems on the theme of China-India friendship, all published in the same collection.

13. On the Foreign Languages Press, see Yan Jia, "Beyond the 'Bhai-Bhai' Rhetoric: China-India Literary Relations, 1950–1990" (PhD diss., School of Oriental and African Studies, University of London, 2019), 139–61.

14. *The Indian Cultural Delegation in China* (Peking: Foreign Languages Press, 1955), 21.

15. *Indian Cultural Delegation in China*, 71.

16. *Indian Cultural Delegation in China*, 71.

17. This is my English translation of Yuan's Chinese poem.

18. For one account of poetry recitations in sites of Third World cultural diplomacy, see Roanne Kantor, "'My Heart, My Fellow Traveller': Fantasy, Futurity, and the Itineraries of Faiz Ahmed Faiz," *South Asia: Journal of South Asian Studies* 39, no. 3 (2016): 608–25. Poetry recitation as part of cultural diplomacy intersected well with China's "recitation movement" (*langsong yundong* 朗誦運動), which had grown out of the literary response to the War of Resistance in the late 1930s and gained a further revolutionary tenor at Yan'an in the 1940s. On poetry recitation in twentieth-century China, see John Crespi, *Voices in Revolution: Poetry and the Auditory Imagination in Modern China* (Honolulu: University of Hawai'i Press, 2009).

19. "Asian Writers' Talks Begin Tomorrow: Preparations in New Delhi," *Times of India*, December 22, 1956, 7; "Asian Writers' Conference: India's Contribution to Asian Culture," *Times of India*, December 24, 1956, 8.

20. Ye Junjian 葉君健, "Liang zhang heying" 兩張合影 [Two group photographs], *Xin wenxue shiliao* 新文學史料 3 (1986): 173.

21. On the final day of the conference, the delegates accepted an invitation from Zulfiya, the Uzbek poetess, to hold the next Writers' Conference in Tashkent. This subsequent conference was held in 1958 as the first Afro-Asian Writers' Conference. See "Cultural Co-operation Among Asian Nations: End of Writers' Conference," *Times of India*, December 29, 1956, 3.

22. "Cultural Co-operation," 3.

23. M. V. Desai, "The Asian Writers' Conference, December 1956: New Delhi," *Books Abroad* 31, no. 3 (1957): 245.

24. "The Asian Mind," *Times of India*, August 6, 1956, 6.

25. "Asian Mind"; "Spread Message of Peace: Call to Asian Writers," *Times of India*, December 24, 1956, 8.

26. "Cultural Co-operation," 3.

27. Desai, "Asian Writers' Conference," 245.

28. My reading of literary consequentiality here is informed by Nan Da's study of Sino-U.S. literary exchange during the late nineteenth and early twentieth centuries. Referring to that context, Da writes, "Serving as proxies for contact, [literary exchange] encouraged a particular association of textual circulation with being in the world as a nation. . . . Because literary exchange was normativized under the logics of recognition and reciprocity, the movement of books became synecdochially linked to desired patterns of international cooperation." Nan Da, *Intransitive Encounter: Sino-U.S. Literatures and the Limits of Exchange* (New York: Columbia University Press, 2018), 15–16.

29. *Indian Cultural Delegation in China*, 71.

30. Mulk Raj Anand, "Mulk Raj Anand Remembers," *Indian Literature* 36, no. 2 (154) (1993): 183.

31. Mangalagiri, "Culture of Cultural Diplomacy," 209.

32. Anand, "Mulk Raj Anand Remembers," 183.

33. "Current Topics," *Times of India*, November 28, 1956, 6.

34. "Renewed Split Emerges Among Organisers: Asian Writers' Conference," *Times of India*, December 21, 1956, 9.

35. "Renewed Split Emerges."

36. "Renewed Split Emerges."

37. Hualing Nieh, ed., *Literature of the Hundred Flower*, vol. 1: *Criticism and Polemics* (New York: Columbia University Press, 1981), 23. All quotations cited from this volume contain Nieh's English translations.

38. Nieh, *Literature of the Hundred Flowers*, vol. 1, 131.

39. Nieh, 18.

40. Ye Shengtao 葉聖陶, *Lvtu riji wuzhong* 旅途日記五種 [Five travelogues] (Beijing: Shenghuo dushu xinzhi sanlian shudian, 2002), 188. The writer Ye Shengtao summarized Pan's remarks in a private diary he maintained while in India. The diary was recovered and published posthumously by Ye's son in 1988.

41. Ye's strategy mirrors that adopted by other newspapers and journals during the Hundred Flowers period. For example, *Wenyibao* 文藝報, a newspaper closely allied with the official Chinese Writers' Association, began to include content explicitly in support of the campaign's aims. On *Wenyibao*'s Hundred Flowers transformation, see Zhong Yuan 鐘媛, "1957 nian 'Wenyibao' de gaiban" 1957 年《文藝報》的改版 [The 1957 revised edition of *Wenyibao*], *Modern Chinese Literature Studies* 中國現代文學研究叢刊 11 (2017): 90–98.

42. Ye Junjian 葉君健, "Yazhou zuojia huiyi qianhou" 亞洲作家會議前後 [On the Asian Writers' Conference], *Wenhuibao* 文匯報, February 10–March 15 1957, February 10, 1957, 4.

43. Nieh, *Literature of the Hundred Flowers*, vol. 1, 24, 30.

44. Ye, "Yazhou zuojia," 4.

45. Ye.

46. On Mao's use of figurative language, see Ch'i Li, *The Use of Figurative Language in Communist China* (Berkeley: Center for Chinese Studies, 1958). On "the active adoption and elaboration of Mao's imagery by individual writers both inside and outside the party's sphere of institutional control," see Dayton Lekner, "A Chill

in Spring: Literary Exchange and Political Struggle in the Hundred Flowers and Anti-Rightist Campaigns of 1956–1958," *Modern China* 45, no. 1 (2019): 37–63.

47. Ye, "Yazhou zuojia," 4.

48. "Writer Must Be Free to Write What He Feels," *Times of India*, December 25, 1956, 8.

49. "Writer Must Be Free," 8.

50. "No One Should Come Between Writer and Reader: Accent on Freedom at Delhi Conference," *Times of India*, December 26, 1956, 11.

51. Popescu, *At Penpoint*, 67, 76.

52. As a political construct in the postwar and decolonial context, "Asia" first took shape at the Asian Relations Conference held in New Delhi in 1947. See Mangalagiri, "The Culture of Cultural Diplomacy," 204–5; Sen, *India, China, and the World*, 340–47; and Vineet Thakur, "An Asian Drama: The Asian Relations Conference, 1947," *International History Review* 41, no. 3 (2018): 673–95.

53. Jed Esty and Colleen Lye, "Peripheral Realisms Now," *Modern Language Quarterly* 73, no. 3 (2012): 269.

54. "No One Should," 11.

55. Nieh, *Literature of the Hundred Flowers*, vol. 1, 48. A version of Lao She's essay appeared in January 1957 in the English-language magazine *People's China*, printed by the Foreign Languages Press.

56. "Extent of Curbs Put by Society on Writers: Keen Controversy in Asian Conference Commission," *Times of India*, December 28, 1956, 5.

57. Xiao San 蕭三,"Ji Yazhou shiren de huijian" 記亞洲詩人的會見 [Remembering the Asian Poets' Meeting], *Shikan* 詩刊 3 (1957): 82. Xiao San's memoir includes a Chinese translation of Anand's letter.

58. *Shikan* was established as part of the Hundred Flowers campaign in early 1957, presenting a forum for experiments in poetry.

59. Xiao San, "Ji Yazhou shiren de huijian," 84.

60. Urdu *mushaira* tradition of courtly poetry recitation and contest involved an intimate interplay between poet and audience, with vocal responses and instant feedback from the audience. In the twentieth century, the Urdu *mushaira* informed the development of the Hindi *kavi sammelan* (poets' meet). On the latter, see Francesca Orsini, *The Hindi Public Sphere, 1920–1940: Language and Literature in the Age of Nationalism* (New Delhi: Oxford University Press, 2002), 80–90. For a different but resonant account, see Faiz's description recounted in Kantor, "My Heart, My Fellow Traveller," 621.

61. Peggy Phelan, *Unmarked: The Politics of Performance* (Oxon: Routledge, [1993] 1996), 146–47.

62. Phelan, *Unmarked*, 148.

63. Édouard Glissant, *Poetics of Relation*, trans. Betsy Wing (Ann Arbor: University of Michigan Press, 1997), 159.

64. Faiz, "Ghazal (Song)," in *Poems by Faiz*, ed. Victor G. Kiernan (London: George Allen & Unwin, 1971), 222. The English translation here is Kiernan's with minor changes. Ye Junjian translated Faiz's couplet into Chinese as follows: *Liu zai xinli de bushi shanghen er shi yi duo hua* 留在心裡的不是傷痕而是一朵花. Ye, "Yazhou zuojia," 4.

65. Ye.

66. In a brief preface to the poem, Xiao San writes that he originally composed the poem a year ago, and although it has since been translated into English and Russian, it is yet to be published in Chinese. The preface reiterates the poem's "continued relevance to today's situation." Xiao San 蕭三,"Cong Yindu guilai" 從印度歸來 [Upon returning from India], Shikan 詩刊 1 (1958): 18.

67. In further contrast with Xiao San's diplomacy-inflected portrayal of Nehru's visit, Ye's report quotes Nehru as explicitly addressing the writers of Asia in the Hundred Flowers idiom: '"A writer takes root in the particular environment in which he has been brought up,' Nehru emphasized, 'but he can use all measures to grow his branches in many different directions, so that lush leaves can grow and beautiful flowers blossom.'" Ye, "Yazhou zuojia," 4.

68. In this line, Xiao San refers to the Afro-Asian Solidarity meeting in Cairo in late 1957, which he was unable to attend.

69. Xiao San,"Cong Yindu guilai," 18.

70. Merle Goldman, "The Party and the Intellectuals," in The Cambridge History of China, ed. Roderick MacFarquhar and John K. Fairbank (Cambridge: Cambridge University Press, 1987), 257. For statistics on the persecutions, see also Richard Kraus, "Let a Hundred Flowers Blossom, Let a Hundred Schools of Thought Contend," in Words and Their Stories: Essays on the Language of the Chinese Revolution, ed. Ban Wang (Leiden: Brill, 2010), 255; and Roderick MacFarquhar, The Origins of the Cultural Revolution: Contradictions Among the People, 1956-1957 (London: Oxford University Press, 1974), 268.

71. Dinkar did not visit China as an Indian governmental representative or as part of an official delegation. In his travelogue, he writes of receiving an invitation to visit China from the Chinese Writers' Association. As a guest of the association, he would have received the party's sanction for his visit. His trip was organized by both the Chinese Writers' Association and the Indian embassy in Beijing. As his travelogue indicates, while in China he was treated and introduced as a national representative of India and Indian culture. Ramdhari Singh Dinkar, Merī yātrāeṁ [My travels] (Patna: Udyacal, 1970), 85.

72. On the title of "national poet," see Onkar Sarad, ed., Maithilisaran Gupt (Bombay: Vora, 1970). The title has also been bestowed on Hindi poet Maithilisaran Gupt (1886-1964), a major influence on Dinkar.

73. For an overview, see Harish Trivedi, "The Progress of Hindi, Part 2: Hindi and the Nation," in Literary Cultures in History: Reconstructions from South Asia, ed. Sheldon Pollock (Berkeley: University of California Press, 2003), 958–1022.

74. For example, Dinkar interpreted Zhou Enlai's decision not to use his (limited) English during their conversation as follows: "The Premier was saying that, if I knew Hindi, then I would certainly speak with you in Hindi. Even though I know English, I will not speak with you in English. I wish those Indians could learn this lesson, who despite knowing Hindi, consider speaking in Hindi below them." Dinkar, Merī yātrāeṁ, 118.

75. On Chāyāvād poetry, see Karine Schomer, Mahadevi Varma and the Chayavad Age of Modern Hindi Poetry (Berkeley: University of California Press, 1983); and Namvar Singh, Chāyāvād (Delhi: Rajkamal Prakashan, 1955).

76. Initially a member of the All-India Progressive Writers' Association, Dinkar later withdrew his membership. Carlo Coppola, ed., *Marxist Influences and South Asian Literature* (East Lansing: Asian Studies Center: Michigan State University, 1974), 52.

77. On Dinkar's views on "New Poetry," see Ramdhari Singh Dinkar, *Miṭṭī ki or* [Toward the soil] (Patna: Udyacal, 1946), 203; and Ramdhari Singh Dinkar, *Sīpī aur śaṅkh* [Shell and conch] (Patna: Udyacal, 1966), iii.

78. It is difficult to assign a static political label to Dinkar's views and literary practice. In current parlance he is considered a "nationalist." He certainly did not fall within the same camp as the other more avowedly leftist Indian visitors to China in the 1950s, such as Mulk Raj Anand. From 1952 to 1964, Dinkar served as a member of the Indian Parliament's upper chamber (Rajya Sabha) as a member of the Indian National Congress (the political party then under Nehru's leadership).

79. Dinkar published several versions of his China travelogue, all compiled from the diary he maintained during his visit, letters he wrote to friends and family while in China, and writings he retrospectively appended to it. Following his return from China, excerpts appeared in the magazine *Dharmayug* in November 1958 and were later amended and included in a six-volume collection of Dinkar's correspondence. See Ramdhari Singh Dinkar, "Cīn ke samsmaraṇ" [Memoirs of China], *Dharmayug*, November 9, 1958, 10; Ramdhari Singh Dinkar, *Dinkarnāmā*, vol. 2, ed. Diwakar (Nawada: Chaitanyam Prakashan, 2004), 441–94. The most complete version appeared in the 1970 volume of travelogues I refer to in this chapter, which also contains accounts of Dinkar's travels to Europe (London and Poland, 1955), Mauritius and Kenya (1967), and Germany (1968).

80. Dinkar met Zhou along with Sushila Nayar, an Indian doctor-activist then in Beijing at the invitation of the All-China Women's Federation. An announcement of the meeting appears in the November, 4, 1957, issue of the *People's Daily* (*Renmin ribao* 人民日報).

81. Kanhaiyalal Fulfagar, *Dinkar ke patr* [Dinkar's letters] (Calcutta: Dinkar sodh samsthan, 1981), 179.

82. The volume contains Dinkar's translations of poems originally written in Portuguese, Spanish, German, French, Russian, Polish, and Malayalam (all via English translation, with the exception of the Malayalam poem, which Dinkar translated in conversation with the poet). Dinkar, *Sīpī aur śaṅkh*, i.

83. Dinkar, iv.

84. Robert Payne, ed., *Contemporary Chinese Poetry* (London: Routledge, 1947), 117. Dinkar also translates poems by He Qifang 何其芳, Feng Zhi 馮至, Zang Kejia 臧克家, and Wen Yiduo 聞一多, all from Payne's volume.

85. For selected studies on Ai Qing, see Eugene Eoyang, "Editor's Introduction," in *Selected Poems of Ai Qing* (Bloomington: Indiana University Press, 1982), i–x; Angela Palandri, "The Poetic Theory and Practice of Ai Qing," in *Perspectives in Contemporary Chinese Literature*, ed. Mason Y.H. Wang (University Center, MI: Green River, 1983), 61–76; and Guiyou Huang, "A Newer Realm of Poetry: Whitman and Ai Qing," *Walt Whitman Quarterly Review* 15, no. 4 (1998): 172–79. See also

translated criticism in Hualing Nieh, ed., *Literature of the Hundred Flowers*, vol. 2 (New York: Columbia University Press, 1981).

86. Dinkar, *Merī yātrāeṁ*, 66–67.

87. For an introduction to Vinoba Bhave, see Geeta Mehta, *Philosophy of Vinoba Bhave: A New Perspective in Gandhian Thought* (Bombay: Himalaya, 1995).

88. Kraus, "Let a Hundred Flowers Blossom," 255.

89. On the persecution of Ding Ling and her associates, see Hong Zicheng 洪子誠, *1956—baihua shidai* 1956—百花時代 [1956—The Hundred Flowers era] (Beijing: Beijing daxue chubanshe, 2010), 166–87.

90. Quoted in Goldman, "Party and the Intellectuals," 255.

91. Nieh, *Literature of the Hundred Flowers*, vol. 2, xxxv.

92. Kraus, "Let a Hundred Flowers Blossom," 255. Ai Qing later wrote that he was sent to a "state farm in the northeast to 'observe and learn from real life.' [He] was deputy head of a tree farm and spent a year and a half there living together with lumberjacks. . . . In the winter of 1959, [he] went to Xinjiang where [he] spent sixteen years in a reclamation area with a production and construction corps." Ai Qing 艾青, "Author's Preface," in *Selected Poems of Ai Qing* (Bloomington: Indiana University Press, 1982), 11–12.

93. Dinkar, *Merī yātrāeṁ*, 107.

94. Dinkar, 112–13. Dinkar also asked the Indians he met in China about Ai Qing. He records one such conversation with P. C. Joshi, the former general secretary of the Communist Party of India, with whom Dinkar crossed paths in China: "I asked Joshiji who China's greatest poet is, Ai Qing or Guo Moruo. He responded that Guo Moruo occupied the same position in the Chinese literary sphere as that of Nirala in the Hindi literary sphere. Joshiji declined to discuss Ai Qing." Dinkar, 100.

95. Dinkar, 107.

96. Dinkar, 99. In early 1957, Zang served as the editor of *Shikan*. The journal carried writings critiquing the party by both Zang and Ai Qing during the Hundred Flowers period. By the time of Dinkar's visit, however, the journal had shifted its tone in line with the policy. The brevity of Zang's remarks to Dinkar stand in stark opposition to the lengthy article he had published the previous month publicly denouncing Ai Qing's recent works. See the translated excerpt of Zang's "What Has Been Expressed in Ai Qing's Recent Work?," in Nieh, *Literature of the Hundred Flowers*, vol. 2, 278–82.

97. Dinkar had his own theory about Ding Ling's fate. Although Mao had earlier praised Ding Ling as "the brightest ray of communism," Dinkar writes, this same Ding Ling "is understood today as opposing communism and is made to work in the offices of the Writers' Association as a mere custodian." Dinkar, 113.

98. Dinkar, 122. Such allegations of promiscuity are consistent with contemporaneous published denunciations. The poet Feng Zhi, for example, attacked poems Ai Qing wrote in the 1930s about his time in France. Feng Zhi accused Ai Qing of identifying with "the decadent youth" of Paris, whose "actual goal was to embrace and enjoy Paris as they would a tawdry, promiscuous girl." Nieh, *Literature of the Hundred Flowers*, vol. 2, 83.

99. Dinkar, 122.

100. The happier accounts include Dinkar's visits to the main tourist attractions and museums in each of the cities he traveled to, visits to villages to glimpse agricultural and rural life, conversations with students at Peking University in Beijing and Sun Yat-sen University in Guangzhou, and so on. Dinkar's itinerary reads very much like the visits of foreign visitors to Maoist China discussed by Lovell, mentioned above.

101. Dinkar, *Merī yātrāeṁ*, 162.

102. Nieh, *Literature of the Hundred Flowers*, vol. 2, 102. Translation from the Chinese is Nieh's. A literal English translation of Dinkar's Hindi rendition reads: "In the spring season when a hundred flowers / were laughing their enticing laugh / and luring butterflies, / she devoted herself to the winter's snow." Dinkar, 164. Both Nieh and Dinkar introduce line breaks into Liu's prose poems.

103. For one such denunciation, see Sha Ou's 沙鷗 essay translated in Nieh, *Literature of the Hundred Flowers*, vol. 2, 105–14.

104. Dinkar, *Merī yātrāeṁ*, 162.

105. Nieh, *Literature of the Hundred Flowers*, vol. 2, 102.

106. Dinkar, *Merī yātrāeṁ*, 164.

107. Dinkar, 166.

4. Word and World in Crisis

1. For historiographical scholarship on the war, see John Garver, *Protracted Contest: Sino-Indian Rivalry in the Twentieth Century* (Seattle: University of Washington Press, 2001); Amit Das Gupta and Lorenz Lüthi, eds., *The Sino-Indian War of 1962: New Perspectives* (New York: Routledge, 2017), 57–58; and Tansen Sen, *India, China, and the World: A Connected History* (Lanham, MD: Rowman & Littlefield, 2017), 379–470.

2. One picture book-style text (*lianhuanhua* 連環畫) published in 1972 offers a rare example of a Chinese literary depiction of the 1962 China-India war. The storybook, entitled *Landmine Detonating Hero Luo Guangbian* (*Gunlei yingxiong Luo Guangbian* 滾雷英雄羅光變), tells of its titular hero's journey from his humble beginnings in a peasant family to a hero and martyr on the front lines in the 1962 war. Luo rises in the ranks through his hard work and commitment to Mao Zedong's teachings, persevering through injury to defend his nation. On the front lines, he sacrifices his life to detonate a land mine that secures China's victory. The book explains the war as instigated by "American imperialism and Soviet revisionism," which led to an "unbridled anti-China sentiment" among the "Indian reactionaries," resulting in India's invasion of China (57). The book follows the format of heroic stories popular at the time, which upheld model peasants, workers, or soldiers as examples of heroic spirits for young readers to emulate (the story of Lei Feng is perhaps the best known of this kind). See Political Divison of Unit 7969 of the People's Liberation Army 中國人民解放軍七九六九部隊政治部, *Gunlei yingxiong Luo Guangbian* 滾雷英雄羅光變 [Landmine

detonating hero Luo Guangbian] (Shanghai: Renmin chubanshe, 1972). I thank Tansen Sen for this reference.

3. *Dharmayug* grew out of an earlier magazine, *Navayug*, until the latter was acquired by the Times of India publishing group in Bombay. In 1949, the modified magazine appeared as *Dharmayug* and soon became a staple in middle-class homes. It was one of the few magazines of the time that was printed in color, with attractive photographs and illustrations. Through the 1950s, its annual tear-away calendars, printed in color and featuring various deities, ubiquitously adorned homes and shop fronts (these calendars were discontinued under Bharati's editorship, when the magazine focused more on texts of journalistic and literary merit).

4. For studies on postindependence-era Hindi magazines, see Aakriti Mandhwani, "Everyday Reading: Commercial Magazines and Book Publishing in Post-Independence India" (PhD diss., School of Oriental and African Studies, 2018); and Aakriti Mandhwani, "*Sarita* and the 1950s Hindi Middlebrow Reader," *Modern Asian Studies* 53, no. 6 (2019): 1797–815.

5. For a study of *Dharmayug* under Bharati's editorship, see Jyoti Vyas, *Dharmavir Bhāratī aur unkā* Dharmayug [Dharmavir Bharati and his *Dharmayug*] (Kanpur: Annapurna Prakashan, 2010). The volume also includes interviews with members of *Dharmayug*'s editorial teams, and frequent contributors and readers.

6. Pra. Ma., "Ek Pairodī" [A parody], *Dharmayug*, December 30, 1962, 11.

7. Ma., "Ek Pairodī."

8. Ma.

9. The poem originally appeared in Shamsher's first poetry collection, entitled *Some Poems* (*Kuch Kavitāeṁ*), published in 1959. Subsequent references to the poem in this chapter are from the 1962 *Dharmayug* reprint of Shamsher's poem.

10. Shamsher Bahadur Singh, "Cīn" [China], *Dharmayug*, December 30, 1962, 11.

11. On Shamsher, see "Shamsher Bahadur Singh," *Hindi: Language, Discourse, Writing* 1, nos. 3–4 (2000–2001): 199–261; Mahavir Agraval, ed., *Śaṁśer: Kavī Se Baṛe Ādmī* [Shamsher: from poet to great man] (Kasaridiha Durg: Sri Prakashan, 1994); Ranjana Argare, *Kavīyoṁ kā Kavī Śaṁśer* [The poets' poet Shamsher] (New Delhi: Vani Prakashan, 1988); Rahul, *Śaṁśer aur unkī Kavitā* [Shamsher and his poetry] (New Delhi: Bhavna Prakashan, 1999); and Namvar Singh, "Śaṁśer kī Śaṁśeriyat" [The Shamsher-ness of Shamsher], in *Pratinidhi Kavitāeṁ: Śaṁśer Bahādur Siṃh* [Representative poems: Shamsher Bahadur Singh], ed. Namvar Singh (New Delhi: Rajkamal Prakashan, 1990), 5–8.

12. Agyeya, ed., *Dūsrā Saptak* [The second heptad] (New Delhi: Pragati Prakashan, 1951), 83.

13. *Tār Saptak* was the first in a series of four such anthologies; following *Tār Saptak*'s publication in 1943, *Dūsrā Saptak* appeared in 1951, *Tīsrā Saptak* in 1959, and *Cauthā Saptak* in 1979. For selected translations, see *Selections from the Saptaks*, trans. S. C. Narula (New Delhi: Rupa, 2004).

14. Vijayadev Narayan Sahi, "Śaṁśer kī Kāvyānubhūti kī Banāvat" [The structure of Shamsher's poetic emotion], in *Śaṁśer: Kavī Se Baṛe Ādmī* [Shamsher: from poet to great man], ed. Mahavir Agraval (Kasaridiha Durg: Sri Prakashan, 1994), 84.

Sahi's essay has been translated into English by Raji Narasimhan in "Shamsher Bahadur Singh," 220–38.

15. Agyeya, *Dūsrā Saptak*, 89.

16. Prabhakar Machwe, *From self to Self: Reminiscences of a Writer* (New Delhi: Vikas, 1977), 41. Machwe's interests in existentialism led him to translate the Czech philosopher Paul Roubiczek's *Existentialism: For and Against* (1966) into Hindi; see Paul Roubiczek, *Astitvavād: Pakṣ aur vipakṣ* [Existentialism: for and against], trans. Prabhakar Machwe (Bhopal: Madhya Pradesh Hindi Granth Academy, 1976).

17. Machwe, *From self to Self*, 126–33.

18. Machwe and Shamsher were likely close friends. Shamsher's second poetry collection, *Some More Poems* (1961), contains a poem dedicated to Machwe entitled "A Correspondence." The poem presents in poetic form letters exchanged between the two. See Shamsher Bahadur Singh, *Kuch Kavitāeṁ va Kuch aur Kavitāeṁ* [Some poems and some more poems] (New Delhi: Radhakrishna Prakashan, 1984), 110–11.

19. Prabhakar Machwe, "Ādhunik Cīni Kavitā Mem Bheṛiyā-Vṛtti" [Traits of treachery in modern Chinese poetry], *Dharmayug*, December 30, 1962, 18.

20. Machwe, "Ādhunik Cīni Kavitā," 19.

21. These are my English translations of Machwe's Hindi translations.

22. On Alley's life and activities in China, see James Beattie and Richard Bullen, "Embracing Friendship Through Gift and Exchange: Rewi Alley and the Art of Museum Diplomacy in Cold War China and New Zealand," *Australian and New Zealand Journal of Art* 16, no. 2 (2016): 149–66; Anne-Marie Brady, *Friend of China: The Myth of Rewi Alley* (London: RoutledgeCurzon, 2003); and Anne-Marie Brady, "Who Friend, Who Enemy? Rewi Alley and the Friends of China," *China Quarterly* 151 (1997): 614–32.

23. The movement aimed to collectivize refugees displaced by Japanese bombing and to engage them in manufacturing efforts, in an attempt to address the refugee crises instigated by the heavy bombing, produce supplies for the Chinese armies, and recover Chinese industry which had suffered during the wartime.

24. For an annotated bibliography of Alley's translations, see Duncan Campbell, "Labouring in the 'Sheltered Field': Rewi Alley's Translations from the Chinese," *New Zealand Journal of Asian Studies* 16, no. 2 (2014): 95–96.

25. Duncan Campbell makes this point in his study of Alley's translations of classical Chinese poetry. Campbell characterizes Alley's practice as a translator as guided by an "insistence on the connection between the poetry of the past in China and contemporary realties as testified to by his own China experiences." Referring to Alley's translation of a poem by the Tang dynasty poet, Li Bai, Campbell writes, "Mis-readings of the original of one kind or another occur on almost every line . . . and through means of both commission and omission, Li Bai is made to address directly contemporary concerns." Campbell, "Labouring in the 'Sheltered Field,'" 81–82.

26. *The People Speak Out: Translations of Poems and Songs of the People of China*, trans. Rewi Alley (Beijing: Rewi Alley, 1954), iii.

27. *People Speak Out*, iii.

28. As Bonnie McDougall notes, in the 1950s, the talks "served as official policy," but only implicitly so; "it was not until the Cultural Revolution that the 'Talks' resumed its former prominence." Bonnie McDougall, *Mao Zedong's "Talks at the Yan'an Conference on Literature and Art": A Translation of the 1943 Text with Commentary* (Ann Arbor: University of Michigan Center for Chinese Studies, 1980), 39.

29. McDougall, *Mao Zedong's "Talks,"* 66.

30. *People Speak Out*, 75.

31. I discuss Payne's volume further in chapter 3 of this book.

32. On the PRC's publishing apparatus during its early years, see Cagdas Ungor, "Reaching the Distant Comrade: Chinese Communist Propaganda Abroad (1949–1976)" (PhD diss., State University of New York at Binghamton, 2009).

33. In his anti-China writings, Machwe often referred to texts he had read in *Chinese Literature*. In an article entitled "The Decline of Chinese Art," Machwe translates selections of poetry and literary commentary from *Chinese Literature* published in 1960–1961 with the aim of denouncing contemporary Chinese literature's overtly political agenda. Prabhakar Machwe, "Cīn kī Citrakalā kā Paṭan" [The decline of Chinese art], *Dharmayug*, February 24, 1963, 17.

34. *People Speak Out*, iv.

35. *People Speak Out*, 103. For the original Chinese poem, see Ai Qing 艾青, "Yingjie yi jiu wu san nian" 迎接一九五三年 [Welcome to 1953], *Renmin Wenxue* 人民文学 1 (1953): 9.

36. Alley's translation is heavy handed. For instance, he translates Ai Qing's simple "he" (*ta* 他) as "our men," literalizing Ai Qing's protagonist into a collective figure of the solider (a gesture that remains implicit in Ai Qing's poem).

37. Machwe, "Ādhunik Cīni Kavitā," 18.

38. *People Speak Out*, 61.

39. Machwe, "Ādhunik Cīni Kavitā," 19.

40. *People Speak Out*, 63; Machwe, 19.

41. Sahi, "Śamśer kī Kāvyānubhūti," 84.

42. Singh, "Cīn," 11.

43. For an introduction to the New Poetry movement, see Lucy Rosenstein, *New Poetry in Hindi* (Delhi: Permanent Black, 2003); and Lucy Rosenstein, " 'New Poetry' in Hindi: A Quest for Modernity," *South Asia Research* 20, no. 1 (2000): 47–62.

44. Agyeya, *Dūsrā Saptak*, 83. On the influence of English poetry and imagism on Hindi "New Poetry," see Suresh Chandra Pandey, *Ādhunik Hindī Kavitā par Aṁgrezī Kavitā kā Prabhāv* [The influence of English poetry on modern Hindi poetry] (Kanpur: Anubhav Prakashan, 1983); Urmila Varma, *Influence of English Poetry on Modern Hindi Poetry with Special Reference to Technique, Imagery, Metre, and Diction* (Allahbad: Lokbharati Prakashan, 1980); and Sri Bhagvan Tivari, *Bimbvād, Bimb aur Ādhunik Hindī-Kavitā* [Imagism, the image, and modern Hindi poetry] (Bombay: Aravind Prakashan, 1992).

45. Agyeya, 86.

46. Ezra Pound, "A Few Don'ts by an Imagiste," *Poetry* 1, no. 6 (1913): 200.

47. Pound, "Few Don'ts," 201, 205.

48. Quoted in Rosenstein, *New Poetry in Hindi*, 53.

49. Gajanan Madhav Muktibodh, "Śaṁśer: Merī Dṛṣṭi Meṁ" [Shamsher: in my view], in Śaṁśer: Kavī Se Baṛe Ādmī [Shamsher: from poet to great man], ed. Mahavir Agraval (Kasaridiha Durg: Sri Prakashan, 1994), 57–58.

50. Fenollosa's manuscripts have been published in Ernest Fenollosa and Ezra Pound, The Chinese Written Character as a Medium for Poetry: A Critical Edition, ed. Haun Saussy, Jonathan Stalling, and Lucas Klein (New York: Fordham University Press, 2008).

51. Haun Saussy, "Fenollosa Compounded: A Discrimination," in The Chinese Written Character as a Medium for Poetry: A Critical Edition, ed. Haun Saussy, Jonathan Stalling, and Lucas Klein (New York: Fordham University Press, 2008), 4.

52. For a selection of scholarship on Pound and China, see Christopher Bush, Ideographic Modernism: China, Writing, Media (New York: Oxford University Press, 2010); Eric Hayot, Chinese Dream: Pound, Brecht, Tel Quel (Ann Arbor: University of Michigan Press, 2004); Robert Kern, Orientalism, Modernism, and the American Poem (Cambridge: Cambridge University Press, 1996); Zhaoming Qian, ed., Ezra Pound and China (Ann Arbor: University of Michigan Press, 2003); and Ming Xie, Ezra Pound and the Appropriation of Chinese Poetry: Cathay, Translation, and Imagism (New York: Garland, 1999).

53. Some Poems contains thirty-six poems originally composed between 1939 and 1958. The volume was reprinted along with Shamsher's second poetry collection (Some More Poems) in 1984. See Singh, Kuch Kavitāeṁ.

54. Singh, Kuch Kavitāeṁ, i.

55. Shamsher's Chinese characters appear on the page in a similar fashion to those interspersed throughout Pound's Cantos. In both, the Chinese characters appear as larger in scale than the lines of verse. However, Pound intersperses Chinese characters throughout the body of the text, whereas Shamsher positions his exclusively in the margins.

56. Singh, Kuch Kavitāeṁ, i.

57. "Creative Writing in the Present Crisis," Indian Literature 6, no. 1 (1963): 78–79.

58. "Creative Writing in the Present Crisis," 85.

59. "Creative Writing in the Present Crisis," 82.

60. "Creative Writing in the Present Crisis," 96.

61. "Creative Writing in the Present Crisis," 76.

62. The phrase "hundred flowers" alludes to the Maoist political campaign of 1956 in which officials invited artists and intellectuals to air criticisms of the party. The campaign also promised writers and artists greater autonomy than previously afforded in artistic experimentation. I discuss the Hundred Flowers campaign in greater detail in chapter 3.

63. "Creative Writing in the Present Crisis," 77.

64. For a brief introduction to Parsai in English, see Vishnu Khare, "Introduction," in Inspector Matadeen on the Moon: Satires by Harishankar Parsai, ed. C. M. Naim (New Delhi: Katha, 2003), 7–12. Parsai's works have been collected in six volumes; see Kamala Prasad, Dhananjay Varma, and Syamsundar Misra, eds., Parsāī Racănāvalī [Collected works of Parsai], 6 vols. (New Delhi: Rajkamal Prakashan, 1985). In addition to "New Madman's Diary," Parsai wrote other China-related stories following the 1962 war. A second satirical story, "The Chinese Doctor Ran

Away: The Story of a Patriot," tells of a man who, in an act of nationalistic outcry, accuses his town's Chinese doctor of spying and successfully campaigns
his townspeople to run the doctor out of town. This "patriotic act" is soon
revealed to be a farce; the man had been scheming to instate his relative as the
town's doctor all along. See Harisankar Parsai, "Cīnī Dāktar Bhāgā: Ek Deśbhakt
kī Kathā" [The Chinese doctor ran away: the story of a patriot], in *Parsāī
Racănāvalī* [Collected works of Parsai], 6 vols. (New Delhi: Rajkamal Prakashan,
1985), 1:192–95.

65. I translate the title of Lu Xun's short story as "A Madman's Diary" as opposed
to the more commonly used translation "Diary of a Madman" for two reasons.
First, "A Madman's Diary" resonates better with Parsai's subtle modification of
the title as "New Madman's Diary." Second, this translation preserves the ambiguity in Parsai's title of whether the adjective "new" modifies "madman" or
"diary" (or both).

66. Harisankar Parsai, "Naye Pāgal ki Dāyarī" [New madman's diary], *Dharmayug*,
February 24, 1963, 9.

67. Translations are Julia Lovell's. Lu Xun 鲁迅, *The Real Story of Ah-Q and Other Tales
of China: The Complete Fiction of Lu Xun*, trans. Julia Lovell (New York: Penguin,
2009), 22.

68. Parsai, "Naye Pāgal ki Dāyarī," 9. The image of a "yellow flower" here has racial
overtones, in line with the idea in circulation at the time that China's attack
on India proved indicative of a Chinese assertion of racial supremacy over Asia.

69. Parsai, 9–10.

70. Parsai, 9–10.

71. Parsai, 9.

72. I discuss the practice of comparing Lu Xun and Premchand in chapter 5.

73. Krishnanand Prasad Singh, *Dhokebāj paṛosī* [Backstabbing neighbor] (Bhagalpur:
Mohan, 1966), 2.

5. On Correspondence

1. Premchand delivered his famous speech "The Purpose of Literature" (*Sāhitya
kā uddeśyǎ*) at the 1936 inaugural meeting of the All-India Progressive Writers'
Association. On the speech, see Carlo Coppola, "Premchand's Address to the
First Meeting of the All-India Progressive Writers Association: Some Speculations," *Journal of South Asian Literature* 21, no. 2 (1986): 21–39. For Lu Xun's involvement in the League of Left-Wing Writers (*zuoyi zuojia lianmeng* 左翼作家聯盟),
see Wang-chi Wong, "A Literary Organization with a Clear Political Agenda: The
Chinese League of Left-Wing Writers, 1930–1936," in *Literary Societies of Republic
China*, ed. Kirk Denton and Michel Hockx (Plymouth, KY: Lexington, 2008),
313–38; and Wang-chi Wong, *Politics and Literature in Shanghai: The Chinese League
of Left-Wing Writers, 1930–1936* (Manchester: Manchester University Press, 1991).

2. For a sample of such studies on Lu Xun and Premchand, see Li Hongyan 李紅艷
and Wang Jipeng 王吉鵬, "Lu Xun yu Puliemuchangde" 魯迅與普列姆昌德 [Lu Xun

and Premchand], *Yancheng shifan xueyuan xuebao* 鹽城師範學院學報2 (2004): 73–78; Liu Anwu 劉安武,"Puliemuchangde he Lu Xun de xiaoshuo chuangzuo" 普列姆昌德和魯迅的小說創作 [Premchand and Lu Xun's fiction writings], in *Yindu wenxue he Zhongguo wenxue bijiao yanjiu* 印度文學和中國文學比較研究 [A comparative study of Indian literature and Chinese literature] (Beijing: Zhongguo dabaike quanshu chubanshe, 2015), 271–81; Liu Dengdong 劉登東, "Puliemuchangde yu Lu Xun xiaoshuo bijiao tan" 普列姆昌德與魯迅小說比較談 [Comparing Premchand and Lu Xun's fiction], *Chongqing shifan daxue xuebao* 重慶師範大學學報4 (1990): 62–67; and Wang Xiaodan 王曉丹,"Puliemuchangde he Lu Xun" 普列姆昌德和魯迅 [Premchand and Lu Xun], *Nanya yanjiu* 南亞研究 1 (1991): 65–71.

3. For a helpful overview of criticism on comparative literature's tendency to impose a normative standard of measure, see Susan Stanford Friedman, "Why Not Compare?," *PMLA* 126, no. 3 (2011): 753–54.

4. See, for example, Wang Chunjing 王春景, "Puliemuchangde he Lu Xun bixia de nongmin xingxiang" 普列姆昌德和魯迅筆下的農民形象 [The image of the peasant in the works of Premchand and Lu Xun] *Nanya yanjiu* 南亞研究 S1 (2005): 39–44.

5. Friedman, "Why Not Compare?," 754.

6. Friedman, 754.

7. Premchand's editorial writings on a wide range of international affairs offer an exception. In the early 1930s, for example, Premchand wrote several articles condemning Japan's encroachment into China. These appeared in the magazine *Jāgaraṇ*, which Premchand edited. See Kuo-hui Ts'ai, Yung-ming Ch'ien, and Mrityubodh, eds., *Cīnī Samālocăkom̐ ki Nazar Mem̐ Premcand* [Premchand in the eyes of Chinese critics] (Beijing: Foreign Languages Press, 1988), 138–39. This volume (published in Hindi translation) collects essays written by Chinese critics on Premchand on the occasion of a conference, "Premchand and Indian Realist Literature," held in Guangzhou in 1986, celebrating the fiftieth anniversary of Premchand's death.

8. See, for example, Ji Xianlin's introduction in Ts'ai, Ch'ien, and Mrityubodh, *Cīnī Samālocăkom̐*. As quoted in chapter 4, Parsai uses such a designation in his pastiche of Lu Xun's "Madman's Diary," "Naye Pāgal ki Dāyarī" [New madman's diary]. Additional examples are cited in Yan Jia, "Beyond the 'Bhai-Bhai' Rhetoric: China-India Literary Relations, 1950–1990" (PhD diss., School of Oriental and African Studies, University of London, 2019).

9. Quoted in Jia, "Beyond the 'Bhai-Bhai' Rhetoric," 158. Translation is his.

10. Readers interested in such a project can find a study of translation and reception in Jia, 192–240. For a chronology of Chinese publications on and translations of Premchand, see Ts'ai, Ch'ien, and Mrityubodh, *Cīnī Samālocăkom̐*. Among the earliest Chinese translations of Premchand's stories (including "A Tale of Two Bullocks," discussed in this chapter) are the following volumes: Premchand, *Bianxin de ren* 變心的人 [He who had a change of heart], trans. Zheng Qiu 正秋 (Shanghai: Shaonian ertong chubanshe, 1956); and Krishan Chander, Premchand, Mulk Raj Anand, Navtej Singh, Ibrahim Jalees, and Manik Bandopadhyay, *Yindu duanpian xiaoshuo ji* 印度短篇小說集 [Collection of Indian short stories], trans. Yuan Ruo 袁若 (Shanghai: Chaofeng chubanshe,

1953). These early Chinese translations relied on Russian translations of Premchand's works. The first piece of criticism on Premchand in Chinese was published in 1957; see Mi Wenkai 糜文開, *Yindu wenxue xinshang* 印度文學欣賞 [An appreciation of Indian literature] (Taibei: Sanmin Shuju, 1957). Premchand's seminal novel *Godan* was first translated into Chinese the following year, in 1958: Premchand, *Gedan* 戈丹 (Godan), trans. Yan Shaoduan 严绍端 (Beijing: Renmin wenxue chubanshe, 1958). Subsequent Chinese translations of *Nirmalā* and *Raṅgbhūmī* were published in 1959 and 1980, respectively. Lu Xun's stories circulated in India in English translation decades before their translation into Hindi. According to Jia Yan, the earliest translation of Lu Xun's works into Hindi is Nur Nabi Abbasi, *Ah Kyū* [Ah Q] (Delhi: National Publishing House, 1955).

11. Adhira Mangalagiri, "At the Limits of Comparison: Literary Encounters Between China and India in the Colonial World" (PhD diss., University of Chicago, 2017), 157–97.

12. For a theorization of the epistolary logic of correspondence, see Liz Stanley, "The Epistolarium: On Theorizing Letters and Correspondences," *Auto/Biography* 12 (2004): 201–35.

13. Lu Xun 魯迅, *Lu Xun zhu yi biannian quanji* 魯迅著譯編年全集 [Lu Xun's writings and translations, arranged by year of composition], ed. Wang Shijia 王世家 and Zhi An 止庵, 20 vols. (Beijing: Renmin chubanshe, 2009), 1:251. As I expand on later in this chapter, Lu Xun borrows the word "Mara" from Buddhist texts, in which "Mara" "meaning 'the destroyer or tempter' was the demonic 'evil one' who attempted to obstruct the Buddha's enlightenment under the *bodhi*-tree, and who was vanquished in the process." Robert Beer, *The Handbook of Tibetan Buddhist Symbols* (Chicago: Serindia, 2003), 252.

14. Lu Xun, *Lu Xun zhu yi biannian quanji*, 1:249.

15. Pu Wang, "Poetics, Politics, and 'Ursprung/Yuan': On Lu Xun's Conception of 'Mara Poetry,'" *Modern Chinese Literature and Culture* 23, no. 2 (2011): 34.

16. Lu Xun, *Lu Xun zhu yi biannian quanji*, 1:276.

17. Lu Xun, 1:275.

18. Lu Xun, 1:247.

19. Lu Xun, *Lu Xun zhu yi biannian quanji*, 1:247.

20. Lu Xun, 1:247.

21. Lu Xun, 1:247.

22. Lu Xun, 1:248.

23. Mark Gamsa, *The Chinese Translation of Russian Literature: Three Studies* (Leiden: Brill, 2008), 233.

24. Lu Xun, *Lu Xun zhu yi biannian quanji*, 15:75.

25. On Lu Xun's critique of Tagore see Sisir Kumar Das, "The Controversial Guest: Tagore in China," in *Across the Himalayan Gap*, ed. Tan Chung (New Delhi: Gyan, 1998), 311–33; Stephen Hay, *Asian Ideas of East and West: Tagore and His Critics in Japan, China, and India* (Cambridge, MA: Harvard University Press, 1970), 191–205; Tan Chung and Amiya Dev, eds., *Tagore and China* (New Delhi: Sage, 2011); and Xiaoqun Xu, "Cosmopolitanism, Nationalism, and Colonial Hierarchy: Chinese Responses to Russell, Eroshenko, and Tagore," in *Cosmopolitanism, Nationalism, and Individualism in Modern China* (Plymouth, KY: Lexington, 2014), 53–88.

26. Saiyin Sun, *Beyond the Iron House: Lu Xun and the Modern Chinese Literary Field* (New York: Routledge, 2017), 86.

27. Lu Xun 魯迅, "Qingnian bidu shu" 青年必讀書 [Essential reading for youth], *Jingbao Fukan* 京報副刊 67 (1925): 8.

28. Lu Xun, *Lu Xun zhu yi biannian quanji*, 8:43–44.

29. The flickering line between "ancient" and "new" is most visible in Lu Xun's linguistic style. Like the other essays Lu Xun published in Japan, "Mara Poetry" is "written in a *wenyan* [classical] style more archaic than the mainstream classical Chinese of the day." Lu Xun's choice of language presents one of several examples critics have discussed as demonstrating "the basic gesture of the entire essay: in searching for new origins from foreign voices, Lu Xun is also reactivating ancient characters and words." Wang, "Poetics, Politics, and 'Ursprung/Yuan,'" 37, 47.

30. Lu Xun, *Lu Xun zhu yi biannian quanji*, 1:249.

31. Significantly, Lu Xun refers to "India" as "*Yindu*" 印度 in his description of it as a silent, declining nation, and to the "India" from which he borrows "Mara" as "*tianzhu*," 天竺 with the latter appellation denoting an older term for "India" commonly used in Chinese Buddhist texts. Lu Xun uses "*tianzhu*" throughout "Mara Poetry," with the significant exception of one use of "*Yindu*" when he refers explicitly to India's (colonial) enslavement alongside that of Poland (印度波蘭之奴性). Lu Xun, 1:249.

32. Patrick Hanan, "The Technique of Lu Xun's Fiction," in *Chinese Fiction of the Nineteenth and Early Twentieth Centuries* (New York: Columbia University Press, 2004), 223.

33. Lu Xun, *Lu Xun zhu yi biannian quanji*, 8:43, 42.

34. Lu Xun, 8:41, 43.

35. Lu Xun, 8:43.

36. David Der-wei Wang, "From Mara to Nobel," in *A New Literary History of Modern China*, ed. David Der-wei Wang (Cambridge: Belknap Press of Harvard University Press, 2017), 224.

37. The *Panchatantra* was translated into Arabic in the eighth century AD and found extensive literary afterlives through the Arabic *One Thousand and One Nights* and the Greek *Aesop's Fables*. On the Panchatantra and its literary journeys, see Ibrahim Dawood, "'The Panchatantra,' 'Kalilah Wa Dimnah,' and 'The Morall Philosophie of Doni'" (PhD diss., Indiana University, 1983); and Katharine Gittes, "The Frame Narrative: History and Theory" (PhD diss., University of California, San Diego, 1983).

38. Gamsa, *Chinese Translation*, 62.

39. V. Sorokin, "Zheng Zhenduo: Man and Scholar," *Far Eastern Affairs* 1 (1989): 108–9.

40. Zheng Zhenduo 鄭振鐸, *Chatuben Zhongguo wenxue shi* 插圖本中國文學史 [Illustrated history of Chinese literature] (Beijing: Pushe chubanbu, 1932), 227.

41. On Zheng Zhenduo's early literary practice (prior to 1927), see Zheng Zhenwei 鄭振偉, *Zheng Zhenduo qianqi wenxue sixiang* 鄭振鐸前期文學思想 [Zheng Zhenduo's literary thought in his early years] (Beijing: Renmin wenxue chubanshe, 2000).

42. Zheng Zhenduo 鄭振鐸, "Yindu yuyan" 印度寓言 [Indian fables], *Xiaoshuo yuebao* 小說月報 15, no. 12 (1924): 2.

43. P. V. Ramaswami Raju, *Indian Fables* (London: Swan Sonnenschein, Lowrey, 1887), title page.

44. Gamsa, *Chinese Translation*, 63; Zheng Zhenduo, "Yindu yuyan," 2.

45. For examples of nineteenth- and twentieth-century collections of "Eastern" fables, see Frances Pritchett, "Folk Narrative," http://www.columbia.edu/itc/mealac/pritchett/00litlinks/lit_folk.html (accessed January 28, 2022).

46. Raju, *Indian Fables*, iii.

47. Raju, vii.

48. In his "Introduction" to *The Tales of the Sixty Mandarins*, Raju's colleague Henry Morley writes, "This is a real book of new Fairy Tales. Gatherings of legends of the people, partly Indian, partly Chinese, have been touched by the genius of a writer, himself from the East, who brings his own wit and fancy to the telling of his tales, and is as ready to invent as to hand down tradition." P. V. Ramaswami Raju, *The Tales of the Sixty Mandarins* (New York: Cassell, 1886), xi.

49. Zheng Zhenduo 鄭振鐸, "Lun yuyan" 論寓言 [On fables], *Wenxue zhoubao* 文學週報181 (1925): 1.

50. Jie Gao, *Saving the Nation Through Culture: The Folklore Movement in Republican China* (Vancouver: University of British Columbia Press, 2019).

51. Zheng Zhenduo, "Lun yuyan," 1.

52. Zheng Zhenduo, "Yindu yuyan," 2.

53. The fable's capacity for enacting subversion lies at the heart of the genre from its very inception, as centuries of fable readers from Lessing to Hegel to Paul de Man and Derrida have pointed out. On the intellectual lineages of fables as subversive texts, see Annabel Patterson, *Fables of Power: Aesopian Writing and Political History* (Durham, NC: Duke University Press, 1991); and Sara Forsdyke, *Slaves Tell Tales: And Other Episodes in the Politics of Popular Culture in Ancient Greece* (Princeton, NJ: Princeton University Press, 2012).

54. On Lu Xun's engagement with what Eileen Cheng terms "literatures of enchantment" (myths, legends, supernatural tales), see Eileen Cheng, "Disenchanted Fables," in *Literary Remains: Death, Trauma, and Lu Xun's Refusal to Mourn* (Honolulu: University of Hawaii Press, 2013), 192–218.

55. Francesca Orsini, "Introduction," in *The Oxford India Premchand* (New Delhi: Oxford University Press, 2012), ix.

56. Amrit Rai, "Soze Vatan Yānī Deś kā Dard" [The dirge of the nation, or the country's pain], in *Soz-e-vatan* (Allahabad: Hans Prakashan, 1988), 3.

57. Rai, "Soze Vatan," 3.

58. One copy of *Dirge of the Nation* apparently survived the censors, and years after Premchand's death, the book was recovered and republished by Premchand's son, Amrit Rai.

59. Premchand, *Soz-e-vatan* [Dirge of the nation] (Allahabad: Hans Prakashan, 1988), 28.

60. Premchand, *Soz-e-vatan*, 5.

61. Premchand, 11.

62. Premchand, 13.

63. Premchand, 15.

64. Premchand, 17.

65. "*Soz-e-vatan* is not important for what it actually attains in absolute standards of art," one critic writes, "but for the author's endeavor to pull the Urdu short story out of the dreamland of the 'dastans' (fantasies) . . . the impact of dastans of all the five stories is too loud to be ignored." Mohan Lal, ed., *Encyclopedia of Indian Literature*, vol. 5 (New Delhi: Sahitya Akademi, 1992), 4149. Urdu and Persian literary influences feature centrally in Premchand's early writings, influences considered "foreign" in form, imagery, and tone. At the turn of the twentieth century, critics accused genres of Urdu literature of promoting escapism and being "more familiar with Baghdad than Banaras." Robert Swan, *Munshi Premchand of Lamhi Village* (Durham, NC: Duke University Press, 1969), 55. In *Dirge*, Premchand's experiments with the *dāstān* answer to both these criticisms: by infusing *dāstān* writing with "real" nationalistic concerns, Premchand combats the escapism of the fantastical *dāstān*, and by using the *dāstān* to express Indian patriotic sentiment, Premchand roots the "foreign" *dāstān* within the political landscape of India.

66. Frances Pritchett, *Marvelous Encounters: Folk Romance in Urdu and Hindi* (Riverdale, NY: Riverdale, 1985), 3.

67. Pritchett, *Marvelous Encounters*, 5.

68. Pritchett, 8.

69. I am referring here to Amrit Rai's 1988 reprinting of *Soz-e-vatan* in the Devanāgarī script. In his preface to the book, Amrit Rai clarifies that "all the stories are presented in the same form as the original 1909 Urdu edition." Rai, "Soze Vatan," 3.

70. Premchand, *Soz-e-vatan*, 14.

71. Lu Xun, *Lu Xun zhu yi biannian quanji*, 1:276.

72. Jon Kowallis, "Lu Xun and Terrorism: A Reading of Revenge and Violence in Mara and Beyond," in *Creating Chinese Modernity*, ed. Peter Zarrow (New York: Peter Lang, 2006), 97.

73. Premchand, *Soz-e-vatan*, 11.

74. Charu Gupta, "Portrayal of Women in Premchand's Stories: A Critique," *Social Scientist* 19, no. 5 (1991): 89.

75. Orsini, "Introduction," xxiii.

76. Orsini, xxiii–xxv.

77. Rekha Sigi, *Munshi Premchand* (Delhi: Diamond, 2006), 23.

78. Women's issues feature centrally in Premchand's writings from the 1920s onward, in which "perhaps the subject of his single greatest concern was that of the many problems of women, family life, and marriage." Swan, *Munshi Premchand of Lamhi Village*, 98. "The Most Valuable Jewel" pre-dates Premchand's most sustained engagement with women's issues, as well as the influential role Gandhi's ideas played in Premchand's views on women's societal position.

79. Lata Mani, *Contentious Traditions: The Debate on Sati in Colonial India* (Los Angeles: University of California Press, 1998), 28.

80. Mani, *Contentious Traditions*, 79.

81. Ania Loomba, "Dead Women Tell No Tales: Issues of Female Subjectivity, Subaltern Agency, and Tradition in Colonial and Post-Colonial Writings on Widow Immolation in India," *History Workshop* 36 (1993): 212.

82. Loomba, "Dead Women Tell No Tales," 212.
83. Mani, *Contentious Traditions*, 2. Gayatri Spivak makes a similar argument. She describes the history of the Hindu widow's repression as having a double-origin, "one hidden in the [legal] maneuverings behind the British abolition of widow sacrifice in 1829, the other lodged in the classical and Vedic past of Hindu India, the *Rg-Veda* and the *Dharmasastra*." Gayatri Chakravorty Spivak, "Can the Subaltern Speak?," in *Marxism and the Interpretation of Culture*, ed. Cary Nelson and Lawrence Grossberg (Urbana: University of Illinois Press, 1988), 297. For Spivak, both these origins commit epistemic violence through a narrative of codification of the legal and scriptural bases of widow immolation. Taken together, the double origins of the Hindu widow's repression mark the disappearance of the subaltern woman from the discourse that has historically constituted her and that claims to represent her.
84. Zhou Zuoren 周作人, "Ren de wenxue" 人的文學 [Humane literature], in *Modern Chinese Literary Thought*, ed. Kirk Denton (Stanford, CA: Stanford University Press, 1996), 156–57. Translation is Ernst Wolff's.
85. Zhou Zuoren, "Ren de wenxue," 156.
86. Zhou Zuoren, 158.
87. Lu Xun, *Lu Xun zhu yi biannian quanji*, 4:210.
88. Lu Xun, 4:210.
89. Andrew Jones, *Developmental Fairy Tales: Evolutionary Thinking and Modern Chinese Culture* (Cambridge, MA: Harvard University Press, 2011), 154.
90. Lu Xun, *Lu Xun zhu yi biannian quanji*, 4:210.
91. Lu Xun, 4:210.
92. Lu Xun, 4:206. English translations of Lu Xun's Chinese translation of Eroshenko's "A Narrow Cage" are Andrew Jones's, with minor modifications.
93. Spivak, "Can the Subaltern Speak?," 296.
94. Spivak, 306.
95. Mani, *Contentious Traditions*, 161.
96. Mani, 164.
97. Mani, 178.
98. Premchand, *Soz-e-vatan*, 12.
99. Premchand, 12.
100. Jones, *Developmental Fairy Tales*, 168.
101. Jones, 168.
102. Jones, 167.
103. Jones, 172.
104. Lu Xun, *Lu Xun zhu yi biannian quanji*, 4:652.
105. For a selection of studies that discuss the iron house parable at length, see Carolyn Brown, "The Paradigm of the Iron House: Shouting and Silence in Lu Xun's Stories," *Chinese Literature Essays Articles Reviews* 6, nos. 1–2 (1984): 101–20; Leo Ou-fan Lee, *Voices from the Iron House: A Study of Lu Xun* (Bloomington: Indiana University Press, 1987); Lung-kee Sun, "To Be or Not to Be 'Eaten': Lu Xun's Dilemma of Political Engagement," *Modern China* 12, no. 4 (1986): 459–85; and Xiaobing Tang, "Lu Xun's 'Diary of a Madman' and a Chinese Modernism," *PMLA* 107, no. 5 (1992): 1222–34.

106. Jones, *Developmental Fairy Tales*, 37.
107. "A Tale of Two Bullocks" has yet to receive sustained critical attention; it is most often cited as an example of Premchand's pedagogical children's stories and included in anthologies of Premchand's writings targeted toward a younger readership. Contrary to this treatment, I read the story as closer to what Andrew Jones terms, in the context of Lu Xun and Eroshenko, the "modernist fairy tale, one in which the very premises of the genre are subject to self-reflexive critique." Jones, 160.
108. Premchand, *Premcand Racănāvalī* [Collected works of Premchand], vol. 14 (Delhi: Janvani Prakashan, 1996), 534.
109. Premchand, *Premcand Racănāvalī*, 534.
110. Premchand, 535.
111. Premchand, 535.
112. Premchand, 528.
113. Premchand, 529.
114. Lu Xun, *Lu Xun zhu yi biannian quanji*, 4:198.
115. Jones, *Developmental Fairy Tales*, 167.
116. Jones, 170.
117. Jones, 169.
118. Jones, 173. Lu Xun's 1919 short story, "Diary of a Madman" (*Kuangren riji* 狂人日記) famously employs a similar, cyclical narrative structure: "The prefacelike passage that introduces the story reassures the reader that the Madman 'has recovered some time ago and has gone elsewhere to take up an official post.' In other words, he has returned to the system against which he once desperately revolted with all his strength." Tang, "Lu Xun's 'Diary of a Madman,'" 1230.

Conclusion

1. Sallie Marston, John Paul Jones III, and Keith Woodward, "Human Geography Without Scale," *Transactions of the Institute of British Geographers* 30, no. 4 (2005): 423.
2. Tim Cresswell, "Friction," in *The Routledge Handbook of Mobilities*, ed. Peter Adey, David Bissell, and Kevin Hannam (Abingdon: Routledge, 2013), 108, 111.
3. Anna Lowenhaupt Tsing, *Friction: An Ethnography of Global Connection* (Princeton, NJ: Princeton University Press, 2011), 1.
4. Tsing, *Friction*, 1, 8.
5. Tsing, 1, 4.
6. Hedley Bull, *The Anarchical Society: A Study of Order in World Politics*, 2nd ed. (London: Macmillan, [1977] 1995), 206.
7. Bull, *Anarchical Society*, 165.
8. Bai Yun 白云, "Gei Yindu Asan" 給印度阿三 [Ode to the Indian Asan], *Shidai zhishi* 時代知識 1, no. 7 (1936): 43. I discuss this poem in chapter 1.
9. Donna J. Haraway, *Staying with the Trouble: Making Kin in the Chthulucene* (Durham, NC: Duke University Press, 2016).

10. Kathleen Stewart, *Ordinary Affects* (Durham, NC: Duke University Press, 2007), 128.
11. Tsing, *Friction*, 5.
12. Anne Toner, *Ellipsis in English Literature: Signs of Omission* (Cambridge: Cambridge University Press, 2015), 10.
13. Pierre Macherey, *A Theory of Literary Production*, trans. Geoffrey Wall (London: Routledge & Kegan Paul, 1978), 87; emphasis in original.
14. Macherey, *Theory of Literary Production*, 131–32.
15. Gayatri Chakravorty Spivak, "Can the Subaltern Speak?," in *Marxism and the Interpretation of Culture*, ed. Cary Nelson and Lawrence Grossberg (Urbana: University of Illinois Press, 1988), 285.
16. Édouard Glissant, *Poetics of Relation*, trans. Betsy Wing (Ann Arbor: University of Michigan Press, 1997), 62.
17. Glissant, *Poetics of Relation*, 189–90.
18. Glissant, 193.
19. Natalie Melas, *All the Difference in the World: Postcoloniality and the Ends of Comparison* (Stanford, CA: Stanford University Press, 2007), 31.
20. Melas, *All the Difference*, 43.
21. Melas, 37.
22. Emily Apter, *Against World Literature: On the Politics of Untranslatability* (London: Verso, 2013), 2.
23. Apter, *Against World Literature*, 3.
24. Emily Apter, "Untranslatability and the Geopolitics of Reading," *PMLA* 134, no. 1 (2019): 197.
25. Apter, *Against World Literature*, 3.
26. Apter, "Untranslatability," 198.
27. Melas, *All the Difference*, 36.
28. Melas, 36–37.
29. Apter, *Against World Literature*, 35.
30. Apter, "Untranslatability," 199.
31. Apter, 199.
32. Stephen Gould has helpfully schematized the workings of contingency as follows: "E, the phenomenon to be explained, arose because D came before, preceded by C, B, and A.... Thus, E makes sense and can be explained rigorously as the outcome of A through D. But no law of nature enjoined E." Contingency constitutes "the central principle of all history," in which "a historical explanation does not rest on direct deductions from laws of nature, but on an unpredictable sequence of antecedent states, where any major change in any step of the sequence would have altered the final result." Stephen Gould, *Wonderful Life: The Burgess Shale and the Nature of History* (New York: W.W. Norton, 1989), 283.
33. Liane Carlson, *Contingency and the Limits of History* (New York: Columbia University Press, 2019), 4.
34. "The essential thing is contingency," Jean-Paul Sartre's protagonist Antoine Roquentin realizes. "I mean that one cannot define existence as necessity. To exist is simply to be there ... contingency is not a delusion, a probability which

can be dissipated; it is the absolute." Jean-Paul Sartre, *Nausea*, trans. Lloyd Alexander (New York: New Directions, 1964), 131.

35. Carlson, *Contingency and the Limits of History*, 33.

36. Reinhart Koselleck, *Futures Past: On the Semantics of Historical Time*, trans. Keith Tribe (Cambridge, MA: MIT Press, 1985), 121.

37. Giorgio Agamben, *Potentialities: Collected Essays in Philosophy* (Stanford, CA: Stanford University Press, 1999), 261–262.

38. Agamben, *Potentialities*, 257, 267.

39. David Wellbery, "Contingency," in *Neverending Stories: Toward a Critical Narratology*, ed. Ann Fehn, Ingeborg Hoesterey, and Maria Tatar (Princeton, NJ: Princeton University Press, 1992), 245.

40. Wellbery, "Contingency," 239.

41. Wellbery, 245.

42. Tsing, *Friction*, 3.

43. Pheng Cheah, *What Is a World? On Postcolonial Literature as World Literature* (Durham, NC: Duke University Press, 2016), 35.

Bibliography

"The Asian Mind." *Times of India*, August 6, 1956, 6.

"Asian Writers' Conference: India's Contribution to Asian Culture." *Times of India*, December 24, 1956, 8.

"Asian Writers' Talks Begin Tomorrow: Preparations in New Delhi." *Times of India*, December 22, 1956, 7.

"Benbao fuyin" 本報附印 [Printed in this newspaper]. *Shenbao* 申報, March 11, 1907, 18.

"China-India Photo Exhibit, Major Attraction at New Delhi Book Fair." *China Daily*, January 7, 2020. Accessed May 3, 2022. https://global.chinadaily.com.cn/a/202001 /07/WS5e13f027a310cf3e35582e8a_2.html.

"Creative Writing in the Present Crisis." *Indian Literature* 6, no. 1 (1963): 66–99.

"Cultural Co-Operation Among Asian Nations: End of Writers' Conference." *Times of India*, December 29, 1956, 3.

"Current Topics." *Times of India*, November 28, 1956, 6.

"Extent of Curbs Put by Society on Writers: Keen Controversy in Asian Conference Commission." *Times of India*, December 28, 1956, 5.

"Final Communiqué of the Asian-African Conference of Bandung (24 April 1955)." In *Asia-Africa Speak from Bandung*, edited by the Ministry of Foreign Affairs of the Republic of Indonesia, 161–69. Djakarta: Ministry of Foreign Affairs, 1955.

"Gandi kang Ying yundong" 甘地抗英運動 [Gandhi's anti-British movement]. *Guowen zhoubao* 國文週報 7, no. 20 (1930): 8–9.

"Hongtou Asan yu lacheren" 紅頭阿三與拉車人 [Hongtou Asan and the rickshaw puller]. *Shiyong Yingwen banyuekan* 實用英文半月刊 2, no. 4 (1937): 49–50.

"Message to King." *Times of India*, December 24, 1929, 11.

"No One Should Come Between Writer and Reader: Accent on Freedom at Delhi Conference." *Times of India*, December 26, 1956, 11.

"Renewed Split Emerges Among Organisers: Asian Writers' Conference." *Times of India*, December 21, 1956, 9.

"Shamsher Bahadur Singh." *Hindi: Language, Discourse, Writing* 1, nos. 3–4 (2000–2001): 199–261.

"S. H. Vatsyayan: A Chronology." *Mahfil* 2, no. 1 (1965): 1–2.

"Spread Message of Peace: Call to Asian Writers." *Times of India*, December 24, 1956, 8.

"Writer Must Be Free to Write What He Feels." *Times of India*, December 25, 1956, 8.

"Yindu Asan meirongshu" 印度阿三美容術 [The beautification methods of the Indian Asan]. *Shijie Huabao* 世界畫報 3, no. 5 (1941): 32–33.

"Yindu zhi fan Ying yundong" 印度之反英運動 [India's anti-British movement]. *Dongfang zazhi* 東方雜誌 27, no. 8 (1930): 1–3.

A Ying 阿英. *Xiaoshuo xiantan* 小說閒談 [Casual discussions on fiction]. Shanghai: Gudian wenxue chubanshe, 1958.

Abbasi, Nur Nabi. *Ah Kyū* [Ah Q]. Delhi: National Publishing House, 1955.

Agamben, Giorgio. *Potentialities: Collected Essays in Philosophy*. Stanford, CA: Stanford University Press, 1999.

Agraval, Mahavir, ed. *Śaṃśer: Kavī Se Baṛe Ādmī* [Shamsher: from poet to great man]. Kasaridiha Durg: Sri Prakashan, 1994.

Agyeya. *Agyeya Racănāvalī* [Collected works of Agyeya]. Vol. 3. Edited by Krishnadutt Paliwal. New Delhi: Bharatiya Gyanpith, 2011.

——. "Author's Introduction." In *Shekhar: A Life*, xi–xvii. Translated by Snehal Shingavi and Vasudha Dalmia. Gurgaon: Penguin Random House India, 2018.

——. *Smṛti-lekh* [Memoirs]. New Delhi: National Publishing House, 1996.

Agyeya, ed. *Dūsrā Saptak* [The second heptad]. New Delhi: Pragati Prakashan, 1951.

Ai Qing 艾青. "Author's Preface." Translated by Eugene Eoyang. In *Selected Poems of Ai Qing*, 1–22. Bloomington: Indiana University Press, 1982.

——. "Yingjie yi jiu wu san nian" 迎接一九五三年 [Welcome to 1953]. *Renmin wenxue* 人民文學 1 (1953): 9.

Alternburger, Roland. *The Sword and the Needle: The Female Knight-Errant (Xia) in Traditional Chinese Narrative*. Bern: Peter Lang, 2009.

Anand, Mulk Raj. "Mulk Raj Anand Remembers." *Indian Literature* 36, no. 2 (1993): 176–86.

Andolfatto, Lorenzo. *Hundred Days' Literature: Chinese Utopian Fiction at the End of Empire, 1902–1910*. Leiden: Brill, 2019.

Ang, Ien, Yudhishthir Raj Isar, and Phillip Mar. "Cultural Diplomacy: Beyond the National Interest?" *International Journal of Cultural Policy* 21, no. 4 (2015): 365–81.

Apter, Emily. *Against World Literature: On the Politics of Untranslatability*. New York: Verso, 2013.

——. "Comparative Exile: Competing Margins in the History of Comparative Literature." In *Comparative Literature in the Age of Multiculturalism*, edited by Charles Bernheimer, 81–96. Baltimore, MD: Johns Hopkins University Press, 1995.

——. "Untranslatability and the Geopolitics of Reading." *PMLA* 134, no. 1 (2019): 194–200.

Argare, Ranjana. *Kavīyoṁ kā Kavī Śaṃśer* [The poets' poet Shamsher]. New Delhi: Vani Prakashan, 1988.

Ba Jin 巴金. *Siqu de taiyang* 死去的太陽 [The setting sun]. Shanghai: Kaiming shudian, 1931.

Bai Yun 白云. "Gei Yindu Asan" 給印度阿三 [Ode to the Indian Asan]. *Shidai zhishi* 時代知識 1, no. 7 (1936): 43–44.

Ballantyne, Tony. *Between Colonialism and Diaspora: Sikh Cultural Formations in an Imperial World*. Durham, NC: Duke University Press, 2006.

Beattie, James, and Richard Bullen. "Embracing Friendship Through Gift and Exchange: Rewi Alley and the Art of Museum Diplomacy in Cold War China and New Zealand." *Australian and New Zealand Journal of Art* 16, no. 2 (2016): 149–66.

Beer, Robert. *The Handbook of Tibetan Buddhist Symbols*. Chicago: Serindia, 2003.

Benjamin, Walter. *Illuminations*. New York: Schocken, 1969.

Brady, Anne-Marie. *Friend of China: The Myth of Rewi Alley*. London: RoutledgeCurzon, 2003.

——. "Who Friend, Who Enemy? Rewi Alley and the Friends of China." *China Quarterly* 151 (1997): 614–32.

Brown, Carolyn. "The Paradigm of the Iron House: Shouting and Silence in Lu Xun's Stories." *Chinese Literature: Essays, Articles, Reviews* 6, nos. 1–2 (1984): 101–20.

Bull, Hedley. *The Anarchical Society: A Study of Order in World Politics*. 2nd ed. London: Macmillan, [1977] 1995.

Bush, Christopher. *Ideographic Modernism: China, Writing, Media*. New York: Oxford University Press, 2010.

Butler, Judith, and Gayatri Chakravorty Spivak. *Who Sings the Nation-State?* Calcutta: Seagull, 2007.

Cai Yuan. "Zhang Taiyan and the Asiatic Humanitarian Brotherhood, 1907." In *Pan-Asianism: A Documentary History, Volume 1, 1850–1920*, edited by Sven Saaler and Christopher Szpilman, 177–84. Lanham, MD: Rowman & Littlefield, 2011.

Campbell, Duncan. "Labouring in the 'Sheltered Field': Rewi Alley's Translations from the Chinese." *New Zealand Journal of Asian Studies* 16, no. 2 (2014): 77–98.

Cao Yin. *From Policemen to Revolutionaries: A Sikh Diaspora in Global Shanghai*. Leiden: Brill, 2017.

Carlson, Liane. *Contingency and the Limits of History*. New York: Columbia University Press, 2019.

Chander, Krishan, Premchand, Mulk Raj Anand, Navtej Singh, Ibrahim Jalees, and Manik Bandopadhyay. *Yindu duanpian xiaoshuo ji* 印度短篇小說集 [Collection of Indian short stories]. Translated by Yuan Ruo 袁若. Shanghai: Chaofeng chubanshe, 1953.

Chatterjee, Partha. "The Nationalist Resolution of the Women's Question." In *Recasting Women: Essays in Colonial History*, edited by Kumkum Sangari and Sudesh Vaid, 233–53. New Brunswick, NJ: Rutgers University Press, 1989.

Cheah, Pheng. *What Is a World? On Postcolonial Literature as World Literature*. Durham, NC: Duke University Press, 2016.

Chen Jiazhen 陳嘉震 and Ouyang Pu 歐陽璞. "Ruci Shanghai" 如此上海 [Such is Shanghai]. *Liangyou* 良友 89 (1934): 21.

Chen Kangtai 陳康泰. "Hongtou Asan" 紅頭阿三 [Hongtou Asan]. *Nanyang gaoji shangye xuexiao xueshenghui jikan* 南洋高級商業學校學生會季刊 1 (1927): 39–41.

Chen Kuan-hsing 陳光興. "Zuowei fangfa de Yindu" 作為方法的印度 [India as method]. *Dushu* 讀書 12 (2010): 10–15.

Chen Linghong 陳凌虹. "Xu Zhuodai liu Ri jingli ji zaoqi chuangzuo huodong kao" 徐卓呆留日經歷及早期創作活動考 [Xu Zhuodai's experiences in Japan and early works]. *Zhongguo xiandai wenxue yanjiu congkan* 中國現代文學研究叢刊 11 (2016): 60–69.

Cheng, Eileen. "Disenchanted Fables." In *Literary Remains: Death, Trauma, and Lu Xun's Refusal to Mourn*, 192–218. Honolulu: University of Hawaii Press, 2013.

Cheng Guan 澄觀. "Yindu Asan mingcheng zhi youlai" 印度阿三名稱之由來 [The reason behind the Indian Asan's name]. *Hongguang* 宏光 5 (1923): 61.

Chow, Rey. "The Old/New Question of Comparison in Literary Studies: A Post-European Perspective." *ELH* 71, no. 2 (2004): 289–311.

——. "On Chineseness as a Theoretical Problem." In *Sinophone Studies: A Critical Reader*, edited by Shu-mei Shih, Chien-Hsin Tsai, and Brian Bernards, 43–56. New York: Columbia University Press, 2013.

——. *Woman and Chinese Modernity: The Politics of Reading Between West and East*. Minneapolis: University of Minnesota Press, 1991.

Clifford, Nicholas. *Spoilt Children of Empire: Westerners in Shanghai and the Chinese Revolution of the 1920s*. Hanover, NJ: University Press of New England, 1976.

Coppola, Carlo, ed. *Marxist Influences and South Asian Literature*. East Lansing, MI: Michigan State University Asian Studies Center, 1974.

——. "Premchand's Address to the First Meeting of the All-India Progressive Writers Association: Some Speculations." *Journal of South Asian Literature* 21, no. 2 (1986): 21–39.

Crespi, John. *Voices in Revolution: Poetry and the Auditory Imagination in Modern China*. Honolulu: University of Hawai'i Press, 2009.

Cresswell, Tim. "Friction." In *The Routledge Handbook of Mobilities*, edited by Peter Adey, David Bissell and Kevin Hannam, 107–15. Abingdon: Routledge, 2013.

Da, Nan. *Intransitive Encounter: Sino-U.S. Literatures and the Limits of Exchange*. New York: Columbia University Press, 2018.

Dalmia, Vasudha, ed. *Hindi Modernism: Rethinking Agyeya and His Times*. Berkeley: University of California, 2012.

Damrosch, David, Haun Saussy, and Jacob Edmond. "Trying to Make It Real: An Exchange Between Haun Saussy and David Damrosch." *Comparative Literature Studies* 53, no. 4 (2016): 660–93.

Damsteegt, Theo. "Violence in the Age of Gandhi—Ajneya's Early Short Stories." *Studien Zur Indologie und Iranistik*, 11–12 (1986): 311–52.

——. "Violent Heroines: Ajneya and Violence—Revisited." In *Violence Denied: Violence, Non-Violence, and the Rationalization of Violence in South Asian Cultural History*, edited by Jan Houben and Karel Kooij, 341–72. Leiden: Brill, 1999.

Das, Sisir Kumar. "The Controversial Guest: Tagore in China." In *Across the Himalayan Gap*, edited by Tan Chung, 311–33. New Delhi: Gyan, 1998.

Dawood, Ibrahim. "'The Panchatantra,' 'Kalilah Wa Dimnah,' and 'the Morall Philosophie of Doni.'" PhD diss., Indiana University, 1983.

Deepak, B. R. *India-China Relations in the First Half of the Twentieth Century*. New Delhi: APH, 2001.

——. "Revolutionary Activities of the Ghadar Party in China." *China Report* 35, no. 4 (1999): 439–56.

Derrida, Jacques. *Specters of Marx: The State of Debt, the Work of Mourning, and the New International.* New York: Routledge, 1994.

Desai, M. V. "The Asian Writers' Conference, December 1956: New Delhi." *Books Abroad* 31, no. 3 (1957): 243–45.

Diedie 喋喋. "Chao Yindu xunbu" 嘲印度巡捕 [Mocking the Indian policeman]. *Huaji Shici* 滑稽詩詞 2 (1913): 34.

Dinkar, Ramdhari Singh. "Cīn ke samsmaraṇ" [Memoirs of China]. *Dharmayug,* November 9, 1958.

——. *Dinkarnāmā.* Vol. 2. Edited by Diwakar. Nawada: Chaitanyam Prakashan, 2004.

——. *Merī yātrāeṁ* [My travels]. Patna: Udyacal, 1970.

——. *Miṭṭī ki or* [Towards the soil]. Patna: Udyacal, 1946.

——. *Ramdhari Singh Dinkar Racănāvali* [Collected works of Ramdhari Singh Dinkar]. Vol. 10. Edited by Nandkishore Naval and Tarun Kumar. New Delhi: Lokbharati Prakashan, 2011.

——. *Sipi Aur Sankh* [Shell and conch]. Patna: Udyacal, 1966.

Djagalov, Rossen. *From Internationalism to Postcolonialism: Literature and Cinema Between the Second and Third Worlds.* Montreal: McGill-Queen's University Press, 2020.

Duara, Prasenjit. "Asia Redux: Conceptualizing a Region for Our Times." *Journal of Asian Studies* 69, no. 4 (2010): 963–83.

Duara, Prasenjit, and Elizabeth Perry, eds. *Beyond Regimes: China and India Compared.* Cambridge, MA: Harvard University Asia Center, 2018.

Dublish, Kaushalya Devi. *Revolutionaries and Their Activities in Northern India.* Delhi: BR, 1982.

Eoyang, Eugene. "Editor's Introduction." In *Selected Poems of Ai Qing,* i–x. Bloomington: Indiana University Press, 1982.

Esty, Jed, and Colleen Lye. "Peripheral Realisms Now." *Modern Language Quarterly* 73, no. 3 (2012): 269–88.

Faiz. "Ghazal (Song)." In *Poems by Faiz,* edited by Victor G. Kiernan, 220–23. London: George Allen & Unwin, 1971.

Fenollosa, Ernest, and Ezra Pound. *The Chinese Written Character as a Medium for Poetry: A Critical Edition.* Edited by Haun Saussy, Jonathan Stalling and Lucas Klein. New York: Fordham University Press, 2008.

Forsdyke, Sara. *Slaves Tell Tales: And Other Episodes in the Politics of Popular Culture in Ancient Greece.* Princeton, NJ: Princeton University Press, 2012.

Fox, Richard. *Lions of the Punjab: Culture in the Making.* Berkeley: University of California Press, 1985.

Fried, Daniel. "A Bloody Absence: Communist Narratology and the Literature of May Thirtieth." *Chinese Literature: Essays, Articles, Reviews* 26 (2004): 23–53.

Friedman, Susan Stanford. "Why Not Compare?" *PMLA* 126, no. 3 (2011): 753–62.

Fu Jianzhou 付建舟. "Wan Qing Zhe ji zuojia Yadong Pofo shengping zhushu kao" 晚清浙籍作家亞東破佛生平著述考 [The life and writings of Yadong Pofo, a Zhejiang writer in the late Qing dynasty]. *Suzhou jiaoyu xueyuan xuebao* 蘇州教育學院學報 33, no. 5 (2016): 12–18.

Fulfagar, Kanhaiyalal. *Dinkar ke patr* [Dinkar's letters]. Calcutta: Dinkar sodh samsthan, 1981.

Gamsa, Mark. *The Chinese Translation of Russian Literature: Three Studies.* Leiden: Brill, 2008.

Gao, Jie. *Saving the Nation Through Culture: The Folklore Movement in Republican China.* Vancouver: University of British Columbia Press, 2019.

Garver, John. *Protracted Contest: Sino-Indian Rivalry in the Twentieth Century.* Seattle: University of Washington Press, 2001.

General Reports on the Progress of the Delhi Conspiracy Case. File No. F-4-13 1930. National Archives of India, Home Department Political.

Ghosh, Arunabh. "1950s China-India Chronology." Accessed January 28, 2022. https:// histecon.fas.harvard.edu/chinaindia1950/.

——. "Before 1962: The Case for 1950s China-India History." *Journal of Asian Studies* 76, no. 3 (2017): 697–727.

Gittes, Katharine. "The Frame Narrative: History and Theory." PhD diss., University of California, San Diego, 1983.

Glissant, Édouard. *Poetics of Relation.* Translated by Betsy Wing. Ann Arbor: University of Michigan Press, 1997.

Goldman, Merle. "The Party and the Intellectuals." In *The Cambridge History of China,* edited by Roderick MacFarquhar and John K. Fairbank, 218–58. Cambridge: Cambridge University Press, 1987.

Gould, Stephen. *Wonderful Life: The Burgess Shale and the Nature of History.* New York: W. W. Norton, 1989.

Govind, Nikhil. "Agyeya: Enmeshments of Revolutionary Subjectivity." In *Love and Freedom: The Revolutionary in the Hindi Novel,* 109–33. New Delhi: Routledge, 2014.

Gupta, Amit Das, and Lorenz Lüthi, eds. *The Sino-Indian War of 1962: New Perspectives.* New York: Routledge, 2017.

Gupta, Charu. "Portrayal of Women in Premchand's Stories: A Critique." *Social Scientist* 19, no. 5 (1991): 88–113.

Gvili, Gal. "Pan-Asian Poetics: Tagore and the Interpersonal in May Fourth New Poetry." *Journal of Asian Studies* 77, no. 1 (2018): 181–203.

Hanan, Patrick. "The Technique of Lu Xun's Fiction." In *Chinese Fiction of the Nineteenth and Early Twentieth Centuries,* 217–50. New York: Columbia University Press, 2004.

Haraway, Donna J. *Staying with the Trouble: Making Kin in the Chthulucene.* Durham, NC: Duke University Press, 2016.

Harrell, Stevan. "The Concept of Soul in Chinese Folk Religion." *Journal of Asian Studies* 38, no. 3 (1979): 519–28.

Hay, Stephen. *Asian Ideas of East and West: Tagore and His Critics in Japan, China, and India.* Cambridge, MA: Harvard University Press, 1970.

Hayot, Eric. *Chinese Dream: Pound, Brecht, Tel Quel.* Ann Arbor: University of Michigan Press, 2004.

He Zou 何奏. "You Gandi dao Nihelu: Yige Yindu xunbu de gushi" 由甘地到尼赫鲁：一個印度巡捕的故事 [From Gandhi to Nehru: the story of an Indian policeman]. *Xin shaonian* 新少年 3, no. 9 (1937): 54–58.

Hegel, G. W. F. *Philosophy of History.* Translated by J. Sibree. New York: P. F. Collier, 1905.

Hon, Tze-ki. "National Essence, National Learning, and Culture: Historical Writings in Guocui Xuebao, Xueheng, and Guoxue Jikan." *Historiography East and West* 1, no. 2 (2003): 242–86.

Hong Zicheng 洪子誠. *1956—baihua shidai* 1956—百花時代 [1956—The Hundred Flowers era]. Beijing: Beijing daxue chubanshe, 2010.

Hsia, C. T. "Obsession with China: The Moral Burden of Modern Chinese Literature." In *A History of Modern Chinese Fiction*, 533–54. Bloomington: Indiana University Press, 1999.

Huang, Guiyou. "A Newer Realm of Poetry: Whitman and Ai Qing." *Walt Whitman Quarterly Review* 15, no. 4 (1998): 172–79.

The Indian Cultural Delegation in China. Peking: Foreign Languages Press, 1955.

Isaacs, Harold, ed. *Straw Sandals: Chinese Short Stories, 1918-1933*. Cambridge, MA: MIT Press, 1974.

Jackson, Isabella. "The Raj on Nanjing Road: Sikh Policemen in Treaty-Port Shanghai." *Modern Asian Studies* 46, no. 6 (2012): 1672–704.

Jaidev. *The Culture of Pastiche: Existential Aestheticism in the Contemporary Hindi Novel*. Shimla: Indian Institute of Advanced Study, 1993.

Ji Xianlin 季羨林. *ZhongYin wenhua jiaoliu shi* 中印文化交流史 [A history of Sino-Indian cultural exchanges]. Beijing: Zhongguo shehui kexue chubanshe, 2007.

Jia, Yan. "Beyond the 'Bhai-Bhai' Rhetoric: China-India Literary Relations, 1950-1990." PhD diss., School of Oriental and African Studies, University of London, 2019.

Jiang Guangci 蔣光慈. "Asan" 阿三 [Asan]. *Tuohuangzhe* 拓荒者 1, no. 1 (1930): 57–61.

Jiang Jingkui 姜景奎. "Lun ZhongYin guanxi de fenqi wenti" 論中印關係的分期問題 [On the periodization of Sino-Indian relations]. *Journal of Guangdong University of Foreign Studies* 23, no. 3 (2012): 5–10.

Jin Xuan 錦軒. "Hongtou Asan" 紅頭阿三 [Hongtou Asan]. *Qianfeng zhoubao* 前鋒週報 6 (1930): 46–47.

Jones, Andrew. *Developmental Fairy Tales: Evolutionary Thinking and Modern Chinese Culture*. Cambridge, MA: Harvard University Press, 2011.

Kang Youwei 康有為. "Yu tongxue zhuzi Liang Qichao deng lun Yindu wangguo youyu ge sheng zili shu" 與同學諸子梁啟超等論印度亡國由於各省自立書 [A letter to fellow scholar Liang Qichao and others on India's colonization due to the independence of its provinces]. In *Kang Youwei quanji* 康有為全集, edited by Jiang Yihua 姜義華 and Zhang Ronghua 張榮華. Beijing: Zhongguo renmin daxue chubanshe, [1902] 1998.

Kantor, Roanne. " 'My Heart, My Fellow Traveller': Fantasy, Futurity, and the Itineraries of Faiz Ahmed Faiz." *South Asia: Journal of South Asian Studies* 39, no. 3 (2016): 608–25.

Karl, Rebecca. " 'Slavery,' Citizenship, and Gender in Late Qing China's Global Context." In *Rethinking the 1898 Reform Period: Political and Cultural Change in Late Qing China*, edited by Rebecca Karl and Peter Zarrow, 212–44. Cambridge, MA: Harvard University Asia Center, 2002.

——. *Staging the World: Chinese Nationalism at the Turn of the Twentieth Century*. Durham, NC: Duke University Press, 2002.

Kern, Robert. *Orientalism, Modernism, and the American Poem*. Cambridge: Cambridge University Press, 1996.

Khare, Vishnu. "Introduction." In *Inspector Matadeen on the Moon: Satires by Harishankar Parsai*, edited by C. M. Naim, 7–12. New Delhi: Katha, 2003.

Kieschnick, John, and Meir Shahar, eds. *India in the Chinese Imagination: Myth, Religion, and Thought*. Philadelphia: University of Pennsylvania Press, 2014.

Koselleck, Reinhart. *Futures Past: On the Semantics of Historical Time*. Translated by Keith Tribe. Cambridge, MA: MIT Press, 1985.

Kowallis, Jon. "Lu Xun and Terrorism: A Reading of Revenge and Violence in Mara and Beyond." In *Creating Chinese Modernity*, edited by Peter Zarrow, 83–98. New York: Peter Lang, 2006.

Kraus, Richard. "Let a Hundred Flowers Blossom, Let a Hundred Schools of Thought Contend." In *Words and Their Stories: Essays on the Language of the Chinese Revolution*, edited by Ban Wang, 249–62. Leiden: Brill, 2010.

Ku, Hung-Ting. "Urban Mass Movement: The May Thirtieth Movement in Shanghai." *Modern Asian Studies* 13, no. 2 (1979): 197–216.

Kumar, Sharat, and Geeti Sen. "Interview with Ajneya (S. H. Vatsyayan)." *India International Centre Quarterly* 10, no. 4 (1983): 527–49.

Kwa, Shiamin, and Wilt Idema, eds. *Mulan: Five Versions of a Classic Chinese Legend with Related Texts*. Indianapolis: Hackett, 2010.

Lal, Mohan, ed. *Encyclopedia of Indian Literature* Vol. 5. New Delhi: Sahitya Akademi, 1992.

Lee, Leo Ou-fan. *Voices from the Iron House: A Study of Lu Xun*. Bloomington: Indiana University Press, 1987.

Lee, Yu-Ting. " 'Tagore and China' Reconsidered: Starting from a Conversation with Feng Youlan." In *Beyond Pan-Asianism: Connecting China and India, 1840s-1960s*, edited by Tansen Sen and Brian Tsui, 209–35. New Delhi: Oxford University Press, 2021.

Lekner, Dayton. "A Chill in Spring: Literary Exchange and Political Struggle in the Hundred Flowers and Anti-Rightist Campaigns of 1956–1958." *Modern China* 45, no. 1 (2019): 37–63.

Levan, Valerie. "The Meaning of Foreign Text in Yu Dafu's *Sinking* Collection." *Modern Chinese Literature and Culture* 24, no. 1 (2012): 48–87.

Levenson, Joseph. *Confucian China and Its Modern Fate: A Trilogy*. Vol. 1. Berkeley: University of California Press, 1968.

Li, Ch'i. *The Use of Figurative Language in Communist China*. Berkeley, CA: Center for Chinese Studies, 1958.

Li Hongyan 李紅艷, and Wang Jipeng 王吉鵬. "Lu Xun yu Puliemuchangde" 魯迅與普列姆昌德 [Lu Xun and Premchand]. *Yancheng shifan xueyuan xuebao* 鹽城師範學院學報 2 (2004): 73–78.

Liang Qichao 梁啟超. "Yindu yu Zhongguo wenhua zhi qinshu de guanxi" 印度與中國文化之親屬的關係 [The kindred relation of Indian and Chinese culture]. *Chenbao fukan* 晨报副刊 (May 3, 1924): 1–3.

Liu Anwu 劉安武. "Puliemuchangde he Lu Xun de xiaoshuo chuangzuo" 普列姆昌德和魯迅的小說創作 [Premchand and Lu Xun's fiction writings]. In *Yindu wenxue he Zhongguo wenxue bijiao yanjiu* 印度文學和中國文學比較研究 [A comparative study of Indian literature and Chinese literature], 271–81. Beijing: Zhongguo dabaike quanshu chubanshe, 2015.

Liu Delong 劉德隆. "Shuang linghun" 雙靈魂 [Twin souls]. *Ming-Qing xiaoshuo yanjiu* 明清小說研究 2 (1996): 231–35.

Liu Dengdong 劉登東. "Puliemuchangde yu Lu Xun xiaoshuo bijiao tan" 普列姆昌德 與魯迅小說比較談 [Comparing Premchand and Lu Xun's fiction]. *Chongqing shifan daxue xuebao* 重慶師範大學學報 4 (1990): 62–67.

Liu Yongguang 劉永廣. "Zhimin chiru yu wenhua xixue: 'hongtou Asan' xingxiang de suzao yu chuanbo" 殖民恥辱與文化戲謔: '紅頭阿三' 形象的塑造與傳播 [Colonial shame and cultural irony: the portrayal and circulation of the image of Red-head Asan]. *Lishi Jiaoxue* 歷史教學 12 (2018): 20–30.

Loomba, Ania. "Dead Women Tell No Tales: Issues of Female Subjectivity, Subaltern Agency, and Tradition in Colonial and Post-Colonial Writings on Widow Immolation in India." *History Workshop* 36 (1993): 209–27.

Lovell, Julia. "The Uses of Foreigners in Mao-Era China: 'Techniques of Hospitality' and International Image-Building in the People's Republic, 1949–1976." *Transactions of the RHS* 25 (2015): 135–58.

Lu Xun 魯迅. *Lu Xun zhu yi biannian quanji* 魯迅著譯編年全集 [Lu Xun's writings and translations, arranged by year of composition]. Edited by Wang Shijia 王世家 and Zhi An 止庵. 20 vols. Beijing: Renmin chubanshe, 2009.

——. "Qingnian bidu shu" 青年必讀書 [Essential reading for youth]. *Jingbao Fukan* 京報副刊 67 (1925): 8.

——. *The Real Story of Ah-Q and Other Tales of China: The Complete Fiction of Lu Xun.* Translated by Julia Lovell. New York: Penguin, 2009.

Luan Weiping 欒偉平. "Jindai kexue xiaoshuo yu linghun: You 'Xin Faluo xiansheng tan' shuo kaiqu" 近代科學小說與靈魂——由《新法螺先生譚》說開去 [Early modern fiction and the soul: starting from *New Tales of Mr. Braggadocio*]. *Zhongguo xiandai wenxue yanjiu congkan* 中國現代文學研究叢刊 3 (2006): 46–60.

Ma., Pra. "Ek Pairodī" [A parody]. *Dharmayug*, December 30, 1962, 11.

MacFarquhar, Roderick. *The Origins of the Cultural Revolution: Contradictions Among the People, 1956–1957.* London: Oxford University Press, 1974.

Macherey, Pierre. *A Theory of Literary Production.* Translated by Geoffrey Wall. London: Routledge & Kegan Paul, 1978.

Machwe, Prabhakar. "Ādhunik Cīni Kavitā Mem Bheṛiyā-Vṛtti" [Traits of treachery in modern Chinese poetry]. *Dharmayug*, December 30, 1962, 18–19.

——. "Cīn kī Citrakalā kā Paṭan" [The decline of Chinese art]. *Dharmayug*, February 24, 1963, 17.

——. *From self to Self: Reminiscences of a Writer.* New Delhi: Vikas, 1977.

Malinar, Angelika. "The Artist as Autobiographer: Sekhar Ek Jivani." In *Narrative Strategies: Essays on South Asian Literature and Film*, edited by Vasudha Dalmia and Theo Damsteegt, 229–42. New Delhi: Oxford University Press, 1998.

Mandhwani, Aakriti. "Everyday Reading: Commercial Magazines and Book Publishing in Post-Independence India." PhD diss., School of Oriental and African Studies, 2018.

——. "*Saritā* and the 1950s Hindi Middlebrow Reader." *Modern Asian Studies* 53, no. 6 (2019): 1797–815.

Mangalagiri, Adhira. "At the Limits of Comparison: Literary Encounters Between China and India in the Colonial World." PhD diss., University of Chicago, 2017.

——. "The Culture of Cultural Diplomacy: China and India, 1947–1952." *China and Asia: A Journal in Historical Studies* 3 (2021): 202–16.

Mangalagiri, Adhira, and Tansen Sen. "Introduction: Methods in China-India Studies." *International Journal of Asian Studies* 19, no. 2 (2022): 169–85.

Mani, Lata. *Contentious Traditions: The Debate on Sati in Colonial India*. Los Angeles: University of California Press, 1998.

Manjapra, Kris. *Age of Entanglement: German and Indian Intellectuals Across Empire*. Cambridge, MA: Harvard University Press, 2014.

——. *M. N. Roy: Marxism and Colonial Cosmopolitanism*. New Delhi: Routledge, 2010.

Mao Dun 茅盾. *Hong* 虹 [Rainbow]. Shanghai: Kaiming shudian, 1930.

Marston, Sallie, John Paul Jones III, and Keith Woodward. "Human Geography Without Scale." *Transactions of the Institute of British Geographers* 30, no. 4 (2005): 416–32.

Marx, Karl, and Friedrich Engels. *The Communist Manifesto: With Selections from the Eighteenth Brumaire of Louis Bonaparte and Capital*. Edited by Samuel Beer. New York: Appleton-Century-Crofts, 1955.

Mattana, Alessio. "The Allure of Synthesis: Science and the Literary in Comparative and World Literature." *Comparative Critical Studies* 17, no. 3 (2020): 351–72.

McDougall, Bonnie. *Mao Zedong's "Talks at the Yan'an Conference on Literature and Art": A Translation of the 1943 Text with Commentary*. Ann Arbor: University of Michigan Center for Chinese Studies, 1980.

Mehta, Geeta. *Philosophy of Vinoba Bhave: A New Perspective in Gandhian Thought*. Bombay: Himalaya, 1995.

Melas, Natalie. *All the Difference in the World: Postcoloniality and the Ends of Comparison*. Stanford, CA: Stanford University Press, 2007.

Meltzl, Hugo. "Present Tasks of Comparative Literature." In *The Princeton Sourcebook in Comparative Literature: From the European Enlightenment to the Global Present*, edited by David Damrosch, Natalie Melas and Mbongiseni Buthelezi, 41–49. Princeton, NJ: Princeton University Press, 2009.

Meng, Yue. *Shanghai and the Edges of Empires*. Minneapolis: University of Minnesota Press, 2006.

Mi Wenkai 糜文開. *Yindu wenxue xinshang* 印度文學欣賞 [An appreciation of Indian literature]. Taibei: Sanmin Shuju, 1957.

Mittler, Barbara. *A Newspaper for China? Power, Identity, and Change in Shanghai's News Media, 1872-1912*. Cambridge, MA: Harvard University Asia Center, 2004.

Moffat, Chris. *India's Revolutionary Inheritance: Politics and the Promise of Bhagat Singh*. Cambridge: Cambridge University Press, 2019.

Muktibodh, Gajanan Madhav. "Śaṁśer: Merī Dṛṣṭi Meṁ" [Shamsher: in my view], in *Śaṁśer: Kavi Se Baṛe Ādmī* [Shamsher: from poet to great man], edited by Mahavir Agraval, 56–65. Kasaridiha Durg: Sri Prakashan, 1994.

Murthy, Viren. *The Political Philosophy of Zhang Taiyan: The Resistance of Consciousness*. Leiden: Brill, 2011.

—— "Rethinking Pan-Asianism Through Zhang Taiyan: India as Method." In *Beyond Pan-Asianism: Connecting China and India, 1840s-1960s*, edited by Tansen Sen and Brian Tsui, 94–128. New Delhi: Oxford University Press, 2021.

Nehru, Jawaharlal. "Foreword." In *Prison Days and Other Poems*, 5–6. Benares: Saraswati, 1946.

Nieh, Hualing, ed. *Literature of the Hundred Flowers*, vol. 1: *Criticism and Polemics*. New York: Columbia University Press, 1981.

——. *Literature of the Hundred Flowers*, vol. 2: *Poetry and Fiction*. New York: Columbia University Press, 1981.

Nijhawan, Shobna. *Women and Girls in the Hindi Public Sphere*. New Delhi: Oxford University Press, 2012.

Okakura Kakuzō. *The Awakening of Japan*. New York: Century, 1904.

Orsini, Francesca. "Domesticity and Beyond." *South Asia Research* 19, no. 2 (1999): 137–60.

——. *The Hindi Public Sphere, 1920–1940: Language and Literature in the Age of Nationalism*. New Delhi: Oxford University Press, 2002.

——. "Introduction." In *The Oxford India Premchand*, vii–xxvi. New Delhi: Oxford University Press, 2012.

Palandri, Angela. "The Poetic Theory and Practice of Ai Qing." In *Perspectives in Contemporary Chinese Literature*, edited by Mason Y. H. Wang, 61–76. University Center, MI: Green River, 1983.

Paliwal, Krishnadutt. "Agyeya: Jel Jīvan kī Manobhūmikā" [Agyeya: the state of mind of imprisonment]. In *Agyeya: Jel ke Dinoṁ kī Kahānīyāṁ* [Agyeya: stories from his jail days], edited by Krishnadutt Paliwal, 11–26. New Delhi: Vani, 2013.

Pan Jienong 潘子農. "Yinbu zhi si" 印捕之死 [Death of an Indian policeman]. *Kaizhan* 開戰 5 (1930): 31–46.

Pandey, Suresh Chandra. *Ādhunik Hindī Kavitā par Aṁgrezī Kavitā kā Prabhāv* [The influence of English poetry on modern Hindi poetry]. Kanpur: Anubhav Prakashan, 1983.

——. *Agyeya: Sāhityǎ Vimarś* [Agyeya: literary discussions]. New Delhi: Naman, 2010.

Parsai, Harisankar. "Cīnī Dāktar Bhāgā: Ek Deśbhakt kī Kathā" [The Chinese doctor ran away: the story of a patriot]. In *Parsāī Racǎnāvalī* [Collected works of Parsai], vol. 1, 192–95. New Delhi: Rajkamal Prakashan, 1985.

——. "Naye Pāgal ki Dāyarī" [New madman's diary], *Dharmayug*, February 24, 1963, 9–10.

Patterson, Annabel. *Fables of Power: Aesopian Writing and Political History*. Durham, NC: Duke University Press, 1991.

Payne, Robert, ed. *Contemporary Chinese Poetry*. London: Routledge, 1947.

Peng Changqing 彭长卿. "Yadong Pofo zhuanlue" 亞東破佛傳略 [A biography of Yadong Pofo]. *Qingmo xiaoshuo yanjiu* 清末小說研究 5 (1981): 26–39.

The People Speak Out: Translations of Poems and Songs of the People of China. Translated by Rewi Alley. Beijing: Rewi Alley, 1954.

Petrie, David. *Communism in India, 1924–1927*. Edited by Mahadevaprasad Saha. Calcutta: Editions Indian, 1972.

Phelan, Peggy. *Unmarked: The Politics of Performance*. Oxon: Routledge, [1993] 1996.

Political Division of Unit 7969 of the People's Liberation Army 中國人民解放軍七九六九部隊政治部. *Gunlei yingxiong Luo Guangbian* 滾雷英雄羅光變 [Land mine detonating hero Luo Guangbian]. Shanghai: Renmin chubanshe, 1972.

Pollock, Sheldon, and Benjamin Elman, eds. *What China and India Once Were: The Pasts That May Shape the Global Future.* New York: Columbia University Press, 2018.

Popescu, Monica. *At Penpoint: African Literatures, Postcolonial Studies, and the Cold War.* Durham, NC: Duke University Press, 2020.

Posnett, Hutcheson Macaulay. *Comparative Literature.* New York: D. Appleton, 1892.

Pound, Ezra. "A Few Don'ts by an Imagiste." *Poetry* 1, no. 6 (1913): 200–206.

Prasad, Kamala, Dhananjay Varma, and Syamsundar Misra, eds. *Parsaī Racănāvalī* [Collected works of Parsai]. Vols. 1–6. New Delhi: Rajkamal Prakashan, 1985.

Premchand, ed. *Bianxin de ren* 變心的人 [He who had a change of heart]. Translated by Zheng Qiu 正秋. Shanghai: Shaonian ertong chubanshe, 1956.

——. *Gedan* 戈丹 [Godan]. Trans. Yan Shaoduan 严绍端. Beijing: Renmin wenxue chubanshe, 1958.

——. *Jāgaraṇ* [Awakening]. Vols. 1.1–2.52, 1932–1934.

——. *Premcand Racănāvalī* [Collected works of Premchand]. Vol. 14. Delhi: Janvani Prakashan, 1996.

——. *Soz-e-vatan* [Dirge of the nation]. Allahabad: Hans Prakashan, 1988.

Pritchett, Frances. "Folk Narrative." Accessed January 28, 2022. http://www.columbia .edu/itc/mealac/pritchett/00litlinks/lit_folk.html.

——. *Marvelous Encounters: Folk Romance in Urdu and Hindi.* Riverdale, NY: Riverdale, 1985.

Qian, Zhaoming, ed. *Ezra Pound and China.* Ann Arbor: University of Michigan Press, 2003.

Question in the Legislative Assembly. File No. 7.22/37/35 1935. National Archives of India, Home Department Political.

Rahul. *Śamśer aur unkī Kavitā* [Shamsher and his poetry]. Delhi: Bhavna Prakashan, 1999.

Rai, Amrit. "Soze Vatan Yānī Deś kā Dard" [The dirge of the nation, or the country's pain]. In *Soz-e-vatan,* 3–4. Allahabad: Hans Prakashan, 1988.

Raju, P. V. Ramaswami. *Indian Fables.* London: Swan Sonnenschein, Lowrey, 1887.

——. *The Tales of the Sixty Mandarins.* New York: Cassell, 1886.

Ramakrishnan, E. V. *Making It New: Modernism in Malayalam, Marathi, and Hindi Poetry.* Shimla: Indian Institute of Advanced Study, 1995.

Ramnath, Maia. *Haj to Utopia: How the Ghadar Movement Charted Global Radicalism and Attempted to Overthrow the British Empire.* Berkeley: University of California Press, 2011.

Rana, Bhavan Singh. *Chandra Shekhar Azad: An Immortal Revolutionary of India.* Translated by Brij Bhushan Paliwal. Delhi: Diamond, 2004.

Rand, Gavin, and Kim Wagner. "Recruiting the 'Martial Races': Identities and Military Service in Colonial India." *Patterns of Prejudice* 46, nos. 3–4 (2012): 232–54.

Rea, Christopher. *The Age of Irreverence: A New History of Laughter in China.* Berkeley: University of California Press, 2015.

——. "Introduction: 'Charlie Chaplin of the East,' Xu Zhuodai." In *China's Chaplin: Comic Stories and Farces by Xu Zhuodai,* 1–29. Ithaca, NY: Cornell University East Asia Program, 2019.

Rigby, Richard. *The May 30 Movement: Events and Themes.* Canberra: Australian National University Press, 1980.

Rosenstein, Lucy. *New Poetry in Hindi*. Delhi: Permanent Black, 2003.

——. " 'New Poetry' in Hindi: A Quest for Modernity." *South Asia Research* 20, no. 1 (2000): 47–62.

Roubiczek, Paul. *Astitvavād: Pakṣ aur vipakṣ* [Existentialism: for and against]. Translated by Prabhakar Machwe. Bhopal: Madhya Pradesh Hindi Granth Academy, 1976.

Roy, M. N. *Revolution and Counter-Revolution in China*. Calcutta: Renaissance, 1946.

Sahi, Vijayadev Narayan. "Śamśer kī Kāvyānubhūti kī Banāvat" [The structure of Shamsher's poetic emotion]. In *Śamśer: Kavī Se Baṛe Ādmī* [Shamsher: from poet to great man], edited by Mahavir Agraval, 74–98. Kasaridiha Durg: Sri Prakashan, 1994.

Sarad, Onkar, ed. *Maithilisaran Gupt*. Bombay: Vora, 1970.

Sartre, Jean-Paul. *Nausea*. Translated by Lloyd Alexander. New York: New Directions, 1964.

Saunders, Frances Stonor. *The Cultural Cold War: The CIA and the World of Arts and Letters*. New York: New Press, 2000.

Saussy, Haun. "Fenollosa Compounded: A Discrimination." In *The Chinese Written Character as a Medium for Poetry: A Critical Edition*, edited by Haun Saussy, Jonathan Stalling and Lucas Klein, 1–40. New York: Fordham University Press, 2008.

Sawhney, Simona. "The Mark of the Political in *Shekhar Ek Jivani*." In *Hindi Modernism: Rethinking Agyeya and His Times*, edited by Vasudha Dalmia, 41–58. Berkeley: University of California, 2012.

Schomer, Karine. *Mahadevi Varma and the Chayavad Age of Modern Hindi Poetry*. Berkeley: University of California Press, 1983.

Selections from the Saptaks. Translated by S. C. Narula. New Delhi: Rupa, 2004.

Sen, Tansen. "The Emergence, Development, and Current State of China-India Studies." *Journal of Asian Studies* 80, no. 2 (2021): 363–87.

——. *India, China, and the World: A Connected History*. Lanham, MD: Rowman & Littlefield, 2017.

——. "The Materiality of Friendship: Kongfuzi as a Source for China-India Interactions During the 1950s (Part I)." Accessed May 31, 2022. https://storymaps.arcgis.com/stories/20b8d81ad58a4146ba24d1e0a832183c.

Shaw, Miranda. "Hariti: Goddess of Motherly Love." In *Buddhist Goddesses of India*, 110–42. Princeton, NJ: Princeton University Press, 2006.

Shi Jiu 拾玖. "Hongtou Asan kao" 紅頭阿三考 [On Hongtou Asan]. *Shenbao* 申報, August 24 1935, 5.

Shigemi, Inaga. "Okakura Kakuzō and India: The Trajectory of Modern National Consciousness and Pan-Asian Ideology Across Borders." *Review of Japanese Culture and Society* no. 24 (2012): 39–57.

Shih, Shu-mei. *The Lure of the Modern: Writing Modernism in Semicolonial China, 1917-1937*. Berkeley: University of California, 2001.

Shingavi, Snehal. "Agyeya's Unfinished Revolution: Sexual and Social Freedom in Shekhar: Ek Jivani." *South Asia: Journal of South Asian Studies* 39, no. 3 (2016): 577–91.

Sigi, Rekha. *Munshi Premchand*. Delhi: Diamond, 2006.

Singh, Daswandha. "Let China and India Unite for the Holy Cause." *Jingbao Fukan* 京報副刊 206 (1925): 6–8.

Singh, Krishnanand Prasad. *Dhokebāj paṛosī* [Backstabbing neighbor]. Bhagalpur: Mohan, 1966.

Singh, Namvar. *Chāyāvād.* Delhi: Rajkamal Prakashan, 1955.

——. "Śamśer kī Śamśeriyat" [The Shamsher-ness of Shamsher]. In *Pratinidhi Kavitāeṁ: Śamśer Bahādur Siṃh* [Representative poems: Shamsher Bahadur Singh], edited by Namvar Singh, 5–8. New Delhi: Rajkamal Prakashan, 1990.

Singh, Shamsher Bahadur. "Cīn" [China]. *Dharmayug,* December 30, 1962, 11.

——. *Kuch Kavitāeṁ va Kuch aur Kavitāeṁ* [Some poems and some more poems]. New Delhi: Radhakrishna Prakashan, 1984.

Sorokin, V. "Zheng Zhenduo: Man and Scholar." *Far Eastern Affairs* 1 (1989): 105–11.

Spivak, Gayatri Chakravorty. "Can the Subaltern Speak?" In *Marxism and the Interpretation of Culture,* edited by Cary Nelson and Lawrence Grossberg, 271–313. Urbana: University of Illinois Press, 1988.

Stanley, Liz. "The Epistolarium: On Theorizing Letters and Correspondences." *Auto/Biography* 12 (2004): 201–35.

Statement of Kailashpatti an Import in the Delhi Conspiracy Case. File No. 11/15/1931. National Archives of India, Home Department Political.

Stewart, Kathleen. *Ordinary Affects.* Durham, NC: Duke University Press, 2007.

Streets, Heather. *Martial Races: The Military, Race, and Masculinity in British Imperial Culture, 1857–1914.* Manchester: Manchester University Press, 2004.

Sun, Lung-kee. "To Be or Not to Be 'Eaten': Lu Xun's Dilemma of Political Engagement." *Modern China* 12, no. 4 (1986): 459–85.

Sun, Saiyin. *Beyond the Iron House: Lu Xun and the Modern Chinese Literary Field.* New York: Routledge, 2017.

Swan, Robert. *Munshi Premchand of Lamhi Village.* Durham, NC: Duke University Press, 1969.

Tan Chung, and Amiya Dev, eds. *Tagore and China.* New Delhi: Sage, 2011.

Tang Xiaobing. "Lu Xun's 'Diary of a Madman' and a Chinese Modernism." *PMLA* 107, no. 5 (1992): 1222–34.

Tang Xiaobing, and Michel Hockx. "The Creation Society (1921–1930)." In *Literary Societies of Republican China,* edited by Kirk Denton and Michel Hockx, 103–136. Plymouth, MA: Rowman & Littlefield, 2008.

Thakur, Vineet. "An Asian Drama: The Asian Relations Conference, 1947." *International History Review* 41, no. 3 (2018): 673–95.

Tibebu, Teshale. *Hegel and the Third World: The Making of Eurocentrism in World History.* Syracuse, NY: Syracuse University Press, 2010.

Tivari, Sri Bhagvan. *Bimbvād, Bimb aur Ādhunik Hindī-Kavitā* [Imagism, the image, and modern Hindi poetry]. Bombay: Aravind Prakashan, 1992.

Toner, Anne. *Ellipsis in English Literature: Signs of Omission.* Cambridge: Cambridge University Press, 2015.

Trivedi, Harish. "Agyeya and His Shekhar: The Second Greatest Novel in Hindi?" *Indian Literature* 55, no. 1 (2011): 78–83.

——. *Colonial Transactions: English Literature in India.* Manchester: Manchester University Press, 1993.

——. "The Progress of Hindi, Part 2: Hindi and the Nation." In *Literary Cultures in History: Reconstructions from South Asia*, edited by Sheldon Pollock, 958–1022. Berkeley: University of California Press, 2003.

Ts'ai, Kuo-hui, Yung-ming Ch'ien, and Mrityubodh, eds. *Cīnī Samālocăkoṁ ki Nazar Meṁ Premcand* [Premchand in the eyes of Chinese critics]. Beijing: Foreign Languages Press, 1988.

Tsing, Anna Lowenhaupt. *Friction: An Ethnography of Global Connection.* Princeton, NJ: Princeton University Press, 2011.

Ungor, Cagdas. "Reaching the Distant Comrade: Chinese Communist Propaganda Abroad (1949–1976)." PhD diss., State University of New York at Binghamton, 2009.

Van der veer, Peter. *The Value of Comparison.* Durham, NC: Duke University of Press, 2016.

Varma, Urmila. *Influence of English Poetry on Modern Hindi Poetry with Special Reference to Technique, Imagery, Metre, and Diction.* Allahbad: Lokbharati Prakashan, 1980.

Vyas, Jyoti. *Dharmavīr Bhāratī aur unkā Dharmayug* [Dharmavir Bharati and his Dharmayug]. Kanpur: Annapurna Prakashan, 2010.

Wagner, Rudolf. " 'Dividing up the [Chinese] Melon': The Fate of a Transcultural Metaphor in the Formation of National Myth." *Transcultural Studies* 8, no. 1 (2017): 9–122.

Wang Chunjing 王春景. "Puliemuchangde he Lu Xun bixia de nongmin xingxiang" 普列姆昌德和鲁迅笔下的農民形象 [The image of the peasant in the works of Premchand and Lu Xun]. *Nanya yanjiu* 南亞研究 S1 (2005): 39–44.

Wang, David Der-wei. *Fin-de-Siècle Splendor: Repressed Modernities of Late Qing Fiction, 1849–1911.* Stanford, CA: Stanford University Press, 1997.

——. "From Mara to Nobel." In *A New Literary History of Modern China*, edited by David Der-wei Wang, 219–25. Cambridge, MA: Belknap Press of Harvard University Press, 2017.

Wang Hui. "Discursive Community and the Genealogy of Scientific Categories." In *Everyday Modernity in China*, edited by Madeleine Yue Dong and Joshua Goldstein, 80–120. Seattle: University of Washington Press.

Wang, Pu. "Poetics, Politics, and 'Ursprung/Yuan': On Lu Xun's Conception of 'Mara Poetry.' " *Modern Chinese Literature and Culture* 23, no. 2 (2011): 34–63.

Wang Ruliang 王汝良. *Zhongguo wenxue zhong de Yindu xingxiang yanjiu* 中國文學中的印度形象研究 [The image of India in Chinese literature]. Beijing: Zhonghua shuju, 2018.

Wang Xiaodan 王曉丹. "Puliemuchangde he Lu Xun" 普列姆昌德和魯迅 [Premchand and Lu Xun]. *Nanya yanjiu* 南亞研究 1 (1991): 65–71.

Wang, Yang. "Envisioning the Third World: Modern Art and Diplomacy in Maoist China." *ARTMargins* 8, no. 2 (2019): 31–54.

Wasserstrom, Jeffrey. *Student Protests in Twentieth-Century China: The View from Shanghai.* Stanford, CA: Stanford University Press, 1991.

Wellbery, David. "Contingency." In *Neverending Stories: Toward a Critical Narratology*, edited by Ann Fehn, Ingeborg Hoesterey, and Maria Tatar, 237–57. Princeton, NJ: Princeton University Press, 1992.

Wellek, René. "The Crisis of Comparative Literature." In *The Princeton Sourcebook in Comparative Literature: From the European Enlightenment to the Global Present*, edited by David Damrosch, Natalie Melas, and Mbongiseni Buthelezi, 161–73. Princeton, NJ: Princeton University Press, 2009.

Wilcox, Emily. "Performing Bandung: China's Dance Diplomacy with India, Indonesia, and Burma, 1953–1962." *Inter-Asia Cultural Studies* 18, no. 4 (2017): 518–39.

Wong, Wang-chi. "A Literary Organization with a Clear Political Agenda: The Chinese League of Left-Wing Writers, 1930–1936." In *Literary Societies of Republic China*, edited by Kirk Denton and Michel Hockx, 313–38. Plymouth, MA: Lexington, 2008.

——. *Politics and Literature in Shanghai: The Chinese League of Left-Wing Writers, 1930–1936*. Manchester: Manchester University Press, 1991.

Xiao San 蕭三. "Ji Yazhou shiren de huijian" 記亞洲詩人的會見 [Remembering the Asian Poets' Meeting]. *Shikan* 詩刊 3 (1957): 82–91.

——. "Cong Yindu guilai" 從印度歸來 [Upon returning from India]. *Shikan* 詩刊 1 (1958): 18–19.

Xie, Ming. *Ezra Pound and the Appropriation of Chinese Poetry: Cathay, Translation, and Imagism*. New York: Garland, 1999.

Xie Man 謝曼. "Hongtou Asan yu Gandi" 紅頭阿三與甘地 [Hongtou Asan and Gandhi]. *Xin Shenghuo* 新生活 2 (1931): 10.

Xu, Xiaoqun. "Cosmopolitanism, Nationalism, and Colonial Hierarchy: Chinese Responses to Russell, Eroshenko, and Tagore." In *Cosmopolitanism, Nationalism, and Individualism in Modern China*, 53–88. Plymouth, MA: Lexington, 2014.

Xu Zhimo 徐志摩. "Taige'er lai hua" 泰戈爾來華 [Tagore visits China]. *Xiaoshuo yuebao* 小說月報 14, no. 9 (1923): 1–5.

Xu Zhuodai 徐卓呆. "Fenge hou zhi wuren" 分割後之吾人 [My people after partition]. *Jiangsu* 江蘇 8–10 (1904).

Yadong Pofo 亞東破佛. "Yuyan xiaoshuo shuang linghun" 寓言小説雙靈魂 [Twin souls: an allegorical story]. *Shenbao* 申報, March 12–April 6 1907.

——. *Shuang Linghun* 雙靈魂 [Twin souls]. Shanghai: Junyi tushu gongsi, 1909.

Yang Cunren 楊邨人. "Hongtou Asan" 紅頭阿三 [Hongtou Asan]. *Dazhong wenyi* 大眾 文藝 2, no. 3 (1930): 11–15.

Yashpal. *Yashpal Looks Back: Selections from an Autobiography*. Translated by Corinne Friend. New Delhi: Vikas, 1981.

Ye Junjian 葉君健. "Liang zhang heying" 兩張合影 [Two group photographs]. *Xin wenxue shiliao* 新文學史料 3 (1986): 173–74.

——. "Yazhou zuojia huiyi qianhou" 亞洲作家會議前後 [On the Asian Writers' Conference]. *Wenhuibao* 文匯報, February 10–March 15 1957, 4.

Ye Shengtao 葉聖陶. *Lvtu riji wuzhong* 旅途日記五種 [Five travelogues]. Beijing: Shenghuo dushu xinzhi sanlian shudian, 2002.

Yoon, Duncan M. " 'Our Forces Have Redoubled': World Literature, Postcolonialism, and the Afro-Asian Writers' Bureau." *Cambridge Journal of Postcolonial Literary Inquiry* 2, no. 2 (2015): 233–52.

Yu Dafu 郁達夫. "Sinking." In *The Columbia Anthology of Modern Chinese Literature*, edited by Joseph Lau and Howard Goldblatt, 31–55. New York: Columbia University Press, 2007.

Yuan Shuipai 袁水拍. *Gesong he zuzhou* 歌頌和詛咒 [Praises and curses]. Beijing: Zuojia chubanshe, 1959.

Zhang Taiyan 章太炎. "Ji Yindu Xipoqi wang jinianhui shi" 記印度西婆耆王紀念會事 [A report on the meeting commemorating the Indian king Shivaji]. *Minbao* 民報 13 (1907): 19–26.

Zheng Zhenduo 鄭振鐸. *Chatuben Zhongguo wenxue shi* 插圖本中國文學史 [Illustrated history of Chinese literature]. Beijing: Pushe chubanbu, 1932.

——. "Lun yuyan" 論寓言 [On fables]. *Wenxue zhoubao* 文學週報 181 (1925): 1–2.

——. "Yindu yuyan" 印度寓言 [Indian fables]. *Xiaoshuo yuebao* 小說月報 15, no. 12 (1924): 3–12.

Zheng Zhenwei 鄭振偉. *Zheng Zhenduo qianqi wenxue sixiang* 鄭振鐸前期文學思想 [Zheng Zhenduo's literary thought in his early years]. Beijing: Renmin wenxue chubanshe, 2000.

Zhong Yuan 鐘媛. "1957 nian 'Wenyibao' de gaiban" 1957年《文藝報》的改版 [The 1957 revised edition of *Wenyibao*]. *Modern Chinese Literature Studies* 中國現代文學研究叢刊 11 (2017): 90–98.

Zhou Zuoren 周作人. "Ren de wenxue" 人的文學 [Humane literature]. Translated by Ernst Wolff. In *Modern Chinese Literary Thought*, edited by Kirk Denton, 151–61. Stanford, CA: Stanford University Press, 1996.

Index